617 SQUADRON
THE DAMBUSTERS AT WAR

617 SQUADRON
THE DAMBUSTERS AT WAR

Tom Bennett

Patrick Stephens, Wellingborough

First published in 1986
First paperback edition 1987

British Library Cataloguing in Publication Data

Bennett, Tom
617 Squadron: The Dambusters at war.
1. Great Britain, *Royal Air Force, Squadron
No. 617*   2. World War, 1939–1945—Aerial
operations, British
I. Title
940.54′4941   D786

ISBN 1-85260-041-1

*Patrick Stephens Limited is part of the
Thorsons Publishing Group*

Photoset in 10 on 11 pt Plantin by
Avocet Marketing Services Limited.
Printed in Great Britain on Onslow White Wove
Vol 18 80 gsm, and bound, by Biddles Limited,
Guildford, Surrey, for the publishers,
Patrick Stephens Limited, Denington Estate,
Wellingborough, Northants, NN8 2QD, England.

Contents

Acknowledgements

I offer my warmest and heartfelt thanks to all the wartime aircrew of 617 Squadron who contributed so enthusiastically and unreservedly to all aspects of this book and without whom it would not have been possible. My grateful thanks to Group Captain Leonard Cheshire and Air-Marshal Sir Harold Martin for their insights into aspects of the 617 Squadron history previously unrevealed. I am particularly indebted to Sir Harold for permission to use material that he holds in personal copyright. I owe a debt of gratitude to Mrs Trudi English of Corringham, Essex, and Mrs Walker of Shoeburyness, Essex for their unstinting help in the translation of German documents and to Mrs Diana Kahl of Hockley, Essex for her unfailing assistance with French translation. Mats Overby of Pitea, Sweden, generously translated Swedish documents. Mr Ole Saelensminde of Os, a very active member of the Norwegian Aviation Historical Society, was a tower of strength when it came to the detailed and deep research required to establish the facts of 617 Squadron's involvement in Norway in January 1945, whilst the University of Bergen also afforded investigative assistance into this phase of the Squadron's operations. Group Captain Laddie Lucas has my grateful thanks for his encouragement and well-founded advice at a very crucial stage of the preparation of the manuscript. My thanks are also due to the staffs of the Public Record Office at Kew and the Air Historical Branch in London for their enthusiastic and generous help in providing data and research facilities.

Many other friends and relatives provided encouragement throughout the period of preparation and production. I hope that they, together with all those who rendered more active assistance, will feel that their efforts have been justified and rewarded between the covers of this book.

Introduction

'And it came to pass'

My introduction to 617 Squadron was somewhat involuntary and back-door. I finished my first tour of operational duty in February 1943 having flown with No 49 Squadron in No 5 Group since August 1942. I was posted for duties in the operations room at 5 Group headquarters at St Vincent's Grantham, where I stayed for six very informative months. At my own request, I was posted for instructional duties at No 1654 Heavy Conversion Unit at RAF Wigsley and performed the duties of a radar navigation instructor. In April 1944 I was posted to RAF Wyton, near Huntingdon, for a second tour of operations with Pathfinder Force (PFF), No 8 Group, Bomber Command.

I arrived at the Officers' Mess, Wyton, at about 16.30 hours on the Easter Monday, having been granted a 48-hour pass to spend the Easter holiday with my family in Ilford, Essex. Tea was being served in the ante room, so I left all my luggage in the foyer and went in. I knew that many of my former aircrew friends were already serving at Wyton and so I was not really surprised to hear a yell of welcome as I collected my tea. I turned to see Squadron Leader Tommy Blair bearing down on me, a broad smile across his round moustachioed face. Tommy had been the bombing leader during my tour with 49 Squadron and, strangely enough, had been the very first officer to greet me when I entered the Officers' Mess at RAF Scampton for the first time as a newly-commissioned Pilot Officer, after having served five months on the squadron as an NCO . . . 'Bloody glad to see you, Ben' he boomed, putting my cup of tea in jeopardy as he pumped my hand, 'It's about time 5 Group started to send us some *real* navigators!' I settled down with him, avidly talking about the 'old days' on 49 Squadron, under Wing Commander Leonard Slee.

Suddenly our lively conversation was rudely interrupted by the Mess tannoy: 'Would Flying Officer Bennett please come to the 'phone!' I ignored the call, since I felt that doubtless there were other 'doubles' about the place, and who would know that I had reported in but a short time previously? However, when the message was repeated plaintively for a third time, and Tommy had moved off to speak to another officer, I went out to the telephone, merely to reassure myself that it was someone else that was being paged. 'Hello, Ben' came a voice that I recognized immediately as that of Gerry Fawke, the pilot with whom I had been 'crewed-up' at No 19 OTU, RAF Kinloss, in February 1942 and with whom I had shared my first tour. I listened uncomprehendingly as he continued, 'I'm sending a "gharri" over to Wyton for you, Ben—to bring you across to Warboys with all your gear. It's on its way and has been told to pick you up from the Officers' Mess, so don't leave there. We are converting to Mossies at Warboys and then joining 617 Squadron for target-marking duties. I'll give you all the "griff" when you arrive over here, mate' and with that he rang off.

Sure enough, a van turned up and collected me from the Mess. In the interim, I had been unable to find Tommy Blair to explain to him that I had probably spent the shortest tour at Wyton of any aircrew—and if he reads these words today, it will solve a mystery that has been puzzling him for the last forty years! Incidentally, I was to learn many years later that a very similar thing had happened to Dave Shannon. He had arrived as a volunteer for PFF duties at Wyton in late February 1943 only to receive a telephoned invitation from Wing Commander Gibson to return to 5 Group to join a new squadron that he was forming in the Group. Dave returned to Lincolnshire with all haste. I guess it was incidents like this that caused Air-Vice-Marshal D. C. T. Bennett, the AOC No 8 Group, to have rather a querulous attitude towards the upstart 617 Squadron in the later stages of the war.

Gerry told me that he had heard of my PFF posting whilst he had been a staff instructor at the Lancaster Finishing School at RAF Syerston, Lincoln. At the same time, the 'bush telegraph' had passed the message that Leonard Cheshire was seeking aircrew to man Mosquito aircraft for 'low-level target marking' and there weren't many takers. Gerry had leapt into a Lancaster and headed swiftly for RAF Woodhall Spa. He managed to get an interview with the 617 Squadron commander, who was impressed by Gerry's record and accepted him for the role. Gerry blurted out the story of my posting to PFF and that he was certain that I would only be too pleased to join forces with him again. 'I will get the necessary posting amendments put in hand immediately' said 'Chesh', 'and Flying Officer Bennett can join you at Warboys for the conversion course and return to Woodhall with the other lads.'

Well, that's how it all came about. I knew very little about 617, save what was general knowledge around 5 Group and Bomber Command. The very real feeling of thankfulness that I had in knowing that I was going back to war in 5 Group and with Gerry Fawke did much to dampen down any secret qualms I may have had about the posting and, anyway, I could always console myself with the thought that at least I had maintained the old Service tradition of not volunteering for anything!

617 Squadron was officially formed at RAF Scampton on 1 April 1943, April Fool's Day and the 25th anniversary of the formation of the Royal Air Force. The Dams raid, which was carried out so magnificently on the night of 16/17 May 1943, remains the most outstanding individual bomber squadron feat of the whole war. Quite properly, it stands as a lasting memorial to the courage and devotion of all bomber aircrew

throughout the conflict. Besides lifting the civilian morale, it boosted the spirits and efforts of the thousands of aircrew with other Bomber Command squadrons then engaged in the bitter bomber battles against the German enemy. It has rightly secured an imperishable niche in British history.

Wing Commander Gibson relinquished command of the Squadron after the Dams raid and was succeeded by Squadron Leader George Holden DSO, DFC, who had previously served in No 4 Group in Yorkshire. On 6 July 1943, he led six aircraft against electric power installations at Aquata Scrivia (near Genoa), whilst another six aircraft attacked the transformer station at San Polo D'Enza. All twelve aircraft flew on to North Africa after the bombing and landed at RAF Blida without loss. They left Blida on 25 July and bombed the harbour and shipping at Leghorn en route for Scampton. On 29 July the Squadron carried out leaflet raids on the large towns of Northern Italy. Again they landed at Blida and returned later to the United Kingdom, this time without attacking any enemy target on the way back.

The Squadron transferred en bloc from RAF Scampton to RAF Coningsby on 30 August 1943. For two successive nights, 14/15 and 15/16 September, the Squadron's target, at low level, was the Dortmund-Ems Canal at Ladbergen in Germany. In that short period, six of the nine crews detailed were lost without the canal being breached, the cause being the fog that enveloped the target area. Among the casualties was George Holden and, with him, practically the remainder of the crew that had flown with Guy Gibson on the Dams raid. Some thirty minutes after landing after the second of these attacks, Flight Lieutenant Mick Martin DSO, DFC, captain of one of the three surviving crews, was discussing the reasons for the outcome of the operation with Air-Vice-Marshal Sir Ralph Cochrane, AOC No 5 Group, who had hastened to Coningsby and was obviously shocked by the losses sustained. Mick told of the poor visibility en route, the dense fog at the immediate target area, the presence of unexpected light-flak defences and the long search for the target. Suddenly Sir Ralph said, 'You are a Squadron Leader as from now and acting commander of 617!'

On the very next night, 16/17 September, the Squadron was required to supply six aircraft for a raid on the Antheor Viaduct in Southern France, near Nice. Three of the 'Dams crews' of Les Munro, Joe McCarthy and Ken Brown, were supplemented by Bunny Clayton, Ted Youseman and Dave Wilson. No 106 Squadron also contributed six aircraft to this operation with their Squadron commander, Wing Commander Abercrombie, in overall command of the whole force. The raid was not a success and the aircraft again flew on to Blida, returning to the United Kingdom some days later without operating against any enemy target.

In the considered opinion of Leonard Cheshire, many years later, Mick Martin was the greatest operational pilot that the Air Force produced. He had long been a devotee of the 'straight, hard and low' approach to bomber operations and had so developed these tactics personally as to know instinctively how to combat and nullify enemy reaction. The fact that he survived the war unharmed, despite a very long operational career is proof that he never made a mistake under pressure.

Mick had assumed command of 617 Squadron very much aware, through his regular and thorough contacts with Barnes Wallis, that 'Tallboy' bombs were off the drawing-board and in production and that the larger 'Grand Slams' were being planned. The scientist had used wind-tunnel tests to evolve perfect aerodynamic contouring for the Tallboy. He had set the tail-fins at an angle of three degrees to the longitudinal axis of the bomb. In flight, this caused the bomb to rotate around that axis at ever-increasing revolutions until the whole bomb became stabilized, like a gyroscope. Barnes Wallis required a bombing accuracy of within twenty yards of the target and maintained that these two bombs would be the most perfect and accurate ever conceived. He told Mick, 'If you can attain an accuracy of twenty yards, the explosive power of my beautiful bombs and their "earthquake" effect will do much to smash the Nazi war arsenal.'

Naturally the key factor in achieving the accuracy worthy of the bomb designs was the facility to aim them precisely, and the solution to this lay with the Stabilized Automatic Bomb Sight (SABS). The key mathematical data required to set-up the SABS for such precise results were:

(a) The aircraft's airspeed at the moment of bomb release which conditioned the bomb's trajectory to the effect of wind-speed and direction.

(b) The aircraft and bomb release speed over the ground.

(c) Exact release height above target.

(d) The immediate outside air temperature. This indirectly indicated air density which, in turn, governed the falling velocity and forward pitch of the bomb. A 1° Centigrade error in the outside temperature automatically fed into the system a bombing error of 21 feet. Thus, a 3° Centigrade error meant an error of 21 yards, which was not acceptable.

The reading on the thermometer normally fitted to the Lancaster was found to be unreliable. The indicated reading was raised by the cabin temperature inside the aircraft. Also, despite the use of a deflector, the friction heat generated by the airflow compressing on that part of the thermometer which protruded through the aircraft's skin to measure the temperature of the outside air also raised the reading. The greater the airspeed, the more friction heat was generated and the larger the induced error from this source.

Mick was in constant touch with Arnold Hall (later knighted) and his staff at Farnborough. A thermometer was devised and produced which was calibrated by airspeed, because airspeed meant frictional pressure on the bulb, which, in turn, registered a false ambient heat. The squadron navigators were furnished with a formula with which they balanced two thermometer readings, to arrive at the precise outside air temperature for use in compiling the vital SABS settings. Thus the Squadron aircraft needed to arrive at their bombing height as early as possible, bearing in mind the strategic and tactical requirements of a particular operation.

Consequently, Mick Martin laid great emphasis on SABS training whilst in temporary command of 617 Squadron. He interviewed volunteer crews and accepted only those he instinctively knew had the right attitude for 617's future needs. Soon the whole Squadron was totally absorbed in mastering the intricacies and demands of the SABS. The bomb-sight demanded a long run-up to the target, with airspeed and height rigorously and unflinchingly maintained. At the same time, Mick saw to it that the 'Dambusting' techniques were practised and kept up-to-date.

The survivors of the Dams raid had raised the subject of the feasibility of the low-level and accurate marking of targets visually, as a result of their experiences. Mick Martin had the correct previous operational experience and background in low-level flying to lead and foster these discussions until they crystallized into convictions. The 617 aircrews were convinced that this type of accurate marking was a prime necessity if the SABS was to be used to its very best advantage in delivering bomb-loads to targets.

Wing Commander Leonard Cheshire DSO, DFC, was appointed to command 617 Squadron on 10 November 1943. On 11 November, ten aircraft under the command of Squadron Leader Mick Martin, made another attack on the Antheor Viaduct. Four aircraft attacked the viaduct whilst six attacked a bridge and embankment near Nice. The force again flew on to Blida, returning on 18 November. Ted Youseman and crew disappeared on this transit flight, which was routed via Gibraltar and the Bay of Biscay.

The absence of a large number of the aircrew personnel of the Squadron in North Africa had afforded Leonard Cheshire the opportunity of getting to know the layout and set-up at Coningsby and, more importantly, of introducing himself to the remainder of the aircrew and the very competent NCOs and staff of the Squadron's ground crew. He appreciated that he had a tremendously experienced and devoted aircrew contingent and soon impressed his own very individual personality upon every member of the Squadron.

Leonard Cheshire had been the commanding officer of RAF Marston Moor, in Yorkshire, when the news of the Dams raid broke. The operation was a great boost to Bomber Command morale and Group Captain Cheshire was very impressed and very anxious to know more of how it was achieved, but it never occurred to him for a moment that it was a squadron with which he would become involved. A special dispensation had been necessary from Air Ministry for him to assume his Marston Moor command, but he hated the job. His honesty told him that he did not fit into it, since he just did not know the ground rules, and he was desperate to get out of what was becoming an intolerable position and back to flying again. He realized, however, that there would have to be some special and powerful pleading to get his AOC, Air-Vice-Marshal

Carr, to demote him to Wing Commander rank.

Air-Vice-Marshal Donald Bennett, the AOC, Pathfinder Group, visited Marston Moor and Leonard approached him for a posting into Pathfinder Force. He was taken aback when the AVM said he did not really know, and that in any case it would be necessary for Leonard to go through a trial period to see if he measured up to requirements. Leonard replied, as politely as he could, what the AVM could do with that offer, as he, Cheshire, had already completed three operational tours with Bomber Command. His next step, in desperation, was to go to a psychiatrist and plead that he was heading for a nervous breakdown unless he could be returned to flying duties but he did not hold out much hope that anything would come of that ploy. He kept trying every possible avenue and generally, he now feels, made a nuisance of himself.

617 Squadron never occurred to him as a possibility and he is not sure if he was even aware that George Holden, another No 4 Group officer, had taken over command from Guy Gibson. Quite how it came about he does not recall, but he found himself being driven down to No 5 Group headquarters, at St Vincent's, Grantham, Lincolnshire, to see Air-Vice-Marshal Sir Ralph Cochrane, the AOC. The appointment to the command of 617 Squadron, out of the blue, was an almost unbelievable gift from heaven. Prior to his departure for the interview, Leonard had been warned that Cochrane was a very tough man, with no sense of humour and someone Leonard would not find easy to accept. His own impression was completely different. He felt immediately at home with the AVM and was delighted to be offered the command at the end of a thorough and searching interview. Sir Ralph told Cheshire that Leonard would have to do a two-week course for Lancaster conversion. Somewhat arrogantly, Leonard assured the AVM that this was not necessary, but Sir Ralph just smiled and waved him out of the office. The AVM's judgement proved completely right. The conversion course, with Squadron Leader Gunter as his instructor and mentor, taught Leonard the Lancaster inside out, and also re-taught him one or two fundamentals that he had forgotten.

The Squadron buckled down to the intensive training schedule introduced by Mick Martin. Wing Commander Cheshire avidly absorbed all the knowledge he could from Mick's operational experience of low flying and acknowledges that all he ever knew and learned about the low flying game came from Mick Martin, albeit he never really reached Mick Martin's ability and stature in this sphere. Cheshire had long advocated that bombing accuracy should be improved, if the full fruits of the bomber offensive were to be gathered. He was tremendously impressed with the commitment to this ideal that permeated 617 Squadron and realized that a weapon was being forged that could revolutionize bomber tactics, given the right tools and encouragement.

On 9 December 1943, four crews were detached to RAF Tempsford to assist in the supply-dropping operations to French Resistance groups. Two of these crews were lost on 11 December. Several times the

Squadron was briefed for operations against flying-bomb sites but the weather interfered and the operations were cancelled. It was to be 16 December before Chesh was able to lead his Squadron against these sites.

On 9 January 1944, 617 Squadron moved 'up the road' from Coningsby to RAF Woodhall Spa. The early operations in the following period were allied to PFF marking which proved totally inadequate for the bombing purposes of 617. At a meeting in Bomber Command Headquarters, Chesh stated that the Squadron's requirement was for a maximum 20 yards marking error. Air-Vice-Marshal Donald Bennett stated that this was totally beyond achievement, to which Cheshire replied, 'Not if the marking is done at low level.' The AVM dismissed this as impossible because of the danger to the pilot, who would inevitably fly into the ground if he attempted a complicated marking operation at 200 feet at night. Eventually, the matter was thrown back to 617's own resources, with the strict proviso that it was not to be carried out below 2,500 feet and that a high-level bomb-sight was to be used. Cheshire argued that the bomb-sight would not work effectively at this height and that they would get the worst possible conditions for both light and heavy ack-ack fire. In effect he was told to 'lump it' and returned to the Squadron somewhat disheartened, but his spirits were soon raised by the enthusiasm and bonhomie of his aircrew. The flying-bomb targets were to be discontinued by Bomber Command but Sir Ralph managed to get some sites set aside for 617 to pursue its objectives, initially against lightly defended targets.

On 24 January 1944 the Squadron carried out its first 'independent' operation, with Chesh and Mick as the marker crews. They made it a point of honour to endeavour to mark the target from height, but this proved a total failure, so they resorted to a low level run, with Mick going in first to show how it could be done. The target was then accurately marked and bombed. A similar sequence on 25 January brought a similar result and Cheshire made Sir Ralph privy to the procedure. Sir Ralph was then convinced that the low level method was feasible whereas the medium level failed. He gave very strong support to further operations, with this low level marking as the featured method of target-marking and on 8 February 1944, the crucial Limoges raid was carried out. The results were almost unbelievable. Specific workshops and buildings in the industrial complex were completely destroyed with no casualties to the French population. The Squadron was on its way.

On 12 February 1944, ten aircraft positioned at RAF Ford, advanced base for a third attack on the Antheor Viaduct. The raid was not a success, for various reasons and factors, but is remembered for Mick Martin's epic flight to Sardinia, after being very badly damaged by the defences around the viaduct area. His bomb-aimer, Bob Hay, was buried at Cagliari, in Sardinia. Bob had been the 5 Group Bombing Leader before joining 617 Squadron. An Australian, he was universally popular throughout the Group for his bombing knowledge and capability and also for his marvellous personality and general love of life. The news of his death in action was a cause of great sadness to the whole of 5 Group, where every squadron mourned his passing.

This proved to be Mick Martin's last operation with the Squadron. He was awarded a Bar to the DSO and, on 21 March, was posted to Headquarters, No 100 Group, to commence a career that was to lead him, through a succession of well-merited promotions and commands to appointment on the Air Staff as Air Member for Personnel and eventual retirement with the rank of Air-Marshal as Sir Harold Martin KCB, DSO and Bar, DFC and 2 Bars, AFC. His influence on the development of the 617 technique of target marking remained paramount for the rest of the war.

The Squadron continued its successful way, still using Lancasters in the low level marking role against specific French and Belgian targets but Leonard Cheshire was agitating for a smaller and faster aircraft, if the system was to be employed against tougher targets. On 27 March, he commenced a short detachment to RAF Coleby Grange in Lincolnshire to convert to Mosquito flying. On 5 April, he used a 'Mossie' for the marking role against an aircraft repair depot at Toulouse. The results confirmed the aircraft's outstanding suitability for the role. Sir Arthur Harris authorized a further three Mosquitos for the 617 marker force on the express understanding that 617 would retain the Mossies only if Munich was severely mauled as a result of their use in a marking role.

Operational success continued to come 617's way and Munich was duly severely damaged on the night of 24/25 April 1944 when 5 Group squadrons were led in by the markers of 617. There followed a five-week lay-off from operations to solve and develop the technique for 'Operation Taxable' . . . 617's feat of imposing a huge invasion convoy on the enemy radar screens in the Pas de Calais area, using the silver foil strips 'Window' and the Gee navigation grid. On 8/9 June the 12,000 lb Tallboy bomb made its operational debut against the Saumur Tunnel, effectively sealing the German reinforcements from Southern France in transit to the Normandy battlefields. With this operation began another 'peak' in the Squadron's history. Leonard Cheshire had fashioned a highly motivated and dedicated squadron from the very experienced aircrew who had come from all over Bomber Command to join 617. The tremendous regard in which he was held by all ranks, added to the superb leadership he continuously demonstrated, made them feel they could achieve the impossible and the Saumur Tunnel raid heralded a run of success that was to last into July.

Their technique made for the destruction of a large number of German E-boats in Le Havre on 14 June with quite severe damage being inflicted on the submarine pens in the inner harbour by Tallboys. The Squadron was given the task of destroying the huge concrete structures that the Germans were building in the Pas de Calais. 617 was the only squadron in Bomber Command that had the capacity to deliver Tallboys accurately against these targets. The crews were kept on continual stand-by, waiting for the cloud to clear from the target area and it was not until 24 June that they were able to open their offensive. With the exception of a very successful operation on the night of 3/4 June against the underground flying-bomb rocket stores at St Leu D'Esserent, all 617's operations were concentrated specifically against these sites until 28 July when the Allied armies over-ran the area and captured the sites.

Wing Commander J. B. Tait DSO, DFC, assumed command on 12 July 1944. A very different type of personality but a very effective leader by example, 'Willie' Tait led 617 to more glory. The submarine pens in ports in France and Holland felt the hammer-blows of 617 until the end of August when training was undertaken for a new target. With the Allied advance on the Continent, 617 had no further need for their Mosquito aircraft which were withdrawn and the Squadron reverted to being an all-Lancaster outfit. Willie led them on all three raids to finally sink the German battleship *Tirpitz* at her anchorage in Tromso, interspersed with the breaching of the Kembs Barrage across the Rhine near Basle. With the British love of alliteration he became known as 'Tirpitz' Tait.

Willie handed over command to the Canadian Group Captain, Johnnie Fauquier on 28 December 1944. 617 Squadron continued their 'special duties' role and were especially active in the campaign to isolate the Ruhr valley area in front of the advancing Allied armies by destroying railway and road bridges. The fearsome 'Grand Slam', a much larger version of the Tallboy, was added to their armoury and the Bielefeld Viaduct capitulated to its awesome power. The German pocket-battleship *Lutzow* was another naval scalp for the Squadron and the submarine pens at Farge, in Hamburg, felt the weight of Tallboys and Grand Slams. On 25 April 1945, the aircraft of 617 were airborne for the last time in anger, taking part in the symbolic daylight raid on Hitler's 'Eagle's Nest' at Berchtesgarten.

No 5 Group Bomber Command was a 'tails up' Group throughout the war and to have served operationally within the Group was an honour indeed. To have additionally served on 617 Squadron within that Group was a privilege for which the favoured aircrew of that Squadron have never ceased to give thanks.

This then is 617 Squadron 'after the dams', a compendium of the personalities and the outstanding operations which more than maintained the enviable reputation established by Guy Gibson and the other 'Dambusters' on 16/17 May 1943.

Chapter 1

Per Ardua

The evening of 20 January 1944 was as murky and unpleasant as only the Lincolnshire winter could provide. Flight Lieutenant Tom O'Shaughnessy's crew had been briefed to carry out a low-level night simulation bombing exercise at the southern area of the Wash, whilst other Squadron aircraft carried out similar details farther north.

Four members of the crew stood beneath the wing of the Lancaster, stamping and moving around to fend off the chill of that winter evening. 'Whatever could have happened to those bloody gunners and the flight engineer?' asked O'Shaughnessy, of no one in particular, but the only reply was a concerted shrugging of three pairs of shoulders. 'I expect they thought the exercise would be scrubbed' remarked Flying Officer Arthur Holding, looking at Pilot Officer Arthur Ward, whose hands were filled with the operational paraphernalia of the wireless operator. 'Well, let's get aboard and get cracking' continued O'Shaughnessy, 'If it was going to be "scrubbed", we would have heard by now—and, anyway, it'll be warmer in the kite, and Flying Control can contact us that more easily if we're "on the air"—not that we really need the engineer and gunners on this exercise' he went on, 'If they're not here when it's time to roll, we'll go off without them.' The four aircrew began to make their way to the open entrance door of the Lancaster. The captain was the first to mount the aircraft ladder, still talking as he did so, obviously concerned about the missing members of his crew. 'Been all the same if it had been a bloody op' he grumbled, 'I'll have a few words to say to that bunch when I do see them!'

Some minutes later, the four engines of the Lancaster roared successively into deafening life. The bomb-aimer, Pilot Officer George Kendrick stood beside the pilot, performing the duties of the flight engineer during the start-up phase. The Lancaster's layout was such that almost any member of the 'up front' aircrew could 'stand-in' for the flight engineer during starting, taxying and take-off, under the close supervision of the pilot. The pre-flight checks completed and satisfactory, O'Shaughnessy signalled the chocks away and the aircraft began to move, slowly and carefully, to the take-off point. Clearance for take-off was given by the control tower and also by a green Aldis lamp signal from the caravan at the side of the runway. The Lancaster gathered speed down the runway and was soon 'unstuck' and heading for the exercise area at a height of 2,000 feet. 'Airborne 19.30 hours' was the entry with which Arthur Ward commenced his wireless log that night—and little did he know, as he made that entry, that he was to be one of the two survivors of that routine night exercise, and the only one to see the end of the war in Europe.

Over the Wash, the Lancaster turned on to the first course of the exercise. The detail was to dive shallowly from a height of 600 feet to 60 feet, using the spotlights mounted in each wing to settle on the optimum height, and to carry out a mock bombing run at that height, keeping the two lights correctly positioned with observations by the navigator. Arthur was listening attentively to his set. He was tuned-in to the base frequency, anticipating the signal which would recall the aircraft to Woodhall Spa. He had listened on the aircraft's intercom, as George Kendrick took his place in the nose of the aircraft and positioned himself for his part in the exercise. He heard the pre-run patter from the pilot 'Bomb doors open—Spotlights on—Height 600 feet—Airspeed 180 knots—commencing first run now'—and the bomb-aimer's confirmatory acknowledgements. He switched back to his set and sent off the signal, '20.05 hours. Commencing first run.' 'That might remind them that we are out here' he thought, thinking longingly of the warm Mess at the Petwood, unaware that time was moving inexorably towards the tragic climax of that night.

Suddenly there was a tremendous crash and smoke billowed up the fuselage and into the front compartment. Instinctively, Arthur disconnected himself from his set and sped to his allocated crash position. He did not have far to go—it was just over the main spar beside his seat—and there he automatically braced himself for what he assumed would be a 'ditching', since his reason told him that the aircraft was over water. Instead, there came a terrifying shriek of tearing metal! The aircraft rocked crazily and violently! Arthur was flung upwards and then he crashed back against the main spar, unconscious. From then on, his awareness of events ebbed and flowed with his consciousness. He 'came to' momentarily, to find himself lying on the ground just outside the aircraft. He felt the cold chill of that winter's night clamping down on him, even as he watched the flames licking greedily at the wings and nacelles of the stricken aircraft. He observed this in detached fashion, vaguely wondering what he was doing outside the aircraft, but then merciful oblivion claimed him again.

Arthur emerged as from a mist, to realize that he was in some sort of a dimly-lit hut. He sank into unconsciousness again, to surface amid voices that sounded Canadian, but he just knew they were not. Off into unconsciousness again, to rally as a person he assumed to be a doctor urgently asked him how many there had been in the aircraft. 'Are my three pals all safe, then?' he asked. He was again sinking into the depths when he heard a voice say 'He has leg and arm injuries', just before he lost consciousness yet again. He lost all track of time. Next time he surfaced into awareness, he heard a doctor talking and Arthur said, 'When are you going to do something to my arm and leg, which, I understand, were injured in some way?' The doctor replied, 'Don't worry, old chap, your injuries have been patched up very neatly, and we are now putting you to bed for the night—for a nice long rest!'· This puzzled Arthur, for he was certain that no one had attended to him—he hadn't felt anything! But the implied invitation to take a nice long rest was irresistible and he abandoned himself to merciful sleep.

Next morning he had miraculously recovered his full faculties and was able to piece together much of the story of the previous night's happenings. Arthur had sustained a dislocated right elbow and a fractured left fibula, as well as much bruising. The instinctive dash for the crash position had undoubtedly saved him from more massive injuries. Tom O'Shaughnessy and Arthur Holding had both been killed instantly. George Kendrick had been in the nose of the aircraft at the time of the incident. He had suffered massive head injuries and cuts and, although he was still alive, he was not expected to survive. Apparently, the aircraft had hit the water at the bottom of the shallow dive, reared up and then plunged downwards on to the beach, slithering along until it finally crashed into the sea-wall near Snettisham. It was fortunate that some Americans were immediately close at hand and they had managed to get all four crew members out of the wreckage before the flames had taken a real hold on the aircraft.

The next two months were largely a routine of plaster and X-rays, followed by the introduction to gentle arm and leg exercises. Arthur was pleased to hear that George Kendrick had rallied in the most amazing manner and was now considered out of danger, to the great delight and surprise of the medical staff. Arthur felt the death of his two crew-mates very deeply, and was constantly astonished that he should have survived such a crash with comparatively little injury. But deep in his mind was the desire to get well and back with the Squadron, and this aim motivated him throughout the period of his convalescence.

Arthur was transferred to the RAF rehabilitation unit at Loughborough College. There, each case was examined individually and a special course of developing treatment prescribed. In the 'early leg class', Arthur found himself walking very carefully at first, with the requirements increasing until, a few weeks later, he was playing fairly strenuous games, which were followed by cycling and cross-country rambling. Parallel to this treatment was the 'arm class', initially gentle stretching exercise, developing into rowing-machine sessions and weight-lifting. Finally, both courses merged into a programme of badminton and squash. At the outset of this phase of rehabilitation, Arthur had to play these games with his left hand and, although his first few attempts were most frustrating, he surprised himself by getting used to it quite quickly. He was delighted, however, when his right arm was sufficiently strong to allow him to resume his normal game. Compared with some of the other cases at Loughborough, Arthur's case was a minor one, and he was elated when, at the end of April 1944, he was pronounced fully recovered. His aircrew medical category was restored without any reservations. After a very enjoyable week's leave at Exeter, he returned to the Squadron at Woodhall Spa.

He was welcomed back to the Squadron by Wing Commander Cheshire, who made it abundantly clear to Arthur that he was under no obligation to resume operational flying after his traumatic experience. The station medical officer asked him if he really felt fit enough mentally to resume flying with the Squadron, and advised Arthur to undertake a few training flights, to make sure that the experience was behind him and that there were no lingering after-effects that might impair his operational efficiency and endanger other aircrew with whom he would be operating.

Arthur met up again with the flight engineer and air-gunners who had missed the ill-fated flight. They had arrived late at the crew room, just after the crew bus had left on its rounds, and the WAAF driver had returned direct to the MT section, completely unaware of their predicament. All three of them had 're-crewed' during Arthur's absence and were now an integral part of the crew of Flight Lieutenant Bill Reid VC. Arthur's main problem was to get settled into a regular crew and this proved to be a most depressing experience. He was able to 'stand-in' on several training flights and recapture his wireless proficiency in the air, but he was unable to get airborne operationally with the Squadron. It was no easy task to sit, day after day, in an empty Mess, awaiting the return of the Squadron, especially when he knew personally practically every aircrew operating. The Squadron had been engaged during his convalescence on highly-successful operations against factories working for the Germans in France, perfecting a bombing technique that was to be adopted as standard by 5 Group a few months later. A very full part was played in the interdiction raids that preceded D-Day, and Operation Taxable was very creditably performed on the eve of D-Day . . . but Arthur was left kicking his heels on the sidelines during all this activity.

Then came the series of operations against the mammoth and mysterious rocket-sites in the Pas de Calais. 617 Squadron was the only squadron equipped with the Tallboy weapon and the battle against these sites was their own private preserve. As these sites were an unknown quantity, aircraft were allowed to carry front-gunners, in addition to the usual crew. Arthur managed to get a few trips in this role with Flight Lieutenant 'Bunny' Clayton, since Arthur was trained in air-gunnery, but he longed for the settled life of a wireless operator in a regular crew.

At last it seemed that Fate had relented! Arthur found himself crewed with Squadron Leader Les ('Smiler') Munro. Les had been on the Squadron since its formation. His wireless operator became 'tour expired' and Arthur was overjoyed to step into this very experienced crew. He had known Les Munro at the OTU at North Luffenham. It was an added responsbility for Arthur that Les was leading the Squadron on operations at this time in the temporary absence of the Squadron commander. However, after only three sorties against the rocket sites, Bomber Command Headquarters irrevocably decided to 'pension off' many of the veteran crews of 617 Squadron, most of whom would have continued on operations until the end of the war, had the choice been theirs! Joe McCarthy . . . Dave Shannon . . . Terry Kearns . . . Dave Wilson . . . Nicky Ross . . . Les Munro . . . all were affected by the Command decision . . . and Arthur was 'crewless' again!

The Squadron's delight knew no bounds when it was announced that Wing Commander Leonard Cheshire had been awarded a Victoria Cross, for his devotion to duties with Bomber Command throughout the war. Chesh was affected by the Bomber Command Headquarters edict, and, along with all the others, was given a superb 'sending-off' party in the Mess. Arthur was pleased to hear that George Kendrick was making a most remarkable recovery. George had visited Woodhall Spa during his convalescence and had vowed that he would resume operational duties with the Squadron before the end of the war!

The Squadron Commander was now Wing Commander Willie Tait. Under his able leadership the battle of the rocket-sites was finally won and the Allied Armies over-ran the sites, to find that the relentless 617 pressure had destroyed Hitler's vaunted V3 before it had had the opportunity to wreak its havoc on the city of London. The Squadron's effort was then diverted to submarine-pens and E-boat nests on the Occupied Channel coast. The underground stores of the V1 (flying bomb) also came in for decisive attention from the Tallboys, which penetrated their underground silos and destroyed the bombs, either by explosion or by the massive falls of rock that accompanied the carnage. Arthur was able to get in a few operations during this phase by flying as mid-upper gunner with Flying Officer Geoff Stout and Flight Lieutenant John Williams—but he still felt out of things without a regular crew!

At teatime in the Officers Mess at the Petwood Hotel, Arthur was asking the gunnery leader, Flight Lieutenant Scott-Kiddie (known as 'Stop Kidding') if any additional air-gunners would be needed on the next operation. 'Why not come with me as my wireless operator?' suggested a very quiet voice. Startled, Arthur turned to face the speaker, and found himself looking into the almost-apologetic face of Willie Tait! It transpired that Willie had decided that his wireless operator, Flight Lieutenant Larry Curtis, the current Squadron signals leader, had done enough operations with his score at 93, and was sending him off for a well-earned rest, despite Larry's pleas, and howls of disapproval! Arthur could scarcely believe his luck, but accepted Willie's offer with alacrity. He was pleased to find that the similarly 'homeless' Danny Daniel, a Canadian, had been recruited as bomb-aimer to the same crew.

So, after four months of 'champing at the bit', Arthur found himself permanently established in the Squadron commander's crew. The 'new look' crew's first operation was against the U-boat pens at Brest in mid-August 1944. It was Arthur's tenth operational trip since re-joining the Squadron in May. He began to operate regularly with his new crew, but the Squadron suffered a grievous blow in late August, when, over a daylight target, Bill Reid's aircraft was struck by the bomb-load of an aircraft of main force and was sent spinning to destruction. Arthur's three old crew-mates—who had missed the fatal night exercise in January—were all posted as missing, along with the rest of the crew. Jock Hutton, Chunky Stewart and Bert Holt—Arthur remembered these three light-hearted friends and felt their loss very keenly. He was overjoyed, with the rest of the Squadron, when the news eventually came through that Bill Reid had survived the calamity and was a prisoner-of-war. Jock, Chunky and Bert all died in the crash, having been unable to get out of the spiralling aircraft before it thundered into the ground.

Arthur continued to operate with Willie Tait until Willie relinquished command of the Squadron to Group Captain Johnny Fauquier on 28 December 1944. Arthur's trips with Willie included all three assaults on the *Tirpitz* in Norwegian waters—raids on the huge rocket sites—several operations against Brest—the daylight low-level raid on the Kembs Barrage, controlling the Rhine waters, on the German-Swiss border—and many other operations. His personal operational score when Willie left was 49 operations and he was the proud holder of the Distinguished Flying Cross and a Mention in Despatches. He continued to fly with the Squadron commander, as Johnny Fauquier took over most of Willie Tait's crew, reaching a final total of 53 operations. On 6 June 1945, he was posted to RAF Mildenhall to join No 15 Squadron. He met up with another ex-member of 617 Squadron, Squadron Leader Brookes and stayed with this crew until his demobilization in September 1945.

It is a continual source of wonder to Arthur that he survived that nightmare training crash in January 1944. He still feels sad at the loss of five of the crew with whom he joined 617 Squadron. George Kendrick was as good as his vow. He literally fought his way back to aircrew fitness, only to lose his life when operating over Bergen (see Chapter 7) in daylight in January 1945. He was serving as bomb-aimer with Flight Lieutenant John Pryor's crew when their Lancaster was shot down by German Fw 190 fighters.

Chapter 2

The unique 'Aspro'

Colin Keith Astbury—or 'Aspro' as he was more colloquially known to the aficionados of No 5 Group, Bomber Command—was a flamboyant Australian character, around whom legend and fact were woven from the time he joined 49 Squadron at RAF Scampton on 24 April 1942. Sergeant Astbury, as he was then, was on the Squadron strength as a bomb-aimer. He was in the crew of the then commanding officer of the Squadron, Wing Commander Leonard Slee. The navigator of the crew was also an Australian, Flying Officer Arthur Grant (later DSO, DFC), who particularly distinguished himself as the lead navigator of 5 Group's famous daylight raid on the Le Creusot armament works in France on 17 October 1942. But 'Aspro' had begun to emerge from the pack long before that, as a character in a Group that already had its fair share of characters.

On 6 November 1942, Wing Commander Slee's crew was one of three crews of 49 Squadron briefed for a 'Moling' operation. 'Moling' was the code-name given to daylight operations when total cloud cover over Germany was forecast by the Met experts. Aircraft made their way to their designated primary targets at around 20,000 feet in this cloud cover, burrowing through the cloud like moles through the earth. Generally, they were briefed to descend to 15,000 feet over the target, at which height it was hoped that they would have a clear view for their bombing run. Should the primary target not be visible at this height, the aircraft turned for a secondary target. If this target was not visible at the lower height, the orders were to drop the bombs on ETA and return to base. Crews were abjured *NOT* to descend below 15,000 feet under any circumstances over Germany—and this order was stressed several times by Slee during the briefing. All three Lancasters were loaded with fourteen 1,000 lb GP bombs—one on each of the bomb stations in the Lancaster's capacious bomb-bay.

Consequently, Aspro was somewhat surprised, but not at all put out, when the aircraft finally broke cloud at around 10,000 feet very close to their primary target, Osnabruck. He busied himself with the bomb-sight settings and selector switches, as the pilot positioned himself for a bombing run on the industrial area of the city. Aspro was patiently waiting for the bombing run to commence, when he caught sight of a

German fighter, which had obviously not seen the Lancaster at that time. He reported the position of the fighter with great alacrity to Wing Commander Slee, who received his report quite laconically and instructed his gunners to keep their eyes open for fighter attack. The aircraft settled into its bombing run and Aspro crouched over the bombsight, concentrating on his duty, but with the thought of that fighter still niggling away at the back of his mind. He was relieved when the bombsight automatically began the release of the bombs and the selector arm started its traverse across the bomb station commutator. He took the opportunity to look around the sky, in an effort to locate the fighter. To his horror, he saw that the fighter had seen them and was beginning to get very interested in the Lancaster, though somewhat uncertainly at first, as if the German pilot couldn't believe his eyes.

Hurriedly, Aspro burst into the silent intercom and made a hurried report to the captain. 'Thank you, bomb-aimer' replied Slee, placidly, 'but I can't do much about it yet, as we have not yet finished the bombing run!' Aspro could hardly believe his ears! Over Germany in broad daylight, with an enemy fighter getting more interested in their antics every second, and the pilot talking as if they were over Wainfleet Bombing Range! Added to that, the selector arm seemed to be dwelling on its journey across the bomb-release panel, and it looked to Aspro as if the 1,000 pounders would never stop falling from the Lancaster's bomb bay. There appeared to be only one thing left to do, and Aspro never shirked that for a single moment. He began to tell the Wing Commander, in many well-chosen words, spiced with many a choice epithet, just what he thought of a bod who chose to ignore all the instructions he personally had given out at the briefing and who was persisting in placing Aspro's precious life in jeopardy for the sake of a few last lousy bombs! In the midst of this tirade, Aspro saw that the selector arm had finally come to rest at the end of its traverse. 'Bombs Gone!' he yelled joyfully. 'Bomb doors closed' replied Slee, dutifully, and, to Aspro's great satisfaction, the mighty Merlins surged as they were fed climbing 'revs and boost', and the Lancaster turned on to the course for Scampton, heading for the enveloping cloud cover some few hundred feet above. To Aspro's great relief, the Lancaster made it before the fighter could get in an attack, and he settled back in the nose of the Lancaster, to enjoy his rations and assist in the return flight wherever possible.

Leonard Slee made no reference to the interlude over the target at any time during the return flight. In fact, he said nothing to Aspro until after the debriefing, when the crews were enjoying mugs of the hot, sweet milky tea with which returning bomber crews were always welcomed. Aspro was surrounded by many of his Squadron contemporaries, who had waited anxiously for the return of the three 'moles'. These aircrew were anxious to learn all there was to learn, against the day when they might be selected for 'Moling' duties. The Wingco drifted over to the throng and said, in the measured tones that endeared him to the crews of 49 Squadron, 'Sergeant Astbury, you have the foulest tongue of any man

I've ever known in this Air Force!' 'And I'm bloody glad to be back in this room, in one piece, and hear you say that, sir!' retorted Aspro calmly. The other aircrew regarded Aspro with a new-found respect. In a Command whose members were well able to express themselves vividly and forcefully, this statement by the Wingco was an accolade indeed, and Aspro had many free pints in the Mess that night on the strength of it—and the story behind the 'award'!

In early 1943 Keith finished his first operational tour. He had been commissioned during its run and had been awarded a well-earned DFC. He had taken a very keen interest in bombing techniques and bomb-sights and was engaged in lecturing on the Mark XIV bomb-sight with which the 5 Group Squadrons were being re-equipped. But he missed the intimate camaraderie of the operational squadron and yearned to return to operational duty. His opportunity came when Wing Commander Leonard Cheshire took over command of 617 Squadron. On 12 November 1943, Aspro presented himself personally to Chesh as an applicant to join this special duties squadron. Chesh, with all his plans for the revolutionizing of existing bomber operations procedures, recognized the full worth of Aspro and welcomed him not only to the Squadron, but to his own crew. Aspro was delighted! He flung himself wholeheartedly into the training of the Squadron with the Stabilized Automatic Bomb Sight. Soon the results began to make people sit up and take notice. Specified areas of French factories working for the German war machine were 'taken out' of complexes by night, without anything more than superficial damage to surrounding locations.

When the Squadron was called upon to demonstrate the feasibility of the new technique over 'hotter' targets, and eventually on the German targets of Brunswick and Munich, four Mosquito aircraft were provided for the low-level marking of these objectives, Cheshire flying one of these, with Pat Kelly as his navigator. Aspro managed to continue his operational career, flying with such well-known Squadron personalities as Les Munro, Bob Knights, Kit Howard, and Nicky Knilans, an American who flew with the Squadron even though he was a Lieutenant in the USAAF. Aspro added a valuable contribution in the battle of the huge rocket sites the Germans were building in the Pas de Calais, on an arc of radius 60 miles from London. He was still on the Squadron when Leonard Cheshire's courage and devotion to bomber operations over the whole period of the war was recognized by the award of the Victoria Cross—and Aspro, in conjunction with the rest of the delighted aircrew, celebrated in suitable style. When the Squadron came under the leadership of Wing Commander Willie Tait, Aspro continued to operate wherever possible until, with his personal operational sorties total at 78, higher authority saw fit to retire him from operations and Aspro was posted to the Air Ministry in London.

He found it a most boring job. He visited factories on the 'Bull Shit Tour', as it was dubbed by the irreverent aircrew. His heart leaped with envy when he read of 617's successful foray against the German battleship *Tirpitz* from a Russian base, which had resulted in the battleship suffering great damage. As a result *Tirpitz* moved round from Kaa Fiord to a new anchorage at Tromso but her new home brought her within range of Lancasters operating from forward bases in the Moray Firth area.

Aspro was delighted to receive a guarded telephone call from a fellow Australian, Arthur Kell, a pilot on 617 Squadron. Arthur indicated that his own bomb-aimer was 'non-effective sick' and that there could be an interesting operation available for Aspro. Keith awarded himself a 48-hour pass and sped to Woodhall Spa, where he was received with great delight by the aircrew.

Group Captain 'Monty' Philpott was the station commander at Woodhall Spa at this time. He lived on his nerves most of the time, never seeming to be able to fathom aircrew—always wondering what new escapades they would get up to—just a bit out of step with them most of the time. He had no idea of the real reason for the reappearance of Aspro and thought that he had probably decided to spend a leave at Woodhall. Aspro thought it best not to disabuse his mind at this time.

On 28 October, the Squadron moved out to advanced bases in the Moray Firth area, and Arthur Kell's aircraft was airborne and away before Monty became aware that Aspro had been included in the crew. Around 02.00 hours on 29 October, the Lancasters took off from Lossiemouth on the long haul to Tromso. Initially, they followed the same track they had used for the earlier journey to Yagodnik in Russia, darting across the narrow waist of Norway into Sweden. But, once well inside the Swedish border, they turned northwards and hurried to the rendezvous position, where the operational gaggle formed for the run to Tromso. Everything went according to plan, but, unfortunately, strips of cloud covered the battleship at the critical time on many bombing runs, and aircraft kept peeling off in frustration, and making fresh runs, in the hope of getting a clear sight of the *Tirpitz*. Kell's aircraft was no exception. After several unsuccessful attempts, Arthur adjourned from the area, hoping that the cloud would clear sufficiently for Aspro to get in a telling blow with the Tallboy . . . but it was not to be. On their return to the target area, they came in for a lot of accurate attention from the main armament of the battleship, and eventually the hope of bombing *Tirpitz* had to be reluctantly abandoned and they made tracks for Scotland.

It was then that they realized how long they had stayed in the target area, for they discovered that there was insufficient petrol on board to reach Lossiemouth. However, plans for such a contingency had been laid on at the briefing and the aircraft headed for the diversion airfield at Sumburgh in the Shetlands. Without any further trouble or excitement, they duly reached Sumburgh, entered the circuit and contacted Flying Control in the normal manner and asked for permission to land. 'Have you a bomb load aboard?' asked the duty controller. 'Yes,' replied Arthur. 'You are to go out to sea about twenty miles, jettison the bomb load and then return for landing instructions.' 'Willco' replied a stupefied Arthur as he turned the aircraft dutifully away and out to sea. There was dead silence in the aircraft as the crew strove to grasp the ground control's instructions. Throw a Tallboy away into the sea? Such sacrilege had never happened before! 617 Squadron ALWAYS landed with their Tallboys on, if they had been unable to bomb the target! Woodhall Spa Control never even raised the matter. Tallboys were far too precious to be tossed away like 500 lb GP bombs! Aspro was the first one to recover his equilibrium. 'We are not going to give this Tallboy to the fishes, Arthur', he declared flatly over the intercom. Kell instantly agreed and relief flooded into the minds of the other aircrew. 'Open your bomb doors and fly low, Arthur' continued Aspro, 'and they'll assume we've jettisoned it when we return.' In due course they reported back to Sumburgh and were given permission to land, without any further query. They landed safely without the slightest trouble and taxied into the grass dispersal area, where the brakes were applied and the four engines switched off.

As he checked that all the bomb-sight gear was off, and gathered up the rest of his stuff to leave the aircraft, the thought suddenly struck Aspro that the Lancaster had supported its considerable bomb-load for nearly 48 hours and he knew there was a danger of permanent damage to the main spar of the aircraft if the load was left on too long. He conferred with Arthur Kell over the intercom and they both agreed it would be a good idea to let the bomb fall safe on the grass beneath the aircraft. Kell opened the bomb doors to complete the bombing circuit. Aspro checked that all the bomb switches were on 'SAFE' and, without further thought or ado, pressed the bomb-tit. They felt the Tallboy thump on the ground. Satisfied, the bomb doors closed, all services switched off and they began the laborious chore of getting down the fuselage and out of the Lancaster.

What they didn't know was that the commanding officer of RAF Sumburgh had never seen an operational Lancaster close up. He had jumped into his car and sped out to the dispersal to inspect the mighty war-bird. His first surprise came when the bomb-doors opened and revealed the menacing beauty of the Tallboy. His second came as he froze, horrified, in his tracks when the brute suddenly fell from the bomb bay and landed some three feet from him!

This was the sight that greeted Aspro as he emerged from the Lancaster's fuselage. He realized immediately what had happened and a great beaming smile spread over his ruddy Australian countenance. 'That Pommy didn't exactly have his fingers in his ears', he recounted later, 'but he certainly was convinced that he was about to face his maker . . . and him never having fired a shot in anger, or hurt a fly!' Aspro dropped all his flying gear close to the foot of the ladder and walked over to the paralyzed Group Captain. 'It's quite alright, sir, never you fear' he said, comfortingly. 'I dropped it "safe" and it's not going to go off! We'd have heard the bang by now if it was' he added, as an afterthought. He patted the stricken senior officer on the shoulder reassuringly, and strode on, to thump the Tallboy several times on its nose and belly. He turned to face the Group Captain, who shook his head, like one coming out of a trance, smiled weakly at the grinning Aspro and tottered drunkenly over to his car without saying a word. He drove off very slowly.

The Lancaster crew had a short rest and a meal whilst the aircraft was being supplied with ample fuel to get to Lossiemouth. They took off for Lossiemouth to rejoin the rest of the aircraft at that advanced base, in readiness for the return to Lincolnshire. 'I never did get to know that CO's name' commented Aspro, some days later. 'In fact he never spoke a word to me during the whole of the two hours we were in the Mess. For some reason, I got the distinct impression that he viewed me with great disfavour!' Keith returned to his appointment at the Air Ministry and resumed his factory visits. But it wasn't the life for which he yearned and his thoughts constantly winged their way, unbidden, to the Squadron he loved at Woodhall Spa. In addition, the Air Ministry was not very liberal with expenses and he found himself getting 'in the red' with his bankers. However, he learned through an Air Ministry contact that he was due to be sent to Bournemouth very shortly, to the holding unit for repatriation to Australia. He also learned that 617 was to take on the *Tirpitz* for a third time. Sensing in his bones that this could very well be the 'kill', he hied himself off post-haste to Woodhall Spa.

Once again, the aircrew were delighted to see him and Arthur Kell welcomed him with open arms. Arthur was still short of a regular bomb-aimer and Aspro's arrival out of the blue was most fortuitous. Monty Philpott was not all that at ease with Aspro's reappearance, and Keith felt it best to be as forthright as the situation demanded. 'I heard that Arthur was still short of a bomb-aimer, sir' he said, jovially 'so, having nothing better to do, I thought I'd oblige him again.' 'That's all very well, Keith' replied Monty, 'but how do you think I'll feel if you go missing?' 'And how the bloody hell d'ye think *I'd* feel!' demanded Aspro, feelingly. The station commander was far from being reassured and looked speculatively at Keith over the next couple of days. He would have been even less happy if he had known that Keith's draft to the holding unit at Bournemouth had materialized, and that he was very much AWOL!

On 12 November, the Lancasters of 617 once again sought their advanced bases in Scotland. Keith was feeling very pleased with life. He guessed that this was going to be the very last time he would be operational with his beloved 617 Squadron. He had been afraid that signals would have flashed from the Air Ministry by now and that he would have been detailed to return forthwith. The aircraft took off in the early hours of 13 November, to follow exactly the same route and plan as for the previous visit to Tromso. There was unspoken concern amongst some of the very experienced aircrew. Intelligence sources had established that a German fighter squadron had recently moved into Bardufoss, the airfield that covered the *Tirpitz* anchorage. Again, the Lancasters had no mid-upper turrets and the fuselages were lined with auxiliary petrol tanks. The armour plate was missing from the back of the pilot's seat. The Germans would note that the tactics being employed were a direct replica of those employed on the previous raid. Thus, there was a distinct possibility that fighters would be encountered over the target and, flying 'petrol bowsers' as the Lancasters were, damage that would normally be superficial could, in this instance, send the aircraft down in flames.

None of these thoughts troubled Aspro. He was too wrapped up in the absolute joy of his 'swan-song'. He checked all his equipment several times and, when at last the aircraft had settled into the long bombing run, he checked the bomb-sight settings meticulously with the navigator, before settling down, for the last time, to bomb a German target—and what a target! To his credit, Aspro made no specific claim about the results of his own bombing, but he was inwardly certain that he had done the battleship a lot of no good. What he did know was that the Squadron had finally sunk the pride of the German Navy, and that satisfied his professional pride. Their aircraft landed at Peterhead where the news had gone ahead from a recce Mosquito sent over the *Tirpitz* an hour after the Lancasters had left. *Tirpitz* was capsized within her protective nets in the Tromso anchorage. Once again, they stayed purely for a meal and some fuel, then sped across to Lossiemouth to join in the general roistering in the Messes.

Next day, the Squadron returned in triumph to Woodhall Spa, where the celebrations involved the whole of the station personnel. But Monty wasn't at all pleased with Keith! He had been dumbfounded to discover that Keith was AWOL from the Air Ministry and that he had 'ducked out' of his repatriation posting to come to Woodhall to operate against the *Tirpitz*. The Squadron aircrew realized that they would see Aspro no more once he left the station and they refused to let him go without an appropriate farewell party for a great warrior, to show the high esteem and respect in which they held him. Eventually, Monty had to insist on Keith's departure and he was given a rousing send off by the whole station.

He returned to the Air Ministry, and was soon escorted to Bournemouth, after having the 'Riot Act' read to him. He was kept under very close surveillance during his few days at the holding unit, but they needn't have bothered. Aspro had been able to end his European operational career on a summit note—anything else would have been anti-climax! On his return to Australia, he was posted to Advanced Command Headquarters, Brisbane, as Command bombing leader and managed to get in a further eleven sorties in Beaufort aircraft. This gave him a war total of 91 operations and he had also been awarded a Bar to his DFC at the official conclusion of his operations with 617 Squadron. He ended his war service flying as a passenger in a Ventura-Moroti aircraft to Darwin—and avers that this one trip, in an aircraft that was not at all rated by aircrew, gave him a dose of 'Tropical Ulcers!'

Aspro is remembered with great delight by many of the wartime 5 Group personnel, and especially by the members of the wartime 617

Squadron which he graced for so long. His sudden reappearances at Woodhall had inaugurated a new game for the aircrew there. For months after Aspro's repatriation, Monty was not allowed to forget him. When the aircrew thought that Monty was getting too set in his ways, one of them would approach him and engage him in casual conversation about things in general, and then add, almost as an afterthought, 'Was that Aspro I saw at breakfast in the Petwood, as I came out to get the 'bus to the Flights, sir?' Monty would almost collapse and gasp, 'Not that bloody man again, surely! Do you know, he haunts me! I shan't be satisfied that he really is in Australia until he sends me a personal letter from there!'—and then he would hurry off to check with the Adjutant whether Aspro was indeed again on the premises!

A great deal of delighted chortling went on all over England when news was received that Aspro—that doyen of the unpredictable and the outrageous—was now a Justice of the Peace—a Commissioner of the Supreme Court—and a church vestryman to boot! It doesn't really tie up with the recollections that the wartime Aspro left behind in England! His many friends all over the world relished the thought of a reformed Aspro. As one of them rightly observed, 'Even if he has become all those grandiose things, I bet his bloody halo is on crooked!'

Chapter 3

Survival of the fittest

Squadron Leader David Shannon DSO, DFC, sat at his desk in the 'A' Flight commander's office of 617 Squadron. He was one of the original captains that had launched the new squadron with the tremendous success of the 'impossible' Dams raid, and had been one of the only three crews to survive the traumatic attack on the Dortmund-Ems Canal on the night of 15/16 September 1943. He was not yet 22 years of age but somehow managed to look much younger than even those tender years. He was wearing the dark blue serge of the Royal Australian Air Force and there was a popular 'tongue-in-cheek' theory held in the Squadron to explain his very youthful looks. It was averred that Dave actually was a young Air Training Corps cadet who, with a flash of inspiration and a tremendous interest in flying, had managed to kit himself out with the uniform of a pilot in the Royal Australian Air Force and infiltrate one of the courses on an RAF Station his unit had been able to visit. Of course nobody in the Royal Air Force would dare question the presence of yet another Aussie about the place, and so he was able to carry out the subterfuge without discovery and become a fully-fledged captain in Bomber Command. This story, however, failed to take into account the fact that he did draw full pay from the RAAF, even if it did offer some reason for that youthful appearance!

It was Friday 31 March 1944, and the Squadron aircrew were on 'stand-down' after a period of intensive training. The Squadron's last operation had been against an aero-engine factory at Lyons, in France, on the night of 25/26 March. As it was the end of the month, most of the 'A' Flight aircrew had summarized their log books for the month's activity, and these blue books were now piled on his desk, awaiting his signature, before being passed to the commanding officer for his confirmatory signature.

This 'office work' was one of the less attractive aspects of the post of Flight commander in David's private estimation, but he consoled himself with the fact that he only had to sign the books of one single Flight—Chesh had to sign the book of every Squadron aircrew member every month! And at least it was not the traumatic experience for him as it was for big Joe McCarthy, the 'C' Flight commander. 'Hell!' Joe had expostulated to Dave, 'How I hate to sign those books! I'm here to fly, not to give autographs!' But the main cause of Joe's distaste for the chore was the fact that he had a slow and laborious hand and it did take him a long time to get through the task. This fact had been quickly noticed by the signals leader, Larry Curtis and, consequently, it was Larry's forte to get all the 'C' Flight aircrew in Joe's office as early as possible on the first day of each month, and badger Joe to sign their log books, so that they could go over to Chesh and be returned as soon as possible, to be available for subsequent new month's entries.

Joe had a horror of performing this task with onlookers, and he would find reasons for not getting down to the job. He would make suggestions designed to get the aircrew out of his office but the astute Curtis always had a reason why such suggestions were not practicable and would continually remind Joe of the 'urgent necessity' of signing the books, until, in desperation, Joe would get down to the disagreeable task. Joe, with his bear-like bulk and his utter unshakeability in the tightest operational situation, was probably the most popular American in Britain at that time, and certainly his Flight aircrew thought the world of him, but it was their monthly treat to see this giant of a man literally running with sweat over the simple task of signing their books. Curtis was the ringleader in this monthly performance, always reminding the aircrew to get into Joe's office on the morning of the 1st. Perhaps Larry's greatest triumph was to come in later months when he persuaded Joe that 'Joseph C. McCarthy' was a much more impressive signature and was really the form of signature the ordinary Britisher expected from an American. Joe complied, and only succeeded in adding to his nightmare!

Dave had just pulled the first pile of books in front of him when the door of his office swung open and in came the ruddy-complexioned and beaming Keith Astbury, the Squadron bombing leader, followed by a figure that Dave immediately recognized as Squadron Leader Dick Richardson, and another person who was unknown to Dave. 'Dave', began Keith ' "Talking Bomb" and his friend here have come up to do a few low-level bombing runs with the SABS, in order to see how it performs as a fixed sight. The armourers are bombing-up *"N for Nuts"* and I wonder if you would be so kind as to take us to Wainfleet for the exercise.' Dave greeted Dick Richardson and his friend, even as he was getting ready to accede to Aspro's request. 'I'll see about getting a crew together, Keith' he began, but Aspro cut him a bit short. 'Hell, Dave, this is a bit of a rush job! We've got no time to run around for other bods!' 'But I'll need a flight engineer, at least,' said Dave. 'Dave, I can do all that and map-read you to Wainfleet and back! Surely four of us can manage a simple detail like this?' Dave thought for a few moments—it might well take a time to get bods from the various Messes and it did seem a straightforward detail. 'OK then, Keith. I'll just enter the details in the authorization book and we'll be off.' As good as his word, he completed the flight authorization book and signed it. He stood up and collected his flying helmet from the book behind his office door. 'Let's go, Keith' he said, 'my van is outside, so we can go to the dispersal in that.' Twenty minutes later, they were airborne in the Lancaster and heading for Wainfleet and a routine bombing exercise at low-level.

Wainfleet Bombing Range was almost at the northern extremity of the Wash. It was some twenty miles from RAF Woodhall Spa and the exercise had been cleared by Aspro, prior to his coming across to see Dave. Consequently, some ten minutes after taking-off from Woodhall, the aircraft was engaged on the detail. Aspro had performed all the take-off duties of the flight engineer competently, with the two passengers seated at the wireless operator and navigator positions for the take-off. When the take-off had been satisfactorily completed and the aircraft had been settled on the course for Wainfleet, Aspro lingered in the cockpit area only long enough to take the thermometer readings that he needed in the calculation of the height to be fed into the bomb-sight, and then he and his two companions passed into the nose of the aircraft, out of Dave's sight. Aspro plugged into the intercom socket and directed the exercise from his forward position.

The first run was made at 300 feet, followed by a wide sweep and a drop down to 200 feet for the second run. This was completed without incident and Dave had just brought the Lancaster round for the third run at a much lower level when he felt a looseness in the hand-grips of the control column. He manipulated them gently so that the Lancaster should have commenced a starboard turn but there was no response from the aircraft. He looked out along his port wing and saw the aileron vibrating in the slip-stream, and a glance at the starboard aileron showed it to be behaving in similar fashion. He realized immediately that the aileron control cable had broken and he had lost the facility to bank the aircraft into a turn. He switched on his mouth-microphone and spoke to Aspro. 'Hello, Keith. I am afraid that we shall have to cancel the rest of the exercise. I've lost my ailerons!' There was a moment's silence, before Aspro said, 'Are they important, then?' in a deceptively innocent voice. Dave smiled involuntarily—trust Aspro to have some such comment readily available. 'Important enough for you three bods to get back up here' he replied, 'and for me to head this kite for Woodhall immediately.' 'OK Dave, Willco' came Aspro's imperturbable reply, as Dave put the Lancaster into the flattest possible turn to port and headed for base. He informed the bombing range that he had had to terminate the exercise early, due to a mechanical failure and this was acknowledged by the range controller.

Once he had the aircraft heading for Woodhall, he climbed the Lancaster gently until he had reached about 800 feet, which enabled him sufficient forward view to pick up his actual position and allow him to make any needed alterations of course gently, in flat turns. He knew that he had to keep the Lancaster's wings level for, although he would be able to correct a lifting wing to some extent with a kick on the opposite rudder and engine manipulation, it was a remedy he did not wish to employ except as a last resort. The three passengers had emerged from the nose, and Aspro was seated in the flight engineer's seat beside Dave, plugged into the intercom. Dave glanced at Aspro who gave him a wink and a grin. 'I think the bugger's enjoying it!' thought Dave, unbelievingly. He switched on his mike and said, 'Keith, go back and settle those two in crash positions behind the main spar, just in case. But tell them it is only a precaution, as I'm pretty certain that everything will be OK,' he added, wishing that he felt as confident as the words he uttered. Aspro gave him a 'thumbs up' and went back to marshal the two visitors into the positions indicated by Dave.

Meanwhile, Dave saw the aerodrome at Spilsby slipping past on his starboard side and knew that he was on reasonable course for Woodhall. He contacted Woodhall control and explained his predicament. He asked them to clear the circuit and for permission to carry out a landing on the runway most suited to his approach heading, for he would be unable to join the circuit and land in the usual and orthodox fashion. He received a 'stand by' rejoinder from control and concentrated on the flying task in hand. Aspro returned to his flight engineer post and very soon the Woodhall control came back to say that the circuit and airfield was clear and permission was granted for an emergency landing to be made on the most favourable runway to his current approach. Dave acknowledged, relieved that he could now concentrate solely on getting the aircraft down safely. Woodhall was now visible and he gently coaxed the Lancaster until he was lined up with a runway, one of the shorter ones, as he noticed. He began to lose height while his mind grappled with the immediate problem of landing. If he did a normal approach and cut back the throttles for the final touch-down, the cross-wind could lift his wing and there was very little he would be able to do except pray and hope.

Suddenly he had an inspiration and switched on his intercom. 'Keith,' he said, 'I'm going to fly her in, aiming to get her wheels on the deck just beyond the peri track. When I give the word, I want you to turn the trimming wheel back gently' and he indicated the trimming wheel at the lower rear of his seat. 'But don't rush it—do it gently, otherwise her nose will come up and anything can happen then!' 'Dave, I'll be as gentle with it as if I was caressing some bird's bottom,' replied Aspro. 'And that's about it' said Dave, unable to restrain a smile at Aspro's sally. He lowered the undercarriage and was relieved to see the 'LOCKED' lights come on. 'All I needed now was some undercart trouble,' he thought, as he continued to lose height and selected the necessary degree of flap down. He came over the aerodrome boundary still with power on and still losing height. 'Now!' he barked as he concentrated on holding the Lancaster in the correct attitude. Aspro performed his allocated task superbly and Dave felt the wheels touch and stick to the runway. He cut back on all four throttles and Aspro held them back, as Dave used the brakes to slow and finally stop the aircraft.

He turned to grin with great relief at Aspro and realized he was absolutely bathed in sweat. 'Well done, Dave,' beamed Aspro, 'I reckon we could have dropped those other four bombs, if you'd thought about it!' Dave said nothing but reported to the control tower that everything was OK and that he was returning to dispersal. He thanked them for their assistance and noted the emergency services returning to their normal posts. Aspro had nipped back and recalled the two passengers from their crash positions, and the looks of relief on their faces were witness to the trauma they'd suffered in the confined crash position, without any knowledge of what was going on up front.

Once the aircraft was correctly positioned in dispersal, Dave shut down the engines and carried out the usual drills before leaving the Lancaster. Aspro left the aircraft and told the ground-crew Sergeant about the aileron trouble, and before Dave descended the ladder from the Lancaster, the members of the ground-crew were already preparing to remedy the fault. 'Sorry about that, sir' said the Sergeant apologetically to Dave. 'No fault of the ground-crew's, I'm sure, Sergeant' replied Dave, 'and there's no harm done, as it turned out.' 'Probably be a "hangar job" for the repair, sir' said the Sergeant, 'I'll get on to R and I as soon as we've had a good look at it, and get the aircraft in as soon as I can.' 'Fair enough' said Dave 'and it might be a good idea to get the aileron cables of all the aircraft checked as soon as possible.' 'I'll get on to that straight away, sir—and I'll let the NCOs in charge of the other Flights know the score, as well.'

Dave nodded in agreement and was about to make his way over to the van in which his passengers were now ensconced when an airman came running up to him, saluted and said, 'Excuse me, sir, but the station commander is on the 'phone and wants a word with you immediately.' 'Thank you,' said Dave, and he made his way to the dispersal hut. 'I wonder what Monty wants?' he mused, as he picked up the receiver, and said 'Shannon here, sir.' 'Oh, David, would you please come across to Leonard Cheshire's office, after you've done all the post-flight nonsense?' 'Of course, sir' replied David, 'I'm just leaving the dispersal now and should be with you in a very few minutes.' He replaced the receiver and went across to his van. 'Come on, hero' greeted Aspro, 'There's at least three foaming pints awaiting you when we hit the Mess bar—unless you'd rather go to the "Golf" ' he added cagily. 'No, thanks, Keith' answered Dave, 'The Mess bar will do fine. I have no intention of getting involved in one of your well-known sessions in the Golf Hotel!' 'It's all lies and jealousies' grinned Aspro, 'put about by teetotallers and non-holders of liquor!' 'Anyway' said Dave, as they drove from the dispersal 'I've got to see Monty in Chesh's office as soon as I've completed the flight formalities.' 'Well, don't let him keep us waiting, David' warned Aspro, 'otherwise you might find yourself faced with a walk to the Petwood! I can drive a van, you know' he leered. Dave laughed at this sally but when he left his Flight office en route for his appointment with the station commander, he took the precaution of removing the arm from his van's distributor—one never knew with Aspro!

He knocked on the Squadron commander's door and entered when he heard Group Captain Monty Philpott's voice say 'Come in!' He was somewhat surprised to find that the Group Captain was alone in the office for he had expected Chesh to be there, too, but he said nothing. 'Ah, David' said Monty, 'You did a fine bit of flying there, but it cannot disguise the fact that you broke the regulations, and I am bound to take a very serious view of that. You may be "617 Squadron and all that" but regulations are regulations and must be carried out to the full, especially where aircraft are concerned!' David was completely nonplussed. 'Sir?' he asked in complete bewilderment. 'You took off without a full crew, David, and that is totally wrong! You came out of it unscathed, I know, but what would have happened in other circumstances and it was found out that you didn't have a full crew?' 'But if there had been a fatal accident, sir, surely it would have been deemed a blessing that there was *NOT* a full crew on board!' he said, still perplexed by the station commander's obvious agitation and annoyance. 'Not just that, David' came the reply, 'so many other things might have happened. For instance, you might have been attacked by enemy fighters over the bombing range. Such things have happened during this war, and then you would have been in a right pickle.'

David looked at the Group Captain incredulously—German fighters over Wainfleet? Not outside the range of possibility, but, really, highly unlikely. But the station commander was in full flight and paid little attention to the expression on David's face. 'Well, there it is, David. There will be a court of enquiry convened to probe into the matter, and I am very sorry to say that I think it will end in a red endorsement in your log book, as a warning to others on the Squadron. I'm sorry, but that's how it is, and I shall have a word with Leonard Cheshire about setting the court up as soon as possible. That's all I have to say at the moment!' The interview was obviously at an end, so David saluted and made his way back to where Aspro and the others were waiting, somewhat impatiently, in his van. 'Well, what is it Dave?' asked Aspro 'Another "gong"?—Air Force Cross—or the Order of the Garter?' he probed. David started the engine and set the van heading for the Petwood. 'As a matter of fact, Monty is predicting a red endorsement!' 'You're kidding!' chorused the other three in unison. 'No, he seemed perfectly serious' replied Dave, 'I broke the regulations by taking-off without a full crew and might have got shot down by a German fighter over Wainfleet for my pains.' There was a hoot of derision from Aspro but it was a complete anti-climax for Dave. 'It'll never stand up,' comforted Talking Bomb, 'and I'm sure that Chesh will see to that!'

Aspro led them to the Mess bar and soon they were enjoying a pint. 'Ah, here's Chesh' said Aspro and Dave turned to see the Squadron commander making his way over to them. 'Hello, Dave' greeted Cheshire 'I've been off the station this morning, and have just heard that you had a bit of a "shaky do" over Wainfleet.' 'Yes, sir' replied David. 'My aileron cable snapped, and I lost all aileron control, but with Aspro's great assistance we made it down OK.' 'He did all the directing, though, Leonard' remarked Aspro. 'Did you think of getting in at Spilsby, Dave?' asked Cheshire. 'It never crossed my mind' replied Dave, 'never once—I'd taken off from Woodhall, and it seemed only right to land back there. I'd cleared it all with flying control here, which was possibly much simpler than getting in touch with a strange control.'

His mind had been racing ahead, even as he spoke and a shaft of inspiration hit him. 'And it's always so much trouble with a strange airfield. We'd have had to get our own ground-crew over to Spilsby to carry out the repairs, with all that entails—and then there would have been the aircrew to fly it out when it was ready—oh no, sir, it was far better to lob in at Woodhall.' Cheshire laughed as he took the pint of beer that Aspro had bought for him. 'Yes, David, that's very good thinking!' and with that he drank from the tankard in his hand. 'Pity the station commander doesn't think so' said Aspro belligerently. 'The station commander?' queried Cheshire, with his forehead knitting in a perplexed frown. 'Yes, sir' said Aspro 'he thinks it's worth a red endorsement!' A red endorsement?' exclaimed Cheshire, looking helplessly at Dave. 'He feels that regulations were broken by my not taking on a full crew for the exercise' explained Dave. 'He may well be right, but it was a "rush job" after the aircrew stand-down and it wasn't possible to get hold of anyone in time.' 'That's absolutely right, sir' interpolated Squadron Leader Richardson manfully, 'we needed that flight urgently—in fact the two bombs we got off have answered our queries.' 'There will have to be a court of enquiry, David' said Cheshire thoughtfully. 'There always is after such incidents—but I'll have a word with Group Captain Philpott and see about the terms of reference to be laid down for this incident.' 'Oh, by the way, sir' added David as an afterthought, 'I've arranged for all the Squadron aircraft to have their aileron cables checked immediately, in the light of this scare.' 'Thank you, Dave, you did the right thing' smiled Cheshire.

The court of enquiry was duly held and made a recommendation that a *green* endorsement be made in the log-book of Squadron Leader David Shannon DSO, DFC. It reads: 'While engaged on a low-level bombing exercise in a Lancaster aircraft, the aileron control cable broke. In spite of this severe handicap, Squadron Leader Shannon maintained control of the aircraft, returned to base and, showing exceptional flying skill, made a perfect landing.' As required by the regulations, it was signed 'M. G. Philpott, Group Captain, station commander'.

Chapter 4

The Arethusa *Connection*

'Twas with the Spring Fleet she set out
The English Channel to cruise about
When four French ships in show so stout
Bore down upon the Arethusa.
The famed Belle Poule *straight ahead did lie*
The Arethusa *seemed to fly*
Not a sheet, or a tack or a brace did she slack
Though the Frenchmen laughed and thought it stuff
They knew not the handful of men how tough
On board of the Arethusa'

Prince Hoar (1755–1834)

Many historians would have us believe that History repeats itself . . . .

North-west Scotland had endured its normal winter and February 1944 found the Cromarty Firth area still snow-covered, with the wind shrieking its piercing anger at the slightest timorous sign of spring. No 4 OTU, Coastal Command at RAF Alness was back-clothed by the rugged heights of the North-west Highlands, with Ben Wyvis rearing its threatening peak some 3,500 feet above sea level. Stubby Sunderlands rocked gently at their sheltered moorings as the supply tenders fussed between them, whilst, across the coastal plain fanning out to the north-east and east of Alness, the outline of Tarbat Ness was discernible in the limpid clarity of the Scottish atmosphere.

Flight Sergeant Tom McLean stared morosely out of the window of the gunnery section in the instructional block. The ribbon of the Distinguished Flying Medal added a splash of colour beneath the air-gunner brevet on his left breast, and announced him as a man who had seen very close action in the aerial warfare of World War 2. He was not a big man, being some 5 feet 10 inches in height and weighing around eleven stones, with a broken nose that warned here was a man not averse to maintaining his point of view even in the most intimidating of circumstances. The appealing beauty of the rugged scenery outside made no impression on him, for his thoughts were far from Alness, and a fresh wave of depression suffused his being as his eyes took in the moored Sunderlands. Whose bright idea had it been to have him banished to this outlandish place after he had finished his first tour of operations with Bomber Command?—This was the question that had bedevilled his mind more and more often in the past few weeks, to the extent that it was almost becoming an obsession.

He had reported to Alness in the late spring of 1943, after his tour in Halifax aircraft with 102 Squadron at Pocklington in Yorkshire. He had arrived with the firm resolve to do the best job he could in instructing the pupil air-gunners of the unit in operational gunnery technique and the tactical methods of German fighters, but his enthusiasm had been gradually dampened by the attitudes he had encountered from members of the permanent staff of the station. From the outset, Tom had stifled the understandable attitude of almost-envy that hardened Bomber Command aircrew felt for their less battle-scarred brethren of Coastal Command, but he had been completely unable to come to terms with one Flight commander's attitude.

This officer had a tour on 'Coastal' behind him and made it perfectly clear that he attached no importance whatsoever to the air- gunnery lessons, since never had guns been fired in anger during his operational tour. In fact, he made no secret of the fact that he thought that these lectures were a 'giggle' in a Coastal Command set-up and that 'giggle' became infectious, spreading rapidly through the staff and pupils. Oh yes, many of them acknowledged him in the Sergeants Mess and endeavoured to be friendly, showing interest in his bomber experiences and the circumstances of his 'gong', but 'Chiefy' McLean did not make friends easily, and the ignominy of his instructional position did not allow him to be more than correctly polite to such approaches, so that he was more often than not left to his own devices.

He turned from the window and sat down at the table in front of him, raising the large mug of steaming coffee to his mouth and taking a long draught of hot, sweet liquid. His mind slipped down the corridors of memory and he recalled his earlier days in the Royal Air Force. He had originally enlisted as a ground gunner and then, when the call came for volunteers to remuster to air-gunners, with the rapid development of Bomber Command, he had unhesitatingly and enthusiastically responded. A smile played involuntarily around the corners of his mouth. It was strange that the newspapers were always ready to dub pilots who hit the headlines as 'natural born flyers', but, somehow, this description was never applied to any other aircrew grades who came to notice—yet there was a mysterious natural affinity between himself and gunnery which could not be explained by any civilian calling or interest, for he had been a show-card artist in Glasgow for a short period before volunteering. He found himself remembering his 'Halibag' tour and the five 'kills' with which he had been credited. One of these had been on his very first operation—Saarbrucken, 28 September 1942, when he had sent a Me 109 spinning to the sea in flames. Many of his contemporaries had gasped at this achievement, but Tom had taken it in his stride. To his mind, he had applied all the facets of his gunnery training and the result had been inevitable, not surprising, but it had given him a tremendous confidence to face the rest of his tour. There had been a sixth 'kill', but this was left as a 'possible' since no other member of the crew had seen the tell-tale explosion on the ground that marked the incineration of yet another night-fighter.

His face darkened as he recalled other frustrations, even deeper than those he was currently enduring at Alness. As his experience grew in Bomber Command operations, so he began to develop personal theories to improve the 'bite' of his four Browning machine-guns. He had not been satisfied with the laid-down assembly of ammunition belts—ball, tracer, incendiary and armour-piercing bullets in regular rotation. His experiments, and successes, had finally convinced him that the 'meatiest' combination was forty per cent tracer and sixty per cent armour piercing. When he had proved this to his own satisfaction, he had approached the Squadron gunnery leader to discuss it in detail. This officer had initially been taken aback that an NCO air-gunner had been giving thought to such matters and his first hurried reaction was that the make-up of ammunition belts was laid down by the staff of the Central Gunnery School—and anyway, too much tracer ammunition in the combination spoiled the rifling of the gun-barrels.

Tom tried to point out that surely it was far easier and more preferable to replace gun-barrels than bombers and precious aircrew, but the gunnery leader just said that it was something that he would give some thought to, and trundled off.

Tom had waited in vain for the subject to be broached again and when it became patently obvious that it had been consigned to limbo, he produced a paper, outlining his operational experiments and results and sent it direct to the Group gunnery leader. All this provoked was a personal 'rocket', signed by a Flying Officer on behalf of the Group gunnery leader, saying that *ALL* correspondence must be submitted through the proper channels and NEVER direct to Group headquarters! He'd given up then, but his disillusionment with officers began from that day, and he often wondered how many of Bomber Command's heavy losses of 1943 might have been averted by 'The McLean Theory', and how many additional night-fighter pilots might now be resting in their German earth!

He took another swig at the coffee. Memories of Pocklington stirred the recollection of that article in *The Daily Mirror* of Saturday, 22 May 1943 by Vernon Noble—a two-column 'line-shoot' that had made him cringe with embarrassment, especially the headline 'THEY CALL THIS GUNNER "KILLER"!' Nobody at Pocklington had ever called him 'Killer', although many did for a 'seven days wonder' after the article had appeared! He had been interviewed by the author soon after his fourth confirmed victory and it was his first experience of realizing how innocuous remarks made during an interview with an adept journalist could be assembled to give an entirely different and alien picture to his own views. His face hardened once again as his lively memory reminded him that there were quite a few officers who had names for him other than 'Killer'. Tom had never suffered fools gladly and would always dispute the theory facets of air-gunnery that did not stand up to the conclusions he had come to as his operational career developed. He smiled ironically to recall that his 'decorations' in this direction were three severe reprimands, two reprimands and a spell at 'Prune's Purgatory', the popular aircrew name for the Aircrew Rehabilitation Centre at Brighton—nothing criminal, just occasions when his hard-won opinions and short-fuse temper had combined to produce a reaction that his inherent stubbornness had refused to allow him to retract.

However, he had always made a personal point of making himself readily available to new gunners as they joined 102 Squadron as replacements for casualties. He did his level best to prepare them for the pressures and ravages that inevitably lay ahead, unreservedly seeking them out and giving them the benefit of his experience and technique to the full. But, of course, this was normal practice on every front-line Bomber squadron throughout the Command! The battle-hardened veteran aircrew of all grades and callings readily made themselves available to newcomers, recalling vividly their own hesitant and timid arrival, and the help and comfort they had received. During briefings, the senior navigators would make a point of sitting beside the 'sprogs', giving advice about things to watch out for along a particular route and navigational prospects and 'dodges' in relation to the particular target. The same consideration and assistance was readily forthcoming from all the aircrew ranks—God! how he missed that sort of spirit at Alness!

He stood against the window from where he could see the flying-boats and his resentment welled up again inside him. That Flight commander hadn't seen a haddock on his Coastal tour, let alone a Hun, and yet he had been able to frustrate all Tom's good intentions! Tom just hoped that none of the gunners would have cause to regret their neglect of the opportunity they had had to prepare themselves to face the enemy with confidence. Still, it hadn't all been a waste of time, for he had kept himself in full practice with the turret set-up in the sand-pit—he'd probably fired more rounds personally at practice than all the course gunners put together! He had acquired the knack of computing the range of any German fighter, using the ring-and-bead gunsight, to such a degree that he could amaze most of the staff instructors with his instant assessment of the 300 yards range at which the Browning machine-guns became effective—all grist to the mill for his next tour with Bomber Command.

But Tom had to be honest with himself. It was not just the situation at Alness that lay at the root of his present uncertainty and irritability. Some weeks previously, when the restlessness had become almost unbearable, he had written to Flight Lieutenant Jock Hill, a commissioned air-gunner from the Pocklington days who had listened to Tom with a great deal of sympathy during his 'Halibag' tour. In his letter, Tom had poured out his heart to Jock, indicating just how fed-up he was with the situation at Alness and that he was so very desperate to get away that he was thinking seriously of 'taking a walk' and to Hell with the consequences—did Jock have any crumbs of comfort or anything to recommend before he did anything final? Jock's reply had raised his spirits significantly. Jock's old skipper, Wing Commander Cheshire, had assumed command of the 'Dambuster' Squadron at Woodhall Spa in Lincolnshire. Only really experienced aircrew were being accepted on the squadron and Jock's urgent advice was for Tom to write to Chesh direct and apply to join. After all, Chesh would be aware of Tom's reputation from 4 Group days and would give every consideration to an application from Tom. The essential secret was to write DIRECT and leave it to Chesh to cut through the inevitable red tape, for he was an expert at that! An application through the 'usual channels' could take months. It could be turned down en route through sheer cussedness or the protection of 'empires', and it did very much appear as if Chesh did have a sort of *carte blanche* for whatever the future held for 617 Squadron.

Tom had written as soon as he had absorbed the full import of Jock's letter. He had commenced the letter by making a formal application to join 617 Squadron and giving details of his operational experience but then the desperation of his current position had overwhelmed him and he had opened his heart in the latter stages of the letter. He had even stated quite baldly that if his application failed, then he would go absent without leave, so essential was it for him to part company with RAF Alness and his present misery. He had posted the letter as soon as it had been written, lest second thoughts caused him to review it and it was the nagging recollection of his 'threat' that was adding to his present unease. He knew Cheshire only by reputation—and he could make a lot of trouble for Thomas McLean if he reported the letter's contents to higher authority. So many imponderables beset his immediate future that . . . At that moment the shrill ringing of the telephone on the desk brought him sharply back to reality.

He crossed to the table and lifted the receiver to his ear and said into the telephone muzzle 'Gunnery Section. Flight Sergeant McLean speaking.' 'Oh good!' came the voice of the WAAF operator. 'The station Adj' wants a word with you, Chiefy. Hold on a moment!' She went off the line and then came back to say, 'Flight Sergeant McLean for you, sir.' 'Is that Flight Sergeant McLean?' came a voice which Tom instantly recognized as that of the station Adjutant. 'Yes, sir' he replied. 'I'd like you to come down and see me immediately, Chiefy' said the Adjutant. 'It is very urgent—rather bad news, I'm afraid!' 'I'll be down immediately, sir' said Tom. He replaced the receiver and hurried across the office, to struggle into his greatcoat which had been hanging behind the door. Bad news? What could that mean? Family trouble? But then there had been no recent raids on the Glasgow area, so it was hardly likely that jettisoned German bombs or a shot-down bomber had brought disaster to his home in the small village of Kirkmuirhill, some twenty miles south of the city.

Bad news? Unless—and his heart sank a bit—unless recently released chickens were coming home to roost in no uncertain manner! Well, it couldn't be helped now and had to be faced! He stepped out into the cold of that late February morning and strode briskly to station headquarters.

He reported to the station Warrant Officer. 'Flight Sergeant McLean, sir. The station Adjutant sent for me urgently.' 'Ah yes, just a moment, Chiefy', and the Warrant Officer left his desk and put his head around an inside door. 'Here's Flight Sergeant McLean for you, sir,' he said. 'Thank you. Send him in, please' came the reply. Tom was beckoned to the door and he entered the station Adjutant's office, giving the usual courteous salute on entry. The Adjutant carefully shut the door to the orderly room before turning to take his seat at the desk. He picked up a sheet of paper. 'I'm afraid that you have been posted back to Bomber Command for another tour of operations' he said. A great joy lifted Tom's flagging spirits and he smiled involuntarily, but the Adjutant did not notice this reaction, for he was engrossed in the signal in his hand. He went on, 'And not only is it a second tour on Bomber but—' and here he glanced up at Tom, 'it's with that suicide mob 617 Squadron!' He hurried on, 'Nothing we can do about it, I'm afraid, Chiefy. You see, it's been done direct between Bomber Command Headquarters and Coastal Command Headquarters and there's no appeal. I suppose that, somehow, Bomber has a call on you, and have decided to reclaim you now.' He looked up again at Tom, with a look of commiseration on his face. 'Oh, that's OK, sir' replied Tom, 'As a matter of fact, I applied for that particular posting!' 'You applied to go back to Bomber? And, more directly, on to 617?' the Adjutant asked, incredulously. 'Oh yes, sir' answered Tom airily, 'there's really no other RAF life, once you've served in Bomber!' 'Yes, but to apply for that "Death or Glory" mob is something I completely fail to understand' rejoined the Adjutant, shaking his head and scarcely able to believe his ears. 'Well, it's a crust, sir' observed Tom sagely, savouring every moment. The Adjutant, obviously taken out of his stride, pointed weakly to the orderly room door. 'The station Warrant Officer will provide you with the usual clearance certificate for completion before you leave the station—and then all the documents and warrant, with routeing to get you to—' he looked down again at the signal on the desk, 'Woodhall Spa—wherever that is in Lincolnshire—God, you'll have a bit of a nightmare journey getting there, I shouldn't wonder! It just remains for me to wish you the best of luck—and remember!—you volunteered for it, whatever the future brings!' 'Thank you, sir' responded a buoyant Tom, throwing up a really smart salute before returning to the orderly room, to commence the time-honoured ritual for leaving a wartime Royal Air Force station. Five days after posting that letter to Wing Commander Cheshire, he was on his way to join 617 Squadron at Woodhall Spa. 'Yes, Jock' he silently agreed, 'Cheshire certainly does know how to cut through red tape!'

★ ★ ★

The journey to Woodhall Spa proved not to be the traumatic experience the station Adjutant, and a casual glance at the map, had foreshadowed. By dint of enquiry at the motor transport section at RAF Alness, Tom had managed to get a lift on a stores lorry going into Inverness, instead of waiting for the local morning train. This ruse had allowed him to board an earlier London-bound train out of Inverness, which was not overcrowded, and getting a comfortable seat had presented no problem, for a change. He had had a fine meal in the Forces' canteen on Inverness Station before the journey—the voluntary canteens in Scotland were justly famous and popular with all ranks of all Services for the quality and scope of the food offered, and the genuine warmth and feeling of all the wonderful ladies who staffed them throughout the whole of each twenty-four hours. A mutual understanding with an Army Sergeant had ensured that both were able to take full advantage of the similar platform facilities at both Edinburgh and Newcastle, with one taking care of the seats and kit whilst the other 'brought home the bacon'.

He alighted from the main-line train at Doncaster and was pleased to discover that the Lincoln train was due to leave in fifteen minutes. This gave him ample time for a quite leisurely walk to the local platform and to settle himself comfortably in a third-class compartment, which he had to himself. The line ran down to Gainsborough and thence to Lincoln and, as he sat and viewed the flat Lincolnshire countryside rolling past the train, Tom knew he was in 'bomber country' again and the knowledge caused a shiver of excitement and anticipation to run through him.

At Lincoln he discovered that he had almost an hour to wait for the Boston train, which would deliver him to Woodhall Spa. He deliberately kept his greatcoat over his arm as he made his way, carrying his full kit, to the RTO's offices further up the platform. It was a cold late Lincoln winter afternoon, with a hint of sleet in the air, as he pushed open the door and entered the warm office. A Sergeant glanced up at him from his chair at a table, taking in his DFM ribbon as he did so and his manner was at once respectful and welcoming. 'Good afternoon, Chiefy' he began brightly, 'What can I do for you?' 'I'm posted to the Squadron at Woodhall Spa' replied Tom, and he was immediately struck by the surge of interest in the Sergeant's friendly demeanour. 'The train's not for nearly another hour and I've been travelling since quite early this morning from Scotland. I'd like to leave my kit here if I may, for safe custody, and get a 'freshen-up' and perhaps some tea and a bite to eat.' 'Nay trub, Chiefy' replied the Sergeant affably. 'Leave your stuff behind that table over there—no one will touch them, I can guarantee. Then through that door you'll find the wherewithal for a wash-and-brush-up—just warm water, I'm afraid. When you're fit, I'll tell you how to get to one of the best and friendliest teashops in Lincoln.' Minutes later, Tom emerged from the wash-room, with the fatigue of the travel removed from his body and spirit. 'Ah, that better, Chiefy?' asked the Sergeant. 'Don't hurry your meal, as I'll get one of my lads to load your kit on to the Boston train and stand guard on it until you arrive to take over.' He gave Tom lucid directions for the teashop and soon Tom was sitting down, enjoying a very pleasant pot of tea with a fine variety of cakes for wartime—but, above all, he was impressed with the cheerful and friendly way in which he was received by the very busy waitresses, for the teashop was quite crowded. He readily came to the conclusion that the people of Lincoln had taken the bomber aircrew very closely to their hearts—and the nightmare of those last weeks at Alness was already becoming a fast-fading memory.

Like a giant refreshed, he made his way back to the station and found the RTO Sergeant awaiting him at the head of the platform. 'Oh, there you are, Chiefy' he said. 'Have a a nice tea?' 'Very nice indeed' rejoined Tom. 'Thanks for the help.' 'That's alright' replied the Sergeant. 'Now, I've sent my lad down there with all your gear, and he has it all stowed and waiting for you. And I've rung the MT section at Woodhall Spa to let them know what time you'll be at the station, so you shouldn't have to hang about there long in this weather.' 'They're quite good down there' he went on, 'The Adj has asked that we warn them of arrivals where we can, so that they can be met quickly. Well, all the very best, Chiefy, whatever's in store for you—glad to have been of service' and, with a final smile, the Sergeant turned on his heel, and walked off into the gloom. Tom looked after him for a few moments. 'He knows that I'm joining 617, though it was never mentioned' he mused, 'It must be the only squadron at Woodhall Spa—and it must be one hell of an outfit to have that effect on RTO staff!'

He was the only person to alight from the train at the small Woodhall Spa station. He made his way out of the station and peered into the inky blackness that the solitary gaslight lamppost served only to deepen and emphasize. 'Over here, Chiefy' called a cheerful feminine voice, and Tom became aware of the vague outline of a small 15 cwt van that waited across the road, just away from the level-crossing. He lugged his two kit-bags to the rear of the van, and slung them aboard, before opening the nearside door and getting in beside the trim WAAF driver, who smiled brightly at him. 'Not a night for hanging about, Chiefy' she said, as she let in the clutch and the van drew smartly away. 'It certainly isn't' agreed Tom, 'and thank you for being here so promptly.' 'All part of the service, Chiefy' replied the lass, with a laugh. 'Have you come far?' 'I left Inverness quite early this morning' said Tom. 'Gee, and you can't come much farther than that' said the girl, looking at him quickly.

They had reached a small crossroads in the village and turned to the right, soon to leave the houses behind. 'Still, you'll be glad you made the journey, once you've settled in, I can assure you' she continued. She glanced at him, as if awaiting a question, and when none came, she said, 'This is the best and happiest station I've ever been on, and I'd cry my eyes out if I was ever posted away. I don't know why, 'cos it's just the usual conglomeration of Nissen huts and mud, but they're all such a great crowd.' She went on avidly, 'The aircrew are wonderful—but then, so's everyone else! I've never been able to figure it out, but I think that it's got a lot to do with the fact that the aircrew literally worship Chesh, and feeling has spread right down to the lowest "erk". Everyone thinks the world of him—he's marvellous.'

She turned the van in towards a large Nissen hut enclave. 'Sergeants' Mess, Chiefy. You'll find the orderly Sergeant inside, with all the accommodation "gen", etcetera.' Tom unloaded his gear and thanked the WAAF before she drove off into the darkness with an acknowledging wave of her hand. He shouldered his way into the Mess reception area and stood for a few moments blinking in the bright lights. It was warm and comfortable inside and a Sergeant detached himself from a small group of NCOs just inside the ante-room door, and came over to him. 'Flight Sergeant McLean?' he asked. Tom nodded, and the Sergeant continued, 'I'm the orderly Sergeant. Your bunk's all ready, Chiefy. Shall I show you there straightaway or would you prefer a pint and a bite beforehand?' Tom said 'That's the best suggestion I've heard all day,' and allowed himself to be led to the bar. 'Not many in the Mess at the moment, Chiefy. No ops tonight, so most of them have cleared off to Boston, but they'll be back around eleven—most of them anyway, and the stragglers will all be here before "Flights time", you can wager!' There were only a few in the Mess, and all of them were ground NCOs. They nodded in a friendly way to the newcomer, automatically taking in the ribbon on his tunic.

It was a tired Thomas McLean DFM, who finally climbed into his bunk that night. He had made a point of leaving the Mess before the boisterous mob returned from Boston, preferring to meet his peers gradually and in sober daylight rather than to be plunged into the inevitable mêlée of the returning carousers. He was strangely excited about what the morrow and following days would bring. The recollection of his letter and its contents still nagged at his mind. Was his career on 617 to begin with a verbal reprimand from the Squadron commander? He was somewhat surprised to find that he did not want to get off to such a start and that feeling in itself caused him some amazement. 'Is this unit getting to me already?' he thought, remembering the WAAF driver's excited chatter, as he settled down for the night.

* * *

Tom McLean had arrived at RAF Woodhall Spa on the third of March. The weather in Lincolnshire was at its sulkiest, occasional flurries of snow and sleet ensuring discomfort outdoors, whilst longer periods of snow made the planning of bomber operations a continuous alternation between optimism and despair. The Sergeants' Mess began to empty at 08.20 hrs the following day, as the aircrew donned their greatcoats and trudged to the Flight offices, hunched and huddled against the elements. Tom was quite impressed that there had been no queries about the worth of reporting to the Flights in such weather. He had left the main stream and made his way to the Squadron orderly room, which had been pointed out to him by one of his fellow-travellers. The orderly room NCO informed the Squadron Adjutant of Tom's presence and very soon Tom found himself in the inner office. He gave a smart salute on entering, which the Adjutant acknowledged with a smile and a nod, and thus it was that Tom had his first encounter with Flight Lieutenant Humphreys, or 'Humph' as he was colloquially and popularly known to all aircrew.

He saw a man some inches shorter than himself, fair haired and with some kind of old injury to his right eye, for there appeared to be some scar tissue above it. He had an easy-going manner, which put people at their ease immediately, but looked directly at anyone to whom he was talking, as he was to Tom at that moment. 'Good morning, Flight Sergeant, and welcome to 617! Have a reasonable journey down?' 'Yes, thank you, sir' replied Tom. 'Good—and comfortably settled in now, I trust.' As Tom nodded his assent, Humph continued, 'Well, there's the matter of the arrival procedure to be completed now. Wing Commander Cheshire hasn't yet been able to replace that, but I think he's working on it,' he chuckled. 'There is an operations stand-by warning at the moment, so the CO wouldn't have been able to see you today, but I have booked 08.30 tomorrow morning for your interview with him. He sees all new aircrew and is most anxious to have a word with you—knew of you in 4 Group, I understand. Well, just complete the arrival procedure, Chiefy—then visit any of the other sections you feel you should—get the geography of the place—and I'll see you tomorrow morning, a few minutes before 08.30 hours, and usher you into the CO.' He smiled in dismissal, Tom saluted and returned to the orderly room.

It could have been a better day for the arrival formalities, but Tom managed to get all the necessary section signatures on the chit before returning it to the orderly room, for whatever happened to such things once they had been completed. It had been of prime importance that he located the air-gunners section and the armoury, and once the chit had been surrendered, he made his way to the air-gunners section and presented himself to the Squadron gunnery leader. Flight Lieutenant Dave Rodger was a Canadian. He had flown with Joe McCarthy on the Dams raid and was still a member of that crew. He eyed Tom shrewdly, 'Oh yes' he said, 'so you're Tom McLean. Chesh mentioned that you'd be coming here. Got a bit of a reputation, one way and another, haven't you?' he asked enigmatically. Tom's heart sank a bit, but the next words reassured him, 'Well, there's quite a few here with reputations, so you won't feel out of place, and there's no reason why you shouldn't be a big asset to the Squadron. I guess you're not crewed up yet and there is a bit of an ops flap on at the moment, so come in and see me again when Chesh has given you your crew allocation, and we can get down to cases then.'

Tom left the gunnery section and realized that it was lunch-time. He returned to the Mess and immediately became aware of a subtle change in the atmosphere. An op was in the air and a battle order, with all the relevant briefing times, was on display on the Mess notice board. The aircrew clustered around it, with groans from those who found they were stood down for the night and the excitement of those who were on the roster. Tom looked around the ante-room and it struck him forcibly that there were no 'sprog' aircrew amongst this lot. The DFM ribbon was quite common and there was not one apprehensive face to be seen. The air of joviality was not forced in the least, and the 'lunch-time drinks' were probably fewer than usual. He did not feel envious, for there was a great deal for him to do before he personally would be ready for operations again, and the main item for the future was to be crewed-up and have a crew to whom he could relate. He had steadfastly refrained from making the slightest enquiry into the Squadron's present role, but he was aware that they were not operating with the main force. It was obviously something very intriguing which had captured the imagination of the Squadron aircrew for there was an air of suppressed excitement emanating from the battle order aircrew, whilst the disappointment of the others was very real.

Lunch over, he strode down to the Flights, to make the call that was probably the most important of all. He entered the station armoury building and sought out the Warrant Officer Armourer. 'Flight Sergeant McLean, sir' he introduced himself, 'I've just been posted into the Squadron and I'd like your permission to have a word with the NCO i/c the gunnery side. Some things I'd like to discuss with him and get his OK about.' 'Welcome to the madhouse, Chiefy' smiled the WO. 'You'll find the gunnery side in that hut across the way' he continued, indicating a building across from his window. 'Don't know how popular you'll be if you go over there this moment, but I know you won't delay them long—lot of work on with this flap—just as much preparation for a scrub as an op, but then I don't have to tell you that, I'm certain.' Tom thanked him and made his way across to the indicated hut.

Inside was a hive of activity and Tom stood aside, until he had identified the Sergeant in charge. He went and stood beside him until the Sergeant had time to notice him. 'Yes, Chiefy, what can I do for you?' 'Just a "quickie", Sarge' said Tom. 'I've been posted into the Squadron today, and I have a very personal view on the make-up of ammo belts for my own aircraft. I realize you're very busy at the moment, but I'd like to come and see you at a convenient moment in the next day or so. I'd like to assure you that I'll make the belts up myself and see to their installation in the aircraft, so it won't add to your work-load, probably the reverse.' The Sergeant looked at him approvingly. 'Can always use another pair of hands in a flap, Chiefy, so when you're ready, pop in and we'll talk about it, and get it all laid on.' Tom nodded his thanks and returned to the Mess. The tempo of operations had begun on the Flights and no one wanted a "gash" Flight Sergeant getting in the way.

He could not help but be impressed by the attitudes of the aircrew at their pre-operational meal in the Mess. Briefings were over and all was known, but not a word of reference was made to the immediate future.

Instead, the aircrew were enjoying their meal with zest and much leg-pulling and laughter. Whole crews sat together at various tables and the 'mickey-taking' between tables caused continuous roars of laughter around the room. There was a lot of banter with the WAAFs serving the meal to the aircrew—and Tom revelled in the atmosphere he had missed for so very long. But all too soon the Mess became silent and deserted as the time ticked remorselessly past. Eventually Tom heard the roar of engines as successive Lancasters took off for the target until a silence descended which signified that the Squadron was again racing to do battle with the enemy. He had never experienced this situation before. At Pocklington, on the odd occasions when he had not figured on the battle order, he had hied himself off to the fleshpots, glad of a night away from the traumas of operating. This was the first time he had heard a squadron depart and he wasn't at all sure that he liked the sensation.

He stayed in the Mess, reading and listening to the 'Nine O'clock News' on the wireless. Just after ten o'clock he decided that his bed was calling, and he made his way to his bunk. He was soon asleep, but stirred in the night as the sound of Merlins penetrated his slumbers and he uttered a silent prayer that all were back safely, before restoring himself to the arms of Morpheus.

Tom was at breakfast next morning when one of the aircrew engaged in the previous night's operation came and sat at the table. 'All back last night?' asked Tom. 'Yes' replied the Sergeant, 'the bloody op was scrubbed! We found ten-tenths cloud over the target, and Chesh sent us all back home. All that way, and you bring the bombs back!' He added, in frank disgust, 'You'd think the Met bods could do better than that! We'd have had a better night with the popsies in the Gliderdrome at Boston!' Tom smiled but there was an element of relief as well as amusement at the Sergeant's sally. All back! Well, it could have been worse!

He reported to the Squadron orderly room in good time, as instructed. He stood with the twinges of apprehension sparking in his mind, when he heard a car draw up outside the building, a door slam and a figure in blue battledress entered the building by a door farther along the concrete path. Several minutes later, the station Adjutant's office door opened and Humph's head appeared. 'Good morning, Chiefy. This way—the CO's ready for you now!' Tom was ushered across the office to another door, which Humph opened and entered, holding the door for Tom to follow. 'Flight Sergeant McLean, sir' he said. Tom strode into the office and paid the usual courtesies to the figure at the desk. 'Thank you, Humph' came the reply and as Tom heard the door close he found himself facing Wing Commander Cheshire DSO and Bar, DFC and Bar, the commanding officer of 617 Squadron.

He hadn't known quite what to expect, but the figure before him in no way fitted his preconceived ideas. He saw an almost slight figure, but realized that the frame was wiry and sinewy. A rather narrow face, high forehead and somewhat receding hairline—quite piercing eyes which obviously could demonstrate a whole range of emotions but which were looking at him with welcome and—dare he think it!—a certain amount of compassion and understanding. 'Good morning, Mac' said Cheshire, 'So sorry I was not able to see you yesterday, but what with the ops flap and the fact that I like to welcome all my new aircrew personally and at length, it was not possible. Still, you also had a lot to do, so it all fitted in. There doesn't seem to be a lot of hope today, either, judging from last night's "boomerang" on a target at St Etienne, so I can have a nice long chat with you and put you fully in the picture.'

'Take a pew, Mac' he went on, waving towards a chair at the side of his desk and then leaning to his left to give the wall a couple of hearty thumps. 'Two coffees, Humph, please!' he called before turning to face Tom again. 'Smoke if you want, Chiefy' he said, pushing an ashtray within reach. At that moment his telephone rang and he picked up the receiver with a murmured 'Yes?' He listened for a few moments and then said 'Thank you—I'm not at all surprised. It's snowing quite heavily outside at this moment.' He depressed the hook for a moment and then allowed it to rise, 'Would you get me the "A" Flight commander, please?' Again a short pause and then, 'Oh, Dave, there's an ops stand-down today, so I feel it would be a good idea to release the crews for the day, after last night's abortive effort. Some of them were back somewhat late so no doubt they'll be feeling like a rest. Would you pass the word to the other Flight commanders? Good, thank you' and he replaced the receiver. He again turned his attention to Tom, but before he could say anything, the door of the office opened and the orderly room Sergeant entered, bearing a tray with two mugs of steaming coffee. He placed one on the beer-mat beside Cheshire and Tom relieved him of the other mug when it was offered to him. When the Sergeant had gone and they were alone again, the CO took a pull at his drink and began to speak, 'It will be no secret from you that Bomber Command's results are not what they are required to be. A great deal of effort and sacrifice goes into getting the bomb-loads into the target area, but a very low percentage of these are actually dumped near the aiming-point, let alone on it, and in stating this truth, I imply no criticism of PFF or the main force. My own opinion is that things will not greatly improve until we have visual identification and effective marking of all aiming-points. Of course, there is a powerful school of opinion against this view. They prefer to back the use of radar aids and pyrotechnics.

'Well, I was given command of this Squadron as an opportunity to prove my theory and possibly to develop a new method of target attack. My main demand was that I was supplied with battle-proven aircrew. There was no immodesty about this request, simply that there would be no time to spare to train pilots and navigators, etcetera. The main training requirement on this Squadron is bombing practice. There are facilities laid on for crews to get other essential training, but bombing is the main training preoccupation.'

'No new crew is allowed to operate until they have carried out at least three six-bomb practice exercises at Wainfleet. The results are computed to a height of 15,000 feet, no matter what the actual height of a particular exercise. Four of these eighteen bombs have to be within 50 yards of the target. The bombing leader maintains an overall Bombing Error ladder in his office by crews. Crews move up and down the ladder as their bombing results are assessed. Thus, a good exercise this week could be marred, or wiped out, by a carelessly dropped bomb in an exercise the following week. A crew's position on the ladder is determined by the average error of ALL their Wainfleet exercises, right from the time they join the Squadron, and position on the ladder can make the difference in being called to operate and not, and also what bomb-load or duty they are allocated on an operation. Consequently, there is great competition to stay in the top area of the bombing ladder and bombing exercises at Wainfleet get the same careful attention as bombing on actual targets.'

He paused and took a swig at his mug of coffee before continuing '*ALL* squadron aircrew need to develop a fetish about bombs and bombing accuracy, no matter what their aircrew calling! Pilots *TAKE* bombs to targets. Navigators *FIND* targets for bombs. Bomb-aimers *PUT* bombs on targets . . . and gunners *PROTECT* bombs to target—it's all about BOMBS!' Tom listened spellbound, almost afraid to drink lest he miss one of these pearls! No CO had ever spoken to Flight Sergeant Tom McLean so openly and convincingly, and he waited expectantly. Cheshire smiled and leaned forward confidentially, 'And you'll have an extra responsibility on this Squadron, Mac, and that is the responsibility of assessing the fall of your aircraft's bomb in relation to the aiming-point marked. After all, you get the finest "going-away" view of the whole crew!' He smiled broadly and Tom began to appreciate why the station personnel held him in such esteem, and he listened avidly and attentively as Cheshire continued.

'You'll be aware that there are some very, very experienced aircrew on the Squadron, and particularly amongst the gunners. The aircrew are all volunteers, drawn from all over the Command. Every Group is at present represented on the Squadron, even 2 Group, the light bomber group. There are still some of the original crews and aircrew from the Dams era. There is quite a strong bevy of 4 Group bods, which your arrival strengthens and there is little doubt that the Squadron has greatly benefited from these Group experiences. It has been a very uplifting experience for me to have such men under my command.' He shifted his position in his chair and, when comfortable, went on. 'Since last November we have been gradually developing the procedures and getting them right. We have operated mainly against the 'softer' targets in France and Belgium, but are beginning to achieve results that are making people "upstairs" sit up and take notice. We have been taking-out not only factories, but specific important buildings in factory complexes.' He reached for a book lying on his desk. 'For instance on the night of 8 February, our target was the Gnome-Rhône aero-engine factory at Limoges. Admittedly there was negligible flak and a beautiful bright moonlight night, but everything went perfectly, even to being able to do three low-level dummy-runs over the target, to warn the French workers and give them ample time to get clear. Twelve aircraft attacked and nine had aiming-point photos—with not one French death!—Imagine that sort of result on a German target!' Cheshire paused for a moment, as if savouring the thought and then continued to the spellbound air-gunner, 'That does bring out one singularly important aspect of our operations in Occupied Europe—the minimum endangering of the lives of Allied civilians. We have to go to great lengths to secure this, and there is no jettisoning of bombs except under the most extreme circumstances, and this is drummed into all captains and crews from the outset!'

Looking directly at Tom, he went on, 'These results are being achieved using aircraft that are totally unsuited to the marking role. The Lancaster really wasn't designed for the dive-bombing type of approach so necessary to plant the markers on the aiming point, without skidding off. I have every hope that soon our results will convince Bomber Command that we deserve at least a run with Mosquito aircraft to do the marking, for they'll be a "must" when we move on to German targets.'

He broke off and smiled at the Flight Sergeant so attentive before him. 'I'm sorry if I've run on, Mac, but it is a bit of a dream and a hobby-horse with me! Are there any questions you'd like to ask?' 'No, sir' Tom replied, 'but it sounds as if a new era of bomber operations has arrived with a vengeance!' 'Well, it seems to be going OK in the present areas but we all appreciate that Germany will be a much tougher proposition. Still, some members of the Squadron are of the opinion that, even with Mossies, the marker aircraft will be in the nature of suicide squads. I don't subscribe to that view and aim to test it out personally before the role gets passed on to anyone else. Now,' he smiled, 'to get down to cases, Mac. I've heard that you are a very hard "nut", Mac.' He laughed at the changed expression on Tom's face. 'I've had a few words with "Gus" Walker, who, as base commander of 42 Base at Pocklington, was aware of your presence on 102 Squadron.'

'Here it comes!' thought Tom wildly. 'He's broached it gently, but here comes the rocket about my "discip" record and my letter to him!' and he braced himself for what was to come. Cheshire was smiling broadly now, as he proceeded, 'Well, this is a whole Squadron of "hard nuts"! Tough and uncompromising in the air, and many of them similarly disposed on the ground—and I'm putting you with a crew of the hardest cases on the Squadron at the moment—Duffy's mob! They are basically a Canadian crew, very effective and no frills—and certainly no nonsense! Even on a Squadron such as this they have a reputation that stands out! I've arranged for Duffy to stand-by in the Flight office until we've finished. I'd like you to go along and introduce yourself and for you both to get to know each other—have a "heart-to-heart" with Duffy first. I think that will be a less over-awing prospect than meeting the whole crew all at once' and Cheshire laughed out loudly at the thought. Tom's relief was so manifest that he felt quite weak and somehow he sensed that Cheshire was quite aware of the sensations within him, for his eyes were twinkling merrily as he looked across the desk at Tom. 'Now, Mac, I've done all the talking so far, and I don't know when I shall get a similar opportunity to have a word with you so—tell me about those fighters you downed on 102, especially that 109 over Saarbrucken on your very first op!'

* * *

It was an elated Flight Sergeant McLean who left the Squadron headquarters building some thirty minutes later. Not a direct word about his letter and his troubles in 4 Group, yet somehow he felt that Cheshire had understood perfectly and was offering him the opportunity to consign it all to limbo. The falling snow could not dampen his soaring spirits, as he crossed to the Flight offices to meet Flying Officer Duffy, his new skipper. He felt that he could meet the Devil himself and not be intimidated. Life was wonderful again!

A well-muffled figure appeared in the doorway of one of the Flight offices. 'In here, Chiefy' called a voice with a Canadian accent, and Tom entered the office, the door closing behind him. It was not all that warm in the office, but he unbuttoned his greatcoat as he turned to face the only other person present, and beheld his new skipper for the first time.

Flying Officer Duffy was a couple of inches shorter than Tom. His Irvin jacket was unzipped and Tom could see he was of somewhat slight build. He had a firm moustache concentrated on his upper lip, nothing 'handle-bar' about it, and he was studying Tom through half-closed but crystal-clear eyes. His lips were parted and Tom noticed a 'Terry Thomas' gap in his geeth. 'So' he drawled, 'you're the guy Chesh has been promising me to complete my crew!' It struck Tom that perhaps his letter had arrived at a very convenient time for Chesh, too! 'Well, pal, I'll put it to you straight down the line. I've got a nerveless mid-upper gunner, Red Evans, but the huge sonofabitch is too big for the rear-turret. If he did get in, he'd certainly never get out again' and Duffy grinned warmly. It was a genuine, honest grin that made Tom take an immediate liking to this man. 'I know all about you as a rear gunner, and so you'll be our protector at the rear, and we all feel that we're lucky to have you aboard, 'cos we're all kinda anxious to see this bloody war through, and your presence will be a great comfort to the rest of us!'

Tom felt on top of the world. No commanding officer or skipper had ever spoken so openly and frankly to him before and he welcomed the new sensation of respect and understanding that had been evident in both voices. He heard Duffy continue, 'Apart from your talent as a rear gunner, I do know that you have as great a talent for getting into the soup. For instance, I know that you had rather a gory punch-up with a Canadian Squadron Leader outside "Betty's Bar" in York.' Tom looked at Duffy in amazement. He'd certainly done his homework outside the operational sphere! But Duffy pressed on, 'Luckily, I know that bod you mixed it with, and I guess he had it coming to him, especially as he'd thrown first punch at you inside the pub.' He drawled, without pause, 'But then there was the matter of the RAF van that went missing from Pocklington and coincidentally was found within five miles of your home in Scotland when you had gone off on leave! The SIB goons were unable to get you to sing about that, but you did have a spell at Brighton that had its roots in that incident—and your previous Squadron commander wasn't exactly enamoured of you, was he? He described you as—let me see' and Duffy plucked a crumpled sheet of paper from his battledress pocket and laid it on the table, straightening it out with his hands before reading from it. 'Ah yes, here it is . . . "Undisciplined, uncommunicative and insubordinate on many occasions. Refused to fly with a certain captain".' Duffy looked up speculatively before continuing to read from the paper, ' "Unfortunately no action could be taken against McLean, as the captain concerned was killed several hours later".' He finished reading it and, in the silence that followed, folded the paper and returned it to his battledress pocket. A thousand thoughts and memories raced through Tom's mind and with them a mental prayer that those tempestuous incidents at Pocklington were not to be resurrected to blight his time on 617. He looked unflinchingly at Duffy. 'He was killed with all his crew—and not on operations—' he retorted, 'and for me the fact that I am here to discuss it with you rather than than "six feet under" will always vindicate my stand—or "obstinacy", as the Squadron commander dubbed it.'

Duffy stared at him for a few moments, then shrugged his shoulders. 'Yeah, yeah' he said, '4 Group had its own peculiar ways and characters—too many Canadians all together, I shouldn't wonder, with all the implications and complications that can cause!' and, to Tom's relief, he grinned impishly. Taking advantage of the lull, Tom interjected, 'From what I've heard of your crew, they're not "Cranwell stick-men" either! If they were, believe me when I say that no way would I fly with them. I like what little I've heard of them so far and I think I could fit in easily. I'd like to try, anyway, because this Squadron intrigues me greatly, and I want to be a success on this tour with as little hassle as possible.' 'That's the hammer!' said Duffy, offering his hand, which Tom took instantly. ' "What's past is prologue," as some clever bod said once' continued Duffy, 'but we've got a helluva lot to get straight and right, fella, before we operate. We're gonna get as much fighter affiliation, and anti-fighter practice, as we possibly can . . . and continue the exercise until we're in each other's brains when we're in the combat role.' 'I couldn't agree more' said Tom, rather hesitatingly, unsure whether a 'sir' was called for, or expected.

Duffy seemed to sense his dilemma, 'They call me "Duff" generally' he said, adding as an afterthought, 'I don't think they mean my flying, but it could be' he laughed, 'although it'd probably pay us both for a little more formality in the presence of "visiting heads" if you get me.' Tom nodded understandingly. 'Got you completely, Duff' he replied. Duffy went on, 'You and I need bags of co-operation in the air, so that if we get into situations where you and I are the only two that matter for that time, we both know the absolute score! What you get up to on the ground is entirely your own business—within limits—so long as it doesn't interfere with our flying or what is now *OUR* crew. Be on time for briefings—and for all take-offs, whether operational or training—I'd prefer no drinking at all, once we're on the battle order, but certainly only in moderation. Any questions or observations from your side?' he asked.

'Yes, Duff,' said Tom, 'I am delighted that you're so keen on the anti-fighter drill. Can I suggest that I be allowed to go into it without warning, whenever we are in transit to and from the bombing range, and similar occasions—never over the bombing range, of course!' he added hastily. Duffy grinned. 'I guess you've had Chesh's BOMBING lecture—and all very true!' he said 'Yeah, that's a great idea, and it'll get the rest of the crew used to taking their operational positions once we get into that situation.' He began to zip up his Irvin and prepare to face the elements. 'The rest of the crew are in the Nav section—or they'd better be' he said. 'Let's go across and meet them, and you can see what you've let yourself in for—and wish that you had never volunteered for a second tour!'

He led the way from the Flight office to another building. In a smaller office inside sat five members of aircrew. Tom noted that three were commissioned, the bomb-aimer, the navigator and the wireless operator. Of the others, the air gunner was a Warrant Officer and the flight engineer was a Sergeant. The latter was English, whereas the other four sported the 'CANADA' flash on their shoulders. They stood up as Duffy entered with Tom. 'We were just beginning to think you'd gone off to the Petwood and left us here, as one of your jokes' said the smiling bomb-aimer. 'I'd considered it!' cracked back Duffy. He turned to Tom. 'This guy is Roy Wood' he said, 'Our bomb-aimer, who has been known to get the odd bomb on target.' Roy offered his hand to Tom and assured him, 'I've done that a darned sight more times than he's made decent landings!'

'This here is Don Bell, our navigator—has often failed to locate his room in the Mess after a bit of a thrash, but has a much better record where targets are concerned' said Duffy. He and Don Bell grinned at each other and Tom felt a surge of reassurance, as he took the proffered hand. The really good crews always had a captain and navigator who had a mutual respect and trust in each other's ability! 'And this here is Doug Pearce, the wireless operator—can't tell you much about him, except that he always comes with us, and seems to know how to operate the set.' 'Pleased to meet you, Mac' said Doug, shaking Tom's hand vigorously. 'Al Benting, our flight engineer' continued Duffy. 'We have him so that other UK bods don't feel out of it—keeps a good log but is inclined to worry over trifles'—there was a general laugh at this, and Tom guessed that it was a reference to some happening to which he was not privy. 'Great to have another leavening of English on board at last, Chiefy' said

Al, smiling broadly as he took Tom's hand. 'And last we have Red Evans, mid-upper gunner by reason of his bulk and not his inclination' intoned Duffy. Tom looked at the last crew member with interest—the gunner with whom he would have to co-ordinate closely in a fighter attack situation. He was disturbed to see that there was no answering smile from Red, a bear of a man, as Duffy had rightly described him in the Flight office.

There was more than a hint of resentment in the look he gave Tom, but he held out his hand and, as Tom grasped it, he said 'Hi—Killer!' and a grin that was almost a sneer lit his face. The others laughed delightedly, but Tom could see no mirth in the face that kept looking at him and which was hidden from the rest of the crew. 'That was all a right load of "bull" ' he said, taken aback that the news had travelled ahead. Still, with all the other information Duffy had garnered, it was really not surprising that they had knowledge of the article. 'Never mind about that' laughed Woody, 'Just keep up the good work for us, if ever you have to!' 'Too right' yelled all the others, but Red kept silent. Duffy looked at his watch. 'Well, we've just about time to get the transport down to Petwood for lunch. I suggest that we have a few jars in the "Mucky Duck" in Coningsby—say, about 20.30 or thereabouts tonight. It's not going to be much of a night for Boston' he added, looking out the window. 'Bang on, Duff' was the general agreement and they left the navigation section for their Messes.

Red pressed on ahead but Al fell in step with Tom and walked with him towards the Sergeants' Mess. 'They're a good crew, Jock' he said. 'Inclined to talk a lot more on ops than your English crew but they know their stuff and always do a good job. Duffy's a first class pilot and I consider myself lucky to be in this crew.' 'What about Red?' asked Tom. 'Well, he's the odd man out, in a way' said Al blithely, 'He is a colossal extrovert—likes to show off his undoubted strength in the Mess, as you'll no doubt observe in due course.' He looked at Tom, 'Duffy found out about the article and was only too pleased to let the rest of the crew know that they were getting a "gen-man" for the rear-turret, but somehow I got the impression that Red felt a challenge to his ego. I might be wrong, but I don't think his welcome is as sincere as the rest of the crew.' Tom shrugged his shoulders, 'Let's hope that time cures that very quickly. Duffy thinks a great deal of him, I know.'

That evening Tom and Al walked the odd mile and a half to the village of Coningsby from the Sergeants' Mess. They had waited in the ante-room after dinner but Red had not put in an appearance. 'Well, he knows the way' observed Al, 'So it's us for the open road, if you're ready, Jock', and they set out for the rendezvous. Tom was pleased to find that Al was a genial sort of chap, who took his aircrew job very seriously. 'We have to keep a very adequate log on all operations' he confided to Tom, 'Many more entries than were required on our previous squadron. They are handed in at debriefing together with any comments we have to offer and are delivered to the Engineering Warrant Officer next morning. He checks them through and initiates any action that appears necessary. If there's anything they don't quite understand, there's always a message in the Flight office, asking you to go out and see them—and bad, or incomplete, logs mean a rocket from the Flight Engineer leader and a warning as to future behaviour, plus another rocket from the skipper, who watches you with an eagle eye on the next ops trip!' Al laughed and went on, 'But of course that rarely happens—generally only to crews joining 617 for the first time.'

Tom could not see Al's face in the almost impenetrable blackout, but he could tell from his voice that he was chuckling to himself, as he continued, 'D'ye know, Jock, I think that they deliberately "underbrief" new engineers about the log and its importance to aircraft maintenance on this unit! And they get the most gi-normous rollicking from all concerned when they turn in their first log, based on previous squadron standards! Everyone goes into a well-rehearsed act, so stylishly delivered that they all deserve "Oscars"! I'll never forget my baptism in this sphere! It was done so realistically that I was certain that I had had my place on the Squadron, and was so very grateful to be given another chance, that I've never turned a "duff" entry in since, let alone a poor log!' He turned his head towards Tom, 'All aircrew are expected to keep on top line with their jobs' he said, 'without being chased or chivvied. The facilities are all laid on and we are expected to use them without being detailed or instructed.'

They continued to chat until they were into Coningsby village. Al said 'Ah, there's "The Mucky Duck" at last. It sounds pretty full.' He pushed open the door of the saloon bar and allowed a blast of heat and fug to escape into the night. 'Put that light out!' chorused a roar of voices from inside, followed by a great shout of laughter, as they stood blinking in the light of the bar. Al leant over to Tom, 'That's the usual greeting' he laughed. 'The local air raid warden always yells that if he happens to be near when anyone enters the pub, so they all yell like that, in the hope that he will hear them on his rounds and be reassured that they're being good boys!' Tom looked above the bar and saw that the real name of the pub was 'The White Swan'—the nickname was the irreverent aircrews' appellation!

'Over here, Al' came a call and Tom looked across the room, to see Duffy, Woody, Don Bell, Doug Pearce and Red Evans all seated at a corner table, with a jug of beer in the centre, from which they helped themselves as required. There were two spare pint glasses which were pressed into their hands as they settled down with the rest of the crew, and soon they were getting down to a session. Tom reached into his pocket to make his contribution to the 'kitty', but Duffy would hear nothing of it. 'This is your night, Mac' he said 'and it's our way of saying welcome.'

'Mind you,' he added, 'if ever you're guilty of finger trouble, you'll be "in the chair solo", and I guess that'd be a tremendous blow for a Scot.' The others laughed at this sally and so a very merry and pleasant evening proceeded. When at last mine host had persuaded the last aircrew to vacate the premises, Tom found that a very large taxi had been laid on, into which they all piled without ceremony. The three NCOs were dropped at the Sergeants' Mess, whilst the taxi then sped off into the blackness, heading for the Petwood, with the occupants singing lustily. 'What's this "Petwood" they refer to, Al?' asked Tom. 'Oh, it's a fine hotel, standing in its own grounds just outside Woodhall Spa, which has been taken over for an Officers' Mess. I've never been in there, of course, but I understand that it is the envy of many of the other RAF stations, especially the satellite dromes with their Nissen-hut accommodation.' Tom felt that bed was calling, so he bade Al goodnight and made his way to his bunk.

He mused over the evening and the impressions he had got from observing and listening to the others. Duffy—a bit of a lad, obviously very well-thought of by the whole crew and on top of his job. Woody—a proper little 'wise-cracker', never short of an answer but with a directness that signified that he was well able to cope. Don Bell—rather quietly spoken, but with a rare dry wit and sense of humour—an air of quiet efficiency that Tom was delighted to find in that important member of the crew, the navigator. Doug Pearce—again, quiet for a Canadian but with a manner that indicated that here was a man who would not panic under any pressure. Al Bentine—he had made a great appeal to Tom during their walk to Coningsby, so very obviously devoted to his calling and proud of his crew and squadron. Red Evans—here Tom was still somewhat troubled in his mind. Even during the jollity of the evening, Tom was aware of that strange enmity Red nurtured against him. He had used the 'Killer' epithet a few times during the session, and there was a bitterness and edge in his voice that apparently the others didn't notice, but which was plain to Tom—and Red knew that Tom was getting the message. To a certain extent, Tom could understand why, for the rear gunner was looked upon as the senior gunner in the air-gunner hierarchy and no doubt Red resented Tom's appointment to that exalted position. Still, if his build was against his manning the turret satisfactorily, surely he would have to come to terms with the situation. But perhaps Red didn't agree with Duffy's assessment of things. 'It's a pity' thought Tom, 'but if it can't be cured, it'll have to be endured.' However, he felt secretly that things would get worse before they got better where Warrant Officer Red Evans and himself were concerned.

* * *

The following two days saw a continuance of the fretful weather, with the sky full of threatening clouds periodically giving vent to windswept showers of sleet and the cloud-base effectively ruling out any possibility of flying. Tom discovered that the usual routine was for all aircrew to report to their respective Flights, and make their presence known to their captain. Unless there was something specific laid on, the aircrew then split up and went along to their various sections where the leader laid on informal talks or marshalled his flock to the various synthetic training set-ups. Aircrew were expected to employ their time gainfully and to keep well abreast of enemy defence developments and techniques, as well as all the myriad facets of intelligence that were available in the intelligence section. This section was always well patronized by the aircrew, for it was generally warm and there was always a decent mug of tea made available. What was very noticeable was the fact that many of the Squadron navigators developed a great interest in the maps and charts kept in the briefing room, due, no doubt, to the fact that two very attractive WAAFs were the custodians of these stocks.

When his crew were together on the first morning, Duffy said, 'I guess that today is gonna be like yesterday, as far as ops are concerned, so if you other guys care to wander over to your sections, I'd like to take Tom and Red over to the briefing room for our initial discussion on combat drill. 'Of course' he added hastily, 'You will all have your part to play in that situation, but the gunners and I have to get together to make sure we can provide the opportunity for you to play those parts.' Doug Pearce said 'I'll tell the gunnery leader where you are, so that he'll be in the picture' and with that, he and the others disappeared in the direction of the section huts, whilst Duffy, Tom and Red made their way to the briefing room and settled themselves down at a table out of the way of other activities.

'Well, Tom' said Duffy, when they were comfortably settled, 'I guess you had better lead off as you have been in the combat situation enough times to be a "gen" man on procedures and drills. How do you see it, and what are the essentials for survival?' Tom cleared his throat and thought for a moment before beginning to speak. 'The main essential, Duff, is that we see the fighters BEFORE they come in to attack us, so on that score it is down to Red and I to keep a continuous and adequate sky search. My main responsibility will be the quarter areas, whilst Red will be engaged in scouring both the port and starboard beam areas. Very few attacks come from the bows, but you might consider it advantageous for the bomb-aimer to man the front turret and join in when occasion permits once we are in the combat situation. It seems a waste to have two good Brownings available and not use them, even if they act as a surprise and deterrent to the German pilot without inflicting any damage.' Duffy nodded. 'Point taken' he said. Tom continued, 'There's not the slightest doubt that the corkscrew is the finest manoeuvre to use against attack by a fighter, as it puts a lot of the initiative into the hands of the bomber pilot—but I maintain that it needs to be co-ordinated with a sudden reduction of airspeed at a critical time.'

Duffy leaned forward, very interested to hear what Tom was about to say, and Red pricked up his ears at Tom's statement. 'You know the German fighters out-gun us—they can lay outside the 300 yards effective range of our Brownings and stream cannon-fire at us in perfect safety, whilst all we can do is to watch impotently. So, the fighter has to be lured within our range, and before he has opened effective fire with his own armament—and the way to do that is by cutting back on all four throttles when I give the word, so that the Lanc seems to hang in space for a few seconds. When the Hun is coming in, the pilot will have estimated the closing speed between himself and his prey, and his finger will be hovering over his firing button, ready to open fire from about 450 yards. If, when he is at about 600 yards, the Lanc drops its speed drastically, so that he starts closing at almost double the rate he had calculated, his immediate reaction is to wonder what is going on, since his gunsight tells him that he is within firing range, but it has occurred that much more quickly than his own mental calculation. Before he realizes what has happened, he's closed to 300 yards or less, and we're on a more equal footing.'

Duffy considered this, and asked Red for his thoughts. 'It certainly sounds feasible and logical' said Red, with something like grudging admiration in his voice, as he looked at Tom. 'How long do we hang there, Tom?' queried Duffy. 'As soon as you hear the Brownings in action, you can pile the coal on again, skipper' replied Tom, 'and that can be disconcerting for the Jerry pilot, too—if there's anything left of him' he added, with a smile. 'That's your department entirely, gunners' retorted Duffy. 'It most certainly is' smiled Tom, 'but I figure that the corkscrew and the speed cut-back presents most night-fighter pilots with problems they never expected or visualized. I am sure that they reason that a bomber that is being stalked will try and go like a bat out of hell, thus making their job that much easier, but a bomber that can put up a competent fight is something they don't expect. I think they believe a lot of their own propaganda about how easy it is to dispose of the "fat pigs" as they call the four-engined bombers and the more nasty shocks we give them, the better.'

'What about all the running commentary we're supposed to maintain during the corkscrew?' continued Duffy. 'If we practise enough and get into each other's brains, as you so aptly put it, then I don't think the commentary is necessary' replied Tom. 'The crew will all realize that I have to leave my microphone on throughout any combat, and we need to keep the intercom traffic down to an absolute combat minimum. When I want the speed dropped, for instance, I shall just call "DROP!" and leave it to you or the flight engineer to act immediately, for my main preoccupation will be to take advantage of the Jerry's discomfiture and welcomed proximity!'

'One other thing, Duff' he added, 'It's a waste of time and precious ammo to fire at anything out of range and no way will I open fire until the range is correct and lethal. My job is "downing" German fighters, not getting rid of ammo or just scaring the fighters off out of range!' Duffy nodded. 'OK, Mac,' he said, 'I guess the manipulation of the throttles can be left safely to Al. I'll have my hands full executing the corkscrew and it'll help take Al's mind off the predicament.' 'Of course' he went on, 'We are all hoping that we'll never find ourselves in that situation, but I am determined that we shall all be ready should occasion arise.' Tom felt relieved and pleased, both at the attitude Duffy had taken and also at the realization that, almost for the first time, an officer was willing to concede that a gunner's views were worth paramount consideration. He considered broaching the subject of the special composition of his ammunition belts, but decided against it, for the time being, at least.

'Well,' said Duffy, rising from his chair, 'I guess there's not much more we can do until we can "leap into the Luft" and put it all to practice. I'm away now to gen up on the requirements of the corkscrew manoeuvre, as it's some time since I looked at it seriously.' He looked enquiringly at Tom, who said, 'If it's OK by you, skip, I'd like to go over to the armament section and have a few words with the NCO i/c the gunnery angle. I called in there on my first day at Woodhall, to "make my number" and it is important that I follow it up—important to our survival, I mean' he added, with a grin. 'Fair enough' replied Duffy, turning to Red, 'and what are your plans, Red?' 'Oh, I'll go over to the gunnery leader and see what cooks' answered Red. 'As soon as anything develops, I'll 'phone the armaments NCO and pass the message to you, Tom' said Duffy. 'You'll get it from the gunnery leader when the usual message is passed to him' he continued, talking to Red.

Closely buttoned against the weather, Tom made his way direct to the armaments gunnery workshop and was received with a welcoming grin by the Sergeant in charge, who recognized him immediately. 'Just in time, Chiefy! Nicely judged! Corp, another mug of tea for a visitor who may come on the section strength at some future time!' Tom laughed at this sally and it came home to him yet again what a wonderful spirit permeated this Squadron at all levels. He took the proffered mug with a word of thanks and sampled the hot sweet contents. 'Now, Chiefy, what's on your mind?' invited the Sergeant. 'My experience during my first tour of Halibags convinced me that the most lethal combination of ammo is a mixture of 45 per cent tracer and 55 per cent armour-piercing' he began, and was encouraged by the Sergeant's developing interest, 'I'd like your permission to make up the belts myself in the section here, and then go to my aircraft and install them in the reservoirs and so along the tracks to the Brownings in the rear turret.' 'Wing Commander Cheshire encourages us to work hand-in-glove with the air-gunners' replied the Sergeant 'and it works very well—but I've never had a specific request like that before.' He pursed his lips, 'Does Chesh know about this combination?' 'No, he doesn't' replied Tom, 'and, to be quite honest, I'd like to do this on the quiet, for the time being anyway. I know it's against all the "preachings" but believe me, it works. It's brought me and my crew back on quite a few occasions, leaving dead Luftwaffe pilots in Germany.'

The Sergeant made up his mind, 'Right, Chiefy, if that's what you want, who am I to stand in your way? You'll make the belts up, and I'll do a "Nelson" about it! But I can see one obvious snag. It'll be alright, once you've "tanked" up your own aircraft with this witches' brew—but, should you be left off the battle order, and your aircraft allocated to another crew, the rear gunner could be frightened out of his wits when he tests the guns over the sea. It would mean taking out your belts, and substituting the usual make-up!' 'Correct, Sarge' agreed Tom, 'and this is why I said I could be an extra pair of hands on occasion.' The Sergeant nodded approvingly. 'Who's crew are you with, Chiefy?' he asked. 'Duffy's mob' replied Tom. The Sergeant grinned. 'A right good lot' he said, 'and they don't forget this section when their "fag allocation" arrives!' He looked at the chart on the wall behind him and then turned to Tom. 'The very bod' he chortled. 'Just a moment, Chiefy', and he went off down the workshop, returning a few minutes later accompanied by an airman. 'Chiefy, this is LAC MacFarlane—same race as yourself and one of your flight armourers. I suggest you chat over your requirements and arrange the installation yourselves—and don't forget the question of re-arming the kite in the circumstances I indicated. It's the only snag as far as I can see at the moment.'

He walked away and Tom turned to the airman who stood beside him, obviously a bit disconcerted at being left with a strange NCO. Tom set him at his ease with an account of the belt assembly he required and repeated his own personal willingness to assist in every way possible. His own Scottish accent seemed to have an additionally reassuring effect on the airman, and soon he was quite interested in the unusual proportions and constituency of the proposed belts. Tom outlined the difficulty that would arise if their aircraft was used by another crew on operations. 'That presents no real difficulty, Chiefy' came the reply, 'We can always disarm your aircraft and stow the special belts in the section, until they are needed for your own use. I'm only too pleased to be of use, if it means a crew getting back successfully.'

The Sergeant returned with a message: 'Flying Officer Duffy asked me to tell you, Chiefy—it's a "stand-down" and he'll see you in the Flights as usual tomorrow morning.' 'Thanks, Sarge' replied Tom as he turned to the airman once again. 'It's almost lunch-time now' he said, 'I'd like to come back this afternoon and put the belts together and install them in Duffy's kite, with your help!' 'Clear it with the Sergeant, Chiefy, and I'll be only too willing to help. There shouldn't be any difficulty in getting the section transport for the job, as no one else will be using it.' Tom made the necessary arrangements with the Sergeant before making his way to the Sergeants' Mess for lunch.

After lunch he returned to the armaments section and quite impressed his helpful assistant with his ability in making up the novel belts. It took some time but soon the long snakes of ammunition were ready and carefully loaded into the van for transport to Duffy's Lancaster. When they arrived at the dispersal, Tom was relieved to see that ground-crew were working on one engine, for that meant that the aircraft would be unlocked and he would be able to get to the rear turret. 'You wait in the van for a while, and I'll get the fitted ammo disconnected from the guns and extract it from the chutes and reservoirs' said Tom to the airman. He climbed the aircraft ladder and was soon wrapped up in his task. He loved the feel of the belts and the soft sibilant sound that the belts made as he handled them back from the turret along the chutes and into their reservoirs. Once the four reservoirs were filled, it was quite an effort to lift their contents out bodily and carry them to the aircraft's door. He waved to the airman, who immediately backed the van up to the door. Between them, they manhandled the belts into the van, and carried the new belts into the Lancaster. Tom laid the belts very carefully into the reservoirs, checking the clips for security and alignment, and looking for any other defects that might cause a stoppage at a critical time.

The airman watched him intently and Tom said, 'A few minutes spent on this, Jock, can give me a few more years on earth, so it pays to be thorough.' He fed the ammunition along the tracks on the port side until they were ready to be fed to the two port-side Brownings, again with great care and attention. He was pleased to see that the airman was similarly engaged with the starboard tracks, obviously paying great attention to his task. Tom fitted the belts to the Brownings with a dexterity born of long practice then returned to the fuselage where the airman was waiting. 'You've done a good job there, Jock' he said, 'but you mustn't mind if I check the tracks for easy running and no snags. It's no criticism of your work, but I have to be sure in my own mind that the belts will feed freely.' 'Of course, Chiefy' replied the airman, 'but I'm sure you'll find it all OK.' Tom smiled and was pleased to find that the work could not be faulted. He said so to the waiting airman, who beamed with pleasure. Tom climbed back into the rear turret and fitted the starboard Brownings with their ammunition. He checked that the Brownings were not cocked, put the safety switch to 'SAFE' and eased himself out of the turret. He shut and fastened the sliding doors of the turret, and the rather odd pair climbed down the ladder and returned to the van.

'I'll nip you down to the Sergeants' Mess, while we're about it' grinned the airman, 'Why walk when you can ride, especially in this weather!' Tom smiled his acknowledgement and soon the van was heading for the Mess. 'It won't take me long to stow the normal ammo back in the section' said the airman, then he added, looking at Tom, 'You taught me something back there, Chiefy. I'll never arm another kite without being very careful how I handle and feed the ammo. Watching you, I suddenly realized that the aircraft and crew's survival can be put in jeopardy by a careless or rushed job.' 'That's why I always like to double-check my aircraft, Jock. Then if anything happens, it's down to me and no one else' said Tom. 'Not that I don't trust the ground-crew implicitly, but it's my nature to make sure!' he added hurriedly. The van halted and Tom alighted, with a smiling 'Thanks!' to the airman, who lifted his hand in acknowledgement before engaging gear and heading back to the Flights.

Tom was feeling more and more at home in the Mess. There was an atmosphere of bonhomie and joviality about the place that could not but envelop one. It was always a very lively place, with an active and capable messing and entertainments committee. He was surprised to find how many ex-4 Group types there were on the Squadron and was aware that they knew of him from '102' days, and that his reputation had preceded him. Nobody came right out and asked questions but Tom could sense a welcome that was implied rather than put into words. With aircrew of this calibre, Tom was just another bod, and he rather revelled in the anonymity it provided. There were many characters in that Mess—among the gunners was Flight Sergeant Micky Vaughan, a 'straight' gunner, who had been operating since early 1941 and Tom appreciated that there were not many 'straight' gunners still alive and active in Bomber Command. Mick had a great sense of humour, was enthusiastically behind any scheme that could benefit the Mess or lead to a 'giggle'. There was 'Taffy' Dadge, mid-upper gunner with Mac Hamilton's crew, with his sly, dry Welsh wit and a great deal of pre-617 experience behind him, Paddy Blanche, gunner in Nicky Knilans' crew, enigmatic to a degree, but ice-cool and efficient, with more than a dash of devil in him that belied his sombre looks.

But most of all he found himself watching and approving Warrant Officer Paddy Gingles DFM, who seemed to bestride the Mess like some Colossus by the sheer force of his personality. It was impossible to be in the Mess and not be aware of Paddy. He had a magnificent operational record and, on a Squadron with many exceptional pilots, he still stood out. The fact that Paddy had resisted every attempt to make him take a commission endeared him to Tom. Paddy's crew always seemed to be together and the other members of the crew so very obviously idolized their skipper that it would have been a very foolish man who uttered any criticism of him. Paddy's rear-gunner was George Reilly, very experienced and a bundle of energy, always fooling about, very popular with the station WAAFs, but a man who still trained assiduously in the training hours available to the Squadron. He was, to Tom, an ideal type for a rear-gunner, being about 5 feet 8 inches in height and with a wiry physique.

These, with many others, formed a unique Mess, a Mess with one other obvious feature—not one of its members appeared to be counting the sorties to the end of a second tour with Bomber Command. Indeed, many had passed that total, and their attitude seemed to be that they had found their Shangri La and were prepared to see out the rest of the war in harness with 617 Squadron. Certainly the prospect of spending the remainder of the war in a training unit filled them with dismay and horror! But one thing they all appreciated, and of which they were very proud, was the fact that their 'commander-in-chief' had taken to referring to them as his 'Old Lags Squadron'.

Tuesday 7 March 1944, gave very firm indications that the weather had no intention of improving even sufficiently for aircraft to get airborne, let alone operate. Quite early in the morning working hours came the news that no operations were being considered for the Squadron and the aircrew were 'stood down' at lunch-time, with the warning that the forecast for the Lincoln area for the next day was an improvement in conditions, and that an intensive programme of training was being prepared to take advantage of what might well be just a temporary improvement in conditions.

When Tom had met up with Duffy and the rest of the crew that morning, Duffy had said that he had asked for a fighter affiliation exercise to be laid on for his crew, after a bombing detail, should the forecast weather improvement materialize the next day. 'I've been running over the corkscrew commentary, Mac' he said, 'but while it covers the manoeuvre, there's nothing about ceasing to throw the 'kite' about!' 'I know that corkscrewing puts a very appreciable strain on the pilot' said Tom, 'but I feel that one cannot really abandon it, especially during a combat. After an attack, the pilot needs to come out of the full corkscrew, but still "roll" gently, against a renewal of attack.' 'Of course' he added, 'if the next attack comes from a different direction, then the direction of the corkscrew has to be varied. So, when the attack by a fighter has ended, I think my message to you should be "EASY!", until we see what Jerry is up to next. Then, when a further attack develops, I'll say "READY TO CORKSCREW PORT" (or "STARBOARD", as the case may be) and just before the fighter gets to his effective maximum range, I'll give "GO!" and you'll be away again, throwing the aircraft around the sky.' 'Sounds OK, Mac' said Duffy, 'and Al will be standing-by, awaiting any "DROP" you may give, so that he can effect the sudden reduction of airspeed to bring the Hun into your range. After about ten seconds, he'll open the throttles again, to the settings they were previously. Well' he went on, 'I guess it's off to our sections, and see you all tomorrow, hopefully for a bit of airborne time, before we all rust-up!'

Tom made his way to the gunnery section where most of the Squadron gunners were assembled. Flight Lieutenant Dave Rodger came across to him. 'Duffy has booked a figher affil detail for tomorrow' he said, and added, approvingly, 'I'm glad to see that you've all got down to the combat drill. That's very essential when a new gunner comes into a crew, and I'm sure none of you will regret it!' 'What are you thinking of doing now?' he went on. 'Well, if you've got nothing special laid on, sir' he answered, 'I'd like to go over to the intelligence library and bring myself right up-to-date on the German defence layout. They didn't pay much attention to that on the Coastal Command station I was on before I came here!' he added, with a grin. 'Fair enough, Chiefy' smiled Dave, 'and it's "Rog" in the normal Squadron set-up' he added, with a wink. Tom nodded in acquiescence and made his way across to the hut that housed the intelligence library.

Entering, he took off his greatcoat and then went forward to a wall which was covered with a huge map of Europe, with its indications of the German defences. He was surprised to see how it had changed since the time of his first tour. There were many more German night-fighter aerodromes than he recalled, and they were located differently. They seemed to cluster on the 'advertised routes' to targets in the Fatherland, and the 'box' system of fighter operation seemed to have been abandoned. He noticed far more heavy flak positions than heretofore and the Ruhr Valley was one mass of colour. 'The "Happy Valley" hasn't changed much' he thought, ruefully.

He spoke to an intelligence officer who sat at a desk, busy on some new publications that had just arrived. 'Oh yes, Chiefy' said the officer, 'the Germans abandoned the "box system" quite a while ago. They have an efficient system of control that allows them to bring aircraft into a "Ruhr-bound" bomber stream from as far afield as Sylt. In fact, they often commit these far-flung fighters early, until they feel they have correctly estimated the target for the night, when they bring in the more local fighters. This conserves the fuel and armament of these fighters until the last possible moment—and of course the anti-aircraft defences have been increased out of all proportion, mainly with the ubiquitous 88-mm gun, which I trust the Allied Armies in Italy and the Russians duly apprciate.' The officer indicated a table liberally laden with books and publications. 'A browse through those will bring you up-to-date, Chiefy, but I'd like to draw your attention to the areas in which 617 has been generally operating since last November.' He indicated various areas in France and Belgium. 'You'll notice that the night-fighter 'dromes are a bit thin on the ground here, except on the approaches to the Third Reich—and this is borne out by the experience of the Squadron in these areas. The flak defences are quite light, almost non-existent, as the Germans withdrew these arms to reinforce the German Homeland defences. Except around Paris, as you'll observe' he continued. Tom studied the Paris area and nodded. 'Plenty of night-fighter fields there' he agreed, 'And there seems to be a very heavy gun-defence of the capital, too. Still that always seems to have been the case, for I've had a few brushes with fighters in that area on occasion.' The officer agreed, 'It's almost as if the Germans want to demonstrate to the French population that they are eminently capable of dealing with any Allied aircraft that come into the vicinity of Paris—a sort of psychological warfare, aimed at bringing home to the French the apparent invincibility of the Germans against Allied efforts.'

Tom turned to the publications previously indicated, and began to immerse himself in them. Before the officer returned to his previous task, he said to Tom, 'It doesn't seem as if we'll be getting any more customers, Chiefy, so I'll lay on a cuppa with the staff for you—have to look after and encourage our regulars' he added. There was so much to absorb and assimilate in the intelligence library that Tom was quite surprised to be reminded that it was almost time for lunch. He made his way to the Mess, and fervently hoped that the morrow would allow them to get into the air for training that was now becoming urgent.

The forecast improvement did materialize and Tom found himself in the rear turret airborne with his new crew for the first time. The novelty of being airborne again served to combat the tedium of the bombing exercise, but he could not help but be impressed with the rapt attention that was paid to the training. They had endured four dummy runs during the six-bomb exercise, when Woody was not satisfied with some aspect of the run, and he was quite impressed with the bombing results achieved against the tiny yellow dot of the target. When the exercise was completed, Duffy made his way to the Louth area, where they were to pick up a Mosquito, for the fighter affiliation exercise. This went according to plan, and Duffy duly went into the corkscrew when given the word by Tom. It had been previously agreed that the main object of this exercise, as far as the crew was concerned, was to get the commentary right, but Tom was quite chagrined by the exercise itself.

After they had landed and were back in the crew room, Duffy turned to Tom and said, 'Well, how did it go, for a "first-timer"? Let's have it straight from the shoulder—no point in it otherwise.' 'Well, Duff' said Tom, 'You've got the corkscrew off as a manoeuvre, but it's much too gentle at the moment. It has to be done VIOLENTLY, especially in the changes. When we get it right, we'll be able to drop the commentary, as I shall be able to anticipate your moves, and that'll leave you to concentrate on the flying—and me the gunnery.' He added 'Even allowing for the fact that the Mossie pilot almost certainly knew what we were going to do, for he coolly followed us through the corkscrew at cannon-range, I'm sure we were shot down before I managed to get a satisfactory bead on him.' Duffy smiled, 'Well, Mac, it's a case of "Learn and live"—so we'll study the fighter report when it comes through and take the necessary correcting action.'

The weather improvement did not last and next day Tom found himself in the gunnery section, after having rendezvoused with the rest of Duffy's crew initially in the Flight office. He was beginning to be recognized and greeted by the Squadron gunners and, on his part, he was getting to know the high proportion of commissioned gunners on Squadron strength. He was particularly taken with Flying Officer Gerry Witherick, another 'refugee' but from 6 Group, who wore the ribbon of the DFM proudly beneath his brevet. Gerry was a real 'down-to-earth' character, and another holder of the 'Flying Bullet'. He had a tremendous fund of stories and was not averse from making the most outspoken comments from his window on the world. He had completed 65 operations in March 1944, and was wont to add, 'I did numerous anti-submarine patrols and convoy escorts from Beaulieu when I was on 405 Squadron but I never counted them, as all we did was to fly over water!' He avowed that he never saw a submarine during this period but was shot at by the Royal Navy every time he went out to help them! This had left him with a somewhat jaundiced opinion of the Senior Service! Tom was admiringly amused to learn that Gerry's first operation was in 1941 in Eritrea on Wellesley bombers. These were open cockpit aircraft (designed by Barnes Wallis) with a Lewis gun for armament. He claimed one-third credit for the shooting-down of an Italian CR 42 biplane fighter during this period of his war career!

During the morning, Duffy came into the section and approached Tom. 'The fighter-affil has come in, Mac' he said 'and it says that the "corkscrew" needs to be a lot more violent.' He grinned and said, 'Nice to know that I have a gunner who'll keep me in line, and I'll shake the lot of you next time we're airborne.' He left the section and Tom went down to the sand-pit for some ground training with George Riley and a few other gunners. After the practice, they adjourned to the armaments section to clean the Brownings and then returned them to the store. The aircrews were stood down from lunch-time and that evening Tom made his first trip to Boston. It was crammed with aircrew from all the surrounding stations and the departure of the last buses at 22.15 hours from the Market Place was a sight which had to be seen to be believed. He had a most enjoyable evening in company with some of the other gunners and was beginning to feel that he had arrived.

Friday 10 March 1944 was to prove a memorable day in Tom's career. He reported to Duffy as usual, and was intrigued to hear that an 'operations stand-by' had come through. 'It looks as though our weather improvement of two days ago has reached the Continent' observed Duffy sagely, 'so we've a good chance of "leaping into the Luft" tonight.' Duffy's optimism proved justified for a battle order was issued during the morning, and the nominated crews went out to their aircraft to carry out ground checks, before getting airborne for a short night-flying test. The aircraft were then returned to dispersals where the magnificent ground-crews of all trades descended on them, to ready them for the night's operation. The briefings took place in the late afternoon and it was Tom's first experience of a 617 Squadron briefing. He could not help but be struck by the almost implacable intensity with which the captains, navigators and bomb-aimers prepared for the fray. There were no 'sprog' aircrew to be shepherded and somewhat cosseted. These were war-proven aircrew who showed their respect for the enemy with the intentness with which they prepared to go forth and meet him. There was no real specialized briefing for the gunners, but they all studied the intelligence map and committed the night-fighter stations along the route to memory. The target for the night was a factory in the French town of St Etienne, capital town of the Loire Département and some 45 miles south-west of Lyons. The route took the aircraft down to Selsey Bill, across to the enemy coast and the town of Caen and then direct to the target, to return by a slightly varied route. After the briefing was completed, the crews adjourned to their Messes for the 'operational egg' and all the usual pre-operational banter.

At the scheduled time, the Lancasters began to crowd to the take-off point and the Lincoln night was shredded with the sound of roaring Merlins. Tom soon found himself shrouded in what he was to call in later years, 'the Loneliness of the Long-Distance Gunner' but he was inordinately content to be in the rear turret of an operational bomber again. The St Etienne trip was a re-introduction to the operational scene for him and what he was to remember of it was the dedication of the crews to their task. His aircraft 'I for Ink' was carrying ten 1,000 lb bombs in its mammoth bomb-bay. These were to be dropped on a short-stick setting. Duffy and Woody brought the aircraft on to its bombing run at 8,000 feet, after receiving instructions that the aiming-point was the eastern part of the large fire that was raging on the ground below. A steady, accurate run was made to Woody's satisfaction and the stick appeared to fall across the target at 23.42 hours. However, there was some patchy cloud over the target, and this led to restricted reports by the returned crews as to the effectiveness of the attack when they were debriefed. The subsequent reconnaissance photographs were to show that excellent results had been achieved in the target area with almost no damage outside the area. It was a tired but content Tom McLean who climbed into his bunk in the early hours of 11 March. He was back on operations and very satisfied with his initiation with 617 Squadron. His last conscious wish was that his career with the Squadron should continue in the same vein.

Surfacing soon after noon and after a leisurely bath and shave, Tom made his way to the Mess for lunch. In view of the very late return from St Etienne and the inclemency of the weather, the Squadron had been stood down until the following morning. He had lunch with members of other crews who had been operating the previous night and was struck by the uplift in spirits that had been engendered. No crews had been lost, which was always a boost to morale, if it was needed, and the general appreciation of a job well done pervaded the Mess. The ground-crew NCOs were always very interested in hearing about the operations and asked many questions.

Tom had been very impressed with the high quality and technical ability of 617 Squadron ground organization and had discovered that whereas the original aircrews of the Squadron had joined either through the personal invitation of Wing Commander Guy Gibson or by volunteering from other squadrons, every member of the ground-crew had been personally selected. Gibby had been closeted with the personnel section of 5 Group headquarters for two days, sifting through the Group mannings and making his selections for the new squadron, even down to the cookhouse staffing. Many of the ground-crew NCOs admitted that they had been very annoyed to be torn up by the roots from stations where they were comfortably ensconced for the posting to Scampton, and the early 'madhouse' days of the new 617 Squadron only served to increase their resentment. But now, a year later, their fervent wish was to see out the war on the strength of 617. 'There's something about this lot' confided one of them, 'Can't put the finger on it, but somehow you know it's special in every sense and is going to be talked about long after the war has finished!'

When the crew assembled in the Flight office next morning, Duffy was obviously still very much engrossed in the question of combat manoeuvres and action against attacking fighters. 'I want us all to know EXACTLY what each one is to do when we come under fighter attack' he said, 'and we'll take these "Action Stations" whenever we go on fighter affiliation exercises or simulated attacks at any time we're airborne on training flights, so let's all adjourn to the intelligence section for a quiet chat and discussion.' They trooped over to intelligence and settled down at a table. When they were ready, Duffy began, 'We haven't a clue how much warning we'll get before we find ourselves committed' he said 'but the overriding consideration must be that the intercom is left absolutely free to the gunners and myself. You'll all be on, of course, and listening, but only break in if you've something of vital importance to say.' He went on, 'Generally the rear gunner will be in the controlling position so the "traffic" will mainly stem from him. We all know what the gunners' commitment will be—and there's not much else Don will be able to do but to sit in his nav seat and keep an eye on our movements and position, so that we can regain track at the earliest opportunity after a combat.' He turned to Doug Pearce, 'Doug, you'll switch off all your stuff and stand in the astro-dome—another pair of eyes to watch the skies whilst the gunners are concentrating on any obviously developing attacks, so that we don't get taken by surprise by an attack from another quarter.' Doug nodded and Duffy turned to Roy Woods. 'Roy, I'll want you to stay in the nose. You'll make sure that the bomb stations are selected, in case we have to jettison but the load is to be jettisoned 'SAFE' if we are over occupied Europe. Not that that would be very effective if we've a 12,000 pounder aboard' he added ruminatively, 'But still, we jettison only in absolute emergency. You'll lay back the india-rubber bedding from the nose escape hatch, so that there'll be no obstructions to cope with if it comes to abandoning the aircraft at a gallop. I haven't quite decided if you'll be better employed manning the front turret, to have a "pop" if opportunity permits, or to keep you in the nose for jettisoning, or releasing the escape hatch, but that can wait for a day or two.' 'Al' he said, 'I'll have my hands full with the corkscrew, so I want you to fold your seat up, so that it doesn't obstruct any passage to the nose. You'll keep an eye on all the dials, both on my panel, and your own panel at the side, so that we get the earliest possible warning of trouble or damage. In addition, you'll be in charge of the throttles. When you hear Tom give "DROP!", you are to cut all four throttles right back, so that we hang in the air for a few seconds, and then when you hear the sound of the rear guns over the intercom, restore them to their previous settings.'

Al nodded and Duffy turned to the crew generally and asked for questions. They shook their heads and Duffy continued, 'Give it a lot of thought, so that you each know what you're to do—all our lives could depend on each one carrying out his role quietly and efficiently. I can't say when we'll be able to get into the air again—the Met outlook is very pessimistic. It could be days away, but I'll book another fighter exercise for the first available opportunity. If there's nothing else, you can all beat it to your sections—and beyond, I shouldn't be surprised! I can't see that the weather is going to allow us to do much today.'

He took Tom aside for a few moments. 'I hope you don't think I'm making too much of all this Mac' he said. 'Not at all, Duff' replied Tom, 'We all hope we won't have to use it, but let's all know what we're doing if it does arise.' 'Good' smiled Duffy, 'You see, I'm tickled pink to have someone like you in the rear turret, and I feel that it would be a waste of your quality if we didn't back you right up to the hilt and not hinder you in any way. After all, you're the one in the "hot seat". You'll be the object of any fighter's initial attention, and we owe it to you to give you every assistance and chance.' 'I can't ask for more than that' answered Tom, 'and I'm sure we'll get it right before we're very much older!' Duffy nodded in agreement and they left the building together, heading for their individual sections.

Duffy was proved right about the weather prospects. It closed in so badly that aircrews were excused the morning ritual for the next two days. An improvement started around mid-day on 14 March, with a thaw setting in, and there was optimism for what the 15th would bring.

* * *

At 08.30 hours on 15 March 1944, Duffy's aircraft was in the air, en route for Boston and a rendezvous with a fighter affiliation exercise over the Wash. They climbed to a height of 8,000 feet in transit, and, having made visual and voice contact with the fighter, proceeded in company with it over the exercise area. The opposing aircraft was a Mustang, the first Tom had seen in the air but he was fully primed with its vital statistics, important in the calculation of range. The fighter made off and then turned to commence the exercise. It made its first attack from the port quarter. Tom aligned his sight on the approaching fighter and gave the preparatory order, 'Prepare to corkscrew port'. Then, as the fighter closed, 'GO!' The Lancaster gave a leap as the four throttles opened, the wings were banked at about 45 degrees and a violent diving turn to port of about 30 degrees was undertaken. Duffy threw the huge bomber into a climb when the initial manoeuvre had lost about 1,000 feet of height and, just as he was about to change to a thirty degree turn to starboard, with the induced speed of the dive falling off, Tom gave the call 'DROP'. He felt a jolt with the rapid deceleration of the climb and the throttling back, and was delighted to see that the Mustang had obviously been discomfited by the series of events. It was vainly endeavouring to place itself for attack but the rapidly changing deflection shot had prevented it from getting in a blow.

On the contrary, it was what he considered a sitting duck for his own Brownings and he called delightedly over the intercom 'Well done, Duff! We've shattered that bloke's ego, I'm sure.' The fighter pilot came on the air, asking for another effort and so the exercise proceeded. Duffy had really taken Tom's previous observations to heart, and flew the Lanc in the corkscrew with a devilry and audaciousness that really warmed Tom's heart. They got full value out of the manoeuvre, much to the consternation of their opponent. Tom considered that he had 'popped' him so many times that the pilot must have been very inexperienced—or else he hadn't come up against anything like Duffy's corkscrew before! Certainly it was the best 'back-up' that Tom had ever experienced. They had had strict orders not to overstay their airborne allocated time, as an operations 'stand-by' warning had been received before the training programme had been launched, and they were back at dispersal by 10.00 hours.

When they assembled on the tarmac, awaiting the arrival of the Flight transport to return them to the site, a shaken Woody said, 'God, Duff, you certainly threw the kite about today. I was very nearly sick for the first time ever in the air!' 'Better to be airsick and live to tell the tale, Woody' chortled Duffy, 'I certainly enjoyed that exercise more than any other fighter affil I've ever done!'

'How was it, Mac?' he asked, turning to Tom. Tom grinned, 'Superb, skip' he said, 'That Mustang never drew a bead on us once, but I'm sure he was a dead duck several times during the exercise.' Duffy was obviously very pleased and walked towards the aircrew coach with a jaunty step. The ground-crew NCO approached them and Duffy asked him for any news of readying for ops. 'Nothing yet, sir' replied the Sergeant, 'But you won't be going to war in this Lanc tonight, anyway. She's due for a minor inspection now, as soon as R and I can accept her.' Duffy looked a little crestfallen, for crews were not keen on operating in an aircraft that was strange to them. 'Cheer up, Duff' said Don Bell, 'If there's no op and the weather closes down again, she'll be out before we want her.' But the operations warning was still in force when they arrived back at the Flight office, and just before they dispersed for lunch, it was confirmed that there was a target and that a battle order was being drawn up.

Tom had just finished his lunch when he noticed a general scurrying in the direction of the notice board and he knew that the battle order had been posted. He joined the throng eagerly scanning the details and he saw that there were sixteen crews and aircraft detailed. Duffy's crew was among them and the aircraft allocated to them was '*H for Howe*'. He realized that he had a commitment with the armaments staff and, quickly throwing on his greatcoat, he made his way hurriedly to the section. The Sergeant grinned at him as he entered. 'Could have been worse, Chiefy' he acknowledged 'but "*H*" is a brand-new aircraft, never been armed before, so that's one job saved. Young MacFarlane is out at your aircraft now, removing your belts, so I'll have you run out there and you can give him a hand with transferring the load to "*H*". There's another armourer out at "*H*", arming the other turrets so you'll be a great help. Duffy will want to do an air test on a new aircraft, and I'll be pleased to know that our side is all complete before he gets airborne.'

Tom was taken out to his aircraft where he found that MacFarlane had disconnected the Browning feeds and was busy feeding the ammo back along the chutes to the reservoirs. The airman smiled in appreciation as he saw Tom enter the aircraft and soon the pair of them had disarmed the guns and transferred the belts to the van. It was but a short journey to '*H for Howe*' and Tom was struck by the pristine newness of the Lancaster, especially the bright unscratched Perspex of canopy and turrets. When they had heaved the ammunition aboard, Tom said to the airman, 'You give your mate a hand with the arming of the other two turrets, Mac. I'll get on with this—I'd like you to make particularly sure that all is well with the front turret feeds, as I showed you the other day.' 'Righto then, Chiefy' said the airman, 'It will certainly help get this kite ready much more quickly' and he disappeared down the fuselage of the aircraft. Tom applied himself diligently to his task and was soon completely absorbed in the work of checking and feeding the ammunition along each of the four chutes to the waiting Brownings. He checked for the smoothness of the feed, revelling in the soft swish of the ammunition as it glided along the chute towards the turret and its individual gun. He worked quickly and precisely with all the experience of the past eighteen months enabling him to complete the task in a relatively short space of time.

He was surveying his handiwork and had ensured that the feed from each of the four reservoirs was smooth and uninterrupted, when he sensed young Macfarlane beside him and turned to face the lad. 'Done already, Chiefy?' asked the airman, 'The front turret is all ready and checked.' After replying in the affirmative, Tom asked the airman to run him back to the Flight office saying, 'The crew are pretty certain to want to air-test a strange aircraft and they are probably wondering where I am.' MacFarlane nodded and soon Tom was in the Flight office, where the rest of his crew were waiting. Duffy had a look of annoyance on his face. 'Where have you been, Mac? We've been looking all over for you?' 'Sorry, skip' answered Tom 'but when I saw we were operating in a strange aircraft, I shot out of the Mess, and came up here to check that it was armed correctly, especially the rear turret. I was so concerned with getting out to the kite, that I completely forgot to tell Red or Al.' 'No real harm done, Mac' said Duffy, mollified by the explanation, 'Now let's get out there and test this new big bird, and make sure she's ready to take us tonight.' Very soon they were airborne and a short fifteen minute air test proved that the new aircraft was in fine fettle with no snags.

They landed and delivered her to the champing bomb-dump armourers, who were waiting in the dispersal area with a huge 12,000 lb high capacity bomb. It was an ugly brute, looking like an oversized pillar box, but it had an awe-inspiring blast capacity. Duffy and Woody were delighted at the sight. 'No stick bombing tonight, guys' crowed Duffy. 'Our position on the bombing ladder puts us in the "one bomb" category!' They returned to the Flight office where the briefing times had been posted and then departed for their Messes.

Tom was in plenty of time for the main briefing and was admitted with the rest of the gunners and flight engineers at the appropriate time. Specialist briefings, which took place an hour or more before the main briefing, did cut down the overall time of the main briefing, as well as serving to give the fullest and more leisurely briefing to those aircrew trades who were required to accomplish a great deal of preparation before an operation. Tom sat down at the table where his crew were assembled and looked around the room. There were no laid-down rules for briefing room asembly but it seemed to be tacitly agreed by the aircrew in general that the three Flight commanders and their crews should occupy the front three tables, and the other crews ranged themselves behind them. Tom looked at the three Flight commanders, Dave Shannon, Les Munro and Joe McCarthy. All three were survivors of the original Dams raid Squadron as were their crews. Dotted about the briefing room were other 'originals' who had stayed on the Squadron when their crews had decided to call it a day. Tom shared the general, if muted, high esteem in which these 'originals' were held by the other aircrew. One had to be Bomber Command operational aircrew to begin to appreciate just what a task these men had been set, and the professionalism and devotion with which they had accomplished their mission, not forgetting the price that had been exacted. The whole of Bomber Command had received an upsurge in pride and morale after that brilliant raid, at a time when things were not going too well for the Command in general.

Soon the Squadron commander and station commander entered and took their places on the dais at the front of the room. A nod from Cheshire and the briefing began. The target was to be the Woippy aero-engine factory at Metz, close to the Franco-German border. The small 617 force was to cross the coast at Beachy Head, after a southerly run to Newbury from Woodhall. The landfall on the French coast would be at Le Tréport, followed by a run down to a point about 120 miles south-west of Rheims, where the route turned for the target at Metz, furnishing a 'run-in' leg of about 135 miles.

The senior intelligence officer took up the briefing at that point. He pointed out the veritable nest of German night-fighter aerodromes to the east of Paris, which the route traversed. He advised that two other raids were to take place that night. First, three Groups of the Command, led by six aircraft from the Pathfinder Force would attack the Longveau marshalling yards at Amiens, which was about fifteen miles to the west of 617's track. However, it was to be quite a short penetration, and the 131 aircraft involved would attack in two waves, between 21.00 hours and 21.30 hours, so they would be well clear of France before the aircraft of 617 made landfall. Another Command raid in strength was aimed at Stuttgart, about 135 miles to the east of Metz. This force would cross the coast at Selsey Bill and landfall in the Fécamp area of France. A south-easterly track would be followed by a turn on to an easterly course. It was hoped that the Germans would conclude that this raid was aimed at a target in southern Germany and that a sharp turn northwards to Stuttgart would put the German controllers into some disarray. The 'time over target' for this raid was scheduled for 23.10 to 23.30 hours. The force would run right through the target then, through the medium of turns to port on comparatively short legs, it would regain a return route over France designed to follow very closely that of 617's, crossing the French coast at Le Tréport and making landfall at Selsey Bill.

The Met briefing followed and it was not an optimistic forecast in the target area for the conditions the Squadron needed for bombing a French target. The Met man could not offer a better chance than 50-50 that the Metz area would be available for bombing. Strangely enough, this pessimistic forecast pleased most of the crews, for so often they had flown off, with assurance of perfect conditions ringing in their ears, only to find targets 'closed in', that they tended to expect the complete opposite of the forecast conditions prevailing in the target area! The signals leader then ran over the frequencies for the night and general signals information, with the bombing leader detailing the various loads and bombing data.

When this was finished, Cheshire rose and summarized the general plan and situation. 'I would ask the gunners not to relax one iota of vigilance in the face of what the overall Command planning is intended to achieve. It will be to our advantage if it works out that way—but, it COULD react against us. The Amiens raid and the presence of the other large force over France and approaching Germany could effectively stir up the German night-fighter defences so that they may well be very alert and active as our small force tries to slip in. The distance between Metz and Stuttgart has been given as 135 miles. Well, that isn't far as the night-fighter flies and the Stuttgart aircraft will be retiring along our own line. I know that the gunners will not relax their vigilance at any time during the operation.' He went on, 'In view of the target area weather forecast, I will push on ahead and reconnoitre the area—no point in bringing you all on, if there is no prospect of bombing. So, signallers, listen out carefully on the Group frequency, as the cancellation will be notified by me to Group headquarters, who will then broadcast a recall.' He turned to Group Captain Monty Philpott, sitting beside him on the platform. 'Anything you wish to say, sir?' 'Just to wish you all the very best of luck, with the usual "617" results' said the station commander. 'Thank you, sir' replied Cheshire and, turning to the crews, he said, 'Thank you, gentlemen. That is all.'

Duffy's aircraft was about the seventh Lancaster to get airborne that night. The runway still had a light covering of snow but the preceding aircraft had scattered so much of this that the black ribbon of the runway could be seen easily between the runway marker lights stretching off into the darkness. Duffy was very pleased at the smooth way this aircraft answered the controls, as he set the engines at climbing revs and boost to reach the operating altitude of 20,000 feet. Like most navigators, Don Bell liked the aircraft to reach the 'straight and level' altitude as soon as possible. Whilst wind velocities were calculated throughout the period of the climb, these could only indicate the possibilities of the wind velocity at the operating level. Tonight offered a good run down England, with ideal Gee navigational facilities, so that the winds should be taped well before the aircraft reached Beachy Head. The Gee facility would lessen as the German jamming grew stronger with the approach to the Continent, until the signals disappeared into the 'grass' flung up on the time-bases by the jamming transmissions. Experienced navigators would work intently at the screen, deciphering and reading the signals until they were eventually swamped, extending the range of this navigational aid to the last possible yard.

The flight to Beachy Head was smooth and uneventful. The mighty Merlins heaved the heavily-laden aircraft up to its height almost effortlessly, and then sank back into a steady drone as the revs and boost were adjusted for level flight. The more he experienced the handling qualities of this aircraft, the more enthusiastic Duffy became. 'Al, this is a fine aircraft!' he enthused, 'I've a good mind to ask Chesh if we can keep it as our own.' 'The wheels took a bit long to come up, skipper' observed Al. 'They came up, Al, and that's the main thing. She handles and answers so well—quite the best Lanc I've flown for a very long time!' 'If you two guys would lay off the chatter, I'm trying to work back here!' came the plaintive tones of Don Bell. In his lonely perspex igloo which was the rear turret, Tom could not suppress a smile. These navigators! So totally absorbed and wrapped-up in their task, they resented anything that tended to distract them in the least! If any one member of aircrew enforced an iron discipline on the intercom, it was the navigator. Tom was often convinced that they became so deeply engrossed in their task that they lost all touch with the operation, surfacing only to offer fresh courses and navigational data to the captain and the rest of the crew. But Tom was inclined to agree with Duffy—this was a very fine aircraft. His turret traversed immediately and so very smoothly in response to the demands of the controls, whilst all four Brownings elevated and depressed without the slightest hesitation or jarring. Despite all the electrically-heated clothing and the heating feed, the rear turret was still a bitterly cold place in which to go to war. Tom periodically flexed his fingers and banged his hands together to maintain adequate circulation.

Don Bell came on the intercom and gave Duffy a course alteration for Beachy Head. 'We will be there in sixteen minutes, skip.' He went on, 'Woody, if you can give me an "overhead" when we get there, it would be a check, although everything is working perfectly up here.' 'Should be able to do that, Don' replied Woody, 'I've seen plenty of beacons on the trip down, and the cloud below is well broken.' The flight was continued in silence, until the quiet was broken by Duffy about thirteen minutes later. 'I can see the English coast ahead, Don' he said to the navigator. Woody chimed in, 'And you're gonna hit Beachy Head right on the nose, mate—and right on time, I figure.' 'All part of the service, sir' retorted Don, but Tom could sense the pleasure in his voice that things were working out so well. 'Overhead—now' called Woody, and Don swiftly gave the course for Le Tréport to the captain, before immersing himself in the calculations that the pin-point and change of course involved. Some fifteen minutes after leaving Beachy Head, Duffy came on the line. 'OK, gunners, if you want to test your guns, now's the time.' Tom acknowledged, followed by Red. He depressed his guns as far as possible in the fore and aft line of the aircraft and activated the firing controls for a couple of seconds. The four Brownings responded instantly and the angry tracer sped its truculent way into the darkness below the Lancaster.

Tom had purposely pointed his guns in that manner, so that Red would not observe the very unusual characteristics of the burst. He reported 'All guns serviceable, skipper' and this was acknowledged, as was Red's similar report some moments later.

As they approached the French coast, Tom began the systematic sky search which was the bomber's insurance against surprise attack by enemy fighters. He swung his turret round to the starboard quarter and was able to see that the alert Red was also sweeping his allocated areas. Reassured, Tom settled into the concentration of his task and the effort served to distract his mind from the coldness of his surroundings. 'Enemy coast coming up, Don—and we appear to be bang on track.' 'Don't sound so surprised, Woody,' answered Don jovially. 'That's what I'm paid to do!' A few minutes later, the 'overhead' pin-point report was given and, once again, a fresh course took the Lancaster on its mission into enemy territory. 'I can't see anything resulting from that Amiens raid out to port' said Duffy. 'Nor can I, skip' chimed in Woody, 'but it seems as if the lower cloud is thickening up all the time now, which doesn't augur well for bombing tonight. Perhaps the Met man is right, for a change.' They flew on in silence, except for a change of petrol supply effected by Duffy and Al Benting with the minimum of fuss.

Doug Pearce had switched on the Monica set soon after the Lancaster had crossed the French coast and he studied the screen intently. Monica was the device that sent out signals behind the aircraft and would cause a small blip to appear on the screen if any object lay in their path. Most of the experienced crews in Bomber Command looked askance at Monica. Whilst appreciating its usefulness, they could not rid themselves of their instinctive caution. What if the Jerry fighters could pick up the Monica signals? Could they not 'home' themselves on to the transmitting aircraft? On 617, the drill for Monica was to establish its serviceability as soon as the enemy coast had been crossed, and then to use it in short two-minute bursts in areas where the presence of night-fighters could be expected. Doug satisfied himself that no night-fighters scrambled by the Amiens raid were in the area and then switched off the set, to concentrate on the Group broadcast frequency.

About 35 minutes after they had left Le Tréport, Don Bell came back on the intercom. He gave Duffy a substantial course alteration and added, 'This is the course for the target, Duff, which we should reach in about 37 minutes, so we'll need to get down to our bombing height in about twenty minutes time, so that I can get an accurate check on the temperature outside for the usual SABS calculations.' 'Roger' acknowledged Duffy, as he swung the aircraft to port to assume the new course. 'How are things going, Don?' he added. 'I'm still getting Gee' replied Don, 'but I don't think it will last much longer, although it's been very useful right through.' Tom remembered the 'nest of night-fighter bases' that the intelligence briefing had brought to notice in this very area and redoubled his vigilance.

Woody came on the intercom. 'Hell, Duff, this weather is certainly closing up below us! It's been getting worse every mile along this leg. We haven't a snowball's chance in Hell of bombing tonight!' 'Cheer up, Roy' said Duffy, 'It could all clear in the next half-hour and you'll really be earning all that money a grateful government pays you!' Don Bell stood up from his navigation table and looked out of the starboard perspex blister. He shielded his eyes to cut out the dull reflection of the glow of the illuminated cockpit instruments and gazed around the inky blackness outside with great intentness before switching on his microphone. 'It certainly looks as if Woody is right' he said, 'and if Chesh is ahead of us as he intended, we might be hearing from Group very soon.' 'That'll make two of the last three ops as boomerangs' said Al, 'Won't win the war like that!' Silence descended on the line until suddenly an audible click announced that some member of the crew was about to speak.

'Skipper' came the laconic tone of Doug Pearce, 'Just had a message from Group. "All aircraft to return to base immediately. Operation cancelled".' Duffy made a brief but heartfelt observation, before thanking Doug for the message. Don Bell gave Duffy a reciprocal course to steer, as he returned to his chart to commence the calculation of the inevitable amendment to this. Duffy put the aircraft into a slow wide turn to starboard, to bring it round on to the offered heading. 'I'll drop her down to about 15,000 feet, Don' he said, when he had levelled off on the new heading. 'It'll be a bit warmer down there, and possibly the wind speed will be less—and we may lose anyone who's been getting interested in us, too.' Don acknowledged the message and the intention and concentrated his whole attention on the 'grass' interference swamping the Gee time bases, alert for the first reappearance of the stick signals which would afford a position check.

Duffy lost height quite quickly to the new level, but it seemed not a degree warmer to Tom. He had continued his systematic search without cessation and was combing the port quarter area when his attention was arrested by a dark shape some distance back. Just at that moment, Doug Pearce came on the intercom. 'Rear gunner—I'm picking something up on the Monica. It's at 1,200 yards range on the port quarter.' 'I have it, Doug' replied Tom, 'and it looks to be a four-engined aircraft.' 'Could be one of our own Lancasters' observed Duffy, 'After all, we'd all get the recall at the same time, and no one would hang about once the op had been scrubbed. Still, keep your eye on it, Mac.' 'Roger, skipper' replied Tom, sweeping the starboard sky quickly before swinging back to concentrate on the stranger in the port quarter. It was certainly a four-engined job, but there was something about the silhouette that wasn't quite right—and that nagged at his mind. Suddenly, Red came on the intercom, 'Skipper, OK if I go to the Elsan?' 'Get yourself along there, Red, if you must! I don't want you making any mess in this magnificent aircraft, especially if she's ours!' 'Thanks, skip' acknowledged Red, 'Mid-upper off intercom,' and with that he disconnected his lead and commenced the long wrestle to get out of the confining turret, to make his way to the rear of the aircraft where the Elsan closet was situated. The continual weaving action which pilots maintained at all times over enemy territory added an additional hurdle to the cold trek inside the pitch-black aircraft.

Don Bell had been delighted to locate the elusive stick signals on the main time base of the Gee equipment. He arrested them on the two steps and then switched quickly over to the strobe time base where, with an increase in the gain control, he was able to identify them much better and take full advantage of his persistence. The first fix he plotted put the aircraft about ten miles south of track, and when this was confirmed by his next fix, with the indication that the Lancaster was heading straight for the heart of the defences of Paris, he hurriedly gave a correcting course to starboard to Duffy in order to regain the retiring track of the operation as quickly as possible. He had been absorbed in the task of tidying up his navigation following his snap alteration of course, when the intercom interlude between Red and Duffy occurred. Don was decidedly concerned that permission had been given for a gunner to move from his post over enemy territory, especially in the area of known night-fighter airfields and made a mental note to have a word with Duffy about this when they were back at Woodhall. He bent to his task to solve the course that would take them to Le Tréport when the next turning-point was reached.

Don Bell was not the only member of the crew perturbed by Duffy's acquiesence to Red's request. Engrossed as he was in the study of the phenomenon behind them, Tom could not help thinking that it was a rash decision, and it indicated to him that Duffy had accepted the aircraft behind as a Lancaster under recall as they themselves were—but there was something not quite right about the silhouette of the shape that was still making up space on them. Tom found this disconcerting, too, for it was unusual for any Lancaster to travel at a speed higher than the normal cruising rate in normal return circumstances. What was it about the line that was wrong? He concentrated hard as the outline came nearer, then when it was at a range of about 900 yards, he switched on his mike and said 'Skip, that's not a Lanc following us—it's two enemy fighters in formation! They are out on the port quarter at about 900 yards! Prepare to corkscrew port!'

Even as he spoke, he felt the tingling prickle of fear alert his skull and he blinked his eyes rapidly as the astringent emotion traversed right through his body right down to the tips of his flexing toes. He welcomed this reaction which he had felt many times before. He knew that it was his mind's way of reacting to danger—basic mortal danger. He knew that it would clear all extraneous thoughts from his whole consciousness and that he would become a clinical fighting machine, with every facet of his training and experience at his instinctive command. To a certain extent he was oblivious of the rest of the crew. It was himself alone upon whom their survival depended now and he bared his teeth in defiance as he faced the enemy now formating behind.

Doug Pearce had switched off the Monica set as soon as Tom had confirmed visual sighting of the object behind, and returned to his listening watch on the Group W/T frequency. When Tom's fighter warning came over the intercom, he had just returned to the system and his heart pounded mightily and he felt a reaching in the pit of his stomach as the full import of Tom's words enveloped him. He was glad that Duffy had given him instructions as to his station in such circumstances. He switched off all his wireless equipment, and slid sideways out of his seat, to prepare to take his stand in the astro-dome, just forward of the main spar. He saw that Al Benting had folded back his seat and stood poised and ready beside Duffy. Don Bell was still working away at the navigation table.

As he stood up into the astro-dome, Doug wondered if they had been hit by the same queasy reaction as he had—whether they were silently praying, as he was—and opined that they all probably were. He was greatly comforted by the calm detached voice of the rear gunner. No panic down there and that was important to them all! He stared long and hard down the port quarter but could not make out the objects of Tom's scrutiny. He then turned his attention to the port beam area and to his horror he saw the unmistakable outline of a Messerschmitt 109! It was flying abreast of the Lancaster about 500 yards away, and it was burning its navigation lights. There was also a powerful white light flashing on top of the fuselage. It appeared that this fighter had no intention of being unobserved! Doug switched on his mike and swallowed several times to lubricate his dried throat, 'Wireless Operator to Captain. There's an Me 109 keeping station with us on the port beam, at about 500 yards range, and he's lit up like a Christmas tree.' 'OK, Doug, and thanks,' replied Duffy. 'Jesus Christ, Duff! We've got three of them on our plate now!' came Woody's voice. 'Now don't get excited and stay off the intercom, you guys! Woody, if you've prepared the hatch for abandoning, you'd better take your place in the front turret and be ready to join in, if you get the chance!' 'Roger, skip' said Woody, and he seemed calmer for having something to do and a possible part to play. 'What's happening down the back, Mac?' called Duffy. 'At the moment, they seem content to stay on station, skip. I figure that the Me is a decoy, aimed at distracting us sufficiently to make it easier for these birds back here—stand-by, I think there's movement towards us.'

One of the twin-engined fighters broke formation and came hurtling in towards the Lancaster. When it had closed to 800 yards, Tom gave the executive order 'GO!' and Duffy hurled the aircraft into a violent corkscrew to port. Tom framed the approaching fighter in his gun-sight and his hands instinctively moved to build up the pressure on the trigger mechanism of his guns. Suddenly, at a range of about 650 yards, the fighter opened up with its full armament. It broke off its attack at 500 yards, executed a diving turn to port and then ranged up again alongside its companion. Tom was elated to think that the burst had missed the Lancaster, but in reality only the cannon fire had passed above his turret. The machine-gun bullets of the fighter had shattered quite a bit of the starboard perspex of his turret and damaged the starboard rear fuselage of the Lancaster, fortunately without any harm to the ammunition ducts. He gave the word 'Easy' over the intercom and the violent corkscrew eased, though the motion was gently maintained. The adrenalin was now pulsating through Tom's body. His iron will had refused to allow him to shoot at a target out of range. He glanced at his Brownings, crouched like hounds in the slips awaiting the command of their master to enter the fray. He crooned softly to them, 'Very soon, little brothers! Very soon,' and awaited the next onslaught.

Red had made his laborious way to the Elsan, for all the world like a bear coming out of hibernation. He had adjusted his progress to the weaving action of the Lancaster, but not before he had struck the flare chute with his knee and tripped forward on the steel catwalk. He had just prepared himself to use the Elsan when he was sent staggering to the starboard side of the aircraft as it plunged violently to port in its initial corkscrew dive. 'What the bloody hell!' he fumed, and then he realized that the aircraft was in a violent corkscrew. 'Jesus!' he thought and without further pause or ado, strained his way back to his turret. It was fortunate that he had interpreted the sudden change of behaviour of the Lancaster accurately, for the striking hits of the enemy fire would have torn through the upper part of his body, had he been standing at the Elsan closet.

Meanwhile Tom was intently watching the two fighters hovering out of range, like dark clad executioners. It struck Tom that the attack was probably being directed from the Me 109, still on station on the starboard beam and that the main purpose of the lights was to provide a datum for the attacking fighters to regain station quickly—something new to report to the debriefing officer, he thought, grinning to himself. The original attacker was making another pass. 'Prepare to corkscrew port' said Tom into his open mike.

The Me 110 came storming in to within 300 yards, obviously encouraged by the fact that his first attack had drawn no answering fire from the Lancaster. Perhaps he thought that his first attack had killed both gunners—whatever the reason he swooped in for what he obviously thought was the *coup de grace*. As soon as he had closed to 300 yards, Tom opened fire for the first time, just beating the enemy pilot to the draw. Duffy's brilliant corkscrew sent the enemy fire cascading over the top of the gyrating Lancaster. Tom, with his head resting against the port headrest of the turret, revelled in the reassuring stutter of his four Brownings—the vibration of the mountings—the clatter of the spent ammunition cases—the sibilant swish in the ammo chutes as the rounds fed themselves easily and willingly into the hungry, fury-filled guns. He watched as his bursts of tracer struck the port engine of the fighter and knew that their armour-piercing brethren would be performing like a chain-saw on the vitals of the engine and the enemy aircraft. Suddenly, the engine spewed a trail of flame and a long black ribbon of oily smoke engulfed the fuselage of the enemy.

Tom ceased to fire and gave the command 'DROP' over his mike. He felt the Lancaster hang, and the burning jackal came quickly closer. He shifted his aim to the cockpit area and gave it several short bursts. His tracer hurtled gleefully into the enemy, like hounds going in for the kill. The fighter reared up like an animal in its death throes, shuddered on to its back and began the death spiral earthwards. A parachute blossomed out—just one, although the body beneath it dangled like a man just hanged. 'You've got him, Mac—you've got that bastard!' yelled Woody. 'Christ! Look at that bastard burn!' But Tom was already searching the sky for the other fighter and quickly located him in the same position on the port quarter. 'Easy' he barked over the intercom and Duffy, with the sweat streaming from him and saturating his whole being, was glad of the relief. Al Benting, who had reacted resolutely to Tom's command to drop the speed, now bent down and checked the fuel gauges, temperature gauges, and fuel position before scanning the instrument panel. 'No apparent damage, skip' he reported, 'Fuel still as expected and certainly no damage to the engines or wings.' 'Thanks, Al' replied Duffy 'But we're not out of the woods yet, son!'

Tom was watching the second fighter when he heard Red on the intercom. He had overlooked the fact that there was another gunner on board, so completely had he been absorbed in the combat. If he had thought about Red at all, it was to conclude that he had possibly been killed by that first blast of the enemy's attack. He heard Red mumble, 'What the bloody hell's going on?' and he could imagine that the big Canadian had had quite a task getting back into the mid-upper turret, what with his bulk and the gyrations of the aircraft. The next thing he heard was a startled 'Jesus!' from Red and streams of tracer went hurtling towards the Me 109 still on the port station. 'Don't worry about him, Red' Tom called, 'He's a decoy, probably master-minding the whole show! He's been out there right from the start. Our main danger is the Me 110 about 800 yards back on the port quarter. Can you see him?' A few seconds silence and then came, 'I see him' from Red. 'Lay doggo, Red, until I open up, then be my guest' said Tom. 'Roger' replied Red as he prepared himself for the attack to come.

Don Bell had busied himself in deducing the results of his snap alteration of course as soon as he had passed it to Duffy. Successive fixes had indicated that he had over-corrected somewhat and that they would strike the leg to Le Tréport some miles north of the planned turning-point. However, the correction was heading them off the centre of Paris and the northerly interception of the track to the French coast would allow him that much more time to calculate that course, and so he let the situation ride. When the rear-gunner's urgent call came over the intercom, he felt a terrific gut reaction and for a moment he was incapable of clear thought. Then he took a grip on himself, and took a reassuring glance at his parachute handy in its stowage. He saw that Al had stowed his seat and guessed that Woody was busy clearing the escape hatch in the nose. It struck him that they were, in fact, clearing the decks for action, so to speak, and he grinned mirthlessly at the thought. He stowed away all his loose navigational instruments because he knew that Duffy's corkscrew would scatter them all over the cabin if they were allowed to lie on the table. He thrust his perspex ruler into its usual stowage down his right flying-boot, and this simple reaction made him smile. As far as he had been able to ascertain, all navigators had used this stowage for this indispensible item instinctively from their first operation!—and many appeared in the debriefing room with the ruler still so lodged!

There was nothing else he could do, and so he carried on with his navigation procedure. He still logged more fixes and forced himself to calculate the data for the alteration on track for Le Tréport. He was not aware of the first attack of the enemy fighter, save by the corkscrew flight of the Lancaster, but he lined up the Gee signals and noted the time of the second attack when he heard the staccato stutter of the rear turret Brownings. He logged the time at 00.09 hours and also entered the readings of the Gee signals. With luck, he would have time to decipher these into the latitude and longitude of the attack later on the trip, as it was something the debriefing officer would want to know. It struck him that it could all be a futile exercise, but what else was there to do? And it did take his mind off the situation somewhat!

The second enemy fighter had moved into a position almost on the extreme port quarter and Tom watched him intently. The Me 110 was slightly below the Lancaster's altitude. Even as he watched, it flipped over on to its back and came curving in to attack the bomber. Red opened up, just before Tom spat 'GO!' into his mike. Immediately Duffy plunged the bomber into a violent dive to port as he commenced the corkscrew. Red's early reaction caused the Me 110 to dip its nose so that it passed out of Red's sight, and then it resumed its curving climb towards its prey, still upside down. Tom's memory presented the fact that German fighters had not been provided with much armour on their bellies and he smiled grimly as he watched the enemy close almost to suicidal range. 'What a surprise this little lot's going to get!' he thought as the fighter closed to 250 yards. The two aircraft opened fire simultaneously. Duffy's magnificent corkscrew, probably allied with the additional sighting problems the enemy pilot had given himself by his inverted attack, caused the whole of the enemy's fire to pass about ten feet above the rear turret, and his impetuosity had delivered his aircraft into the merciless maw of Tom's four Brownings. Tom gave a long uncompromising burst which chewed its way into the gaunt underbelly of the fighter.

Some of the early tracer bounced off the enemy's hide like a boarding-party being repelled by a resolute crew but the armour-piercing bullets soon opened up the path for all the following stream, which tore into the enemy's innards. The stricken aircraft reared up, its momentum carrying it up to an angle of about 45 degrees on the port side of the Lancaster's rear turret. Instinctively Tom gave the 'EASY' command over the intercom and, as the bomber's gyrations soothed into a gentle phase, he had the enemy fighter hanging almost on the muzzles of his guns. He fired into the cockpit area—a short burst but a very lethal one. He saw the silhouette of the pilot's head just briefly in the glow of the tracer and then the aircraft began to break up in mid-air. Parts of the fuselage were tearing themselves from the underbelly—bits and pieces were detaching themselves from the cockpit area. An internal explosion split the starboard wing and as the fighter burst into flames it began a sickening plunge to the dark earth below. A series of explosions shredded the fuselage like a carrot going through an electric fan. Doug Pearce watched the spectacle, spellbound. Red had taken the opportunity of the fighter's death throes to put a few bursts into the maelstrom of Tom's havoc and then his guns fell silent as the drama played itself out before their eyes. Red watched the Me 110 curve away towards the ground and saw it disintegrate into a million red-hot fragments as it struck the resentful earth.

There was a moment's silence in the Lancaster and then Duffy, who had seen the impact of the fighter with the earth said 'Well done, gunners—keep it up!' 'There's a terrible smell of burning, Duff' interjected Don. 'It's only the cordite fumes from the turrets drifting through' came the calm voice of the flight engineer. 'No damage and all dials reading normal, skipper' he went on. 'Good' rejoined Duffy, 'We're certainly setting the Luftwaffe a few problems tonight.' 'And they won't like it—or give up easily' came the logical voice of the navigator. Don Bell had logged the time and data of the second 'shoot-down'. The queasy feeling had subsided somewhat in his stomach and he was inclined to think that the residue owed more to Duffy's exuberant corkscrew than his own nerves. There was a feeling of resentment building up at the back of his mind. He thought of all the work he had put in, locating the Gee signals in the 'grass' jamming—getting the aircraft back on track and then the calculations for the time to turn and the course to steer for the exit at Le Tréport. The fighter attacks had effectively prevented him from passing any information to Duffy. He saw that they had about six minutes still to run before his calculated interception of the Le Tréport track. He fervently hoped that he would be allowed to get the aircraft on that track at the proper time, otherwise it would mean a mental reassessment of this course as the overshoot proceeded, and that was an affront to his navigational fastidiousness.

Doug Pearce's voice broke urgently into the intercom. 'Skip, that Me 109 is still out to port—and still with all lights burning.' 'Roger, Doug' said Duffy, 'Red, you keep a watchful eye on that character. Anything happening down your end, Mac?' Tom had flashed a rapid glance to the port beam as soon as the fiery second Me 110 had begun its plunge to earth, and the continued presence of the light-burning Me 109 told him that their ordeal was by no means over. With the enemy presence in Red's domain, he telescoped his night search in a narrower starboard and port scrutiny. Doug's warning had caused him to concentrate his efforts on the port segment of his reduced search. His intuition was rewarded by the early observation of the silhouette of an approaching twin-engined fighter—another Me 110. He had just assured himself that this aircraft was unaccompanied, when Duffy's question struck his ears. 'Another fighter has ranged up on the port quarter and is moving to starboard, Duff' he said, 'He's at about 900 yards and laying off—probably getting some "gen" from the 109! Prepare to corkscrew starboard!' The Lancaster steadied out of its gentler port corkscrew and the crew braced themselves for the next trial of strength. 'Can you see it, Red?' asked Tom. 'Got it' answered Red laconically. Tom concentrated on the enemy fighter, giving thanks for the clear visibility and the bright starlit sky around them. The fighter moved into an almost dead astern position, at about 700 yards range. Tom felt the attitude of the Lancaster change and realized that they were in a shallow dive. Duffy came on the intercom, 'There's a bank of layer cloud below ahead. I'm gonna try and make it, and give your friends a few problems!' The enemy pilot immediately appreciated the purpose of Duffy's action, probably forewarned by the shadowing 109. The Lancaster's descent had left the fighter about twenty degrees above the rear turret and slightly to starboard. The Me 110 came swooping in like a striking buzzard. As he crossed the 400 yards barrier, Tom yelled 'GO!' and Duffy abandoned his dive for the corkscrew to starboard.

Almost immediately, Tom gave 'DROP' and the Lancaster's headlong plunge was arrested as though by a giant hand. The diving fighter was taken completely by surprise by the combination of the corkscrew and speed reduction. His flight path had taken him below the sight of the mid-upper turret and his despairing burst of fire passed harmlessly beneath the climbing, hanging Lancaster. His impetuosity had delivered a sitting duck to the calculating rear gunner who made no mistake with his answering fire. Tom's virulent fire chewed its path from the perspex nose of the fighter right down to the tail in a steady traversing stream. His Brownings then spat their destructive loads into the forepart of the stricken fighter. There was a tremendous burst of flame as its port fuel tanks took fire, whilst smoke and fire belched from the starboard engine. It was so obviously dead that Tom ceased his torment.

The fighter, in the final frenzy of its death pangs, turned to starboard and appeared to make a last despairing effort to clamber into the star-laden heavens, away from its executioner. Its nose cone was bereft of all perspex. Tom could see into the mortally-wounded adversary. Sparks danced around the fuselage as severed live circuits suddenly found they had nowhere to go except to earth on the gaping fuselage. He could see the crouched figure in the radar position and the pilot's head lolling about as the aircraft vibrated under the influence of its racing port engine. All this was burned into his memory as the fighter hung in his view for a few short seconds into which an eternity seemed to be concentrated. Then the nose sank and the burning mass went straight down with a wounded whirlygig motion.

It plunged from view into the sheet of cloud some 10,000 feet below the Lancaster. There was a sudden red glow which momentarily lit the cloud sheet as the fighter cremated itself and its occupants. There were no parachutes from that one! 'Bloody hell!' said Doug involuntarily. 'Easy, skipper' called Tom, and the violent corkscrew eased once more. Red came on to the intercom. 'Skipper, that Me 109 has doused his lights. He could be thinking about a run at us. Stand-by!' Tom traversed his turret to the full on the port side. He picked up the lean grey shape of the 109 and his impotence grew as he realized that he could not bring his guns to bear on this enemy if he turned in from his present position. 'I don't think I'm going to be of any help, Red' he called, 'This one's all yours!' 'Thanks very much!' replied Red concentrating on his prey. The fighter made its move, turning almost in its own length and coming in from the port beam. Tom watched impatiently and with a feeling of helplessness as the combat began. He felt that Red opened up a bit early, but, on reflection, decided that this was probably a good move. This particular enemy pilot had seen three of his compatriots shot down in flames and may have been very worried and concerned about the reception that awaited him. Red's streams of ammunition seemed insipid against the fiery fury of his own special belts. Tom pounded the butts of his own Brownings in frustration. A German fighter within range and he couldn't get a bead on it! He saw the winking muzzle flames from the 109's armament and was taken aback when these ceased quite suddenly. Red's fire was quite accurate, as far as he was able to assess. The fighter continued to approach in a shallow dive which took it beneath the Lancaster. Red followed its starboard side retreat with several long bursts until the fighter disappeared from sight. Tom had traversed his turret to the starboard extremity of its orbit, and then began to comb the starboard sky, in case the 109 was craftily playing possum and planning to reappear on a surprise sneak attack. The heavens in the range of his vision were clear. He spent another minute on a meticulous search and then said 'That seems to be it, skipper. We're all alone again!'

Don Bell cut into the intercom, with great alacrity, 'New course for Le Tréport, skip, and turn on to it immediately, otherwise we could find ourselves tangling with the Paris gun defences.' Duffy acknowledged and almost stood the Lancaster on its starboard wing-tip as he brought it round on the new course, appreciating the urgency in Don's voice. When the Lancaster had settled on course, Don said 'We've got about a fifty-minute run to Le Tréport, Duff.' 'Thanks, Don' acknowledged Duffy. 'Well done, gunners—and everybody else! God, that fighter practice was some insurance premium! But I can imagine that the Luftwaffe are hopping mad and may well fling up everything they can on this leg, so let no one relax.'

Tom felt absolutely drained as the reaction to his 'high' set in, but he forced himself into the routine of sky search. He could feel the sweat trickling in the small of his back and his left hand felt almost tacky with sweat. He became aware of a throbbing in that hand. He brought it to his lap, reaching out the long torch he had jammed into his right flying boot. The shielded beam revealed a tear in the lower part of the glove with another on the lower palm. The fleecy lining was blackened but with closer examination under the torchlight, he saw that it was blood. He had been wounded in the very first fighter attack! The bullet had passed right through the fleshy heel of his left hand, but his absolute concentration on the combat had cauterized his mind against the pain and realization. He heard a click as some member of the crew came on the intercom. 'I was so intent on getting on the course for Le Tréport that I forgot to ask if everyone is OK' came Duffy's voice. 'How are you down there, Mac?' 'I've just discovered that I was wounded in the left hand in that first attack, skipper' replied Tom, 'It's bleeding a bit even now, but it's nothing that can't wait for a while.' 'You're sure?' asked Duffy anxiously, 'I can send Woody down with the first-aid kit, Mac, but if you can hang on until we're in safer areas, it would be better. It would be silly to be bounced by more fighters when we've survived what we have.' 'No, it's not urgent, skipper' replied Tom, 'and, by the way, I've just noticed that all the perspex is missing from the starboard side of this turret. That very first burst must have been a lot nearer than I thought, for certainly nothing else hit us throughout the rest of the combat.' 'A miss is as good as a mile' responded Duffy, to which Woody responded, 'No, a miss is as good as a missus, Duff!' The air of tension was passing from all the crew members. Don Bell checked the times of the first and last kill, and saw that 24 minutes had elapsed between the two logged times. 'Add three minutes for the first "pass"' he mused, 'and probably the same for the last effort with the Me 109—that means the running combat lasted for around half an hour—and that's more than enough for one night!'

Duffy came on again, 'Doug, get a message off to Group headquarters. Hell, the Jerries found us without much trouble before, so I don't suppose a W/T transmission is gonna do us any harm. The message is, "Attacked by fighters East of Paris. Three twin-engined fighters definitely destroyed. One single-engined fighter possibly damaged. Lancaster slight damage, nothing serious. ETA base follows later, God willing".' 'Willco, skip' replied Doug, having logged the message as Duffy spoke. He reached for his code book and soon had the message encoded. He busied himself on the preliminaries of transmission and then passed the message to the listening headquarters. He was given a rapid acknowledgement of the message and switched back to receiving. He told Duffy the message had been passed as instructed. 'Thanks, Doug' said Duffy. 'There's enough bad news for the Command these days, so let's put a bit of cheer about! Anyway, I'd hate to think that our achievement back there will go unnoticed if we do have any bad luck between here and Le Tréport.'

The Lancaster had maintained a height of 10,000 feet from the combat zone. Duffy said to the navigator, 'Don, I'm losing off 2,000 feet and opening up a bit, just in case ground control are tracking us. I'll maintain 8,000 until the coast comes into view, and then I'll open up and shallow dive across the coast to foil any flak that's been alerted for us.' 'Roger, skip' replied Don. 'You should see the coast in just seven minutes. The Gee is working well and we are right on track.' This intercom traffic alerted the gunners to even keener efforts in their search. Doug Pearce again took station in the astro-dome—another pair of eyes might well be very useful at this critical stage. 'Le Tréport coming up, skip' sang out Woody. 'Thanks, Woody—I can see it now! Right, Al.'

The four Merlins surged in a shout of defiance and exultation! Duffy put the nose down sharply and the speed rapidly built up as the mighty aircraft crossed the last hurdle. 'Overhead Le Tréport' reported Woody dutifully, then added 'And cleared for bacon and eggs at Woodhall!' Duffy dropped the aircraft to 6,000 feet before levelling out. 'I'll give it a few minutes at this altitude, Don, then get up to 8,000 again a bit sharpish. I'd hate to be shot down now by some trigger-happy convoy or naval gunners!' 'Too right, skip' agreed the irrepressible Woody, 'and we're approaching from just the right direction to give them the excuse.' 'Woody' said Duffy, 'get down to the rear turret and do what you can for Mac's hand.' 'Mac,' he continued, 'I'm sending Woody down to you with the first-aid kit, to make your hand comfortable. You'd best come out of your turret on to the walk-way, so that he can see it better. Red, you'll have to maintain an all-round watch whilst Mac is having his wound dressed, although I am pretty certain that we're safe from fighters now.' 'Roger, skip' acknowledged Red.

Tom centred and locked his turret before opening the sliding doors behind him to gain access to the fuselage. He felt mentally drained and the effort to lever himself backwards out of the confining turret left him panting and physically weak. His wounded hand gave a sharp darting pain when he involuntarily put weight on it and this added to his difficulties in reaching the wider area of the fuselage. He could make out the dark form of the bomb-aimer making his way down towards him in the blackness of the interior of the aircraft. Soon Woody was beside him, lugging a large first-aid box. He put the box down beside Tom and pulled Tom's left earpiece aside to speak to him. 'Get your gloves off for a moment, Mac' he said, raising his voice to combat the incessant roar of the four Merlins. With Woody's help, the leather outer glove and the silken inner glove were slid from the damaged left hand. Tom retrieved the torch from his right boot and beamed the light so that Woody could see what needed to be done.

As he had anticipated, the bullet had passed right through the lower fleshy part of his hand. Woody cleaned the congealed blood with surgical spirit before deftly dressing the wound and applying a covering adhesive medical plaster which allowed Tom to replace his outer glove. Again the tugging aside of the earpiece and, in a very evangelical voice, Woody bawled, 'Don't worry, old pal. That should hold it OK until we reach Woodhall! Then we can have you rushed to sick quarters for amputation at the shoulder!' Tom smiled, in spite of his hand. The cold, which was all-pervading, and a feeling of lassitude had taken over. Woody noticed

Tom's large torch whilst Tom was directing the beam to allow Woody to re-assemble his very adequate first-aid kit. 'That's a helluva great torch, pal' he said, very close to Tom's ear. 'Are you sure you didn't use it to identify those Jerry fighters? Or were you searching the sky with it and that's what brought them all buzzing around us back there?' Tom laughed at the very thought of such a ludicrous suggestion. The large torch contained a very large battery which lasted for a very long period, a factor not to be ignored in the shortages produced by the wartime economy.

Woody moved off down the fuselage and Tom laboriously regained his seat in the turret. The hand was certainly a lot easier now and he relaxed, trying to coax more warmth into his body and limbs. He plugged in his intercom and reported, 'Rear-gunner back on intercom.' 'Great, Mac' came Duffy's eager voice, 'How's the hand now?' 'A lot easier, skip, thanks to that Florence Nightingale you sent down to me!' 'But you had the lamp, Mac' came Woody's sally. Tom smiled—never lost for an answer was the imperturbable Woody! Don Bell's voice cut in, 'Beachy Head in three minutes, skip.' 'I can see it dead ahead now' replied Duffy. Don passed the next course to him and added, 'Turn on when Woody gives the overhead, Duff. I've calculated the ETA base, in case you want to send it to Group, as you indicated in your signal from France.' 'Hell, yes!' replied Duffy 'What is it?' '02.25 hours' came the navigator's immediate response. 'Thanks, Don! Wireless operator, send a follow-up signal to Group. It reads "Crossing coast at Beachy Head. Rear gunner wounded in left hand, otherwise all sound. Aircraft almost undamaged. No control problems. ETA base 02.25 hours".' 'Wilco, skipper' came the unhurried tones of Doug Pearce, who immediately bent to his task.

Woody gave the overhead report and Duffy eased the Lancaster on to its new course, which he knew to be the penultimate correction before the welcome run to Woodhall Spa. He slid the Lancaster down to 4,000 feet, hoping to ease off the cold in the turrets to some extent. It was always so warm in the cockpit area that one tended to forget that some members of the crew had temperature problems. He unbuttoned his face-mask and leaned across to the flight engineer, busily engaged on log entries. 'How about some nice hot drinks and a munch of chocolate for the hard-working crew who have given you such an interesting tour of France tonight, Al?' he grinned. Al turned a beaming smile on him. 'OK, skip—I think they've all deserved it.' Doug Pearce came on the intercom to report that the message had been transmitted and acknowledged by Group. 'Thanks, Doug—would you like to give Al a hand getting some warming liquid and grub around the crew?'

Tom accepted the steaming mug of hot, sweet tea gratefully when Doug passed it to him in his turret. He could almost feel himself thawing out as the welcome liquid coursed down his body. His hands cupped the mug firmly, deriving great comfort from the lifegiving warmth it exuded. He thought dispassionately back to the air battle that they had so miraculously survived—not only survived, but from which they and the

Lancaster had emerged virtually unscathed. There could be nine German aircrew awaiting burial back there in France, if each Me 110 had been carrying its full complement. That one parachute didn't appear to have been supporting a live survivor.

There was no elation in his thoughts, just a self-satisfaction that he had been tried and not found wanting. How fortuitous it had been that Duffy had put the main emphasis on fighter combat since he had joined the crew! He looked at the earth below his turret. The weather had cleared and there was not a cloud to be seen, below or above the aircraft. The myriad stars seemed to twinkle the merrier for their survival from the very jaws of a horrible and excruciatingly painful death. He savoured the very real and almost painful relief, doubtless all of them were feeling to have gained the sanctuary of friendly, welcoming territory—always to be felt at this stage of any operation!

In the operations room at No 5 Group headquarters, the duty Wing Commander smiled his relief when Duffy's ETA signal was handed to him, having been carried at great speed from the signals room by the Sergeant-in-charge. He studied it for a moment and whistled speculatively. A veteran of operations himself, his mind simply refused to grasp the import of the story both signals indicated. The recent history of Bomber Command was littered with reports from crews who had thankfully survived one, perhaps two, fighter attacks, with the occasional claim of having probably destroyed a tormentor—but these signals indicated that this lone Lancaster had not only survived a running battle with a number of fighters, but had probably seen off FOUR of its attackers, with very litte damage to itself or its crew! And it was now proceeding normally to its base, for all the world as if nothing out of the ordinary had occurred. He had been delighted to receive the second signal for two reasons, and the primary one was his unreserved pleasure that the Lancaster had survived and reached the safety of England. The second reason was much more personal, for he had been posed with a problem when the first signal had arrived at the headquarters.

The AOC 5 Group, Air-Vice-Marshal the Honourable Sir Ralph Cochrane, expected to be informed of all unusual occurrences connected with any operation in progress, but then, he would demand the fullest possible information, and the duty officer realized that the first signal hadn't provided that. True, it gave some details of the results of the combat, but it was still over enemy territory when the message was actioned and there was a chance that intensive Luftwaffe reaction could still prevent its return. The AOC would certainly want to know the ETA of the aircraft at its base and that was promised in a later signal. With a muttered prayer that the captain would not forget to transmit this information, he decided to let the matter rest until the details were clarified. He had spent an hour or more on tenterhooks, for he knew Sir Ralph could be very short with officers who took wrong decisions. However, he had telephoned the operations room at Woodhall Spa and given them the gist of the first signal. 'What do you make of that?' he asked, after he had passed the message. 'Well, it's Flying Officer Duffy's crew—very experienced—mainly Canadian—oh yes, and they have got quite a good rear-gunner' came the unexcited reply. 'Thank you' he said weakly as he put the 'phone down in something of a daze. The Woodhall Spa end had taken the news very much in their stride, as if it were a normal operational event, and not surprising in the least!

With the second signal propped before him, he lifted the telephone and asked to be put through to the AOC. He glanced at the operations room clock, 01.15 hours—the AOC was probably still up. He heard the ringing tone stop and a clipped voice said, 'Cochrane!' With a nervous lick of the lips, the Wing Commander launched into his report. 'We had a signal earlier on from a 617 Lancaster still over France at the time, sir. He reported having shot down three enemy fighters, and a fourth probable. The Lanc apparently suffered only slight damage. The message said that an ETA base would be passed later, and that signal has just come in. It is due at Woodhall at 02.25 hours.' 'Flying Officer Duffy, sir, a Canadian—mainly Canadian crew, sir' he answered to the question that the AOC asked tersely. 'Order my car for Woodhall Spa—here in half-an-hour' said Sir Ralph, 'And thank you for the report.' The 'phone went dead and the elated Wing Commander made the necessary calls to have the great man's car at his quarters on time. He did not overlook the time-honoured 'back-scratch'. He telephoned the operations officer at Woodhall Spa and said 'The AOC will be with you by 02.30 hours' and put the 'phone down without further ado. He chuckled, 'My earlier message they may have taken in their stride, but I bet there's a few calls and a few ruffled feathers at Woodhall right now.' He felt elated, both with that thought and also the realization that Sir Ralph had found no fault with his handling of the situation. Life wasn't that bad, after all!

The car carrying Sir Ralph Cochrane sped north towards Lincoln on the Lincoln-Newark road. The road was deserted and forged its dead straight black path into the dark distance. Sir Ralph sat in the back, his thoughts very much to himself. He was a man of slight build, with a hawkish, ascetic face that did not welcome or encourage flippancy. His clipped manner of speaking, with the minimum of words, put people on their guard and often had them at a disadvantage when a sudden question was fired at them. Aircrew tended to be very correct and watchful in his presence, and he was unable to approach them in the informal, 'hail-fellow-well-met' attitude that came so easily to Sir Alec Coryton, his predecessor in 5 Group headquarters. The aircrews felt they could relax in Sir Alec's presence for he had the knack of putting them at their ease, especially with his deep and obvious concern for their operational welfare. That is not to say that Sir Ralph was unpopular with his aircrews—far from it! When he had arrived at 5 Group, he announced his intention to make the German night-fighter profession the most dangerous in the Luftwaffe. He called a series of seminars at his headquarters, then at St Vincent's, just outside Grantham. These were attended by the most experienced of his squadron and headquarters officers throughout the Group. They examined the various operational situations in which a captain could find himself over the Continent and came up with the best method of extrication from a particular situation, be it flak or searchlight in origin. This was all collated into a booklet entitled 'Combat Manoeuvres' and a copy was provided for every operational captain in 5 Group—and they were expected to know it off by heart!

For his assault on the growing night-fighter menace, Sir Ralph trawled farther afield. Some of the best and most experienced of the British night-fighter force were invited to join the seminars and it was from these that the corkscrew method of evasion was evolved. Once this drill had been clarified, Sir Ralph had insisted on a tremendous increase in fighter affiliation training, as well as gunnery lectures and training on squadrons, aimed at raising the standard of air-gunnery in his Group. Up to that time, air-gunners were expressly forbidden to open up on unsuspecting enemy night-fighters, even if they were sitting ducks. The drill was to steal silently away into the night, but Sir Ralph effectively changed all that. 'There's not a man alive who would not have the fright of his life suddenly to find himself the object of a squirt from four Brownings' he averred. Air-gunnery became an obsession with him. He expected captains and gunners to have the standard commentary off pat, and had a disconcerting habit of dropping on individuals, describing a developing combat situation and standing back to hear what commentary could be expected.

He didn't always emerge unscathed from these sudden forays. The aircrews of 5 Group were delighted with one story that went the eager rounds of the Group. Sir Ralph had left Syerston airfield en route for St Vincent's when he noticed a Flight Sergeant wearing an air-gunner's brevet, standing patiently by the Lincoln bus-stop. He ordered his driver to pull up alongside the NCO and beckoned him over. The Flight Sergeant saluted as Sir Ralph wound down the window and he awaited developments. 'Flight Sergeant' began Sir Ralph, 'you are over Germany when suddenly an enemy night-fighter approaches your aircraft from the starboard quarter and closes for an attack. What would you tell your pilot?' and Sir Ralph leaned forward to catch the NCO's reply. 'Nothing, sir' came the unabashed reply. 'Nothing, Flight Sergeant?' came the almost-startled rejoinder from the AOC. 'No, sir' replied the NCO, 'I'm a signaller, sir!' 'Drive on!' said Sir Ralph shortly to his driver, winding up his window and acknowledging the salute of the Flight Sergeant as the car swept away. It is, alas, not recorded if Sir Ralph permitted himself a rueful smile if he thought over the incident later—certainly it caused much laughter in the ranks of Tuscany! This, then, was the man speeding purposefully towards Woodhall Spa in the early hours of Thursday 16 March 1944—determined to discover at first hand what this crew had accomplished and the method of that accomplishment. It was not a job Sir Ralph ever left to reporting subordinates, if he could avoid it. He needed to be on the premises personally, to put all the questions he would want to ask. In such circumstances, Sir Ralph never spared himself.

* * *

Lancaster '*H for Howe*' touched down at Woodhall Spa at 02.30 hours on the fine, clear morning of Thursday 16 March 1944. Most of the crew were in ebullient spirits as the full import of their survival dawned on them. Tom had recovered somewhat from his nervous reaction and now felt his normal self. Woody had reminded Duffy during his landing circuit that the 12,000 lb bomb was still aboard and Tom recalled, with some measure of surprise, that throughout the whole of the running combat, no one had suggested jettisoning the monster. It spoke volumes for the Lancaster that it had coped adequately with all the strains and demands made upon it, even with that bomb-load aboard!

Duffy ran the aircraft to the end of the runway, before turning to port and following the perimeter track back to dispersal. He could see the small ambulance tagging along after them. When the Merlins had been shut down, the vehicle drew up alongside the exit door. Doug Pearce moved quickly down the fuselage, switched on the fuselage light, then opened the aircraft door and locked it back. It was the work of seconds to remove the ladder from its stowage and place it in position. He turned to find that Tom had levered himself out of his turret and was even now approaching the door. 'Can you manage OK, Mac?' Doug asked, unable to keep the admiration out of his voice. He realized he owed his life to the sheer persistence and professionalism of this man. He recalled the unhurried and calm manner in which Tom's voice had come over the intercom throughout the ordeal. Tom nodded and Doug called out to the waiting medical staff, 'Here comes the walking wounded case!', as Tom slowly and carefully descended the ladder. A medical orderly led him to the back of the ambulance. When he was safely aboard, the WAAF driver began the journey to the station sick quarters.

Here Tom was ushered quickly inside. The station medical officer hovered around, whilst an orderly, having expertly cut away the dressing Woody had applied, made the wound ready for the MO's inspection. 'That was quite a neat bit of first-aid' observed the MO, as he gently pressed and felt the area around the wound. 'Amazing!' he pronounced professionally, 'The bullet has gone clean through, without causing any bone damage! I'd say that was a chance in 10,000, but you've pulled it off, Chiefy!' 'From what I recall of the turret damage, Doc' answered Tom, 'If I'd used the starboard head-rest for sighting, instead of my natural port side, your skill would have been tested far more!' The MO laughed. 'Let's be thankful for small mercies, then' he said. He inserted a couple of small stitches to draw the wound together, followed by an antibiotic shot. He turned to the waiting orderly. 'Dress this with a pad and a small bandage, then take the Flight Sergeant to the debriefing room.'

'I doubt if rigor mortis will set in, Chiefy' he observed jocularly. 'If you'll amble down here either later this afternoon or tomorrow morning, I'll have another look at it. By the way, I have to tell you that this rules you out of further operations—you'll be "non-effective" until you get medical clearance, as I have no doubt you fully appreciate.' Tom nodded and thanked him for the attention. The wound was dressed and Tom was delivered to the debriefing room. The visit to station sick quarters meant that he was some 45 minutes behind the arrival of the rest of his crew.

There were not many aircrew in the room when Tom entered. This was not surprising, as Duffy's aircraft had been the last to land, and the debriefing officers had very little to note because of the 'boomerang.' He made his way to where his crew were congregated. Duffy caught sight of him approaching, over the heads of the debriefing officers who had descended on the crew of 'H for Howe' when they arrived. Duffy came to meet him and said, 'How's the hand, Mac? OK?' 'Very lucky, apparently, Duff' replied Tom, 'an "in-and-out" job with the bullet and no bone damage—but I'm non-effective until it's cleared up.' 'We shall always remember that we owe our lives to you' said Duffy, serious for once. 'No one else will be able to appreciate fully what we all went through during that running battle, but it will stay with us for the rest of our lives!' Then the usual smile returned to his mouth and eyes, 'I figure we've shaken the Luftwaffe somewhat tonight, and they'll give Duffy's crew a wide berth in future!' A dark-haired petite WAAF named Sadie came up to Tom and handed him a cup of steaming Bovril. 'I thought you would prefer this to tea, Chiefy—help to restore your strength!' Tom thanked her and continued to the table at which his crew were sitting.

A couple of the debriefing officers looked up at him, smiling. 'Well done, Chiefy. We won't have to bother you as we've got all the facts and details from the rest of the crew. It's unbelievable, really. I still haven't grasped it myself—and I'm sure it will cause a few raised eyebrows when it gets through to Command!' Tom sat silent, sipping his hot drink. He was feeling a bit light-headed—probably something to do with the MO's shot, he thought, but he ruminated on the attitudes of these officers. Certain that he could add nothing to what the captain and the rest of the crew had told them, they were not even concerned to ask him a single question. Circumstances had thrust him into the seat of power and control that night—he had been at the forefront throughout the action—yet his testimony and commentary were not to be sought in the face of the information elicited from the others. 'Same old Air Force' he mused silently. 'It's only the pilots that matter—and occasionally the navigators. The rest of us are only along for the ride, and don't really count!'

He thought this without rancour for the other aircrew trades accepted this as a fact of Air Force life. His train of thought was interrupted by the voice of the Squadron commander, who had come alongside him unnoticed. 'Well done, Mac—the whole Squadron's proud of you!' Tom looked round, startled out of his reverie, and saw Cheshire standing beside him. He began to stand but a gentle pressure on his shoulder made him realize that the Wingco was dispensing with the formalities. 'How's the hand, Mac?' continued Cheshire. 'Oh much better than it might have been, sir. No bone damage, but the MO has put me off ops until it has cleared up.' 'I should think the Luftwaffe will be greatly relieved at that news when it reaches them!' laughed Cheshire. 'Now, I have to take you across to meet someone who has made the journey from Group headquarters especially to have a word with you. It's not often the AOC comes our way at this time of night, but Duffy's signals were sufficient to bring him hotfoot to Woodhall. He's had a word with Duffy and the rest of the crew, but he particularly wants to have a chat with you. Don't be afraid of him. He looks a bit intimidating but you'll soon be comfortable with him. He's genuinely seeking knowledge and not trying to trap you at all. He has a deep personal interest in the demise of German night-fighters and this is the most intriguing episode that has occurred in 5 Group since he assumed command in early 1943. So, when you're ready, I'll take you across and introduce you.'

Tom gulped the rest of his drink and stood up, reaching for his forage cap in his epaulette. 'No need for the cap, Mac' said Cheshire, 'Just come to attention and then you'll be invited to sit. Sir Ralph wants this to be as informal as possible.' He led Tom across the room and up to a table where a group of senior officers had assembled. Tom noticed the station commander was present in the group as well as a couple of senior station 'penguins'. 'This is Flight Sergeant McLean, sir' announced Cheshire. The talking ceased as Tom came to attention and the group of officers dispersed, leaving Tom facing one figure at the table.

It was his first sight of Air-Vice-Marshal Sir Ralph Cochrane. The gold-braided hat had been laid to one side of the table and the sharp features of the AOC were very much in repose although the piercing eyes studied him intently for a few moments before softening into a welcoming glance. 'Pleased to meet you, Flight Sergeant McLean' said Sir Ralph. 'I hear that you've put up a marvellous show tonight! How's the hand?' 'Could have been a lot worse, apparently, sir' replied Tom. 'Good, good!' exclaimed Sir Ralph. 'Have a seat, Flight Sergeant. I'd like to hear from you about the action right from the start.' The attentive Cheshire slid a chair beneath Tom and then withdrew. 'I was afraid that I wouldn't see you here' said the AOC. 'I feared that you might be detained in the sick quarters. Now, what about a cup of tea, McLean—with a tot of rum, eh?' he said, with a fleeting wink. 'That would go down a treat, sir' said Tom, never averse to a drop of the hard stuff. Sir Ralph beckoned to a nearby Squadron Leader who came over almost at the double. 'A drink for the Flight Sergeant and myself, with a few biscuits and a celebration tot of rum, please.'

Within a few minutes the Squadron Leader was back, carrying a tray. On the tray were a cup of tea, a cup of coffee, a double rum, a few crumbling biscuits and, unbelievably, a thick slice of corned beef on a plate. In a very amiable voice, Sir Ralph said 'Take this hash away. Put the rum in a clean glass and then get two cups of good tea, in clean cups and a few presentable biscuits.' The unhappy officer scrambled off and in a very short space of time was back with the items as specified by Sir Ralph.

'I am glad to have this opportunity to meet you, McLean. I read the write-up about you in the press. A lot of padding for public consumption, I know, but basically it presented you as a first-class gunner. No wonder Wing Commander Cheshire was glad to sign you up for 617!' Tom nodded and said 'In spite of what the article said, sir, no one had ever called me "Killer"!' Under the influence of the rum and the informality of the meeting, Tom was thawing out and losing the reserve that had initially descended on him. 'Now, Flight Sergeant, if you're ready, I'd like you to take me through the combat. I've had a quick word with your captain and crew, and they are all adamant that it was your calmness and gunnery that got them back to Woodhall tonight. The navigator told me that the combat lasted for a period of some thirty minutes and the Lancaster was still quite a way inside enemy territory when it finished. If nothing else, it is a remarkable feat of concentration and stamps you as a man out of the ordinary.'

Tom began to recount the whole episode, right from the moment of the spotting of the 'Lancaster' behind them. Sir Ralph listened intently, occasionally asking very searching questions. Tom emphasized the violence of Duffy's corkscrew and its effectiveness in keeping the aircraft virtually unscathed. He mentioned Doug Pearce's contribution from the astro-dome and noted the AOC's nod of approval. He spoke of the pervading calm of all members of the crew whilst their ordeal was in progress, but described graphically every combat detail. When he had finished, Sir Ralph put many questions and had obviously fully grasped the whole episode. He asked Tom if he had come across this 'formating' of attacking fighters before. Tom replied that he had not, but felt that it was a ploy that might take rear-gunners unawares, if developed. He could only hazard his own opinion, in retrospect, that the Me 109 had been a control aircraft, and speculated that it might be an idea that someone on the active side of night-fighting had had in mind for some time. A solitary Lancaster over France may have been deemed to be an ideal opportunity to try out the new procedure before submitting it for employment in the defence of Germany.

Tom was sorely tempted to tell Sir Ralph of his special 'ammo mix' but was still somewhat overawed by the mien of the senior officer. He felt that he might well involve the other 'conspirators' to their detriment, if Sir Ralph took exception to this flagrant departure from standard procedure and decided that it would be best to say nothing. Once the catechism on the night's happenings had finished, Sir Ralph swung the discussion into many facets of air-gunnery, tactics and bomber defence measures. His knowledge amazed Tom, who was more used to pilots knowing very little outside the boundaries of their own flying trade—especially senior officers, with the notable exception of Cheshire.

They discussed angles of deflection, sighting, cones of fire and deficiencies of the .303 ammunition used by the Browning guns. Sir Ralph agreed wholeheartedly with Tom that British bombers needed something akin to the ball-turret of the Fortresses to cover the menacing area beneath them. The talk turned to the relative merits of the Frazer Nash and Boulton Paul turrets, until at last Sir Ralph was satisfied that he had all the information he required. 'Well, thank you, McLean' he said. 'I have no doubt that bed and a good sound sleep have a very great attraction for you right at this moment. Well, you've earned it.' But before you go I must commend you and your captain, Flying Officer Duffy, for getting down immediately to fighter affiliation exercises as soon as you were crewed together. Almost like intuition—or coming events casting their shadows before—something which will not be lost upon the other crews in the Squadron—or the Group!' He went on, 'Thank you for your time—it was a pleasure to speak to you!'

Tom stood up and came to attention, a sincere tribute to a man he had come to respect in a very short time. He turned and left the table, conscious that other senior officers were moving across to the Group commander. 'It's not only Nature that abhors a vacuum!' he thought maliciously and was unable to stifle a yawn. Yes, he was tired and the thought of bed and sleep were attractive. There were no other aircrew in the room, but he caught sight of an engineering Flight Sergeant busy on some paperwork and went across to him. 'Could I leave a message for one of the airmen in the gunnery section, Chiefy?' he said. 'Certainly' answered the NCO, 'What is it?' 'LAC MacFarlane is the bod' said Tom. 'Just to let him know that the rear-turret ammo for 'H for Howe' will need replacing. He'll know what I mean.' The Flight Sergeant thumbed through his sheets. 'Here it is—'H for Howe'—she's due for turret replacement and rear fuselage repairs, according to this engineering report, Chiefy. I'll attach your note to the report and it'll find MacFarlane.' He looked up, as a thought struck him, 'Were you in that aircraft tonight, Chiefy?' Tom smiled 'Right in it—and lucky not to be all over it, I guess!' 'Glad you survived OK . . . and long may it continue' said the NCO with genuine admiration in his voice. Tom was aware of a WAAF standing beside him and turned to see that it was Sadie. 'How's the hand, Mac? Is it hurting?' 'Not hurting, Sadie, but it is throbbing a bit now.' 'Let me kiss it better, then' rejoined Sadie and gently took his bandaged hand in hers and bent to kiss the bandage. She looked up and said, 'I've got the Austin outside Mac. I don't suppose I'll be missed for a few minutes, so let me run you down to the Sergeants' Mess for your supper, before you toddle off to bed.' Tom picked up his Irvin jacket and flying helmet. 'Let's go, then, Sadie' he said and they slipped out into the darkness. No one noticed them go.

Lancaster 'H for Howe' had a turret change and the minor damage at the rear was very quickly and expertly repaired by the efficient ground-crew. The aircraft was detailed on the battle order that night, with Duffy's crew and a replacement rear-gunner. The target was the huge

Above A 22,000 lb Grand Slam bomb being delivered to a waiting Lancaster of 617 Squadron in the spring of 1945 *(Imperial War Museum).*

Below With a Grand Slam aboard and destined for enemy installations, a Lancaster B Mk 1 of 617 Squadron runs up its engines *(Imperial War Museum).*

Above left The moment of departure: a camera mounted aboard a following aircraft captures the instant of bomb release as a Grand Slam, 35 ft 5 in long and 3 ft 10 in wide, is despatched towards a railway viaduct target in spring 1945 *(Imperial War Museum)*.

Left The dramatic end of the *Tirpitz*: hit by at least three 12,000 lb Tallboy bombs, the 45,000-ton battleship begins to capsize at her mooring in Tromso Fiord on the morning of 12 November 1944. Note the surrounding anti-torpedo boom *(Imperial War Museum)*.

Above A ground level view of the capsized battleship with evidence of a near miss by another Tallboy in the foreground.

Right On his triumphant return from his third and ultimately successful raid on the *Tirpitz*, Wing Commander J. B. Tait DSO, DFC, who led the attack, poses by the tail of one of the participating Lancasters *(Imperial War Museum)*.

Above A dud shell, fired by the *Tirpitz* against her attackers, and dug out of a bog 42 km south-east of Tromso in 1967. This memorial was raised by Mr Ingolf Sjursnes on the exact spot where he stood, as a fourteen-year-old boy, watching the Lancaster force en route for Tromso.

Below Flight Lieutenant Keith Astbury 'the unique Aspro', toasts Wing Commander Cheshire on the occasion of the latter's award of the VC.

Facing page On the ground at Porjus in Sweden, Bill Carey's Lancaster *'E for Easy Elsie'*.

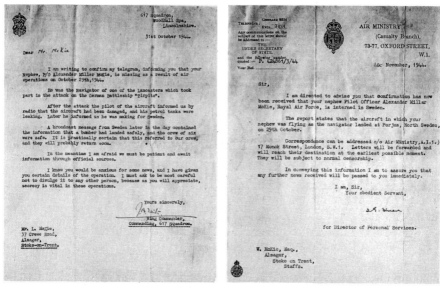

Above Official communications to Alex McKie's next of kin about their nephew's unexpected 'holiday' in Sweden.

Below RAF internees at Falun, Sweden in November 1944. In the back row second from the left is Alex McKie, second from the right is Doug MacLennan. In the front row, second from the left is Gerry Witherick: far right, Curly Young; and second from the right, Les Franks.

Above Standing at the rear of the Petwood Hotel, members of Bill Carey's crew in January 1945. From left to right are Gerry Witherick, Bill Carey, Doug MacLennan and 'Mo' Morieson.

Below A typical 617 Squadron operation against the Gnome Rhône aero engine works at Limoges, 200 miles south-west of Paris. In clear moonlight the attack was made from well under 10,000 ft on 8 February 1944. In this picture target indicators light the factory for the following Lancasters *(Imperial War Museum)*.

Above A remarkable night photograph, taken during the attack on the French powder factory at Angouleme on a bend on the River Charente in Vichy France on the night of 20–21 March 1944. Brilliantly lit by a target indicator, the dense pillar of smoke (centre) marks the explosion of a heavy bomb *(Imperial War Museum)*.

Below The remains of the powder factory at Angouleme after the raid. Direct hits on the compressor plant destroyed all 24 compressors, demonstrating the remarkable accuracy of 617 Squadron techniques *(Imperial War Museum)*.

Michelin rubber factory at Clermont-Ferrand, about 40 miles due west of Lyons, in the Auvergne district of France. It was a tremendously successful operation. Duffy's crew did not think it hard that they should be called upon to operate so soon after their traumatic experiences of the previous night. They were that sort of crew. It was that sort of squadron.

* * *

Extract from *The London Gazette* No 35849 Friday 1 January 1943:

'Distinguished Flying Medal

1059877 Sergeant Thomas Joseph McLean, No 102 Squadron.
1354876 Sergeant Ronald Frank Lillywhite, No 102 Squadron.

One night in December 1942, Sergeants McLean and Lillywhite were mid-upper and rear gunner respectively of an aircraft detailed to attack Mannheim. During the attack the aircraft was intercepted by a Junkers 88. Slight damage was sustained but accurate return fire by Sergeants McLean and Lillywhite caused the enemy aircraft to break away. It flew in again, however, but both gunners met it with devastating fire, causing it to dive earthwards in flames. Almost immediately, two more enemy aircraft made a simultaneous attack. Accurate fire from McLean and Lillywhite frustrated the attack and one of the fighters was shot down. Both these air-gunners displayed great skill, courage and determination.'

Tom McLean's award of the Distinguished Flying Cross was gazetted in the issue No 35849, dated 12 December 1944. No citation was printed, due to lack of space. The citation, which accompanied the recommendation for the award, was not strictly in accord with the facts. It read:

'1059877 Warrant Officer Thomas Joseph McLean DFM, No 617 Squadron. Since being awarded the DFM, this Warrant Officer has destroyed three Junkers 88s in two air combats, and a Me 109, bringing his total victories to seven enemy fighters destroyed. He is a courageous and alert air gunner whose skill, determination and courage have frustrated many attacks by enemy aircraft.'

* * *

Monsieur Jean Chabaud, Managing Director of the newspaper *L'Union*, included an article in the issue of 12 May 1980, which outlined events of the night of 15/16 March 1944. The newspaper is printed in Rheims and circulates throughout the region. It carries news of interest to the various associations of former Resistance members. Readers were asked to write in if they had anything to offer about that night.

The following replies were received:

From M Georges Leroy, of Vaudesson
'I wish to inform you that on the indicated date (but of which I am not absolutely certain) a German single-engined night-fighter (Me 109 or Fw 190) crashed during the night near Fismes, outside Rheims. I remember that detail perfectly because the aircraft came straight down vertically and, although the point of impact occurred only a few dozen metres from the road to Fismes, it was nearly invisible from the road because it literally buried itself in the ground. The point of impact was a few hundred metres from the Demouay farm, in the area of Bazahes, towards Fismes—not far from a monument.

'Unfortunately, I cannot be much more explicit about this incident, being at that time on the run from the Todt Organization. I made no notes and moved around as little as possible.'

From M Jean Boky, of Frignicourt
'I read your article about the English airman who is searching for witnesses to a particular aerial combat. I was witness to such a combat and, although I cannot remember the exact date, it was in March 1944, and I just couldn't believe my eyes.

'I was out that night because we were looking after five escaped Russian prisoners who had been hidden in the woods, and my father and I were taking them food. I was only ten years old at the time but I remember it very clearly. I was living at Samsois, about 20 km south of Vitry-le-François and the combat passed to the north of Samsois, the distance I cannot say, and the shot-down fighters fell in the east.'

From M Marcel Lambert, of Colligis
'I watched a combat between the English aircraft and German night-fighters, but, unfortunately, I do not recall precisely the exact date. What I can state is that the aircraft certainly was a Lancaster. Seven or eight German interceptors took off to engage in combat. Some aircraft fell in flames and we verified that they were all German, because, out of the complement, three or four missed roll-call. This was confirmed by the London Radio the following morning ('Our bombers raided Metz and Brairville without loss'). I cannot confirm that the combat I saw involved that particular aircraft but, all the same, there is a remarkable coincidence.

'I was nineteen years of age at the time and living about 500 metres from the military base at Athies-sur-Laon, a village in the Puiseux district of Chambry, and therefore had a front-row seat. Furthermore, I was in the Land Army from 1942 until the Liberation and we were on the bombers' flight-path to Metz. Also, if memory serves me correctly, all the German aircrew shot down in the district were buried at the base. I myself was press-ganged in the burial of many on several occasions.

'It may be possible to obtain confirmation of this matter, for the airmen in question may have been buried there. The important thing is to confirm that the target for 617 was indeed Metz. If so, then there is no doubt.'

From M R Goujon, of La Neuville-au-Pont
'This is what I saw that night. I was at my parents' house, my daughter gravely ill, in a little village near Ferté-Milon (Aisne). I could not sleep and, between 10 pm and 11 pm, I heard the sound of machine-gun fire. I got up and, at the window of my room on the first floor, I caught sight of a black shadow in the sky (this would be the bomber) and tracer bullets passing in two directions at quite a low height. A short while later a flame sprang from one of the aircraft, which fell in the direction of Château-Thierry/Epernay, as did two others shortly after that. The sky was quite clear and I followed the battle for some time. The next day I went by train to Rheims where I lived, and, from the train, I saw the wing of an aircraft, with a black cross on it, in the marshland which bordered the railway line. I then recalled the events of the previous night.'

Chapter 5

Bill Carey's Swedish holiday

617 Squadron attacked the German battleship *Tirpitz* three times before she was sunk at her moorings in Tromso Fiord on 13 November 1944. The first raid was carried out on 15 September 1944 from a Russian base at Yagodnik, some thirty miles south-east of Archangel on the River Dvina. This outward flight had been routed from the Squadron's home base at Woodhall Spa, Lincolnshire up to North Unst, the northern tip of the Shetlands. Then a northerly course was followed at low altitude to avoid the enemy's radar screen until a point was reached where the aircraft turned due east and sped across the narrow waist of Norway and into Sweden. A climb to a safety height of 6,000 feet was delayed as long as possible on this leg, in order to keep off the enemy's radar screens until the last possible minute, although a radar-investigating aircraft of a research unit had surveyed the area and reported that there was a break in the enemy's radar chain in the area. The further track took the aircraft across Sweden and the Gulf of Bothnia, across Finland and into Russia and to Yagodnik.

On 15 September the attacking aircraft flew direct from Yagodnik to the *Tirpitz'* base at Kaa Fiord, in the North Cape area of Norway, and returned by the same route. The return flight to the United Kingdom was made direct from Yagodnik to Woodhall Spa, and this route took the aircraft across Russia and Finland, passing south of brilliantly-lit neutral Stockholm on their way across Sweden, into the Skagerrak and the straight track to Lincolnshire. It is interesting that this operation involved some 27½ hours of operational flying. British intelligence knew that the Germans could cover the *Tirpitz* with smoke from the permanent smoke-screen pots in ten minutes. It was calculated that the surprise approach from the landward side of Kaa Fiord would afford the Germans seven minutes warning, and thus the whole gamble was laid on the difference of three minutes. The battleship's superstructure was visible to the bomb-aimer of Group Captain Willie Tait's aircraft, which led the formation into the attack. Certainly no other bomb-aimer obtained a view of the *Tirpitz* on this operation.

617 Squadron lost one aircraft on the return from Yagodnik to Woodhall Spa. Flying Officer Levy and crew crashed into the valley of the village of Nesbyen for some unexplained reason. The seven graves are

lovingly tended by the villagers and on the anniversary of the tragedy, the whole village, including the children, congregate in the cemetery and a memorial service is held for these strangers who died in the struggle for the Liberation of Europe.

Raids by high-flying bombers were only feasible when the position of a high-pressure area caused an off-shore wind, otherwise the orographic cloud development caused by an onshore wind greatly hampered the bombers in their bombing runs.

Tirpitz was moved from Kaa Fiord, around North Cape and was re-located at an anchorage near Tromso. This did not have the defence system of Kaa Fiord and, most importantly, the smoke-screen units were not moved down from Kaa Fiord. Naval intelligence could not establish the exact nature of the damage that *Tirpitz* had suffered or what the German Naval staff's intentions were, in relation to the battleship. Was she to be moved to her main base at Wilhelmshaven for repairs? Was it the German intention to establish her as a strong-point for some future Norwegian redoubt? The Royal Navy was most anxious that the *Tirpitz* menace be removed forever, so that their force held in Northern waters could be redeployed for duty in the Pacific, and this redeployment could not be initiated whilst *Tirpitz* was still afloat.

The second operation against the battleship was mounted on October 29. The Squadron operated from advanced bases in the Moray Firth area of Scotland. Their Lancasters had been modified to allow an extra petrol load to be carried and the aircraft's tanks were topped-up after they had arrived at their advanced base. The outward route was basically the same as that followed for the journey to Yagodnik, once they had reached North Unst, except that after crossing into Sweden, they turned on a northerly course at a low altitude to rendezvous at the lake with the town of Porjus at its southern extremity. The passage at low altitude was designed to use the mountainous country to the west of track as a shield from any watching enemy radar. Once the rendezvous had been effected, the squadron assembled itself into its bombing gaggle and set course for the *Tirpitz* anchorage at Tromso. The formation climbed to its operational height of around 16,000 feet and then settled into the long undeviating bombing run demanded by the SABS.

The huge grey outline of the battleship was visible from many miles in the clear Northern air, but fingers and banks of orographic cloud obscured the *Tirpitz* in the crucial stages of the bombing runs. Most of the aircraft were obliged to break-off their attacks, and return to the start of the bombing-run, in the hope of getting a continuous bead on the target. Tallboys were dropped, mostly by allowing the sight to run on and release the load automatically, even though the latter part of the bombing-run was blind. Several near misses were reported but no hits claimed. It is interesting to note that the first bomb was dropped at 07.50 hours and the last bomb dropped was at 08.05 hours, a 'spread' of fifteen minutes, and this takes no account of the many aircraft that toiled well after that time, vainly seeking to have *Tirpitz* in the sight throughout the run, before retiring baffled and frustrated. One Squadron aircraft did not return to the advanced Scottish bases from this raid. 'E for Easy Elsie', badly damaged by fire from the Tirpitz' main armament, made its crippled way back to Porjus, to force-land, without casualties, in the vicinity of the town.

On 12 November 1944, 617 Squadron again moved to advanced bases in the Moray Firth area. Exactly the same flight plan was followed as for the previous visit to Tromso. Intelligence sources gave the rather disquieting information that a fighter squadron of the Luftwaffe had moved into Bardufoss, apparently to cover the Tirpitz' anchorage. The additional petrol tanks along the inside of the fuselage, together with the absence of the mid-upper turret, made the Lancasters a far more vulnerable target than usual. However, the Fates were smiling for this final operation. No cloud whatsoever obscured the battleship from the keen eyes of the bomb-aimers during the whole of the bombing run. Tirpitz fought defiantly and courageously throughout the action, until internal explosions capsized her at her berth. No fighter opposition was encountered during the operation and the eighteen Lancasters of 617 all dropped their Tallboys between 08.41 hours and 08.45 hours on 14 November 1944, in striking contrast to the bombing time-spread of the previous raid. All 617 Squadron aircraft returned safely and undamaged to base, with the knowledge that the menace of the Tirpitz had been removed.

What follows is the story of 'E for Easy Elsie', the stricken Lancaster forced to carry out an emergency landing in Sweden, for what was later dubbed on the wartime squadron as 'Carey's Swedish holiday'.

* * *

On Thursday 26 October 1944, the weather situation in the Tromso area of Norway began to develop the pattern required for another attempt by Bomber Command to sink the German battleship Tirpitz. No 5 Group headquarters issued the preliminary order to prepare the Lancaster aircraft of 617 Squadron for the operation, and thus began a hectic and intensively-busy period for the ground personnel of the Squadron.

During the previous four weeks, the Rolls-Royce Merlin 22 engines fitted to the Lancasters had been replaced by the more powerful Merlin 24s. The aircraft had then been flown on very long cross-country exercises, designed to determine the engine handling that produced the most economical fuel consumption for each individual aircraft. These results had been studied and assimilated by the crew to whom the aircraft had been allocated.

The task of replacing the engines had fallen on the flight-mechanics and engineering staffs, but now all sections of the ground organization were heavily involved. The armour plate was removed from behind the pilot's seat. The entire mid-upper turret assemblies were taken out completely. The rear-turrets were removed, to allow the starboard side of the fuselage to be lined with long, narrow overload tanks taken from Wellington bombers. These tanks then had to be keyed into the aircraft fuel systems, carefully and painstakingly. Carpenters climbed unaccustomedly aboard the aircraft, to shore up these fuselage tanks with timber, so that they would stay firm throughout the operation. The rear turrets were replaced and the aircraft stringently air-tested, particular emphasis being placed on the rigorous proving of the new fuel system.

The aircraft's return to dispersal was the signal for a myriad ground-crew to swarm aboard, to complete their allotted task in the preparation of the aircraft for battle. Armourers loaded the maximum possible ammunition for the remaining six Browning .303 machine-guns. Instrument mechanics checked and re-checked every instrument. The awe-inspiring Tallboys were winched into the yawning bomb-bays. The re-fuelling operation was completed—there was no rest for anyone! The ground-crews worked throughout the night and well into the next day to complete the preparations. Meals and rest periods were rostered to allow the demanding and urgent work to continue uninterrupted. The kitchen staffs of the Messes were embroiled in the arrangements, serving a continuous stream of meals. But, such was the marvellous spirit that pervaded the whole of this Squadron, not one word of complaint was heard from any section. Indeed, there was an atmosphere of suppressed excitement! Everyone knew what the target MUST be and yet no one spoke the word. They all had a supreme confidence in their aircrew to ensure that their hard work would not be in vain. All the toiling ground personnel felt personally involved. Their loyalty to the aircrews made it a matter of personal pride and responsibility that the aircraft were brought to a peak of operational efficiency in every aspect and service.

The aircrews were summoned to the briefing room during the evening of 27 October and fully briefed for the operation. The Squadron was to move out next morning for advanced operational bases in the Moray Firth area of Scotland. There they would be 'topped-up' with petrol and, at the appointed time, would take-off for Tromso and the *Tirpitz*. The flight plan was to fly independently at safety height over Northern Scotland, the Orkneys and Shetlands. Once clear of land, they would descend to around 600 feet and continue their northerly track, flying parallel with the coast of Norway but beneath the probing pulses of the German radar. An easterly turn would be made, to take the aircraft through a reputed gap in the German radar defences and across the narrow waist of Norway. On this leg, the height of 600 feet would be maintained for as long as considered prudent, before the aircraft were put into a climb, to cross the Norwegian coast at a safety height of 6,000 feet. The easterly course was to be held until the aircraft were well inside Sweden and safe from German radar surveillance. A swing on to a northerly track followed, to bring the aircraft to a rendezvous position above a prominent lake after dawn.

The usual operation gaggle formation would then assemble, and course set for Tromso, with the Squadron commander in the van. The formation would climb in good time to be comfortably settled around 16,000 feet for a long, steady bombing run on the target. After bombing, the plan was to put the nose of the aircraft down on a westerly course and clear the mainland as quickly as possible, before turning for the return trip to Scotland, at a height of around 1,000 feet, using the fuel economy techniques. Crews were warned that the small islands off the coast bristled with flak guns of all calibres, whose efficiency had been ruefully reported many times by the Fleet Air Arm. It was also pointed out that *Tirpitz* could be afforded fighter cover from the airfield at Bardufoss, some thirty miles from Tromso, although there was no intelligence report of the arrival of fighter reinforcements since *Tirpitz* had dropped anchor at Tromso.

Royal Navy destroyers would be on station at a certain position, ready to lend all possible assistance to any aircraft in danger of 'ditching'. The necessary VHF channel frequency for voice contact with the Navy was carefully noted by all captains and wireless operators. The call-sign to be used was 'Friend at Position B'. The airfield at Sumburgh, at the southern tip of the Shetlands had been cleared as capable of accepting Lancaster aircraft, should the need arise, and the station would be warned that the operation was in progress at the zero hour for bombing. All the modified aircraft took off without a hitch during the morning of 28 October. Sufficient ground-crews were also airlifted aboard the Lancasters to ensure adequate servicing cover at the advanced bases, without embarrassing the establishments at those stations. As soon as the aircraft were safely marshalled in the dispersals in Scotland, the ground-crews 'topped-up' the fuel tanks. Aware of the inherent dangers of the cold, clammy Scottish winter nights, they continually applied a thin film of glycol to the wing surfaces of all 617 Squadron aircraft, to prevent the formation of lift-destroying ice during the hours before take-off.

The final weather forecast was distributed and the navigators completed their flight-plans. All possible preparations complete, the aircrews adjourned to their respective Messes for the usual pre-operational meal of egg, bacon and chips, with lashings of bread and butter, with hot, milky, sweet tea to wash it all down. Their hosts, delighted to have operational aircrew to look after, did them really proud!

After the meal, the officer aircrew of Flying Officer Bill Carey's crew sat in the Officers' Mess ante-room at RAF Milltown, a satellite airfield of RAF Lossiemouth, with their opposite numbers of Flight Lieutenant Freddy Watts' crew. These two crews had an affinity remarkable even for a wartime Bomber Squadron. They shared a lot of their off-duty pursuits, visiting the local towns together. Bill Carey was an Australian from Mount Gambier, in South Australia. Barely above the minimum height for aircrew, he had been automatically dubbed 'The Australian James Cagney' after a few weeks on the Squadron. As usual with most aircrew nicknames, this fitted him to a T! His navigator was Pilot Officer McKie, newly-commissioned and still finding the surrounds of an Officers' Mess strange but exciting. Bill's rear-gunner was the ubiquitous Flight

Lieutenant Gerry Witherick DFM. The operation against the *Tirpitz* was to be his 95th operation, but he chose to fly with the 'bread and butter' crews of 617, rather than hitch on to the crew of the Squadron commander or one of the Flight commanders. He had been a regular member of Bill Carey's crew for quite a few months and had adopted a fatherly attitude towards the Canadian bomb-aimer, Flying Officer Doug MacLennan, whom he always addressed as 'Junior'.

Freddy Watts had joined 617 on 5 April 1944 from 630 Squadron in 5 Group after completing his first tour of operations. He was a superb Lancaster pilot, confident in his own ability and had the full and unstinted trust of his crew. During the transit flight to Yagodnik for the first raid on the *Tirpitz*, Bill Carey's aircraft *'E for Easy Elsie'* had been badly damaged by Russian flak, which had ceased abruptly when Witherick's guns had chattered their annoyance from the rear turret. It had been impossible to repair the aircraft in time for the *Tirpitz* sortie, so its load of 'Johnnie Walkers' had been transferred to Tony Iveson's aircraft, Iveson having jettisoned his similar load before effecting an emergency landing at another Russian airfield when weather conditions had prevented the location of Yagodnik. Undaunted, Bill Carey and Gerry Witherick had climbed aboard Freddy's aircraft as guests for the trip to Kaa Fiord and quite enjoyed the experience.

The two crews sat talking quietly amongst themselves, whiling away the couple of hours before they would be taken to their aircraft. Some of them had the odd half-pint in front of them, but there was no heavy drinking in progress. Gerry Witherick was a bit pre-occupied and quiet for him. He had operated in Eritrea in the early part of the war, and his experiences in Russia had convinced him that the Northern theatre of war was an unlucky area for him. This would be his 95th trip and, unusually for him, he had an instinct that he would not come back this time. If any of the company sitting around had been apprised of this, they would have laughed in disbelief. Witherick missing? The indestructible Gerry not lording it in the Petwood Mess, back in Woodhall Spa? The very idea was ludicrous and utterly unthinkable. But the thought was very present in his mind, even though he tried to put it from him and join in the general conversation.

Gerry Witherick was not the only member of Bill Carey's crew who viewed the coming operation with more than the usual trepidation. Newly-commissioned Alex McKie, the navigator, had prepared the navigational side of the operation with even more care than usual, but he sensed that this trip was fraught with problems not previously present. The sight of the auxiliary petrol tanks running the full length of the starboard side of the fuselage had been a trifle unnerving for him when he entered *'Easy Elsie'* for the transit trip to Milltown. 'God!' he thought, as he made his way to the front of the aircraft, weighed down with all his navigational gear, 'We're a flying petrol bowser!' He had been unable to shake the memory from his mind and appreciated that a near flak burst, which would normally inflict only superficial damage, could turn the

Lancaster into a fireball in a few short seconds.

The others in the circle had no qualms about the coming trip whatsoever. 'Another night, another trip' was the typical aircrew philosophy with which they approached this latest trip. Freddy Watts was regaling his listeners with a story far removed from the operational sphere. Bill Carey, so intensely proud of being a member of 617 Squadron, was mentally urging the minutes past so that soon his beloved Lancaster would be heading for that date with the *Tirpitz* which the Russian flak had previously denied him and his crew.

Freddy Watts leaned over to him. 'I figure we should get out to our aircraft a while earlier than planned, William' he said. 'I don't like the look of the local weather and I don't intend to be left on this airfield whilst the rest of them are heading for Tromso.' 'Good idea, mate' agreed Bill, 'Give it another quarter-hour and we'll make our way to the dispersals.' When the time had elapsed, Freddy stood up and said, 'Well, lads, let's go!' and the aircrew left their chairs and bunched out of the ante-room. 'Just a moment' came the voice of Witherick, as they passed the bar 'We haven't been able to have much of a drink, so I'm going to leave a pound in the bar, to make sure we have a bit of a session when we come back.' 'Excellent, Gerry' agreed Freddy, 'and my pound will join yours!' They moved into the bar and, with great ceremony, Witherick presented the astonished barman with two one-pound notes. 'Put those just behind the mirror, lad' he said, 'with half of them showing so that we don't forget them—and we'll be drinking your health when we return in the near future'. The barman grinned and did as he was bidden. He watched the laughing throng leave the bar. 'Aircrew!' he thought 'They're a race on their own!'

Bill Carey's crew reached their aircraft somewhat later than they had planned. The wireless operator, Sergeant 'Curly' Young had had to dash off and get some operational cards he had forgotten. Alex McKie had 'flapped' over some maps and charts—the transport had been late—all these incidents confirmed to Witherick that this trip was jinxed from the start. They had managed the time-honoured 'Good Luck' pee over the tail-wheel before climbing into the aircraft and it was there that Gerry discovered that he had not put on his lucky sweater. This meant taking off all his protective clothing before he could put the sweater in its correct sequence of dressing and then dressing again, all in the confined space of the rear fuselage. Because of fears about the local weather, Bill Carey had been very prompt with the pre-flight checks and the Lancaster was taxying along the perimeter track to the take-off point before Gerry had completed his re-dressing. Bill turned the aircraft on to the duty runway. He held the protesting Lancaster on the brakes, as the flight engineer, Les Franks, slowly opened the four Merlin throttles to take-off 'revs and boost'. Bill released the brakes and the heavily-laden aircraft leapt forward down the runway and into the mist that had been visibly thickening for the past hour. Gerry was forced to cease his dressing and brace himself against the fuselage to keep his balance. He glanced out of the small side-window as he felt the aircraft swing slightly on take-off, and he saw the Milltown control tower looming up as the Lancaster strove for height. '*Easy Elsie*' cleared the tower by what seemed to be inches to the watching Witherick.

As the Lancaster settled down to the climb Witherick completed his dressing. 'I bet there's a few frightened "penguins" in that tower, who will remember this night for ever more' he thought sardonically. Yet that 'hairy' take-off served to reinforce the increasing conviction that this was to be a very fraught trip! He eventually settled himself in the rear turret and then set about the drill of proving the turret serviceable. He swung it through its full traverse several times, checking the smooth raising and lowering of the four Brownings in the same action. He checked his gun-sight and, satisfied, he settled back. There was nothing to be seen outside and he looked forward to a long, relaxed run over the sea, before the aircraft entered enemy territory and the long, systematic watch of the Bomber Command rear-gunner began. With no mid-upper gunner, the responsibility for the fighter watch was his alone.

Alec McKie was immersed in his navigation. He had arranged his navigational equipment just as he was wont to do when he had settled down at the navigation table. He felt the aircraft tremble as the pull of the engines built up against the brakes. He sensed the build-up of speed as the Lancaster sped down the runway and heard the terse 'Wheels Up!' call from the pilot to the engineer and moments later he heard the reassuring thuds as the undercarriage tucked itself neatly into the engine nacelles. The mechanics of his task then took over—he had no further time to worry about omens or portents—there was a job to be done!

Bill Carey had striven to control the swing that had developed once the aircraft had 'come unstuck' from the runway. The cross-wind had been the main cause of this swing, but he soon had the Lancaster well in control, even though it had still been 'pretty adjacent' to the roof of the tower as it roared on its way. Still, it wasn't his fault if they built these control towers so high, and then placed them so close to the runway! He brought the aircraft on to the heading required by the navigator and climbed on track to the safety height required for the journey across Northern Scotland. '*Tirpitz*, here we come!' he thought with anticipation.

'*Easy Elsie*' droned on competently in the northern darkness. Pre-flight vexations and presentiments now forgotten, each member of the crew was absorbed in his particular duties. The weather had cleared, as forecast, before they reached the Orkneys and, although the night was very dark, flying conditions at 700 feet were good. The rear-gunner and navigator combined to check the aircraft's drift with flame floats in an area where aircraft navigation was reduced to basics. When the turning-point for the Norwegian coast had been reached, Alex gave the captain the easterly course which would take them over Norway and into Sweden, and immediately he began to calculate the moment when the heavily-laden Lancaster would have to begin the climb to safety height of 6,000 feet, if the mountains barely inland were to be negotiated safely. The aircraft would just about make 150 feet per minute on the climb with its all-up weight. He did the important calculation methodically and accurately and gave prior warning to the captain of the deadline, even as he checked the figures again. 'Time to commence the climb, skip' he said, when the deadline had been reached. The aircraft engines changed to a new note as climbing revs and boost were fed to the powerful units, and the aircraft began the long pull to height.

Alex stood up and peered intently out of the starboard perspex blister, trying to pick up the jutting headland which should be some fifteen to twenty miles south of the aircraft, but could not satisfy himself that he could genuinely see it in the darkness. 'Well' he mused, 'at least I know we're not south of track!' and he resumed his seat at the navigation table. Some fifteen minutes later, Doug MacLennan came on to the intercom. 'I can see the coast ahead, Mac' he said 'and you'll be as surprised as I am to know that we are practically on track!' Alex smiled to himself. Life wouldn't be the same in this crew if these back-handed compliments were not sprinkled about, in disguised admiration for a good performance. 'Thanks, Doug' he replied, 'Let me know when we cross the coast, for a ground-speed check to the next turning-point—and I only hope that your bombing will match my superb navigation when we get to Tromso!' The Lancaster crossed the coast on track but a minute ahead of time. Alex decided not to alter his ETA at the next turning-point, for dawn would soon be breaking, bringing with it the light to identify the ground over which the aircraft would be passing.

Some desultory tracer meandered into the air to the north of them as they crossed the coast, but it was nowhere near *'Easy Elsie'*. It could possibly be aimed at one of the other aircraft that would be crossing the coast at that time. They flew on to the turning-point and then made the northerly turn for the rendezvous—the flight plan was working out perfectly! Bill Carey held the safety height until the position of the aircraft had been indubitably pin-pointed as the light of day developed, and then dropped down to the screening height. The distance to the rendezvous was being devoured, and the crew looked out on the Swedish landscape with great interest. It was the first time any of them had flown over Sweden in daylight. Their maps and terrain corresponded beautifully, and the geographical features were so obviously outstanding, that they made for perfect map-reading. It was no surprise to them when they arrived at the rendezvous on time. What was surprising was that at one moment they were, to all intents and purposes, alone in the Swedish sky and then they were part of a throng of Lancasters circling the rendezvous area!

Squadron Leader Gerry Fawke, in Lancaster *'J for Jig'*, had all his crew searching the sky to identify Willie Tait's aircraft. Gerry's position in the gaggle would be as No 2 to Willie's lead aircraft and he was anxious to place himself conveniently, to be able to take up his correct position as soon as possible, so that the rest of the Squadron could begin to sort themselves out behind. There was no sign of the lead aircraft and the navigator came on the intercom to say that course should be set for Tromso within the next three minutes, if the time-on-target was to be met. 'Willie will give us no marks for hanging about, waiting for him' said Gerry, 'so we'll get the mob heading for Tromso.' He set the required course on his compass repeater and brought his aircraft carefully round on to the heading. In the meantime, the navigator fired off a stream of green Very cartridges which burst continuously in the clear air. The circling Lancasters realized that course was being set on time for Tromso and began to sort themselves out until the gaggle was correctly assembled. 'Here comes Willie now' sang out the rear-gunner of '*J for Jig*' and to Gerry Fawke's great relief, Willie's Lancaster came winging its way above the formation to drop into the lead position. When he had settled in, Willie waggled his wings in obvious approval of his deputy leader's decision.

As they flew farther north, the briefed signal was given by the lead aircraft and the whole formation began the climb to bombing height. Some forty miles from the target, this was achieved, and the bomb-aimers and navigators began their intimate co-operation in meticulously calculating the data to be fed into the SABS, which was 617's pride and joy. The bomb-aimers tested all the bombing circuits several times, fused the mighty Tallboys, selected the appropriate switches, made sure the graticule of the bomb-sight was correctly illuminated for the light conditions and fed in the data supplied by the navigators into the bomb-sight in correct sequence. Then they began to search the scene ahead for a sight of their quarry.

Doug MacLennan whistled involuntarily to himself when he first saw the *Tirpitz*. She was clearly visible through the ultra-clear air of those northern latitudes. She was easily the largest ship he had ever seen from the air, and his bomb-aimer's heart leapt at the prospect of such a well-defined and challenging target. *Tirpitz* lay there, sullen and grey, and, for the moment, silent. It was as if both adversaries were weighing each other up, and calculating the best moment to strike.

In the gun control room aboard *Tirpitz*, Willibald Völsing had been called to 'Action Stations' with the rest of the watch, when the outer ring of radar defences reported the approach of a strong heavy bomber formation. Willibald had a great problem with which to wrestle—of which he had been aware ever since *Tirpitz* had been in the fiords of northern Norway. The complicated ranging system had been damaged during the Fleet Air Arm attacks in the summer of 1944, and given a severe nudge by the bombs of the Lancasters in Kaa Fiord in September of that year. In addition, the effect that the Earth's magnetic field had on the measuring instruments was practically insurmountable. The deviations of five ostensibly checking instruments gave a variation of fifteen to twenty miles in the matter of the distance the attacking formation was from the battleship—and Willibald was the one who had to decide when to open up with the main armament on the enemy aircraft. He uttered a silent prayer for guidance and bent once more to his unenviable task.

The 617 Squadron aircraft were committed to their bombing runs. Bomb-aimers manipulated the controls of their bomb-sights, to keep the target coincident with the travelling graticule. At the same time, they had to give the pilot a coherent and accurate commentary on the run. The pilots listened intently to this commentary and endeavoured to execute the flattest of flat turns whenever the run required. The pilots also had to concentrate on keeping the airspeed indicator needle unwaveringly on the bombing airspeed, and the altimeter reading steady on the allocated gaggle height. Their attention was riveted on these instruments and the commentary in their ears and not on any circumstance outside the aircraft. Navigators, with no current commitment to make to the operation, stood behind the pilot and flight engineer, watching the squat shape of the grey *Tirpitz* disappear from view, obliterated by the nose of the aircraft. The rear-gunners searched the skies methodically for the presence of enemy fighters, and tensed themselves to report the results of the bombing. Suddenly, the *Tirpitz* dropped her mask of indifference and spat flame at the approaching bombers with all the venom her 36 flak barrels could muster, and the 98 guns of the shore-based batteries added their considerable contribution. A curtain of hot steel soared towards the oncoming aircraft, but the initial sighting salvoes were woefully out of range, leaving the bombers to continue their approach unscathed and unmolested. The tension mounted inside the aircraft as the crew members waited for the magical 'Bombs gone!' from the bomb-aimer and then the seemingly endless wait for rear-gunner's assessment of the strike.

* * *

'Any moment now!' thought Alex McKie, 'Bombs gone—and then we'll be away home.' He heard a howl of disappointment from the bomb-aimer. 'Cloud! Stinking, rotten bloody cloud!' wailed Doug. 'I've lost her altogether!' came the anguished lament in Canadian accents. 'Righto, Doug' comforted Bill, 'We'll just peel off and go round again for another run' and, so saying, he turned the aircraft off to port. The aircraft gave a slight heave, which Bill put down to turbulence, caused by the slip-stream of the earlier aircraft. McKie's pre-flight qualms began to flood back into his mind. 'One life gone—and eight to go!' he thought involuntarily.

Witherick had noted with satisfaction the ineptitude of the first salvo of German flak, but he was too experienced to expect this to continue indefinitely. What had really shaken him, though, was the size of the flak bursts, with their unusually large fiery centres, and he realized that *Tirpitz* was using her main 15-inch armament in her aerial defence—something to tell the intelligence officer when they returned to base. He shrugged when MacLennan's disappointment came over the intercom—'just one of those things' he thought—then suddenly the aircraft heaved and he saw a huge yellow cloud of smoke about 100 feet below *'Easy Elsie'*. 'Christ, that was close!' he said to himself and surmised that the aircraft had been saved from a lot of damage, and possible destruction by the Tallboy bomb, slung in the bomb-bay. He was certain that it had absorbed the brunt of the chunks of flying shrapnel the burst would have produced and shielded vital parts of the Lancaster from damage.

They had no better luck with the second bombing run. 'Dummy run!' called Doug, without having to explain further to the rest of the crew. McKie could not contain himself. 'Dummy run?' he ejaculated, 'For God's sake, let's drop the bloody bomb and get to hell out of all this!' 'Steady, Mac' intervened Witherick, 'We've not come all this way to waste the bomb! Junior is going to repay that son-of-a-bitch battleship for hitting us on the first run,' and Bill Carey peeled off yet again, to return to the bombing datum for a further run. But, even as he did so, a mighty burst of flak shook the whole aircraft. Looking out on the port side, where the flak had burst, Les Franks could see precious fuel escaping from No 2 fuel tank and disappearing as a fine white vapour in the Arctic air. Bill Carey continued to seek a new datum for another run, whilst around him Lancasters wheeled in frustration, seeking, like *'Easy Elsie'*, a cloud-free run on the inviting target below. Some aircraft had managed to bomb and were already on the westerly tack for the journey home. Bill was just that bit envious of them as he turned for the third run-in.

Willi Völsing was feeling a lot happier in the gun control room. The first sighting salvoes had been widely dispersed and Willi kept his fingers crossed that the poor ranging would not result in the death of his beloved *Tirpitz*. Fortunately, very accurate flak-spotting reports were coming back, coolly and quickly, from the bridge to gunnery control, together with information that ridges and banks of cloud were obviously interfering with the bombing runs in the later stages. The ship's radar teams reported that the bombers were breaking off their runs and returning to their datums higher up the fiord, to make new bombing runs on the battleship. Aligning the 'spotting' reports with the readings of his suspect instruments, Willi discarded those that did not match up to the flak reports and concentrated his attention on the two remaining instruments that appeared to be the most reliable. He calculated a re-laying of the main armament, based on this data and his own experience. *Tirpitz* had suffered no direct hits so far, but several near misses by the earthquake bombs had strained some of the armoured plates. Willi was certain that, on their next run, the bombers would find that the *Tirpitz* flak still had a deadly sting. He was delighted when the bridge reports indicated that the bursts were now within damaging distance of the attacking bombers. Radar continued to report that bombers were still congregating down the fiord, and turning for further runs, and had not abandoned their struggle with the cloud and the *Tirpitz*. Willi made a few slight adjustments to the gun-laying and waited for the next wave of attackers.

'Easy Elsie' had had very little luck with the cloud. Bill Carey had set

her on course three more times, only for Doug MacLennan to sing out 'Dummy Run!' before the aircraft had come within range of the *Tirpitz'* flak. Now they were committed to the sixth run and it looked as if their luck had changed, for the target was visible throughout the whole of the run. 'Bomb gone!' came the joyful cry from the bomb-aimer's compartment and the whole crew gave a sigh of relief. 'Spot the fall, Gerry' called Bill Carey, as he began the turn to the west—and the aircraft shuddered as it was hit—and hit again!

Freddy Watts had just set his aircraft heading for the *Tirpitz* for the fourth time when Charles Housden, his navigator, tapped him on the shoulder and pointing up the fiord said 'How about that, Freddy?' Freddy looked to where Charles was indicating and saw a large chunk of aircraft fall free as a burst of flak exploded beneath it much farther down the fiord, to be followed by several more dislodgements as another burst wrought its own havoc. There was no way that Freddy could know that it was Bill Carey's aircraft that had been so violently struck, as he turned to Charles and said, 'If you saw that in one of the Hollywood films, you'd snigger in disbelief—and yet here it is happening in real life! That lot'll need some luck to make up for all they've just suffered!'

Inside *'Easy Elsie'* six hearts had momentarily stopped in utter disbelief and fright as the Lancaster rocked and plunged under the two heavy blows she had sustained. Then their instilled discipline took over. Les Franks reported that the port engine had stopped and that there was a heavy fuel loss from Nos 1 and 2 port fuel tanks. Bill Carey had automatically feathered the dead port inner engine on receipt of this information. It registered with him that, with the port inner gone, there were no hydraulic services available for landing. The calm voice of the rear-gunner broke in on the intercom, to announce either a very near miss or a direct hit on the *Tirpitz*, and, whilst this had the effect of temporary cheer, they were soon plunged back into the pressing realities of their situation. They were out of the immediate danger zone now, and Bill found that he could not close the bomb-doors. He concluded that the shrapnel from the burst had severed the hydraulic pipelines and caused any built-up pressure in the lines to be dispersed into the atmosphere.

They were well out of the reach of *Tirpitz* now, and descending on the westerly track. Bill saw a small island off the coast and told Doug that he would track the aircraft over the small town visible on the island, so that Doug could give the navigator accurate data, from which to start the return trip to Scotland. Curly Young, the wireless operator, asked for permission to use the Elsan and, upon receiving Bill's assent, clambered from his position, over the main spar and down the fuselage. Suddenly the small island below erupted in a storm of tracer and heavy flak which engulfed the aircraft. Bill hauled the Lancaster away from the danger, cursing himself for the mental aberration which had caused him to overlook the briefing warning about the flak concentrations on the small islands off the coast. Clear of the danger, he took stock of their position. The port inner engine was dead and the port outer was now beginning to run roughly. The encounter with the island flak had shattered the wireless set and blasted a huge hole in the fuselage where Curly Young would have been if he had not moved off to the Elsan. Even more serious, they had lost about 800 gallons of fuel and it was out of the question to make Scotland, or even Sumburgh. The question to be decided was whether to aim for the Royal Navy destroyers or seek a forced landing in Sweden—and the answer had to be forthcoming very, very quickly!

The Royal Navy and the Royal Air Force had certain reservations about each other throughout the war. These stemmed from the Navy's reluctance to recognize any RAF aircraft as 'friendly' and the Air Force's chronic inability to recognize British submarines! These self-same reservations clouded Bill Carey's mind, as he weighed up the alternatives with which he was now faced. He instinctively 'buttoned' the VHF frequency given to them at briefing to contact the destroyers on station, and called continuously as he circled flatly safely off the coast, but his calls failed to elicit a response. He knew that with the reduced fuel load, there was very little margin for error on either side. The Navy calculated human survival time in these waters at about ten minutes in the depth of winter, and it was late October already. Then again, the gaping bomb-doors would greatly reduce the normally-excellent 'ditching' characteristics of the Lancaster. The dinghy, on which they would have to depend if they failed to contact the destroyers, was stowed in the starboard wing-root. It could well have been seriously damaged during their flak experiences—was it serviceable? Would it eject satisfactorily when wanted? The destruction of the wireless set meant that it would not be possible to broadcast any 'MAYDAY' message—no, all things considered—it *HAD* to be Sweden.

He spoke on the intercom to the rest of the crew. 'I feel that Sweden is the only real answer to our plight' he said, 'What do you think, Mac?' McKie was delighted with his captain's decision. 'It's the only answer, really, Bill' he replied. 'We can get across Norway and into Sweden quite quickly, about a thirty mile run when we hit the coast. I calculate that we have enough fuel to get us back to Porjus, where we rendezvoused on the outward trip, and, from what I can remember of that area, it seemed flat enough for a safe forced-landing. There is one thing, however, and that is we'll need about 6,000 feet on the clock about ten miles this side of the coast. The land rises quite steeply just inside the coast'. 'Righto, let's get on our way' answered Bill, 'But first I'll try and raise Willie Tait and inform him of our decision and reasons.' He switched to the Squadron communication frequency and began calling.

At first he called 'Formation leader' but when that evoked no reply after several calls, he addressed himself to any listening aircraft. There was no reply. It was as if the set was dead. The silence that followed each call was daunting. McKie had an inspiration. He leapt to the Very pistol and began to loose off a succession of red cartridges, to attract the visual attention of any aircraft in the vicinity. He had fired off about four rounds when the agitated voice of the rear-gunner asked him if he was aware that the fuel was still streaming in vapour from the stricken petrol tanks and that the Very lights were bursting in very close proximity to this area and would he kindly desist before he incinerated the whole crew—all this was put in the polite vernacular that aircrew commonly used in such circumstances and Alex' inspiration subsided almost as quickly as it had arisen! But not before it had brought dividends.

Flight Lieutenant 'Mac' Hamilton was on his way from Tromso when the distress signals were sighted, and he wheeled over, to see what he could do. He identified the aircraft at once, and called on the VHF for details. Bill was relieved to know that his set was working OK, and he told Mac that he was Sweden-bound because of damage to the aircraft and loss of fuel. He asked Mac to pass on the message to Willie Tait, with the crew's regrets at not being able to get back to base. 'Mac' Hamilton promised to pass on the message, apologizing for not being able to help in any other way, especially as his own fuel state didn't give him much leeway to hang about. He wished Bill and his crew all the luck in the world with the landing '—and lay off those Swedish maidens, you randy lot of bastards' were his final parting words. Carey brought 'Easy Elsie' on to the course McKie had given him, and the haul for Sweden was on!

All Witherick's pre-flight misgivings came flooding back as the aircraft shuddered and reared as the two giant blows struck 'Easy Elsie'. As he obediently swung his turret round to spot the fall of the bomb, he listened mutely to the traffic on the intercom. Les Franks' information about the engines on the port side was grave. Gerry himself could see the vapourizing fuel dispersing into the air. His eyes were riveted on the *Tirpitz* and a yell of exultation left his lips as he saw her disappear in what appeared to be a great spume of smoke, steam and spray. 'By God, you've hit her, Junior!' he shouted delightedly, his aircraft's predicament momentarily forgotten in the excitement of the achievement. 'Well' he mused to himself, 'if I'm to disappear into this cold Arctic sea, it looks as if the *Tirpitz* will be joining me!' He had just settled himself comfortably again, when all hell broke loose unexpectedly around him. His whole world gyrated madly as the pilot slewed the Lancaster out of the barrage. Incensed at this latest attack, Gerry swung his four Brownings down and gave the retreating island a blast from his guns. Not that he was convinced that it would do any real damage, but it was an automatic reaction to the vexation that seized him. His feathers were still ruffled when Very signals began to leave the Lancaster. To his horror, he saw that they were igniting close to the area of the petrol vapour!! He couldn't switch his mike on quickly enough to berate verbally the stupid cow-son who was busily trying to finish what the *Tirpitz* had started. His tirade was enough to cause the barrage of Very signals to stop immediately. He gradually calmed down and nodded approvingly at the captain's decision to go for Sweden, rather than the Navy. 'Bloody "fish-heads"!' he thought disdainfully 'They never did do the Air Force any bloody favours!'

Les Franks had been fully occupied in safeguarding all possible fuel.

He had kept the engines supplied from no 1 port tank, at the same time manipulating the Lancaster's fuel system controls and pumps to get as much petrol transferred from the damaged no 2 tank into the no 1. When the no 2 tank registered 'EMPTY', he switched the engine supply to the starboard inner petrol tank, and began to pump the petrol from the leaking no 1 port tank into this reservoir.

Bill Carey flew the aircraft carefully down the Malangey Inlet, keeping clear of the land on either side. He had put the aircraft into climbing revs and boost, but she was making very heavy weather of it and her rate of climb would not guarantee that safety height was obtained before the really high land loomed. 'We've got to lighten the old girl' he announced over the intercom, 'so let's get rid of eve1 ything movable we don't need for the run to Sweden'—and at that moment the engines cut out for a fraction of a second which seemed like an eternity to the horrified crew. Les Franks came hurriedly and reassuringly on the intercom. 'I've got all the remaining fuel into the starboard tanks by draining the damaged port tanks. I'm sorry if that "cut-out" gave you all heart-failure, but I was so engrossed in the work that I momentarily forgot that anyone else was aboard!' Relief flooded the minds of his fellow unfortunates and the mobile members of the crew commenced the task of lightening the aircraft.

Bill Carey ordered Gerry Witherick to remain at his post to guard against possible fighter attack and directed that none of the rear turret ammunition should be jettisoned until they were safely inside Sweden. The jettisoning of items was accomplished either through the access door in the fuselage or the bomb-bay inspection panel in the nose of the aircraft. Parachutes, ammunition for the front turret, the front turret Brownings, the damaged W/T set, the VHF receiver—all went cascading out of the aircraft into the waters of the Malangey Inlet, most after being treated to a few judicious jabs with the aircraft axe before despatch. The Gee set was destroyed by using the built-in detonating circuit and the equipment speedily followed the earlier items to the bottom of the sea. MacLennan did an 'axe' job on the SABS, completely wrecking it beyond repair, before taking it from its mounting and further dismantling it. It was then jettisoned piece by piece, to be followed by the F.9 camera, dutifully smashed. The camera magazine was opened and the complete film exposed to the daylight before it too was sent hurtling downwards. Every loose piece of equipment and gear was tossed overboard, and 'Easy Elsie' began to reach the rate of climb necessary to safeguard her from the looming mountains.

It was a relieved McKie who saw the altimeter needle reach the 6,000 feet mark a minute or so before the critical moment. Once straight and level, the ground speed began to increase and Alex map-read the aircraft to the turning-point. They were over Lake Kilpisjarvi, where the borders of Norway, Finland and Sweden met. The next course swung 'Easy Elsie' on to a south-south-west track, designed to take the aircraft to the chosen forced-landing area. This track lay over the higher foothills of the mountain range they had crossed. To starboard, the mountains loomed over the aircraft, rising to some 6,800 feet and sheltering it from any German radar interrogation. McKie had calculated that this leg would take about 36 minutes and Les Franks reported that the conserved fuel should last for at least another fifty minutes—if the gauges were still reading correctly. The whole crew realized that it was still very much touch-and-go, and their survival mainly depended on the terrain they found at the end of this leg.

They were now well on course for their destination. The weather was fine and clear, which augured well for their prospects. Their thoughts began to turn towards the security aspect of their predicament. MacLennon shredded all the maps and charts that neither he nor Alex would require for the rest of the journey and fed them out into the slip-stream at intervals, after he had mixed them well. Curly Young tore up all his radio codes and log books and mixed them inextricably in the navigator's bag. He checked that the small spiked incendiary bombs, which aircraft carried for the purpose of setting the aircraft on fire in the event of a forced-landing on the Continent, were available and secured them carefully against the inevitable impacts that would occur when the captain set the aircraft down.

McKie continued to map-read the track, correcting the course as required and checking the ETA as ground-speed checks became available. He was delighted to see the long, narrow Stora Lulevatten appear on cue ahead of the aircraft. This was a body of inland water, akin to the Caledonian Canal, running in a south-east/north-west direction for a distance of some 70 miles. It was an ideal land-mark for the circumstances in which the crew of *'Easy Elsie'* found themselves. 'That's the area, at the southern end of this lake, Bill' said Alex to the captain. Witherick came on to the intercom. 'I'm ready to throw out all the equipment from the rear-turret, skipper' he said. 'It's all by the rear door, and if Junior could come down and give me a hand, I suggest that you fly down this lake and we drop it all in the water, rather than over land, where it might be recovered, or hurt somebody.' 'Good idea, Gerry' answered Bill, 'and it won't cost us any time either.' Doug MacLennan moved to the rear door and very soon the four Brownings, gun-sight and ammunition supply for the rear-turret were hurtling down and sending up columns of water as they crashed into the placid waters of the lake below. 'All clear, skipper' came Witherick's voice on the intercom when the last of the stores had gone.

Bill Carey acknowledged the message and felt that things were beginning to go their way at last. The remaining fuel would last for another twenty minutes at the outside and he prayed that would be ample time to find a suitable landing place. He noticed that there was a great deal of forest-land in the area and, throttling back, he began a wide sweep of the area, at the same time losing off the height so bravely won. He spotted a large clearing in the forest, close by the shore of the lake, and brought the aircraft round, so that he could inspect it and assess its suitability for a landing. Both Les Franks and Alex McKie helped him with this assessment and it was unanimously decided that, in the present circumstances, it would be foolish to try and better the present offer. He told the crew that, as the field seemed quite flat, he would try a landing with the wheels down. For this purpose, he required that Les Franks should stay beside him, in order to pull the compressed air bottle when required, to force the undercarriage down and lock it. He ordered the rest of the crew to take up their crash positions immediately.

McKie, Young, MacLennan and Witherick made their ways dutifully to the fuselage without fuss, thanks to the routine crash drills they had regularly performed on the Squadron. McKie plugged into the sole intercom socket and reported all crew members in crash positions, which Carey acknowledged. Bill lost a lot of height and then turned to make a long, flat approach to the clearing. When he was nicely lined-up for the landing, he gave the command 'Now!' Les Franks pulled the bottle at the same time as Bill selected 'Undercarriage down' and they were both relieved when the lights showed that the undercart was down and locked securely. Les did not have time to get back to his allotted crash position and so, with Bill's approval, he lowered the second-pilot's seat beside the pilot and strapped himself in as best he could. Bill checked his own safety-straps and concentrated on the approach and landing, the flight engineer standing-by to cut the four throttles right back when given the word by the captain. Les had also decided to press all four fire-extinguisher buttons on the aircraft panel as soon as he had cut the throttles. Satisfied that all possible precautions had been taken, Bill told the crew to brace themselves for the impact and set the Lancaster down just inside the field.

The aircraft touched down perfectly but had run about twenty or so yards when the wheels began to sink rapidly and deeply into the ground. True to his aim, Les Franks had cut back the throttles on command and pressed the extinguisher buttons. The rate of deceleration was tremendous and the tail of the Lancaster rose high in the air as the nose dug in and mud poured in through the forward escape hatch. They had landed in a bog! The advent of the mud was the last thing Les remembered of the inside of the Lancaster, for the next moent, inexplicably, he found himself OUTSIDE the aircraft, in the mud, looking up at the Lancaster as the tail crashed back to the earth!. . . and he without a scratch or injury to mark this rapid transition!

Bill Carey just couldn't relate to what was happening. He had felt the wheels touch and was elated to think that their main dangers were past. Suddenly, the aircraft seemed to stop dead, the nose dipped steeply and the tail rose sharply. Although he was strapped securely into his seat, he felt a tremendous pressure being applied to his back. He grimaced wildly as he thought, 'My back's breaking! I'll be dead in a minute!' Despite the restraining strap, he was thrust forward and his left knee struck the P.4 compass, shooting a searing pain up his thigh as the kneecap dislocated. The tide of mud rushing into the aircraft still further bemused him. With a tremendous reverberating thump, the fuselage crashed back to earth and the pain in his leg and back mercifully numbed. He glanced dazedly out of the port side of the cockpit and was amazed to see Les Franks, liberally bespattered with mud, frantically waving up at him. 'Christ!' he thought, through the pain of his knee, 'It didn't take that old bastard long to get out of *"Elsie"*!'

The four aircrew in the fuselage had opened and fastened back the fuselage door, before taking their crash positions. This ensured their exit, even if the door area was ruptured during the landing. They had braced themselves instinctively when they felt the wheels touch, but they were not really prepared for the tremendous pressure they felt with the rapid deceleration of the aircraft. Doug MacLennan gave mute thanks that crash positions decreed that aircrew would be braced against the main spar, facing the rear turret, for, as the tail reared viciously into the air, a receiver (which they had been unable to release during the lightening phase) broke loose from its mounting and came flying directly for him. He had his hands clasped behind his head, in the recommended manner, but was able to ward off the projectile with his feet. When the tail fell back to the earth, the receiver went crashing back towards the turret. Doug realized that the receiver would have crashed into the recumbent form of Les Franks, had he been in his proper crash position, and he made a mental note to tell Les.

They sat immobile for a few moments, to ensure that the aircraft had finally come to rest and to get used to the silence which had descended upon the aircraft. It was about 11.00 hours and the roar of the Merlins had been the background of life for the past ten hours. Thus the silence was deepened by their shut-off and it was some few seconds before they were accustomed to it. Then a tremendous feeling of elation swept them at their safe deliverance from mortal peril. Laughing with undisguised relief, they began to strip off their parachute harnesses, Mae Wests and such other flying equipment that would impede their mobility. There were urgent security duties now laid upon them and not one of them knew just how long they had to attend to these essential matters.

Alex McKie switched on his mike and spoke to the pilot, 'Well done, Bill! That was bloody marvellous! We're all OK back here and . . .' He was interrupted by a groan and heard Bill Carey say, 'I've dented my left knee on the P.4 compass and it's giving me hell! Les is outside the aircraft—don't ask me how—so I'm on my own up here and I'll never get out of this seat without help.' 'Hang on, Bill, and we'll be right up' said Alex. He switched off, removed his 'electric hat' and told the others of Bill's plight.

Gerry, Doug and Curly all plunged over the main spar and hurried to the cockpit. They were all pretty sure that, with the very low fuel state, there was little danger of *'Elsie'* catching fire, but their survival instincts told them to assume that the danger was present and to react accordingly. It was imperative to get Bill out of the aircraft and at a safe distance from it. Whilst the other two carefully manoeuvred Bill from his seat, Doug looked around the cockpit and noticed that the starboard side of the windscreen was pushed out raggedly. He put his mouth close to the opening and yelled out 'LES! WHERE ARE YOU?' 'I'm down here, in the bog!' came an answering shout. 'Are you alright?' queried Doug, fearing the worst. 'I'm perfectly OK, Doug—I landed on my head!' came the flippant rejoinder. 'About the safest place, too' called out the irrepressible Witherick as he struggled with Bill Carey, 'If it had been anyone else, they'd have been brained!' With great care and gentleness, Bill was lifted over the main spar and down to the open aircraft door.

Les Franks managed to heave himself aboard the Lancaster. He removed the ladder from its stowage and placed it in position for Bill's removal from the aircraft. With the utmost care, Les and Curly supported Bill's legs, whilst Gerry and Doug managed his shoulders and back. They succeeded in getting him out without jarring him or causing him any greater pain than he was suffering already. They sploshed through the mud of the bog, sinking into it just above their shins. They could see the track where the aircraft's weight had rutted two deep trenches from the point of touch-down for some twenty yards. The trenches deepened rapidly along their length until the Lancaster's wheels were scarcely visible above the surface of the swamp. They were clear of the bog after some thirty yards and they carried Bill a further fifty yards, to lay him gently down on a small wooded rise. It was a bright sunny day and reasonably warm but Bill was now shivering, violently and uncontrollably. Curly examined Bill's leg and found no sign of blood, but the kneecap was very obviously dislocated and causing Bill considerable pain. Gerry had noticed a parachute pack beneath the navigator's table. It had been overlooked during the jettisoning interlude, and Gerry gathered it up as he passed back down the fuselage, assisting with Bill. Now he carefully pulled the silver release handle, holding the pack close to contain it in its folded shape. He used a knife to sever the revealed shrouds and then the four of them wrapped Bill warmly in the enveloping silk.

Soon his shivering ceased—but the relief at getting his crew down safely and without injury to them, plus the pain of his injury, produced shock reaction in his system and tears began to roll down his cheeks. The crew members, each of whom knew he owed his life to this man's skill and devotion, watched him with sympathetic understanding. They understood the reasons for his tears, and did their best to comfort and reinstate him to the normal character of their 'Australian Jimmy Cagney'. 'Everything's fine, Bill' consoled Witherick 'and it's all thanks to you, mate! Lie there and rest, whilst we deal with the aircraft—and then we'll get you to hospital where lush blond Swedish nurses will gush all over you—and more besides, with a bit of luck!'

Doug MacLennan sped back to the aircraft where he found Alex McKie doing his level best to destroy the aircraft, as per the book. Alex had climbed out through the pilot's escape hatch, clutching the destructive incendiaries close to his chest. He knelt on the starboard wing and removed the caps from all four bombs. He struck the detonator levers smartly against the side of the fuselage and rammed two of the bombs into the wing, so that they remained upright on their spiked bottoms. He leapt quickly to the port wing and repeated the process, then lowered himself smartly through the open escape hatch, tore down the fuselage and out of the door, putting as much distance as he could between himself and the doomed aircraft. He stood with Doug, waiting expectantly, but nothing happened. After ten minutes, Alex reluctantly decided that the bombs were dud.

He retraced his steps to the wings, seized the reluctant incendiaries and flung them as far as he could into the depths of the bog. Meanwhile, in the fuselage, Doug had attacked the auxiliary tanks with the aircraft axe and was rewarded when petrol began to flow from them. Alex returned from the cockpit, carrying his navigation bag. He upended it into the gathering pool of petrol and the torn radio logs and codes cascaded into the liquid. 'I think we've done everything necessary in here, Doug' he said. 'Just one thing more' said Doug, and he pulled the dinghy release just by the door. Nothing happened—no muffled explosion—no dinghy shot from the starboard wing root. Repeated tugs failed to operate the system. Doug turned to Alex, 'Just as bloody well we didn't choose the wet way home' he said, 'It would have been a long swim!'

They both scrambled out of the aircraft and stood with their backs against the fuselage, to the right of the entrance door. Alex fashioned a torch from the few maps and charts he had brought with him and held it for Doug to light with his Ronson lighter. The aircrew on the knoll watched the scene intently. They saw Alex toss the flaming brand into the open door and then both figures began a dash which would not have disgraced Jesse Owens, even allowing for the clinging properties of the bog. Suddenly there was a distinct 'whoomph' as the petrol ignited and soon 'Easy Elsie' was engulfed in flames. Thick black smoke soared obscenely skywards, into the bright, clear Arctic day. As the fire took firm hold, odd rounds of ammunition exploded—stowed Very cartridges ignited and sent their multi-coloured signals aloft, as if in salute to a dying heroine. Exploding oxygen bottles added their contribution in the fiery farewell to a gallant veteran. Suddenly, there was an external and muted explosion. The aircraft dinghy was flung clear of the flames and lay, smoking, some ten yards from the holocaust. The smoke that issued from it soon ceased and the bright yellow dinghy continued to inflate itself automatically.

They all watched 'Easy Elsie's' funeral pyre with silent sadness and regret. She had borne them proudly and safely on many operations with the Squadron. It seemed such a pity that she should meet her end at the hands of those she had carried to war! But the rules of the game demanded it—and there was no gainsaying them! Soon all that was left recognizable of the Lancaster was the fuselage and engines—the interior was a molten charred mess. Even through their sadness, the crew could view the affair with great satisfaction. They had completely and efficiently discharged the duties laid upon them in such circumstances.

There were no secrets to be learned from *'Easy Elsie'*!

As the aircraft fires were spluttering to their fitful conclusion, Alex turned from the death throes and spoke to his aircrew friends, 'Now's the time to make contact with the local natives and get some creature comforts—and, most important, medical aid for Bill.' They all nodded in assent, so he went on, 'I've a pretty shrewd idea where the lake lies. From there, we can make Porjus—at least, I think that was the name of the town on the map. I suggest that one of you comes with me whilst the rest stay here with Bill. That way we can inform our contacts of your position and they'll be able to get here with the minimum delay.' They all agreed that this was the best plan in the circumstances. Curly Young volunteered to accompany Alex and together they set off at a brisk pace.

Watching the desultory splutter of the dying flames, Doug suddenly remembered the incident during the actual landing, when the receiver had hurtled into the crash position area. 'You've had some extra luck today, Les' he said, 'Getting through that windscreen without a scratch—and that I'll never understand—and then a dislodged receiver crashing on to your crash position.' He continued to relate the affair to Les Franks, who agreed that it did seem to be his lucky day. The recollection stirred Doug's memory still further and he told the others about the failure of the dinghy release. 'You're dead right, Doug' agreed Gerry, 'It was the right decision to come to Sweden. We'd never have found those "fish-heads", I'm convinced, and it's not quite the time of the year for an Arctic swim!'

Mention of the dinghy brought Gerry to his feet. 'I'll go over to the dinghy and get the survival rations' he said. 'We could do with something to eat and I've always been curious about the contents of those packages.' He rose and made his way to the dinghy. It had occurred to him that the tins of soup in the rations were just what they needed now. The tins had a self-contained heating system, and he cursed himself silently that he had not thought of them before. A piping hot drink would do Bill a world of good—and it wouldn't come amiss to the rest of them, either. The pack was in the dinghy and he carried it back to the small rise where the others waited expectantly. They crowded round him excitedly as he tore the adhesive strips away and revealed the contents. There was a dumbfounded silence, as they surveyed the contents—no tins of soup, no chocolate, no biscuits, no Horlicks' tablets—just a few tins of water. That pack should have contained survival rations for a crew of seven for at least three days. Gerry swore softly to himself, his mind unable to grasp what his eyes beheld.

He couldn't believe that the food had been removed on the Squadron—the ground-crew and aircrew were too close for such a despicable theft to be perpetrated there—and anyway, the dinghy stowage couldn't possibly be breached without it becoming obvious to the most casual of inspections. 'No,' he decided, 'it could only have taken place at the factory where the packs are assembled and sealed before being stowed in the dinghy. Probably some "civvy", without thought of the circumstances in which these stores would be vital to the survival of a Lancaster crew, had decided to supplement the meagre civilian rations by adding the missing items to his own personal larder.' His anger mounted as he opened a tin of water and held it for Bill to take a drink. 'Bastards!' he said aloud, 'Rotten stinking bastards! I hope they bloody well choke on them!' The rest of them nodded in assent. The choice of 'ditching' would almost have been unwitting suicide!

Alex and Curly had made good time to the lake. Skirting it to the south, they came across a boat-house on the shore. Inside they found several boats, and chose to launch a small rowing-boat. Fifteen minutes later, they had crossed the lake and beached the boat above the water-line with both pairs of oars safely shipped. A short walk in a northerly direction brought them to the railway line Alex was sure he'd seen from the air and they turned on the southward run and walked along the metals towards Porjus. They met no-one on the way, but soon they were in the outskirts of the town, with large residential houses. They forsook the railway for the road which served these houses. 'I'll try at the next house, Curly, and see what cooks!' said Alex. Suiting the deed to the words, he strode up the short drive and knocked loudly on the wooden door. The door opened and a large old lady stood framed in the doorway, staring at Alex. 'I am a member of the RAF' he began, and ceased, disconcerted, as the door was slammed firmly in his face without further ado. He went back to Curly. 'I dinna think she kenned ma Scotch accent, man' he beamed. 'Let's hope we have better luck lower down.'

They walked on and Alex tried again at one of the other houses. This time a much younger lady answered his summons, and she didn't seem at all put out by his appearance. 'I am a member of the RAF' began Alex again, and paused, to see if there was any hostile reaction, but the lady waited attentively. 'We have made a safe forced landing in this area and we are anxious to contact the Swedish military authorities.' 'Do come in with your friend' came the reply, in excellent English. 'I am sure that you could both do with something to eat and drink first. Then I will contact my husband, who will get all things arranged.' Alex and Curly entered and were soon comfortably seated beside a warming fire, eating home-made biscuits and drinking a large mug of steaming sweet coffee. It was only when he sat down that Alex realized how tired he was. He'd been on his feet, one way and another, ever since they'd turned to limp into Sweden and his legs welcomed the rest. The lady of the house joined them and said that she had contacted her husband by phone and he was getting in touch with the Swedish authorities. It would not be long before they arrived at the house.

It was *not* long before a Swedish Army lorry arrived. They said goodbye to their hostess, thanked her for her hospitality before climbing on to the lorry, under the escort of two armed Swedish soldiers, who looked at them with friendly faces. They were driven to the local gaol in Porjus where they were each shown into separate cells. A few minutes later, a Swedish officer arrived and began to interrogate Alex, but Alex politely cut him short. 'Excuse me, sir' he said, 'I don't wish to be rude, but four of our friends are still in the woods, close to the place where we forced-landed. The pilot has a bad knee injury and is suffering from shock. I would be most obliged if you could send medical aid to them as soon as possible.' 'Please come with me' said the officer and he took Alex to an office where a large-scale map of the locality hung on a wall. 'Can you indicate just where your friends are?' he enquired. Alex studied the map and mentally retraced his hike and row. 'Yes' he said, 'I think they are on a small rise—about here,' indicating an area near the lake. 'Ah yes', rejoined the officer, 'That would tie up with the direction the smoke was observed. Would you please wait here? I will make the necessary arrangements to have your friends picked up—and I will make sure that a stretcher is taken, too.' With that, he left the office and Alex stared curiously about him. 'An interrogation, eh?' he thought, 'Well, I'll be on my guard—but what would the Swedes hope to get out of it?'

Doug MacLennan was beginning to feel restive. Alex and Curly had been gone for well over an hour and he felt that they should have seen some results by now. In his own mind, he was not all that sure that they were out of the reach of the Germans. This probably stemmed from the fact that, for the first time since he had left Canada, there was no stretch of water between him and land-based Germans, and he could not put the thought from his mind that German patrols could venture this far into Sweden. There was also a nagging doubt about the reaction of the Swedes. To him they were an unknown quantity and it was not inconceivable that some of them might hold pro-German sympathies—might even have an arrangement with the Germans across the border to hand over shot-down British aircrew. Intelligence bulletins were always warning aircrew of this danger in the Spanish areas of the Pyrenees—why not here? He was thinking along these lines when the four of them suddenly quietened and listened intently. Faint voices were borne on the gentle breeze which had sprung up during the past hour and they turned to face the direction from which the sounds appeared to be coming. Doug could not recognize the language but its guttural content did nothing to reassure him.

Instinctively, he moved behind a large tree, some yards away from the other three, and loosened the .38 revolver from its holster as he stood awaiting developments. He peered cautiously round the tree and saw two men in uniform approaching. They were wearing uniform, but, reassuringly, wore Red Cross armlets and carried no arms. He returned his pistol to its holster and stepped forward to rejoin his comrades. The men hurried forward when they caught sight of the RAF party, smiling and shaking hands all round. They set down the stretcher they were carrying and gave Bill their attention. When they finished their ministrations they gave him a jab of morphia, before wrapping him efficiently in the blankets they had brought. The injured pilot was then lifted carefully on to the stretcher and secured with webbing-straps. Doug, Gerry and Les realized that Alex and Curly had made contact and had sent help with all possible speed.

One of the orderlies spoke quite good English, and his opening sally startled his listeners considerably. 'Have you seen any snakes whilst you have been here?' he enquired. 'Snakes?' snorted Gerry, 'Haven't we put up with enough since we left England, without being expected to cope with bloody snakes!' 'Anyway' he sniffed, 'there shouldn't be snakes—not in the Arctic—it's too cold for them—but let's get moving in case this bod is not joking!' The orderly laughed delightedly, and he and his companion took the handles of the stretcher and lifted Bill from the ground. They retraced their steps, with the others following in single file. The path was occasionally quite slippery, but the bearers managed to give Bill quite a gentle ride and avoided spilling him, despite slithering on a few occasions. Presently they reached a forest track and the going became much easier.

Les Franks was intrigued with the construction of the path. It was made with tree trunks sawn into lengths of about eight feet and laid athwart the run of the path. To mark the edges of the path, other tree trunks were laid laterally in a pyramid of three. It struck Les that it was certainly an effective way of providing a useful track using 'on the spot' materials. They journeyed about a quarter-mile along this track until they struck a road on which an ambulance was parked. Bill was loaded into the ambulance very carefully and then the rest piled in with one of their forest escorts. The other escort took his place behind the wheel and soon they were en route for Porjus. The orderly inside the ambulance had limited English but became quite interested in Doug's 'CANADA' shoulder-flashes. 'Canada?' he enquired, 'Canada?' and Doug nodded his assent. The man then waved his hand in the direction from which they had come. 'Liberator?' he queried, 'Liberator?'. Doug thought that the man was trying to make him aware that he knew that the Canadian Army was fighting on the Continent to liberate the occupied countries. He nodded his head vigorously and said 'Yes!' several times, in a most emphatic fashion. The incident came back to him next day when he was told by a Swede that the local paper's edition bore a banner headline 'RAF Liberator crashes. All Canadian crew on board!'

* * *

Alex had had time to compose himself whilst the Swedish officer was out of the room. 'Number, rank and name, that's all they're entitled to, and that's all I intend to give them' he mused, and smiled contentedly to himself. At least he was not called upon to face the rigours of a German interrogation, with its adept questioning and probing. The Swedish officer returned to the room. 'An ambulance is on its way' he beamed, 'and now, if you don't mind, I would like to ask you a few questions.' He motioned Alex to a seat on the opposite side of the desk and arranged his papers carefully. 'Your Service number, rank and name, to begin with' he said, and Alex obliged him with these facts. They were written down carefully and checked verbally. 'Your RAF Squadron, next' he said with his pen poised, ready to log the information. 'I am sorry, sir, but all I am required to give you, under the Geneva convention, is my number, rank and name. My squadron information is secret and I must not give it to you', replied Alex evenly.

The interrogator looked bewildered. 'But they will want to know this in Stockholm' he declared. Alex looked at him in silence until the Swede shrugged his shoulders. 'I suppose it is useless to ask you what target you attacked in Norway, but I would guess that it was the *Tirpitz* at Tromso.' He eyed Alex expectantly, but Alex said nothing. 'Why did you land in Sweden? Do you wish to be interned for the rest of the war?' pursued the Swede. 'It was imperative to avoid capture by the Germans, sir—my comrades and I wish to be returned to our Squadron as soon as possible, so that we can resume the struggle to liberate Europe' replied Alex. He felt that he was bound to answer this direct question, which could have a bearing on their immediate future. His answer was recorded, but the next question astounded him. 'Why did you try to destroy the dam which holds our reservoir?' said the officer in the most severe voice he had used throughout their contact.

Alex looked at him unbelievingly. Bomb the dam? What was he talking about? Suddenly it dawned on him—the late jettisoning, just before the 'pancake-ing'! 'Believe me, sir, we did not try to bomb the dam! Sweden is neutral and we value her friendship. We were jettisoning items from the aircraft, to make the forced landing that much safer. We had no bombs on board when we crossed into Sweden, I can assure you. We'd given them to the Germans!' The officer smiled and was obviously mollified by the reply. 'Well, there's nothing else I can ask you—at least, nothing to which you will reply' he went on. 'If you will wait here, I will see if your friend's interrogation is finished. We will be sending you to a small hotel in Porjus, but—' and he looked most apologetic, 'I am afraid that we shall have to mount guards at the door.' He left the room, to re-appear very quickly and beckon Alex to accompany him. Alex saw Curly waiting in the reception room of the gaol. 'Alright, mate?' he queried. Curly winked solemnly, 'Number, rank and name, Alex, as per the book—nothing else, although they guessed the target without me confirming it.'

At that moment an officer came over to them. 'There are some Swedish and Norwegian civilians outside who wish you to join them in a drink. So you can go with them and they will take you to the hotel when you have finished.' They were delighted at the thought of a drink, but Alex couldn't help thinking, 'I'm sure it wouldn't have been like this at Dulag Luft!' Outside the gaol there was a crowd of some twenty men and a cheer went up as they appeared. 'Well done, English!' shouted one enthusiast, 'It will soon be peace and the damned Germans will run out of Norway!' They were slapped on the back and led to what obviously passed for a Swedish pub. Drinks were pressed on them and a very happy mood descended on the company. Songs were sung with great gusto but eventually they asked to be taken to the hotel. Their hosts were loth to oblige until Alex said they wanted to be reunited with their friends, one of whom was wounded. There followed nods of understanding and the whole group moved down the street to the hotel. Alex and Curly turned round just before they entered and waved to their hosts. There was more cheering and waving, and then they pushed their way into the hotel.

* * *

The ambulance drew up outside what proved to be the local gaol. Doug, Les and Gerry alighted and were greeted by a Swedish officer. There was also quite a crowd of civilians, who clapped and cheered loudly. 'Well done English! Soon it will be peace!' were a couple of the cries they recognized. The officer beamed at them, 'You can see what the people think of you, and most people in Sweden think that way. Your wounded comrade will be taken to hospital for such treatment as we are able to give him. If you gentlemen will go into the building, others are waiting to receive you. I am going with your comrade to the hospital.' He stood aside and allowed them to pass into the gaol. He stepped back up into the ambulance and it drove off.

The three aircrew were ushered into separate cells and in a very few minutes each was being subjected to interrogation. Politely but firmly they stuck to the 'number, rank and name' formula of their Intelligence training, and only allowed themselves to be drawn on topics of no military significance. Doug was questioned about the 'bombing' of their dam, and gave an explanation identical to Alex's answer to the same suggestion. His interrogator, however, was loth to leave the subject and asked Doug's advice on the best steps to take to prevent such an occurrence. Doug thought for a moment and then said 'Well, it might pay to fly a Red Cross flag on a mast at each end of the dam—and to paint red crosses on the face of the dam, if possible.' The answer was received very cordially and the officer left the room.

The interrogation of Les Franks followed much the same lines and Gerry Witherick was also subjected to a similar line of questioning, but when his interrogator asked him what kind of aircraft it was, he replied, 'I don't know. We are kept in a small hut and then taken to the aircraft, so we don't really know what type we're flying in.' The officer nodded and said, 'Well, I can tell you it was a Liberator'. 'Thank you, sir' replied Gerry, 'I will now be able to complete my log-book entry correctly when I get back to England'.

After the interrogations had finished, they were reunited in the reception area. An officer came over to them. 'We are accommodating you in a small hotel, rather than in the gaol' he said. 'You will understand that we must retain your small-arms and there will be a guard at the hotel entrance. However, you will have full freedom of movement within the hotel. I am sure you will all like to bath and shave—and perhaps get a few hours sleep, after all your troubles. My commanding officer would be honoured if you will all dine with him tonight in his quarters. We will send transport to the hotel for you at nine o'clock. This way, if you please, gentlemen' he said as he led them out of the gaol and down the street to a small hotel. They received many smiles and admiring glances from many civilians who had obviously been hanging about, hoping to see them.

The hotel was very comfortable. Shaving soap and razors had been made readily available for each of them and they bathed before adjourning to the dining-room, where a meal was laid before them. Alex and Curly had rejoined the party, regaling them with the tale of their adventures. They compared verbal notes in very quiet tones about their separate interrogations and were jointly relieved to discover that the Swedes had not attempted to probe very deeply into military matters once it had become abundantly clear that the RAF aircrew were not prepared to go beyond number, rank and name. Alex and Curly's drinking session was envied by the others. After the meal, they retired to their rooms, slipped out of their aircrew battledress and climbed thankfully into bed for a few hours rest, after arranging with the proprietor for a call at eight o'clock.

The proprietor was as good as his word, and they awoke to find that during their slumber, their battledresses and shoes had been removed for cleaning. All traces of the mud of the bog and other reminders of their sojourn in the open had been removed from their clothing and it lay, cleaned and pressed, waiting for them. Their shoes shone fit to delight the heart of the most demanding station Warrant Officer. They were ready when, promptly at nine, the Swedish Army transport called for them and took them to the Swedish commander's quarters. He was a most courteous and kindly host. The British aircrew had realized by this time that almost everything in Sweden was quite stringently rationed. Coupons were required for everything, but the Swedish commander had used up all his coupons to ensure that cigarettes were available in quantity for his guests. They had some initial drinks and then sat down to a delicious meal of Swedish origin which they all thoroughly enjoyed. 'That was great, sir!' enthused Witherick at the end of the main course, 'What was it?.' 'Be glad you had it to eat' interjected Doug, 'without worrying what it was!'—but his intervention came too late. 'Cow's lung and liver' replied their host. Gerry looked across the table at Doug who shrugged his shoulders and said, 'We've eaten it now, so what's the odds?'

They went into a lounge where coffee was served in steaming mugs. The conversation was naturally confined to the war—its vicissitudes for the Allies, with the gradual change in fortunes which had now brought an Allied victory in sight. Their host revealed a good knowledge of aircraft and Allied operations. He mentioned the Swedish admiration for the Dams raid, but they allowed this to pass without comment. Towards the end of the evening the Swedish commander said to them, 'You will be moved tomorrow by train to Falun, some 120 miles north of Stockholm.

There is a hostel in which British internees are billeted. The journey will take about 36 hours and, naturally, you will be accompanied by guards, but I can assure you that is a mere formality—something we are required to do by international law.'

'The journey will be most comfortable and will give you all an opportunity to see a great deal of Sweden—from the ground this time, gentlemen', he added with a disarming grin. The aircrew burst into spontaneous laughter, realizing that he was referring obliquely to the Squadron rendezvous and forming into gaggle which he had obviously watched with great interest that very morning! 'However' he continued 'I am afraid that your pilot will not be coming with you. He needs an operation on his left kneecap and, for that purpose, he will be going to the hospital at Yokkmukk. I can assure you that he will get treatment that cannot be bettered anywhere in the world, so you need have no worries on that score. It may well be that you will not see him again until you are all back in England—but then, such affairs are beyond my control, and I may be speaking out-of-turn—but, somehow, I don't think you will be detained long in my country.' This news cheered them greatly. They thanked their host for his great hospitality, and apologized that security had so greatly limited their ability to talk with him on military matters. The transport took them back to the hotel and very soon all were sound asleep—having 'a short course of death', as Gerry so aptly put it!

* * *

Bill had been removed from the ambulance with great care and taken into the civilian hospital that served Porjus. It seemed to him that an extraordinary number of staff had assembled to meet him, with many sympathetic smiles. He was prepared for examination which was prompt and thorough. 'We shall insert some stitches in the knee, purely as a temporary measure' said the surgeon, after completing his survey. 'But we shall have to send you to the big hospital at Yokkmukk tomorrow where permanent treatment is available.' The stitching proved to be efficient and painless. Bill was able to bath and don the pyjamas provided by the hospital. He then climbed gratefully into bed, feeling a lot better and somewhat hungry. The door of his private ward opened and a Swedish Army Captain entered. 'I must ask you a few questions' he began, almost apologetically, and settled himself at the bedside, with his papers balanced on his knee. 'Oh, oh!' thought Bill 'I wondered when this would come up! I shall have to watch things here!'

The first question was straightforward enough—number, rank and name, which Bill answered immediately. But further questions on military matters were parried. 'I'm sorry, sir, but that is information I am not prepared to divulge.' At length, the Captain said 'I quite understand your position, Flying Officer Carey, but there are two matters which involve Swedish authority. First, did you drop bombs into the lake before your forced landing?' Bill looked astonished, 'But we had no bombs on

Above Lancaster *'P for Popsie'* of 617 Squadron, the command of Squadron Leader 'Mick' Martin DSO, DFC.

Below Flying Officer Joplin's crew on joining 617 Squadron in August 1944. From left to right, back row to front row: Basil Fish, Loftus Hebbard; Frank Tilley; Bob Yates; Gordon Cooke; Arthur Joplin; Norman Lambell.

Above Flying Officer Duffy's crew. In the back row (left to right) stand Roy Woods, 'Red' Evans, 'Bill' Duffy and Don Bell: in the front row are Al Benting, Doug Pearce, and Tom McLean.

Below The aftermath of the Bergen raid—battle damage to Lancaster *'M for Mike'*, photographed at RAF Sumbrugh on 13 January 1945.

Above The crew of Flight Lieutenant Watts. Back row: D. Cooper; H. Luck; M. McKay; G. Matthews. Front row: C. Housden; R. Heggie; F. Watts.

Below The crew of Flight Lieutenant John Pryor. Back row: Pilot Officer Patterson; Flying Officer Pinder; Flight Sergeant Hepworth; Pilot Officer Telfer. Front row: Flight Sergeant Colyer; Flight Lieutenant Pryor; Flying Officer Pesme.

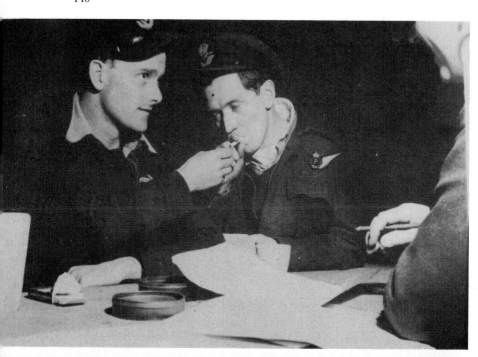

Left Flying Officer Bill Carey at debriefing with an apparently 'flak-happy' Doug MacLennan.

Below left Flight Lieutenant Castagnola's crew. From left to right: Jack Gorringe; Jim Ronald; Bill Eaves; Jimmy Castagnola; Chick Henderson; Norman Evans and Flight Sergeant Salter.

Right Flight Lieutenant J. Castagnola DFC and Bar.

Below and below right Flight Lieutenant George Kendrick, and his grave at Møllendal Cemetery, Bergen, Norway.

Above left Flying Officer Frank Chance.

Above right Warrant Officer Albert Cherrington.

Below The crew of Squadron Leader Ward (centre) with Flight Sergeant Des Phillips on the far left, Flying Officer Basil Fish (left); Flying Officer A. C. Weaver and Flight Sergeant G. H. Webb on the right.

Above left Warrant Officer Tom McLean DFC, DFM.

Above right Squadron Leader David Shannon DSO and Bar, DFC and Bar. From a portrait by Australian artist William Dargie, in the RAF War Memorial Museum, Canberra, Australia.

Below left Flight Sergeant Les Smith.

Below right Flight Sergeant Frank Tilley.

Left Flight Lieutenant Roy Woods DFC.

Below Flying Officer Ted Wass.

board, sir, when we entered Swedish territory, I can assure you!' 'We have had confirmed reports that things were dropped into the lake, nevertheless.' 'Oh yes' said a relieved Bill, 'We were jettisoning items of aircraft equipment which might have caused trouble following the forced landing—no bombs, sir, none at all!' 'The other question then is more of a political nature. Why did the British aircraft rendezvous inside Swedish territory, before going to the target?' Bill thought quickly—he had visions of a diplomatic incident hanging on his reply—and a difficult situation for himself when he returned to Britain. 'We were not routed over Sweden, I can assure you, but the aircraft on which we were to formate must have strayed over Swedish territory. It contained a senior officer, and I can only think that he had made a navigational error. He summoned the rest of us to take up formation positions by Very signals and immediately began to lead us out of Sweden as quickly as possible.'

He looked at his interrogator who was studying a report that he held in his hand. In the ensuing silence, Bill thought, 'Well, most of it was true—and I'm sure Gerry Fawke would forgive my detrimental remarks in the circumstances.' The Captain spoke 'That would seem to tie up with eye-witness reports—except that the aircraft didn't actually follow the shortest route out of Swedish territory. Still, we all know where they were going and quite understand.' He took his leave of Bill, and his departure was the signal for two blonde nurses to bring in some delicious food on a tray, with an ice-cream sweet that Bill greatly enjoyed. A steaming beaker of coffee washed it all down, and Bill settled down in the warm bed, and fell into a deep, refreshing slumber.

Next morning, after another bath, shave and breakfast, he was taken by ambulance to the hospital at Yokkmukk, where his kneecap was re-set with great skill.

* * *

The four aircrew were awakened at about eight o'clock next morning. They performed their usual morning ablutions and ate a hearty breakfast. At about nine-thirty, a Swedish Army Lieutenant came to the hotel and spoke to them. 'Good morning, gentlemen ' he said, 'today you begin the journey to Stockholm. It will take about 36 hours and will be by train. I will be your escorting officer, and I shall have two soldiers with me—not that I expect any trouble' he added hurriedly 'but it is the regulations'. I will call for you in about half-an-hour and we will go to the station'. They thanked the hotel proprietor and his staff for being so kind and when the officer returned, they set off for the station. The news had obviously been circulated around Porjus for they found a crowd of about 200 men and women waiting to accompany them. 'Many of these men are Norwegians' explained the Lieutenant to Les Franks. 'They have left Norway and settled with us until the Germans leave Norway. You can understand how pleased they are to meet members of the RAF who are doing so much for their return.'

The train was waiting for them at the station. Most of the windows were down and many heads craned out of the compartments to catch a glimpse of the RAF aircrew. The attack on the *Tirpitz* had been announced in the BBC bulletins, including the fact that one Lancaster was missing, and there was a buzz of excited conversation as the five of them entered the train. It was spotlessly clean and an electric system. They had a very spacious compartment, sealed off from the rest of the train. The Lieutenant and two soldiers settled themselves comfortably in with Gerry, Doug, Alex and Les, then divested themselves of their tunics and stowed their rifles and small-arms on the luggage racks. Box lunches were provided for each of the party and they proved to be delicious. 'It's a pity this lot don't take over the job of providing us with our aircrew rations' observed Gerry, as he tucked into the lunch. The scenery was beautiful on this sunny bright day and the officer was only too pleased to point out the sights en route. Occasionally they stopped, and, without fail at each stop, a group of local people were on hand to offer them coffee and home-made cakes. The 'bush telegraph' was amazing!

Doug MacLennan, however, had a troubled mind. He had inadvertently brought his pay book with him on the operation—and Bill Carey had done likewise! In the forest clearing, whilst they awaited rescue, Bill had entrusted his pay book to Doug and asked him to destroy it. They were both concerned that, if they fell into the wrong hands, the paybooks could give away their RAF station and, ultimately, the squadron to which they belonged. About an hour out of Porjus, Doug asked the lieutenant if he could go to the toilet and received immediate assent. Neither of the escorts accompanied him, and so he was able to tear up both paybooks and burn the pages with the aid of his Ronson lighter and, finally, flush the ashes down the pedestal. When he was satisfied that no trace of his work remained, he returned to his seat. 'Relieved?' queried Gerry. 'You can say that again!' replied Doug, with a chuckle.

They played cards to while away the time. During the evening, at one of the major stops, they were taken from the train to a beautiful restaurant, where they had a really sumptuous meal, followed by the finest ice-cream they had tasted in years. During the meal, they had a great deal of evidence of the esteem in which the RAF was held in Sweden. Not only did other diners smile and wave at them, but a group of senior Swedish Army officers broke off their meal and came over and introduced themselves. They were most enthusiastic about the RAF's achievements and congratulated the four aircrew on the first-class job their Service was doing. 'They'd have given us the freedom of Sweden if the *Tirpitz* had been sunk' observed Alex sagely. They returned to the train, with more than a suspicion that it had waited for them to finish their meal in comfort. As night drew on, they were able to make up the beds in their compartment, and settled down to a good night's sleep.

An attendant brought them coffee and biscuits about eight o'clock next morning and they dressed and shaved leisurely, before taking their seats to enjoy the passing scenery. 'Did you sleep OK?' enquired their escort.

'Like a top!' replied Alex, but he felt this burst of English was a little too colloquial for the Lieutenant, because he looked quite puzzled. They had a fine breakfast at the next stop. It was all ready for them, and the five of them began to feel that the telegraphs had been buzzing all along the line. Such things just couldn't happen spontaneously. Les said as much to the Lieutenant, but he smiled disarmingly and did not reply. 'I'm absolutely sure that we wouldn't have received all this attention on the German railways en route for Dulag Luft!' mused Alex to the others, and they laughed uproariously. The day wore on and at about ten o'clock in the evening they reached Falun. A car was waiting to convey them to the hotel which had been converted into quarters for interned British aircrew.

Their escorts handed them over officially to the supervising Swedish authority at the hostel. Gerry, Doug, Les and Alex bade a warm farewell to their escorts and thanked them for their care and kindness en route. Alex commiserated with them about the long journey they faced back to Porjus. 'Oh, no—not immediately' grinned the Lieutenant 'you see, we three all live in Stockholm and, as a reward for the heavy duty of escorting desperate RAF aircrew, we have been given four days extra leave!' The whole party laughed heartily and it was on this high note that the two sides parted.

*   *   *

Their new hosts checked their identities and showed them to their rooms. The officers were accommodated in a different part of the building from the NCOs and were introduced to an RAF officer in civilian clothes, the senior British officer of the internment hostel. He greeted them warmly, but all four of them were somewhat reserved in their reactions, since their security training warned them not to confide in strangers, whatever credentials they appeared to possess. 'Come downstairs and I'll introduce you to all the other chaps', said their new acquaintance. He was as good as his word, and the five of them were introduced to about a dozen other aircrew, some in aircrew battledress and some in civvies. They were surprised to find that a few Americans were also present amongst the internees. 'I could do with a nice hot bath, after that rail journey' said Gerry. 'There are no bathing facilities in the hostel' replied their mentor, 'but there is an arrangement with a public baths down the road, which works most amicably. If you're all ready, I'll take you along there' he said with a grin.

They accompanied him along the street, and he told them that they would be going down to Stockholm the next day, and he did not think they would be returning to Falun. They reached the baths, were vouched for and allowed to use the facilities. Initially, they stripped off and entered a hot steam bathroom. When they felt that they had stood as much as they could, they went under an icy shower that really put their backs up. This treatment was repeated until they were satisfied that their pores had been thoroughly cleansed. After the final shower, they disported themselves in a swimming bath until, finally, they were ready to dress. They climbed out of the bath and made their way to the exit door. To their shocked consternation, five women met them, grinning hugely at their obvious embarrassment and, without further ado, dried each one of them with gusto and comments in Swedish, using large warm towels. Doug was standing next to Gerry during this procedure. Gerry leaned across to him and said 'Nothing like this ever happened to me in London!'

They dressed and returned to the hostel, to find the inmates all waiting for them, with broad grins on their faces. 'Enjoy yourselves?' they queried, laughingly. 'That's one of the few Falun perks, mates!' They all sat down to a large evening meal, but the 617 aircrew refused to allow themselves to be drawn into any discussions of a security-risk nature, and were relieved when they finally adjourned to bed. After the usual pre-breakfast ablutions, they presented themselves in the dining-room and enjoyed a good meal. 'Transport will be here about 09.30' said the SBO, 'You will go to Stockholm by rail, and be met at the station by officials from the British Embassy, who will be responsible for you from then on. As I hinted yesterday, you will not be returning here—it's an early repatriation for all of you, you lucky beggars.' Many of the interned aircrew gave them names and addresses in the United Kingdom, and asked them to write, or call, if possible, to assure their relatives that they were all fit and well, and looking forward to early reunions.

The transport arrived on time and the whole crowd turned out to see them off. They caught the train in plenty of time, and settled down comfortably to enjoy the 120 miles journey to Stockholm. 'I wonder why we've been given priority in repatriation?' asked Alex. 'Well, we ARE 617 Squadron' replied Gerry, 'and I expect that the Stockholm embassy has been told. After all, the Squadron will want us on the next *Tirpitz* raid, if they want her sunk!'

The journey to Stockholm passed pleasantly and quickly. A dapper, and obviously British, man was waiting for them and his greeting was barely formal. 'This way, gentlemen, please. I have a car to take you all to the embassy, and I must ask you not to dawdle, as this promises to be a very full day for us all!' They followed his hurrying figure. 'Been here all the bloody war, I expect' hazarded Gerry, as they followed their new contact. 'Never heard a shot fired in anger, and is bleeding annoyed that we've interrupted his social round—always the bloody same, these embassy bods!' The man was holding open the door of a large automobile and almost thrust them inside. He took his seat beside the driver, and they set off into the thin Stockholm traffic. A short drive brought them to the embassy building. They were ushered inside and shown to separate rooms, which brought back memories of the interrogations at Porjus.

Alex McKie's experience was typical. A man entered and introduced himself, after a curt 'Good morning', and said he wanted a statement covering the whole of the episode from the time they had left Tromso after bombing until their arrival at Falun. Alex gave all the information he could, and it was recorded in painstaking silence, except when clipped questions were fired at him to elucidate certain points for the interrogator. All this took the best part of an hour and then the full statement was read over to him and he was required to sign it at the end, agreeing that it was a true statement. The man across the table then looked at him very directly and said, 'Why did the crew decide to make a landing in Sweden? After all, it meant crossing enemy territory in broad daylight, in what you admit was a badly crippled aircraft, that could scarcely climb to safety height.' 'It seemed the best thing to do, all things considered' said Alex. 'The best thing to do!' echoed his listener in a disbelieving tone. 'Were you not given ample facilities for assistance from the Royal Navy if you found yourselves in this sort of trouble? VHF channel—position of the ships—what more could you want?' 'We'd lost a lot of petrol, both over the target and when we were hit again by the flak from the island' replied Alex evenly, 'The flight engineer and pilot reckoned that too much had been lost—about 800 gallons was the figure mentioned, I believe.' 'Yet you were able to climb over the mountains and select the Porjus area deliberately for the landing! Surely the amount of petrol you used would have got you very close to the destroyers, had you attempted that route to safety?'

'It might have done, and it might not' replied Alex, a bit puzzled by this line of questioning. 'The dinghy didn't operate when we tried to let it out after landing, so we would have been in a fine pickle if we had attempted to "ditch" ' he went on. 'But you'd have been near the Navy and they would have had you out of the water in no time!' interjected the inquisitor sharply. 'If the rendezvous had been made correctly, that might well have been so, but don't forget, also, that the bomb doors couldn't be closed, which would have made the "ditching" a bit "hairy" at best' said Alex, somewhat testily. 'But the emergency air-bottle could have been used at the correct time to close those bomb-doors, surely!' persisted his tormentor. 'Hardly likely, if the pipes in the hydraulic system had been fractured by shrapnel' Alex retorted, 'The compression released by the air bottle would have been discharged into the atmosphere by way of these fractures!'

The man shrugged his shoulders with impatience. He looked at Alex speculatively for a few moments and then said, suavely, 'Are you sure that you weren't attracted by the opportunity of opting out of the war—to live out the next few months in safety and comfort until peace restored you to your family?' Alex looked at him in disbelief, unable to credit his ears. Their experiences of the past few days flashed through his mind—over the target—the island—the stagger to Porjus—Bill's superb handling of the forced landing—his injury—contact with the Swedes at Porjus—and here was this bod suggesting that they had just cut and run for it! Trying to keep the edge of contempt out of his voice, he replied, shortly, 'You are quite mistaken. You couldn't be more wrong!' and fell silent. A shrug of shoulders, which Alex took to be non-acceptance of his submission, and then his interrogator gathered all his papers together. 'Please wait in here for a while, until all the others have been interrogated and then you will be instructed about further arrangements.' He left the room, and Alex sat brooding, absolutely dumb-struck as he thought back over the interview again.

Suddenly the door opened and another official stuck his head round. 'Would you please come with me' he said, 'we are about to brief you all about the immediate future.' Alex accompanied his new mentor to another room and was pleased to find his four comrades already seated and facing an embassy official. Alex took his seat beside Doug and listened intently, as if at an operational briefing. 'Well, gentlemen' the official began, 'Thank you for the information you have given about your past few days. You will not be returning to Falun. Instead you will be accommodated at the Hotel Astor until we can get you air passages back to the United Kingdom, which, I trust, will not be long. Immediately, you will be taken to a large department store and allowed to provide yourselves with civilian wear and necessities. The embassy will take care of the bill, but I must warn you that clothes are very expensive in Sweden. I shall issue you each with a temporary identity card, as well as food coupons for one week, plus an allowance of Swedish money. You are required to report to the embassy each morning around 10.30 hours for any instructions and also for your daily allowance of money. Each week we will also issue you with fresh food coupons. Otherwise, you are free to come and go as you choose.

'You are expected to conduct yourselves in an exemplary manner—we do not want any "incidents", please! It is a grave offence against Swedish law to drink on the street, even graver to be found drunk in public. I must advise you that, if you feel at all unsteady after any drinking in hotels or clubs, you are to take a taxi back to the Hotel Astor, rather than risk a brush with the Swedish police. I warn you along these lines since you are likely to have a great deal of hospitality pressed upon you whilst you are in Stockholm—the Royal Air Force is very popular in this country at this moment! But you must remember that you are representatives of that Service, and of the United Kingdom as well, and do nothing that will cause offence. Are there any questions on what I have said?'

Gerry rose to his feet. 'Have you any idea how long we are likely to be here, sir?' he asked. The official shook his head, 'No, not precisely—but I would be surprised if it was much longer than two weeks!' 'Has the Air Force informed our next of kin that we are safe and in good health?' queried Curly. 'The authorities are aware of your presence in Sweden' came the cautious answer, 'but what further action they have taken on the matter, I just don't know. However, it is certain that, as a security measure, your imminent repatriation will not be made known to anyone in the United Kingdom, of that I am sure'.

They collected their identity cards and food coupons, together with what seemed to be a generous amount of kronor, but they reserved judgement on that score until they had had an opportunity to study Swedish prices. They were ushered into an embassy car and taken to a large Swedish store, where they went to the gents outfitters department and spent a hectic hour and a half getting a civilian rig-out—overcoat, suit, shirts, ties, a change of underwear, plus a few toilet requisites—and each bought a handsome fibre suitcase. This sort of outfitting they had not indulged in for quite a number of years and they were captivated by the novelty of it all, almost like children at a treat. Once all their purchases were complete, they tumbled into the car again and were taken to the Hotel Astor. 'It's like an early Christmas!' grinned Gerry, as they sat, swamped in parcels, inside the car.

At the Astor, their escort made the necessary accommodation arrangements and informed the hotel proprietor that the embassy would take care of the charges for bed and breakfast, but that all other expenses were to be charged to the individual concerned at the time such expenses were incurred. Doug and Gerry shared a double room, as did Les and Curly, whilst Alex had a single room. They adjourned to their rooms and changed into their civilian clothes, hanging their aircrew battledresses in the wardrobes. The hotel room staff were only too pleased to clean their shoes for them and eventually they all met down in the hotel bar. How very strange they all appeared to each other! Never before had they beheld their comrades in anything else but uniform! Doug was most intrigued with the material of the suits. It was made from wood fibre, since wool had long since ceased to be available in Sweden, and it was the first man-made fibre any of them had ever seen. 'I don't know whether it'll shrink or sprout in rain!' observed Doug, with a laugh.

Alex took the opportunity to ask them about their interrogations in the embassy, and it appeared that the question about 'opting out of the war' had not been raised with any of the other four. Gerry said, 'My bod seemed quite pleased with the way everything had gone, particularly with regard to security matters.' 'My one was glad that the local Swedes at Porjus had received us so enthusiastically—especially the civilian demonstrations at the hotel and the station' declared Doug. Alex thought it strange that the question had been put to him alone—was it a personal quirk of that particular official? Was it because, in the absence of the pilot, it had been assumed that he, the navigator, would have had most to say in the final decision? It was pretty certain that the suggestion would not have been put to Doug, as a member of the Commonwealth. Witherick, on his 95th trip, could hardly have been accused of dodging out of the war. Perhaps it had been assumed that the wireless operator and flight engineer would have had little say, if any, in the outcome. 'Bill, as an Australian, is in a similar category to Doug, as far as the inference went' thought Alex to himself, and permitted himself a smile at the thought of Bill's reaction if the suggestion was put to him inadvertently. His questioner would find himself faced with a blazing Aussie, quite capable of flattening him without a second's thought! 'No' he decided, 'I was the obvious target for such a question—and being newly-commissioned probably made it easier for them to throw it at me! Still, I gave them my answer and they can do what they like about it!'

They took advantage of their freedom to explore Stockholm. The hotel was in the centre of the city, very close to the Royal parks. In one of these parks was a large statue with an outstretched arm pointing urgently to the east. The inscription beneath the statue was translated for them by one of the very friendly Swedes. It was 'There is trouble in the East'.

They discovered that the Germans and Russians in similar plight were penned into internment camps and subject to quite tight checks. Their daily trek to the British embassy took them past the German embassy. It was strange to be so close to the enemy on the ground! It intrigued them to see the propaganda battle being waged in Stockholm. The British embassy had a display, showing a large swastika with a bayonet stuck right through it. Around this were the front pages of the London newspapers, detailing the advances on the Continent. The German embassy had a display, refuting all these claims and insisting that it was the Germans who were making the advances or holding firm all along the line!

On the morning following their arrival at the hotel, Gerry had failed to find a bathroom, so he made an enquiry at the foyer desk. The desk clerk smiled at him and said that there was no bathroom in the 'Astor' but she could arrange a bath for them at another hotel further down the street, which they also owned. This she did and Gerry and Doug strolled along to this hotel, with memories of their Falun bath very much in mind. On arrival at this hotel, they were shown into a bathroom which had the largest tubs any of them had ever seen. A woman was in process of filling the tubs and she had a huge thermometer, which she thrust into the tubs to take the temperature of the water. She indicated to each of them what the water temperature was, and stood expectantly, as they studied the reading.

'Seems a bit bloody hot' said Gerry, 'We'll know how lobsters feel if we get into that water!' So, using the thermometer, they indicated that they wanted the water temperature dropped. The woman laughed uproariously and proceeded to pour cold water into the tubs until they signed that it was just right. She stood there, facing them. None of them moved until Gerry exclaimed, 'I think she's waiting for a striptease—and she's not my type at all!' he added. He gestured her towards the door. She pointed at them, tossed her head in the air and gave another bellow of laughter. She made her way to the door, looked back at them and then went on her way, closing the door behind her. They could hear her laughing all the way down the corridor. They undressed and clambered into the tubs. It was an invigorating bath, but, somehow, they were secretly disappointed that this time they had no attractive assistants to dry them!

They visited all the places of interest in Stockholm, including museums and art galleries. Everywhere they went they were warmly greeted by the Swedes. In cafés and restaurants, Swedes would come over and chat to them, shake their hands and demonstrate how pleased they were with the progress of the war. Quite often they found that their bills had been paid when they took their leave. In other restaurants, no bills were presented. They were left in no doubt just where the Swedish sympathies lay.

As the Germans retreated in Finland, more and more of them crossed the border into Sweden, preferring internment to capture by the Russians in the Arctic wastes. The Swedish government decided to repatriate one German for every one member of the Allied forces and soon a regular flow of 'repats' was leaving Sweden, heading south or west.

When Gerry, Doug, Alex and Curly reported to the embassy on 6 November 1944, they were told that they were to be flown out from Stockholm airport the next day. That night, they had one final sortie on the fleshpots of Stockholm. They found a posh restaurant that looked more like a night club. Pushing their way through the swing-doors they found themselves in a corridor, with several doors leading off. 'Which one of these do we take?' queried Doug, but Gerry just shrugged his shoulders. 'It's my first time, too, mate!' he said, but just then a lovely blonde appeared at the end of the corridor and called, 'Follow me, fellows', which they did, with great alacrity. There followed a hilarious 'last evening' in Stockholm, one which proved to be very popular with the night club clientele, as well as the hostesses. It had struck Doug that the blonde who had showed them into the club had a transatlantic accent and during the course of the evening, she told them that she had lived in New York for quite a few years. In 1940, she had come over to Sweden to visit her parents and had been trapped in Sweden by the war, so she had sat out the war as a hostess in the night club—but how she longed to be back in the States again!

They dressed in battledress next morning and packed their civilian gear in the fibre suitcases. They took fond farewells of the hotel staff after breakfast, and the staff seemed very sorry to see them go. Embassy cars sped them to the airport where, with the minimum of formality, they were taken to a Dakota aircraft. On the way to the Dakota, they passed three Junkers 88 transports and Gerry said, 'For God's sake make sure we get on the right aircraft! I couldn't bear an Oflag after Stockholm!' They boarded the Dakota and were greeted by the pilot, whose name was Parker. He informed them that they were flying in a British civil airliner and the only armament he had on board was a Very pistol! He told them that their destination was Leuchars airfield, south from Dundee, across the Firth of Tay. They would fly down the Skagerrak straight to Leuchars and it should take about six hours. It was to be a night take-off, for obvious reasons and they would have to wait in the airport lounge until it was time to go. There was no possibility of being allowed to go into Stockholm, and, anyway, the time of take-off was kept secret for as long as possible, to obviate any messages being flashed to German night-fighters in Denmark.

They sat in the lounge until it grew dark and then they saw Mr Parker beckoning to them urgently. Quickly joining him they found that the Dakota was quite full, with about twenty people besides themselves as passengers, although they were the only ones in uniform. There was one cabin attendant who served them with hot coffee from large vacuum flasks and some paste and cheese sandwiches. The journey to Leuchars was cold but uneventful. When they arrived, they were met by Air Force officers, who checked their particulars and then took them off to Air Force accommodation in the RAF part of the airfield surrounds. Next day, they were given warrants to London, identity passes and allowed to travel in their Swedish civilian clothes, as it was not permitted to leave the camp in battledress. They were instructed that they would be met at Kings Cross by intelligence officers and on no account were they to leave the platform until the contact had been made, even if it meant waiting about.

The train journey passed without incident, although they had many strange glances which they took to be more for their suits than themselves. What did strike them very forcibly, however, was the striking contrast between the spotlessly clean and electric Swedish trains against the dirt and scruffiness of their British steam equivalent.

They were literally pounced upon by waiting intelligence officers at Kings Cross and herded very quickly into a crew bus that was waiting almost alongside the barrier. They were whisked away to accommodation in London, where they were given a meal and a room, but instructed not to leave the premises for any reason that evening. They were told quite pointedly not to try to telephone relatives or friends. Their itinerary for next day was quoted to them—medicals, then a debriefing, and, if everything was satisfactory, an allocation of leave before being posted as decided. Doug was told that his future would lie in the hands of the Royal Canadian Air Force and he could very well find himself repatriated.

Gerry asked if there was any news of Bill Carey, since they had had no information about him since they'd parted in Porjus. He was told, quite shortly, that Carey was progressing quite favourably and would be returned to the UK at some future date. 'What about our relatives?' queried Curly, 'We can hardly turn up on the doorstep tomorrow, without them having been prepared in advance—they'll have heart failure!' 'You can expect to be with us for a couple of days, at least' came the reply, 'I can assure you that they will be informed gently in good time for them to be prepared for your arrival, whenever that might be.'

The five of them spent the best part of the evening in the lounge, catching up on the news, before they finally adjourned to their separate rooms for the night. They were all washed, shaved and breakfasted by 08.30 next morning. They sat in the lounge, reading the morning papers and generally preparing themselves for the trials immediately ahead. Promptly at 09.15, their escort of the previous night entered and asked them to come at once. The aircrew bus was waiting and disgorged them at Adastral House in Kingsway. They were hurried into the building and were soon in the throes of the tough aircrew medical examinations. They lost touch with each other as they were separately directed to the various medical specialists, none of whom referred in any way to their Swedish interlude. When they had run the full gamut of medicals and had dressed themselves finally, they were shown to individual rooms and each of them realized that, yet again, an interrogation was to follow.

The disturbing business of the Stockholm embassy interview had gradually faded from Alex' memory under the impetus of their stay in Stockholm, but now it came flooding back into his mind. He sat apprehensively at the desk, awaiting the arrival of the interviewer. After an interval of about a quarter of an hour, the door opened and a Squadron Leader entered briskly. Alex stood to attention and the officer motioned him to sit. He opened a file and began to arrange his papers, which gave Alex a chance to study his interrogator. The first thing that struck him was that the officer wore no aircrew wings of any sort on his tunic. Alex felt that he was making a pretext of studying his papers, as if for the first time.

The officer looked up suddenly and caught Alex's wary look. 'Right then, Mr McKie, let's get on with it. I'd like to know just what took place from the time you commenced the run on the *Tirpitz* until you eventually arrived at the British Embassy in Stockholm. In your own words, just as they come—and I'll just make a few notes as we go.' Once again, Alex found himself relating their experiences, but this time he was a little more careful with his words—perhaps a little slower in his narrative, as he gave the sequence that much more thought. Except for the occasional question to clear a point, he was listened to in silence. When he finally finished, a stillness descended on the room, as the interviewer completed the last of his notes. It suddenly dawned on Alex that his Stockholm interview was quite probably one of the contents of the file that the officer was studying, and he braced himself for what he felt must be the inevitable question. 'Thank you very much, Mr McKie' said the Squadron Leader, 'That seems to bring us right up-to-date. One thing I am bound to ask you, since no advantage was taken of the arrangements made for Naval assistance—was the Swedish decision taken as a cosy way out of the war?' He looked intently at Alex as he asked the question.

Alex could feel his cheeks burning and wondered whether it was with shame at being asked such a question. The apparent inference was that operational aircrew would seek to opt out of the war, given the chance, and he knew that this was a foul calumny as far as his Squadron was concerned. He levelled his gaze at his accuser and answered firmly and quietly. 'This is the second time that suggestion has been made to me, sir, and it's just as false now as it was in the first instance. The decision to get down in Sweden was a reasoned one, bearing in mind the circumstances in which we found ourselves in the Arctic Circle. Subsequent events have confirmed, in my view, that it was the right one and I am prepared to defend it at any level.'

The officer gave no indication about his feelings on the matter. He gathered up all the papers into the file and prepared to leave the room, 'I understand that you will be going on leave from Air Ministry and then you are posted back to 617 Squadron.' 'Thank you, sir. I couldn't be more pleased—and I am sure that goes for the rest of the crew' replied Alex, rising to attention as the officer made to exit. With a final enigmatic look at Alex, the officer closed the door behind him, and Alex sat down again, bewildered by these implications of opting-out.

The door opened and a Warrant Officer came in. 'Come along with me, please, sir', he said with a smile. 'We're off to the orderly room to get you fixed up with leave pass, warrants, ration cards and all the other delights that go into the process of leave!' He held the door open and allowed Alex to pass into the corridor before closing the door and joining him. 'The other members of your crew are already "doing the necessary"' he said, 'You've had quite an interesting holiday in Sweden, from what I've gleaned from Flight Lieutenant Witherick—that is his name, isn't it?—the one with the DFM, "Spam and Coronation"?' 'That's the one and only Witherick' assented Alex, with a laugh. He was beginning to feel better already, surrounded by the familiar Service atmosphere. In the orderly room, he found Doug, Curly and Gerry all busy filling out the apparently interminable forms for fourteen days leave. 'You are permitted to take advantage of the leave facilities laid on in Morecambe for returned aircrew' the Warrant Officer told Alex but Alex declined with a smile. 'I think I'd better go home this time' he answered, 'perhaps I'll get "Morecambe bound" next time.' 'Christ, hark at the optimist' enjoined Gerry, ' "Next time" the man says! Get yourself another rear-gunner, mate, for any similar caper!'

The five of them sat talking whilst the forms went the rounds. Les had decided to sample the delights of Morecambe Rehabilitation Centre, but the others had elected for a more conventional leave. 'I've got to go along to Canada House and make my peace with them' Doug informed them. 'At the moment, it's not certain that I shall be re-posted to the Squadron. It's all in the lap of the gods.' Soon they were on their various ways. They shook hands all round outside Adastral House and disappeared into the milling throngs of London. Gerry and Alex stood together for a while. 'Care for a cuppa before we set course, Gerry?' asked Alex. 'Fair enough, mate' replied Gerry. 'We're a bit short on the "tea stakes" since the Swedish interlude!' They made their way to a restaurant and were soon ensconced at a corner table. Alex asked Gerry if he had been asked about a 'cosy way out' in relation to the landing in Sweden. Gerry waxed indignant. 'Bloody cheek!' he growled, 'No suggestion like that was made to me—and just as well it wasn't!' They drank their tea in silence and Gerry noticed that Alex was quite perturbed by the recollection. 'Don't worry about it, mate! Put it all from your mind!' he said, consolingly, 'After all, what more can you expect from a bloody "penguin", who's never been in anything worse than a bun-fight! He was probably envying us our erotic nights, 'cos I told them about the bath at Falun with great relish—and not a little embroidery!'

After their various leaves, they reported to the Squadron at Woodhall Spa. The welcome from the Squadron was warm without being over-enthusiastic. There was still a war to be won and it was business as usual. Witherick was most disconsolate that the *Tirpitz* had been sunk whilst he was on leave. 'How could you, sir!' he reproached 'Willie' Tait in the Mess bar, 'how could you go and sink the *Tirpitz* before I got back?' 'If you decide on the spur of the moment to go off for a holiday in Sweden' replied 'Willie' imperturbably, 'then you can't very well expect us to hold the war over until you deign to return, Gerry! Anyway, the Germans still have plenty of other ships for sinking!'

Les Franks was a bit aggrieved. 'I didn't expect the flags out and a red carpet laid, Alex,' he confided a few days later, 'but at least I thought that Willie would have had us in and had a few words with us!' 'Not on THIS Squadron, mate, not here!' replied Alex. 'It's business as usual every day—and briefings—and take-offs—and bombing practice—no time to spare for recalcitrant aircrew. God, if it meant a party every time such aircrew returned, they'd all be at it!'

★ ★ ★

Doug MacLennan had reported as ordered at RCAF headquarters in London. He was eventually taken in to see a Wing Commander, who greeted him warmly. 'Damn glad to see you back with us, MacLennan!' he said, shaking his hand energetically, 'and I guess there's a lot more people who'll be glad of the good news! Well, the war's over for you right now! It's repatriation home to Canada and a nice training job until "Civvy Street" beckons!' With that he stood back and confidently awaited Doug's stammered thanks when he had fully assimilated the glad tidings. Doug stood dumbfounded, his mind in a turmoil, but not in the direction that the Wing Commander assumed. Repatriated? Back to Canada? But there was still much more to do! And how would Bill Carey get on with no 'Junior' to curse? And who'd give Alex such magnificent pin-points? And what would days be like without Witherick's blithe and pithy observations? His mind cleared and he faced the beaming expectant Wingco. 'I don't want to go home—not yet, anyway, sir. I can't leave the Squadron now, with so much still to be done! Can't the "repat" be rescinded—for the present anyhow—I'd greatly appreciate that, sir—and a re-posting back to 617 at Woodhall.'

The Wingco's face was a study in amazement. He thought of the number of bods who'd been on that self-same carpet, pleading, almost, for repatriation. 'You're sure of that!' he murmured weakly, 'You'd sooner go back to your Squadron?' 'Yes, please, sir, if it can be arranged—I'd be most grateful.' 'Well,' said the staggered Wingco, 'It was being pushed through with some degree of priority, what with your operational record and the forced landing in Sweden, but I suppose it can be halted—you mean what you say?—You'd sooner go back to your squadron?' 'Yes please, sir' said Doug quickly. 'OK, then I'll fix it' agreed the Wingco, 'I expect you could do with some leave, though.' 'That'd be fine, sir' grinned Doug. 'The rest of the crew will be going on leave and our pilot is still detained in Sweden with an injury. If it's OK by you, I'd like to go to a "Nuffield" hotel'. 'By all means, MacLennan—you've more than earned it', said the senior officer.

He rang a bell on his desk and, a few moments later, a Warrant Officer came in and saluted smartly. 'Take Flying Officer MacLennan away and do all that's necessary to fix him with fourteen days leave at a hotel under the Nuffield Scheme—and he'll want a warrant to take him back to his squadron at the end of his leave.' 'Very good, sir' answered the Warrant Officer. He turned and held the door open for Doug. 'Glad you made it back to us, MacLennan' said the Wingco, and offered his hand. Doug shook it warmly, 'Thank you for all you've done sir, especially for the altered posting.' He stepped back and saluted smartly. The Wingco caught his eye just before he turned to leave. 'MacLennan, that must be one helluva squadron!' he said. 'It sure is!' grinned Doug 'None better!'

The Swedes were as good as their word. Bill Carey had had the finest attention possible and was looked upon almost like a mascot for the whole of his convalescence in the hospital at Yokkmukk. When the news came through on November 14, that the 'Dambuster Squadron' had sunk the *Tirpitz* at Tromso, he found himself treated like a hero. The Swedish CO called upon him to ask Bill to convey his congratulations to the Squadron when he rejoined them. Gifts of flowers, sweets and cigarettes were sent to him by delighted Norwegians. He felt quite embarrassed by all the attention and wished fervently that he had been aloft with the Squadron for the ship's final date with Destiny.

When he was completely recovered, he travelled down to Falun, escorted very comfortably by the officer who had interrogated him in the hospital. It was a very pleasant journey, the memories of which were to stay with him forever. He was sent from Falun to an hotel in Stockholm and then taken to the British embassy, to be instructed by the officials there as had his crew before him, but without any interrogation. He was fitted out with civilian clothes and enjoyed the sights of Stockholm for a couple of weeks.

In due course he flew back to Leuchars and was then directed down to London for an interview at Australia House. He was offered but declined an immediate repatriation to Australia. Instead, thinking that his left leg might not be up to the stresses of flying a Lancaster, he made tentative approaches about flying 'intruder' Mosquitos or some sort of light bomber, such as Bostons, but his enquiries led to polite but firm refusals. He passed his full aircrew medical without trouble, with the medical officers remarking on the fine job the Swedes had done on his knee-cap. He returned to the Squadron at Woodhall Spa after a period of leave, about a month after the other members of his crew. He discovered that they had been doing the odd 'fill-in' operation with other crews and were obviously delighted to see him, and also with the thought of getting 'warborne' again together.

Bill returned to Woodhall on the very day that a Mess party had been arranged. All his uniform and personal effects had been gathered up and sent for safe custody when he was reported missing, and they had not yet reached Woodhall on their return journey. He was called to order by Squadron Leader Jock Calder, who had joined the Squadron whilst Bill had been in Sweden. 'You can't come to a Mess party in battledress, you know!' said Jock, and Bill had to explain the reason for the gaffe. Whilst he was in the middle of the explanation, Willie Tait came over. He made no reference to Bill's dress, except that his eyes seemed to twinkle even more than usual. 'Come with me, Bill' beamed Willie. 'There's someone I want you to meet.' Bill followed in Willie's wake and, to his horror, found himself being introduced to Air-Vice-Marshal Sir Ralph Cochrane, the AOC No 5 Group, Bomber Command! 'God,' thought Bill frenziedly, 'He's going to ask me if I've been over to Bardney yet and apologized to Wing Commander Bazin about that Yagodnik "beat-up"!'

When both 617 and 9 Squadrons had shared the billets at Yagodnik, awaiting the first raid against the *Tirpitz*, there had been quite a bit of inter-Squadron horse-play, which finally culminated in one of the 9 Squadron aircrew being tossed over the side of the boat returning from a visit to Archangel, for a swim in the Dvina. Dennis Oram ('Squire' to the Squadron aircrew) and Bill elected to 'beat-up' Yagodnik airfield after getting airborne for the return trip to Woodhall Spa. The 'beat-up' was carried out most effectively and thoroughly, but prevented any of the 9 Squadron aircraft from taking-off until the exercise was completed. When Willie Tait became aware of this, he sent for Squire Oram and said that he was to make his own way to RAF Bardney and make a personal apology to Wing Commander Bazin for such rank bad manners. This Dennis had done and he had gloatingly told Bill, when Bill returned for Squadron duty, 'And it's your turn next, mate!'

Sir Ralph did not mention this matter at all. He was most interested to find out about the forced landing and the subsequent happenings. Finally, he said in the clipped and precise tones, which were his hallmark 'Your crew's security drill was excellent, Carey, I have been informed—and I am very pleased to hear it! It would have been a markedly different matter if the report had been otherwise.' A few more questions and then Sir Ralph was off to meet other guests. Bill sighed with relief. In the euphoria that had followed the sinking of the *Tirpitz*, his peccadillo had been forgotten, much to the chagrin of Squire Oram!

Some days later, when Bill, Gerry, Doug and Alex were having a drink in the small bar at their Mess in the Petwood Hotel, Gerry suddenly said 'I wonder what has happened to that two pounds Freddy Watts and I left behind the bar mirror at Milltown? Freddy dropped in at Sumburgh on the way back from Tromso, took sufficient juice on board to wing straight back to Woodhall and never touched-down at Milltown at all! Must try and get up there one of these days, on a recovery mission!'—but he never did!

They did ten more operations together before the war in Europe ended.

Alex felt that was the complete answer to the questions that had been put to him personally in Stockholm and London. He only hoped that the interrogators were made aware of that fact!

One echo of their Swedish interlude drifted down the corridors of time for the British aircrew involved. Almost a year after they had returned from Sweden, they received accounts for the clothes they had acquired in Sweden without any thought of cost, and settlement was demanded without delay. Gerry, with the pre-war airman's respect for authority, duly paid up, permitting himself a barrage of cursing on the side as he did so, but Alex McKie was made of sterner stuff. His Scottish ancestry rebelled at the thought of paying for something he had had no choice but to buy. He took the equipment officer who had presented him with the bill into the Mess bar, bought him a few drinks and then discussed the matter of the account with him. It didn't take many more drinks for the equipment officer to agree that there could be some irregularities in the account and decide that it should be sent back to Air Ministry for clarification—and that proved to be the end of the matter in Alex' case.

The only other problem Alex could recall about the affair was explaining to the powers-that-be how the valuable navigation watch, supplied by the Service, came to be ripped off his wrist, and lost, during the forced landing—but then that was an explanation required of countless navigators in similar circumstances throughout the war!

Chapter 6

Politz, 21/22 December 1944

The oil installation at Politz, north-east of Stettin, was the target for No 5 Group, Bomber Command on the night of 21/22 December 1944. It was one of the very few occasions that 617 was called upon to operate at night with the other squadrons of the Group and was undertaken by the 617 crews with a great deal of misgiving. They were to use their Tallboy bombs and all previous experience had indicated that the Pathfinder Force procedure could not mark targets accurately enough for such bombs to be used to the maximum of their devastating effect. Even the OBOE system at its most accurate had proved ineffective for the standard of target-marking required, and Politz was a target at extreme range with very little natural or physical features to help the target-marking crews of Nos 83 and 97 Squadrons. Target indicators of various hues were to be laid and many of 617 aircrew knew from experience that the problem of identifying the most accurate marker could be well-nigh insoluble.

This was to prove an operation of limited effectiveness, but one which for domestic reasons was to provide bitter memories and have a lasting and detrimental effect on the bodies and minds of some of the aircrew who took part. Nothing that has happened over the years has convinced them other than that they were the victims of a foolhardy gamble that should never have been made, in circumstances where those who ordered the gamble were at no personal risk.

The Politz operation was to leave scars within 617 Squadron that would evoke bitter resentment for many years. The conduct of the final stages of the operation demonstrated an almost criminal lack of appreciation of the tiring effect such a long-duration operation inevitably had on aircrew, both physically and mentally. It showed that the best interests of the airborne aircrew were not always paramount in the minds of senior officers on the ground. It also demonstrated churlish and obstinate adherence to rules by support services that even now seems unbelievable.

This episode relates the 617 aspect of this unfortunate night with reference to the experiences of crews of other squadrons affected by decisions which, at best, were risky and which, perhaps, should never have been taken.

* * *

21 December 1944 was a cold and foggy day, with intermittent drizzle, and the aircrews of 617 Squadron were not surprised when the news came through that no operations were planned for the Squadron that day. Lectures and discussions were laid on in the various aircrew sections and the aircrew were informed that they would be 'stood down' after lunch.

Flying Officer Mark Flatman, Flight Lieutenant John Pryor, Flying Officer Slater and Squadron Leader Brookes were readily given permission by Wing Commander Tait to form a duck-shooting party. They set off for the Wainfleet Sands area, armed with their own shotguns and a plentiful supply of ammunition drawn from the clay-pigeon shooting stocks held in the station armoury. Their object was to supplement the poultry supplies to the Messes for the looming Christmas celebrations. Approval had been given for the use of Squadron Leader Brookes' Flight van for the journey to Wainfleet. It was a journey that was to take much longer than they had anticipated with the prevailing weather conditions, but the four officers were not perturbed on that score. They called at a pub for some warming drinks and a bite to eat before continuing to Wainfleet.

When they arrived at the entry gate to the bombing range, a Sergeant SP came to the vehicle and told Squadron Leader Brookes that he was required to telephone Wing Commander Tait immediately. Brooky went into the small guard room to carry out this order. He emerged some minutes later to tell the other officers that they had to return to Woodhall Spa as quickly as possible. The Squadron was required to operate that night. Inevitably, the return journey was a long and tedious one, and they arrived to find that the crews had all been briefed.

617 was to supply sixteen Lancasters all armed with Tallboy bombs for a solely-5 Group raid on the oil installation at Politz north-east of Stettin. Because all Lincolnshire bases were expected to become enveloped in fog before the time of return, diversion bases in the Moray Firth area of Scotland had been allocated at briefing to all the participating 5 Group squadrons. This was a very necessary precaution as the Group effort that night was some 207 Lancasters and the diversion bases had to be alerted to the number of aircraft each would be required to accept, in order that these bases could make the necessary arrangements to handle the aircraft and crews. There was not a lot of enthusiasm for this operation on the part of the 617 aircrew. The many who had operated with main force squadrons were not optimistic that this target at maximum range would be marked accurately enough for the Tallboys to bite home and destroy this panacea target, but they were all firmly resolved to do their best, in the hope that at least some of their bombs would find the right target.

The crews were already on their way to the aircraft in dispersals when the erstwhile duck-shooters arrived back at base. They climbed hastily into their flying-kit and Mark Flatman had the personal services of the station commander, Group Captain Monty Philpott, to get Mark's 'chute and Mae West to the waiting crew-bus. The three pilots were briefed for the operation by their navigators during the period that the original take-off times were delayed.

Flying Officer Arthur Joplin and his crew featured on the battle order in Lancaster 'T for Tare'. For five of the crew it was their ninth operation together, as they had been posted direct to 617 Squadron from the Lancaster Finishing School in August 1944. The two extremities of the aircraft were manned by very much more experienced aircrew. Flying Officer Arthur Walker had taken the place of the crew's regular bomb-aimer, Flight Sergeant Loftus Hebbard, who was 'non-effective, sick' in the station sick quarters. Arthur Walker had been the regular bomb-aimer in Flight Lieutenant Bob Knight's crew from August 1944. He was one of the best bomb-aimers to have served on 617. His knowledge of the SABs and his unswerving application to his calling, whether operationally or on the bombing range, was a great factor in the continuing success of Bob Knight's crew during the latter stages of their operational career.

When Bob and the rest of the crew had ceased operating, with Bob scheduled for training to transfer to the emerging BOAC civil airline, Arthur's total of sorties stood at 44, one sortie short of that required to fulfil two continuous tours of operational duty. This had caused Bob a great deal of concern and he discussed the matter with Willie Tait. With great understanding, Willie had used his prerogative as Squadron commander to allow Arthur to finish operating at his current score. But both had reckoned without Arthur's personal conscientiousness. He thanked Bob sincerely for his efforts, but said that his duty required him to accomplish 45 operations and that is what he intended to do. Arthur had approached 'Joppy' when Lofty Hebbard had reported sick and he was welcomed with open arms. He had been able to advise and assist on their practice bombing achievements and Joppy was delighted with the improvement Arthur's presence and experience had wrought.

The rear turret was manned by Flight Sergeant Jim Thompson. It was his fiftieth trip, although the great majority of his previous trips had been as wireless operator with Flight Lieutenant Mac Hamilton's crew. 'Tommy' had opted to continue his operational career beyond the required 45 sorties and had joined Joppy's crew as rear-gunner when their usual rear-gunner, Sergeant Norman Lambell, had been posted to another squadron to resolve the incompatibility that had developed between him and the rest of the crew, an occasional circumstance to which posting always provided an effective answer.

Joppy's crew was completed by Sergeant Frank Tilley, flight engineer; Flight Sergeant Basil Fish, navigator; Flight Sergeant Gordon Cooke, wireless operator; and Flying Officer Bob Yates, mid-upper gunner. Bob Yates had been so delighted with the Scottish diversion instructions given at briefing that he had packed a bag of 'small kit' on the off-chance that continuing foggy weather in Lincolnshire might present him with the opportunity to spend Christmas with his family in Scotland. Joppy, Basil Fish, Gordon Cooke and Bob Yates were to have their very first experience of a night operation over Germany. Frank Tilley had flown as flight engineer with Squadron Leader Drew Wyness DFC on the night of 22/23 September 1944 when the Dortmund-Ems Canal had been the target.

The crew had settled in their aircraft and carried out all pre-flight checks to the final extent of checking the engines, when the take-off was delayed. The engines were shut down and the crew remained on dispersal until the amended time of take-off had been communicated to them verbally by messenger in one of the Flight commander's vans. Eventually the aircraft began to taxi round the perimeter track to the take-off point. The 617 effort was airborne between 16.34 hours and 17.02 hours.

It was a long trip to the target but relatively uneventful. The target area was well-lit with flares but the target markers were somewhat scattered. Arthur Walker assessed the situation from his own observations and the master bomber's instructions and their Tallboy was eventually aimed at the marker 'recommended' by the master bomber, without any visible result. There was plenty of heavy flak over the target area but if '*T for Tare*' sustained any damage from this, it was of a minor nature and not revealed by any misbehaviour of the aircraft or by dial indications. Once the bomb had gone, and Arthur Walker was satisfied that the photo had been taken, course was set for the nominated Scottish diversion.

Suddenly, Gordon Cooke came on the intercom to inform the captain that a message from 54 Base instructed all aircraft to return to bases. Joppy checked the fuel state with Frank Tilley and was assured that the current fuel load was sufficient to allow the aircraft to reach Woodhall Spa. Basil Fish supplied an amended course and the Lancaster turned on to a south-south-easterly course, heading for Woodhall Spa. Basil picked up the eastern Gee chain signals and after a few minutes gave the pilot a slight change of heading. He calculated the estimated time of arrival and continued his normal navigational role, checking track and ground-speed with a series of Gee fixes to confirm his original ETA. One of the eastern Gee chain stations was in the Louth area of Lincolnshire and this produced an area of ambiguity in the Humberside area, but Basil had confidently assessed the track and ground-speed before this area was reached.

Frank Tilley had begun to express some concern with the fuel state but Basil reassured the captain with the statement that there was but another eight minutes run to base. There was nothing to be seen outside the aircraft but the inky blackness produced by the aviator's continuing worst enemy, fog. Joppy ordered all the crew to keep a sharp look-out for other aircraft. Gordon Cooke reported an instruction from 54 Base by W/T that aircraft should now get down at the first available airfield. The diffused glow of an operating FIDO installation appeared, reflected on the fog banks. Basil established with the aid of Gee that it was Ludford Magna in the Lincolnshire Wolds. He checked the safety height for the area and passed this to Joppy, glancing at his own altimeter to see that the aircraft was above this level. His message was acknowledged by the pilot, who, commenced to circle the area of the FIDO glow, calling for permission to land. Other aircraft were also endeavouring to get similar permission but no answer was heard from the ground by the crew of '*T for Tare*'. Joppy broadcast his request on another channel without success. Frank Tilley informed him that the fuel state precluded any thought of re-diverting to Scotland.

The aircraft continued to circle for a few more minutes until the crew felt a jar and judder on the port side. Frank Tilley, to his horror, had the impression of the area of wing beyond the port outer engine folding upwards. The needles of the engine gauges began a crazy dance and Joppy's immediate and calm reaction was to call for full power on all engines. Frank pushed the throttles straight 'through the gate', giving maximum power to all engines but he had a sickening feeling of no power being delivered and the aircraft beginning to lose height. Still very calm, Joppy ordered all crew to crash positions, whilst broadcasting on VHF '"*T for Tare*" crashing—"*T for Tare*" crashing.' He stuck to his position wrestling with the controls to keep the aircraft on as level a keel as possible.

Basil Fish clambered over the main spar to take up his crash position. He heard his chess mate, Bob Yates, yelling for his parachute. Basil shouted to him to forget the 'chute and get to the crash position. Frank Tilley was in his position beside Basil. Gordon Cooke apparently decided to wedge himself in his crew position and brace himself for the inevitable approaching impact. Basil could feel the aircraft sinking and the overpowering roar of the engines was almost unbearable, but he was aware of a strange peace within him. He was shaken but, surprisingly, found himself not frightened, thinking to himself, 'Well, this is how it ends—this is the way I am to die.' In the rear turret, Jim Thompson had assessed the probabilities. He figured that the impact was imminent and that he could not make the crash position in time, so he decided to stay in the turret. He unstrapped himself and disconnected his intercom lead and oxygen supply, before turning the turret on to the beam and bracing himself within it.

There was a minor bump and the aircraft seemed to rise up before collapsing in a hideous roar and the shriek of tearing metal. The engine roar ceased abruptly but the crew were severely buffeted about as the aircraft slithered to a halt. Basil was flung upwards and his helmeted head struck the fuselage, knocking him unconscious. His next recollection was vaguely hearing Frank Tilley yelling, 'Get out, Basil! IT'S TAKEN FIRE!'—and then Frank was gone. As consciousness gradually returned, Basil found that his feet were trapped and he tried frantically to extricate himself, with the growing realization of his plight. Eventually he slid his feet from his flying boots and was then able to release the boots without too much trouble. He pulled them on again and turned to face the front of the aircraft. The cockpit area and nose had broken away at the final impact and was some twenty yards ahead of the aircraft. He could feel the blood oozing from his head wound and felt the heat growing as fire began to take firm hold of the aircraft. The cold damp air struck him forcibly as he moved clear of the aircraft and he was violently sick.

Jim Thompson had been thrown about in his turret when the aircraft finally hit the ground. The turret doors flew open and he was flung out of the aircraft. He landed on soft earth with a thump which knocked the breath from his body and he lay there for some minutes, collecting his thoughts. He tested his limbs and was relieved to find that they appeared to be undamaged. He became aware of the fire taking hold of the aircaft and rose to his feet to assist where he could. He found it very painful to walk and realized that he had not escaped unscathed.

Basil's head cleared after the final violent retch and soon he was able to assess the stark situation. Frank Tilley had crawled clear of the flames but was unable to stand or assist. Jim Thompson was walking in great pain. Gordon Cooke was clear of the aircraft but had badly-burned hands, especially in the wrist area. He was walking aimlessly around, murmuring in delirium. Basil saw that the kapok of Gordon's Mae West was smouldering and, gently but firmly, coaxed the wireless operator to stand still. Basil undid the ties of the Mae West and removed it from his crew mate. All this time ammunition was exploding and bullets were flying at all angles. It was a veritable inferno. Frank Tilley was yelling to Basil to take cover and get clear of the aircraft and his pleas were reinforced by Jim Thompson, who was not afraid to confess to himself that he was more than a little nervous of the exploding ammunition. Basil's main concern was to establish the whereabouts of his comrades and render what aid he could. He made his way to the torn-off fore part of the aircraft where Joppy was trapped in his seat, moaning softly. Carefully Basil extricated his pilot from the wreckage and carried him clear of the burning fuselage, on the opposite side from where Frank Tilley lay. He was horrified to hear the savage crunch of bones as he lifted his skipper and realized that Joppy had suffered grievous injury.

Five of the crew were now accounted for, but two were still missing. Despite the now-fiery heat, Basil approached the open forefront of the aircraft, shielding his face with his hands as best he could and ignoring the ever-present danger from the exploding ammunition. He managed to get partly inside and glimpsed what he took to be one (or was it two?) charred bodies. The intense heat drove him out before he could verify this impression and the developing hold of the hungry flames prevented him from essaying another attempt to get inside the fuselage. A wave of sadness engulfed him at that moment at the realization that two of his comrades had died that night.

Basil then turned reluctantly from the blazing aircraft. The wound in his head had stopped bleeding and the dried blood matted his hair. He realized that he was the sole member of the crew with mobility, for Gordon Cooke was still in a state of shock from the severe burns he had suffered and was muttering incomprehensibly as he wandered about the area. Basil ensured that Joppy was as comfortable as possible and arranged for Jim Thompson to settle down beside the unconscious pilot. He led Gordon Cooke gently to the other side of the burning fuselage and coaxed him to sit down beside Frank Tilley. Basil told Frank that it was his plan to set off in search of help.

The fire had passed its peak and Basil began to feel the bitter cold and damp of that foggy mid-winter Lincolnshire night. His fellow crew-members, except for the rear-gunner, had very little protective clothing to shield them from the cold and Basil appreciated that injured men needed warmth if they were to survive, which made it all the more imperative to locate aid. He told Frank that he would want an answering blast from Frank's whistle as soon as Frank heard Basil signalling on his own whistle that he was leading a rescue party to the scene. Basil crossed to Jim Thompson and made a similar arrangement. He then studied the local topography as best he could in the appalling conditions that prevailed but there was no natural feature that stood out to pinpoint the crash position. It was impossible for Basil to have any choice in the direction of his walk. The fog was thick and the stars completely hidden. With a muttered prayer that he would be going in the best direction, he set off.

It was the most nightmarish journey of his life. Visibility was limited to a few yards. It was bitterly cold with a slight but penetrating drizzle. By now Basil's head was aching furiously and his exertions caused the head-bleeding to start again. He stumbled and fell many times as he literally staggered across ploughed fields and rough terrain. He had no option but to fight his way through hedges and after what seemed to be an eternity, he began to doubt if he would ever reach assistance. In desperation and to raise his own hopes, he began to give intermittent blasts on his whistle but there was no response. He found himself on a small road or path and turned to walk along it. Suddenly a farmhouse loomed out of the murk ahead. Basil located the front door and hammered on it, shouting for help. The occupant of the house eventually answered the door and Basil explained the situation as best he could, asking if there was a telephone to use to obtain medical assistance. Unfortunately no 'phone was available but the farmer asked Basil to wait whilst he donned some clothes and said he would take Basil to the nearest village. The farmer reappeared with a big Tilley lamp and escorted Basil to a public telephone kiosk, which turned out to be in the village of Tealby. The farmer was most helpful and showed much concern for Basil who must have appeared to be in a dreadful plight, being covered with mud and blood. Basil asked the telephone operator to put him through to the nearest RAF station or hospital and was somewhat stunned when the operator told him to put twopence in the coin-box. The nature of the emergency was explained and the urgency of getting medical assistance as soon as possible to the crash site. He was quickly put through to the nearest RAF station which proved to be Ludford Magna. With the farmer's help, Basil identified his exact location and was told to wait there until the rescue party arrived.

It was not long before the rescue team from Ludford Magna arrived.

Basil's head injuries were cleaned up by an officer who proved to be Flight Lieutenant Freeth, the station medical officer. Taking the farmhouse as his starting-point, Basil related the details of his journey in reverse to the best of his ability—how long he had been on the road that had led him to the farmhouse—the type of terrain he had crossed and a rough description of the crash site. Flight Lieutenant Freeth, who struck Basil as being a very 'clueful' type, formed an opinion of where the crash had occurred and the whole party set off under his direction. After a while, Basil began to send a series of 'SOS' signals in Morse Code on his whistle. The whole party strained their ears in the intervals between the signals and there was great relief when the first faint answering replies were heard. They 'homed' on the strengthening replies until in the fog ahead they saw the flames of the burning fuselage and sped directly towards them.

Headlamps and torches revealed an almost indescribable scene. Flight Lieutenant Freeth noted the time of reaching the crash as 05.30 hours, 22 December 1944. Ludford Magna logged the time of the crash as 02.45 hours, with Basil's call for assistance recorded at 04.45 hours. Thus, two and three-quarter hours had passed from the time of the crash until the arrival of the rescue team.

It was ironic that the search revealed a parachute pack not ten yards from Frank Tilley. The 'chute could have been used to provide cover and warmth for the injured men. Flight Lieutenant Freeth diagnosed that the pilot had suffered two broken legs, the flight engineer had a broken leg, the wireless operator had a fractured skull and the navigator and rear-gunner were deemed to have minor injuries. The bodies of the mid-upper gunner, Bob Yates, and the bomb-aimer, Arthur Walker, were recovered from the wreckage when the flames had been extinguished and the wreckage cooled. Joppy, Frank Tilley and Gordon Cooke were sent directly to Louth County Infirmary. Basil Fish and Jim Thompson were taken to station sick quarters at RAF Ludford Magna and put to bed, just as they were, after being liberally dosed with pills. All they both remembered for a considerable number of hours was the WAAF orderlies constantly renewing the myriad hot-water bottles with which they had been surrounded on being put to bed and the administering of more pills if ever they appeared to be 'surfacing'. A further and more comprehensive examination revealed that Jim Thompson had suffered a spinal fracture and he was immediately transferred to the RAF Hospital at Rauceby, near Sleaford, Lincolnshire, to which the other three injured crew members had also been transferred from the county infirmary.

Basil Fish returned to Woodhall Spa a couple of days later. He was greeted enthusiastically by Flight Sergeant Ross and other members of the ground crew responsible for 'T for Tare', who had waited up all that fatal night, hoping that the Lancaster would return safely. It is recorded in the RAF Woodhall Spa operations record book, with reference to the crash: 'Station Sick Quarters, Ludford Magna reported that Flight Sergeant Fish, with great presence of mind, released fellow members of the crew and instructed them to blow their aircrew whistles to attract assistance and, though suffering from shock and minor injuries, walked three miles through heavy country for aid'. The actual weather summary for 21/22 December 1944 is also logged as 'Fog or mist all day. Continuous rain from 22.00 hours to 04.00 hours. Fog persisted all day'.

After another medical check-up, Basil was sent home on leave for seven days. On his return, he was subjected to a series of medicals, particularly X-rays to the head but was finally cleared to return to operational flying with 617. Frank Tilley suffered a broken right leg and severe bruising to the other leg. He was a patient in the 'crash ward' at Rauceby and counted himself lucky when he saw the terrible injuries other aircrew had suffered in crashes. After his legs had been healed, he had six months convalescent treatment at Hoylake, Cheshire. When he returned to Woodhall Spa he found that the Squadron had gone. Several items were missing from his personal kit and a few vital parts of his motor cycle had been removed. This did nothing to raise his spirits. For eighteen months after the crash his nerves were bad and his morale was very low. With VJ-Day having been celebrated, he just could not wait to be demobbed.

Gordon Cooke had suffered burnt tendons of one hand, in addition to the fractured skull diagnosed on the spot. Basil visited him and the other crew members during their spell at Rauceby Hospital. He saw some terrible sights in the 'burns unit', which was supervised by Sir Archibald McIndoe, the New Zealand surgeon, noted for his work with badly-burned aircrew. Jim Thompson went through the necessary hospital treatment and convalescence to recover from his spinal injuries. Arthur Joplin suffered a broken left ankle, which was re-set, and his left foot and leg put in plaster up to the knee. His right leg was broken below the knee and, because of the angle of the break, it could not be re-set, eventually having to be screwed or pinned together. During his short stay in Louth County Infirmary, he was completely unaware that two of the crew had died in the crash. During his transfer to RAF Hospital Rauceby, in an ambulance from RAF Woodhall Spa, the ambulance crew halted the ambulance and entered the body of the ambulance, to ensure that Joppy was comfortable and untroubled. In the conversation that ensued, Joppy happened to say how lucky it was that all the crew had survived. The two airmen looked at each other and reluctantly, under Joppy's insistent questioning, told him that the bomb-aimer and mid-upper gunner had died in the inferno. This unexpected news was a shattering mental blow to Joppy and he was in very low spirits throughout his stay at Rauceby.

What has been crystal-clear and unfaltering over the years is the survivors' conviction on two points. Primarily, they owed their lives to the quiet skill and devotion of their pilot in the circumstances into which he was plunged without warning very early in his operational career. Only just secondarily, their survival was due to the devoted and relentless determination of their navigator, Basil Fish, in dragging them clear of a burning aircraft and getting the medical assistance they so desperately needed that bleak early morning in December 1944. When the story was eventually known on 617 Squadron, there was a sense of pride that the aircrew involved had performed in the traditions of the Squadron. It was confidently predicted that Basil Fish would receive some award to acknowledge his great gallantry.

It should be appreciated that large-scale diversions of operational bombers was anathema to commanding officers, since it generally involved the loss of operational opportunity whilst the force eventually reassembled in their home bases.

RAF Coningsby records: 'Very foggy all day but with the hope of suitable diversions in North Scotland, a battle order was put out. The crews took off into very foggy weather (16.24–16.53)—in fact aircraft could not be seen getting airborne. The weather at base was not as bad as expected, so orders were transmitted to aircraft to cancel diversion instructions and return to Coningsby. However, at the last minute, conditions deteriorated and although several aircraft managed to land, a large proportion had to report to Metheringham and their FIDO aid. Some four crews landed in Scotland.' The two Coningsby PFF Squadrons had put a total of 28 Lancasters on the Politz operation and of these seven aircraft of 83 Squadron landed at Dallaghy and five of 97 landed at Wick.

RAF Waddington records: 'Aircraft took off in conditions of bad visibility and crews were briefed for most probable return to bases in North of Scotland. This was to be confirmed or otherwise on W/T when aircraft were in a position near the NW coast of Denmark on their way back. ETA base and ETA diversion bases were, from that position, approximately the same. It would appear that there was some ambiguity in the orders issued, as they were construed differently by some crews, which resulted in some crews arriving at base in hopeless conditions of visibility with insufficient fuel left to reach a safe diversion airfield.'

RAF Strubby records: '17 Lancasters of 619 Squadron to Politz. 619 'P' F/O Botham returned—early sickness of pilot—and landed at Banff. Sixteen diverted to Scotland owing to weather at Base.'

No 5 Group records: '212 Lancasters and one Mosquito took off. 12 returned early: 9 failed: 3 missing: 6 crashed: 182 Lancasters and one Mosquito returned safely', but Bomber Command records: '207 aircraft detailed: 24 aborted: 183 attacked: 6 Landing Accidents: 145 aircraft landed in Scotland.' However, not all the aircraft landed in Scotland. Acklington, Carnaby and Fiskerton (1 Group) were also gratefully used by returning aircrews, obeying the instruction to get down at the first available airfield and very relieved to do so in safety. From the figures available it is safe to assume that about forty Lancasters of the force involved actually returned to the Lincolnshire area after carrying out the full operation against Politz. The rest either did not receive the diversion cancellation or sanguinely decided that discretion was the better part of valour, in view of their own knowledge of the return forecast, and carried on to Scotland. For this, the powers-that-were in 5 Group at that time must have heaved a sigh of relief, for a major disaster would have struck the Group if all the aircraft had returned as ordered by their respective bases.

One aircraft of the 617 effort aborted. Wing Commander Jock Calder had a port-inner engine failure soon after take-off. He carried on whilst the flight engineer tried to remedy the fault but the engine obstinately refused to give power, forcing Jock to abandon the operation and land at his briefed diversion airfield at Milltown.

Freddy Watts' SABS was found to be completely unserviceable on test. Mervyn Mackay tried his best to get the bomb-sight to work but had to admit defeat after his efforts. It could not be used as a fixed sight as this had been forbidden at briefing, due to the proximity of a concentration camp a few hundred yards from the aiming point. Freddy's aircraft was within half-an-hour's flying time of the target when his bomb-aimer finally declared the bomb-sight unserviceable, so Freddy decided to contribute his mite to the concentration of aircraft and did a run through the target. He also did one orbit of the area, to try and assess the effectiveness of the operation before setting course for Scotland. He obeyed the recall to Lincolnshire messages, to find Woodhall Spa 'out' when he arrived in the circuit. The FIDO at Metheringham had been brought into operation and reminded Freddy of Dante's Inferno, with plenty of aircraft trying to land against the back-drop of the flaming fuel.

He decided to have another look at Woodhall Spa and picked up the Coningsby beacon flashing its red 'CY' characteristics. He called up Coningsby and was invited to land if he felt he could make it. Freddy was to report that with the aid of a continued rate four turn, gravity and a few 'Hail Marys', he managed to get down safely on the Coningsby runway. It was a trip he was to remember as being his sole experience of bringing his bomb-load back. Four other 617 aircraft also returned with Tallboys, due to the unsatisfactory nature of the target-marking. Six aircraft diverted to use the Metheringham FIDO with Woodhall Spa fogbound. Three of these were the aircraft of the 'aborted' duck-shooters.

Six aircraft crashed in Lincolnshire that night. Flight Lieutenant Kynoch (467 Squadron) crashed beside the runway at Waddington, with none of the crew injured. Flying Officer Halsted (463 Squadron) crashed two miles north-east of Waddington, six of the crew being killed. Squadron Leader Hatcher, AFC, DFM (83 Squadron) crashed off the runway at Metheringham, with six members of the crew killed. Flying Officer Stockhill (630 Squadron) crashed at Scrafield Farm, Scrafield, east of Horncastle, again with six of the crew killed. Flying Officer Read (9 Squadron) crashed just off the airfield at Bardney, killing two and badly injuring the remaining five aircrew. Flying Officer Joplin (617 Squadron), with two killed and four injured, was the sixth casualty. Of the 42 aircrew involved in these incidents, 22 were killed, eight seriously injured, one injured and eleven escaped with minor injuries and a severe shaking-up, seven of these latter being accounted for by the complete crew of Flight Lieutenant Kynoch of 467 Squadron.

Group Captain D.J.R. King, the station commander of RAF Ludford Magna received a request from Headquarters, 5 Group, through his own

No 14 base headquarters at 01.15 hours on 22 December to bring the FIDO installation into operation. He consulted his specialist officers and was told that with Ludford Magna being some 500 feet above mean sea level, and the clamp-down almost to the foot of the Wolds, previous experience of lighting the FIDO in these conditions had proved the facility to be grossly ineffective. He reported this back to his base. However, 5 Group repeated the request to the point of insistence and the installation was lit at 02.30 hours. Conditions remained hopeless for landing aircraft but the glow of the FIDO attracted aircraft to the area. Ludford Magna logged the 617 crash as 02.45 hours, three miles north-west of the runway. Group Captain King concluded that the pilot had descended to investigate the possibility of a landing on FIDO and had hit the ground.

The time of the crash of the 630 Squadron aircraft was 02.15, with Joplin's crash at 02.45. These were the only two aircraft to crash away from their bases or diversions but it is impossible that they could have been in collision, with points of impact sixteen miles and thirty minutes apart. Yet Frank Tilley remains adamant that the accident to 'T for Tare' WAS caused by a mid-air collision. The crews of 617 who landed at Metheringham that night went back to Woodhall Spa by road transport. They returned next day to collect the Lancasters and Mark Flatman recalls that Ian Ross was unable to fly his Lancaster, as it was discovered that it had sustained damage to one of the wings. The damage was more consistent with the wing having been struck into rather than damaged by enemy action. Ian Ross' crew were lost on the Bergen operation in January 1945 and no corroboration is now available.

The Lancaster 'B for Baker' of 630 Squadron, piloted by Flying Officer Stockhill, had taken off from RAF East Kirkby with definite instructions for diversion to RAF Tain in Scotland, as it was expected that the base would be unfit for return. During the flight to the target, the pilot told the crew that the aircraft was consistently flying starboard wing low and that he could not trim it out. The crew agreed to carry on with the operation and encountered only the usual and expected problems over the target area. After bombing, the Lancaster set course direct for the Scottish diversion base. A W/T message was received, cancelling the diversion instructions and ordering a return to base. When they arrived at East Kirkby, the crew found that the fog was worse than it had been on departure. The pilot made three abortive attempts to land and was then instructed to divert to RAF Strubby, on the Lincolnshire coast.

The navigator gave the required course to the captain and the aircraft duly set off for Strubby. For some reason, the pilot asked the navigator to call out the airspeed constantly, and apparently the wheels and flaps of the aircraft were still down. No other messages or calls came over the intercom except the airspeed reading, which the rear-gunner, Sergeant Les Pooley, recalled was 120 knots. His next recollection was regaining consciousness in an eerie silence. He lay for a while gathering his thoughts, realizing that the aircraft had crashed. He appreciated that his turret was at an angle but he managed to open the doors which allowed some light to filter in. He wriggled and squirmed and succeeded in extricating himself on hands and knees. He discovered that the fuselage had snapped off just by the rear door.

He examined himself very carefully, moving all his limbs gingerly and was relieved to find nothing broken. The fog was very thick and the night bitterly cold. He stood very still, listening intently for sounds from his other crew members, but foggy silence blanketed the area. There was no sign of the rest of the aircraft. Les had had to remove his helmet before escaping from his inverted turret as he had been unable to reach the connecting plug and the slight drizzle began to wet his head. He decided to seek help and set off, climbing over fences and through hedges until he came to a road. Completely unaware of his whereabouts, he turned right along the road and had the great good fortune to locate a house very quickly. It proved to be a large farmhouse and he knocked heavily on the door. It was opened by a lady who proved to be a Mrs Odlin, who was in the house with her daughter. Les explained that his aircraft had crashed and he was trying to get help for the crew. Mrs Odlin said that her husband and others had heard the crash and were even then out, trying to locate the aircraft and render all possible aid. She ushered Les into the living-room and provided him with hot tea and cigarettes. He began to talk to Mrs Odlin and was amazed to find that she actually came from the same village as he did, Terrington St Clements, near Kings Lynn in Norfolk, and that her brother was still farming there!

Later a Police Sergeant arrived and said that they had been searching the fields for Les after they had discovered the empty turret. Les asked about the crew and was told that one member was being brought to the house but the Sergeant did not know who it was. The inert figure was making terrible noises but the Sergeant refused to let Les look at him. He did describe the brevet and Les knew it was the wireless operator. An ambulance arrived from RAF Woodhall Spa, with the station medical officer and an orderly. The medical officer told Les to ride in front with the driver, saying that should he feel sick during the journey, he would be better able to open the door and be sick out of the ambulance, but Les felt this was a subterfuge to keep him away from the stricken wireless operator. Les was admitted to the station sick quarters at Woodhall Spa and a thorough medical examination confirmed facial injuries and a shaking-up but otherwise nothing wrong.

Mr George Young, of Queen Street, Horncastle and Mr C Sharp, of Raithby, near Spilsby were both part of the spontaneous rescue team that night. George recalls that the aircraft 'came down like a whirlwind'. Mr Odlin had telephoned the police immediately the incident had occurred and organized a search party of his farmworkers. They found the empty rear-turret and said that Les Pooley had crossed two fields in dense fog before coming to the farmhouse. The main wreckage, which had not taken fire, was located some 300 yards from the rear turret and five bodies were extricated from the wreckage, with only the wireless operator alive but in great pain. The remaining body was found in a ditch later that morning. The four dead bodies and the wireless operator were carried as gently as possible to the farmhouse on improvised stretchers made from sheep trays. The ambulance delivered the wireless operator to Tattershall Military Hospital where he died. Later a vehicle arrived to collect all five dead bodies and deliver airmen to guard the wreckage.

George recalls that visibility that night was 'nil' and that Providence and sheer good luck had brought Les to the house from which the search had been organized. Mr Sharp remembered a shout of 'Bombs Gone!' as they carefully approached the wrecked aircraft, which reassured the rescuers considerably, but the source of that shout is a mystery. Mr Sharp's original thought was that Les Pooley had shouted the information from his broken-off turret, but Les was already on his staggering trek before the rescuers arrived on the scene, so it is more likely to have come from the aircrew whose body was later found in the ditch, though it could have been the wireless operator's last conscious reaction.

All aircraft accidents were the subject of investigation as to the cause, and aircraft crashes were subject to courts of enquiry. These were mounted for all six crashes that occurred on 22 December 1944. During the two days that he was detained in station sick quarters, RAF Woodhall Spa, Les Pooley was visited by a Squadron Leader who told him he was investigating the cause of the crash. Les told him the full story of the operation and the subsequent events as he recalled them. The Squadron Leader told him that the starboard wing of the Lancaster had struck a tree.

Les was discharged from sick quarters and returned to his unit on 28 December 1944. During his scramble to get help, Les had lost his flying gloves. He was allocated to the crew of a Flying Officer Scott and went to the equipment stores for replacements for helmet and gloves. To his astonishment, 'Issue on Repayment' forms were raised by the equipment officer and a charge sheet, Form 252 was raised in respect of the loss of flying clothing. When this charge sheet was presented to the 630 Squadron commander for action, Wing Commander Grindon tore it up in disgust. The same fate befell two replacement charge sheets and eventually the disciplinary measure was dropped. The equipment officer remained obdurate, however, on the matter of the repayment and Les had to pay for the replacement kit with which he was issued. Regulation-bound 'emperors' like this caused occasional bitterness in aircrew ranks during the war, refusing to pay attention to the exceptional circumstances surrounding such losses and demanding their 'pound of flesh'. Les was to discover later that a Mr Dent, a worker on Scrafield Farm, found the gloves in a hedge and had excellent wear out of them for six years!

Arthur Joplin had been placed in a room on his own on arrival at Rauceby. He appreciated the solitude for he was in an indescribable state of mental anguish which dulled any pain from his injuries. His mind throbbed with the memory of Bob Yates, the very first member of his crew—they had got into conversation on the train taking them to No 17 OTU, RAF Silverstone and had crewed up almost by mutual consent. His tortured thoughts switched to Arthur Walker. Joppy knew that it was the bomb-aimer's forty-fifth and final operation and Joppy had welcomed him for this sortie. Now both were dead—two fine officers and friends—Joppy wanted to awaken from this nightmare, but his brain kept him in touch with the reality of the situation.

He became aware that a figure was standing by the bedside—a Wing Commander, he believed—who began to interrogate him about the circumstances of the crash. Arthur was really in no fit state, physically or mentally, to cope adequately with such an interview. The deaths of his crew members weighed heavily on his mind, and the injuries he had suffered were quite painful. The officer seemed to be somewhat aggressive in his manner and suggested that Arthur must have had influence to have been posted direct from training to 617 Squadron. The Wing Commander did concede that the altimeter setting was correct and that ordering the crew to crash stations had undoubtedly saved some lives, but his general demeanour was one of thinly-disguised hostility. Joppy's morale and spirits dropped lower and lower as the interrogation progressed. He signed the statement proffered to him at the end of the session without reading it. By this time he was convinced that he alone was completely responsible for the crash and he could not shake the thoughts of his two dead friends from his mind.

Basil Fish was interviewed after his return from survivor's leave. He clearly remembered the offhand attitude of the officer and considered some of his questions irrelevant, especially in the checking of the 'Dead Reckoning' track to Woodhall Spa against the Gee lattice homing. The overall impression Basil gained was that the interview was merely a formality to tidy up the paperwork relating to the accident, for the officer did not seem in the least interested in the immediate post-crash period.

Some weeks later Basil was sent for by Flight Lieutenant Humphreys, the 617 Squadron Adjutant. He had no firm idea why Humph should want to see him and en route for Squadron offices could not help but wonder if an award had been notified. He was shown into Humph's office and, to his utter consternation, was told that his log book was to be endorsed. Humph asked Basil to deliver the log book to him as soon as possible and added that Flying Officer Joplin's book was to receive a similar endorsement. Basil was absolutely dumbfounded and, at the same time, both disgusted and resentful at the injustice and nonsense of it all.

* * *

'No 5 Group Bomber Command Standing Orders' was a thick publication in which were embodied rules and regulations to cover all aspects of flying procedures within the Group. On the operational navigation side, it laid down that aircraft returning from operations should 'home' along specified Gee lattice lines, designated for each operational station in the Group. The intention was to prevent collisions in the air. Unfortunately no copy of these orders is preserved in public research facilities but it would appear that the relevant order specified Gee homing values when aircraft were returning from the east or from the south. From the east, aircraft were required to pick up their homing lattice at the coast. From the south, the lattice was picked up in the Stamford area. These were the two general directions of return from operations. There is some doubt whether the order covered the unusual return from the north or north-east.

What cannot be disputed is that few operational crews adhered faithfully to these instructions. One obvious weakness was that although the order laid down the track to be followed, returning aircraft were not given individual heights at which to carry out the homing and, in the minds of many captains, this tended to add to the risk of collision rather than diminish it. They preferred a straight, unfettered run to base, with navigation lights on in the Group area and a sharp look-out for other aircraft from all aircrew stations. Higher authority seemed to have been aware of this situation, for the '5 Group Monthly Magazine' often raised the matter of the 'Gee Homing' in its 'Navigation' pages, with quizzes raising the question 'Do you use the homing procedure laid down in Group Standing orders?'

The post-operational report of Flying Officer Hudson, a pilot of 463 Squadron, who managed to get his Lancaster back into RAF Waddington, makes interesting reading. 'Did not get the diversion signal at Position A but heard other squadrons getting theirs, so decided to make for Lossie. When we arrived at Position 57°00'N 05°00'E at 01.12 hours heard recall to base. At 02.29 hours received message to return to Lossie. We then sent message to base informing them that we were short of petrol and must land. Landing was difficult owing to poor vis.'

Unfortunately most of the accident report records were destroyed in the years after the war. However, by great good fortune, the RAF Air Historical Branch has in its possession record cards Form 412 in the matter of three of the crashes on December 22 1944. These cards summarize the enquiries and conclusions of the investigating officers, and the action taken. The card in relation to the No 9 Squadron crash (Flying Officer Read) states: 'Pilot briefed to expect diversion to Lossiemouth at Position A. This was to be confirmed. No confirmation at Position A so pilot set course for Lossiemouth. Recalled to base. Base conditions deteriorated but owing to fuel shortage aircraft had to be landed. Two killed: Two injured: Three slightly injured. These findings were concurred by the station commander, the AOC 5 Group and the AOC-in-C, Bomber Command.'

Bearing in mind that the sole testimony available for the circumstances of the No 630 Squadron crash (Flying Officer Stockhill) was that of Sergeant Pooley, the only survivor, and that the prevailing weather conditions made independent observation of the aircraft impossible, the summary on the card for this incident makes strange reading: 'Pilot failed to check altimeter while circling the airfield after abortive attempt to land. Pilot fatigued after long ops trip, controlling aircraft flying starboard wing low. In low flight—after carrying out overshoot procedure due to bad vis, pilot was checking that his undercarriage was locked up when aircraft flew into ground. Unable to land and was being diverted.' These findings were agreed by the station commander, the AOC 5 Group and the AOC-in-C Bomber Command. Les Pooley's comments on being apprised of this record were, 'The pilot had made three attempts to land and we had set course for diversion before the crash happened. It makes you sick when a dead man takes the blame, without being able to defend himself.' In neither of these cases was the question of homing raised and it seems to have been tacitly assumed that as both aircraft had reached their home bases, they had carried out the mandatory procedure.

The summary card for the 617 crash did not refer to being recalled from diversion. It did not mention pilot fatigue after a long ops trip or Basil Fish's fortitude and courage. What it does record is this: 'Did not adopt correct homing procedure. Navigator did not check aircraft's position. Pilot was under impression he was near base. Broke cloud whilst uncertain of position. Aircraft should have been homed on an Eastern lattice. Pilot called on R/T using studs A and B but got no reply. Primary cause: Bad weather. Recommends that Captain's and Navigator's logs endorsed. The Station commander concurred. The AOC 5 Group says, "Endorse 'disobedience'" AOC-in-C concurred.'

The court of enquiry findings were confirmed history and unchallengeable when the red endorsements became known at aircrew level at Woodhall Spa. A post-operational plotting exercise indicated that if Basil Fish had altered the aircraft's course to pick up the specified lattice line on the Lincolnshire coast, the aircraft would not have had sufficient fuel to reach fog-bound Woodhall Spa. It also ignored the cancellation of diversion orders and then the urgent instructions to captains to land at the first available airfield. Surely the whole affair is put into its proper perspective by the fact that Basil Fish, still serving on 617 Squadron within 5 Group, Bomber Command, was commissioned in April 1945, without any reference being made to the endorsement! Recommendations for commissioning had to be approved at *every* level of command, from the actual Squadron commander right up to Bomber Command level. Basil never allowed the findings to affect him. He knew in his own mind that he was blameless. In the later stages of the war, he flew with the 'A' Flight commander of 617, Squadron Leader Ward. The endorsement was made on a page of his log book that he subsequently removed without trace. In this he followed the example of many wartime aircrew, ill-used by higher authority.

Joppy was less fortunate. His red endorsement was made on the inside cover of his log book and was thus irremovable. He never rejoined the Squadron, for the war was over in both spheres before he was considered fit enough to be repatriated to New Zealand. He was visited in hospital by Basil Fish, Jim Thompson, Mark Flatman and a few other aircrew, but it hurt him that his Flight commander or Squadron commander never paid a visit. It was perhaps very unfortunate that the command of the Squadron was being handed over by Willie Tait to Johnny Fauquier during this period, a task that was quite time-consuming and formidable, with all the inevitable 'Hellos' and 'Goodbyes' that the change required. Joppy was unaware of this and in his depressed state concluded that the Squadron CO held him responsible for the deaths of two aircrew. He carried this mental burden for many years and was doubtful about attending the reunion arranged by the Australian element of the 617 Squadron Association in Adelaide during April 1980, fearing that he would be ostracized if he appeared. He kept his 617 Squadron service very much to himself when he settled back in Auckland, in case the dark secret of his endorsement should become public knowledge, without proper appreciation of the true facts behind the stark and condemning words. His wife Betty persuaded him to attend the reunion and, to their intense relief and joy, he was heartily welcomed as a full and worthy member of the association, with the truth of the episode well known within the organization.

He had always felt that too much was asked of him by pitch-forking his crew on to 617 without any previous operational experience. He was always conscious of the additional effort he and his crew had to make to match their vastly more experienced comrades. He wondered if this aspect was ever considered by whoever decreed that 'green' crews should be posted direct to the Squadron. More to the point, did the powers-that-were, in their determination to find scapegoats for the tragedies of 22 December 1944, ever give thought to the mental anguish they were to cause a very young and badly-injured New Zealander for over forty years? And is there no way, even now, that justice can be seen to have been done to both Joppy and Basil?

Chapter 7

Bergen, 12 January 1945

On 12 January 1945, 617 Squadron carried out orders to bomb targets in the Norwegian port of Bergen. Four of the Squadron's longest-serving captains were given specific targets in the harbour. These included a submarine mother ship and a large floating dock. The remaining twelve aircraft were ordered to attack the submarine pens.

The Squadron commander, Group Captain Johnny Fauquier DSO, DFC, accompanied by the Squadron navigation leader, Flight Lieutenant Joe Bayne DFC, was to act as master bomber in a Mosquito aircraft. The attack was to commence at 13.00 hours. The flight plan required that the Lancasters should fly north and rendezvous with an escort of Mustang fighters, flown by Polish pilots, before heading across the North Sea for Bergen. Two Fw 190 fighter squadrons were stationed at the German base at Herdla, and fighter opposition could be expected. Most of the 617 Squadron stalwarts were on the battle order and it was an operation many aircrew were to remember for the rest of their lives. Two aircraft were destined not to return. Nine aircrew were to become prisoners-of-war and eight others would make the supreme sacrifice. It was also an operation to be remembered by the aircrew of one Lancaster for their survival against seemingly impossible odds. That they did is due solely to the expertise and fortitude of these crew members. Details of the successes scored during the operation were not to be known until quite recently. A mystery was to remain, a source of discussion and speculation for many years to come. This is the story of that raid, to set the record straight and to place it in its niche in the wartime history of 617 Squadron.

* * *

Flight Lieutenant John Pryor DFC, turned his car into the gravel-strewn drive of the Petwood Hotel at Woodhall Spa, in Lincolnshire. The tyres crunched the gravel as he negotiated the winding drive between the high rhododendron bushes which loomed on both sides until he entered the large quadrangle in front of the hotel. This was the very comfortable Mess for the officers of the wartime 617 Squadron, and it was the envy of other squadrons in 5 Group. He parked the car and looked at his watch. 'Five past seven' he mused to himself, 'Not at all bad! And I'm still not late back from leave!' He permitted himself a smug smile. Officers were afforded the privilege of a leave extension until 08.00 hours, instead of the usual 23.59 hours that appeared on other leave passes. It was Friday 12 January 1945, and, from the weather portents, it promised to be quite a pleasant winter's day.

He got out of his car in which he had driven up from his farm home at Navestock, Essex. He was in battledress and leaned over into the rear to collect his greatcoat and cap, which he had unceremoniously tossed on to the rear seat. He became aware of the crunch of heavy wheels on the gravel, and seconds later, a crew bus turned into the quadrangle and came to a halt close to the entrance of the Mess. 'Looks as if it's to be a busy day!' thought John as he made his way into the building. He strode to the Mess notice board and was not surprised to find a battle order neatly pinned in a prominent position. He examined it closely and saw that he and his crew had been nominated as a reserve crew. Reassured, he returned to his car, and retrieved the rest of his luggage from the boot. He was just entering the foyer when he heard his name called. He looked in the direction from which the call had come, and saw Flying Officer Mark Flatman hurrying towards him.

John liked the tall, fair Mark, with his wind-ruddied face. They had a common interest, for Mark's family farmed in the Lancaster district. 'I'm glad to see you, John' beamed Mark, 'My crew were delayed going on leave against your return, and "Brooky" said that if you got back OK and were agreeable, you would take our place on the battle order.' 'Of course, Mark' replied John, 'Nay trouble! What time's briefing?' 'That's all been completed, John' rejoined Mark 'Most of your crew have been duly briefed with the rest of us. However, I've got to fill you in on specific detail—it's that sort of operation—and I can't very well do that here!' 'I'll just get a cup of coffee from the dining-room' said John, 'and then we can adjourn to my room for the transfer of information.' 'Good' replied Mark, 'That'll give me time to get on to the Sergeants' Mess and tell my crew that they can doddle off on leave. I'll meet you back here in a few minutes.'

John collected a large cup of coffee but declined the offer of breakfast from the WAAF waitress. He very rarely ate breakfast, and certainly didn't feel like eating at that moment. He returned to the foyer and was soon joined by Mark. 'Don't know why, but my lot cheered when they heard the news' he grinned, 'Bet they're nearly at Boston by now!' He took John's luggage and John retrieved his greatcoat and cap. Together they mounted the stairs and made their way to John's room. It was empty, and Mark set the luggage down, whilst John tossed his gear on the bed, and put the cup of coffee on the bedside table. Mark produced a large photograph. 'The target is Bergen, John' he said, automatically lowering his voice. 'Take-off time is 08.35 hours. Time on target is 13.00 hours. Intelligence is aware that there are two Fw 190 squadrons at Herdla, just north of Bergen, so the plan is that we toddle up north to Peterhead and pick up an escort of Polish Mustangs, before heading for

Bergen. No weather troubles are expected en route or over the target. Whilst the main Squadron effort is to concentrate on the submarine pens, four crews have been given specific targets within the harbour area itself.' He produced a large photograph which John instantly recognized as Bergen harbour and its environs. The photograph was covered by a grid. Mark continued, 'The grid has been superimposed so that captains can identify their particular target and attack the right one. My target—or rather, your target now, is this submarine mother-ship' and he pointed to a ship moored in one of the basins. 'Jock Calder is leading the gaggle whilst Johnny Fauquier does the master bomber role in the Mossie. He will carry out a visual recce immediately prior to the attack, and alter targets by the grid reference if there have been shipping movements since PRU took these photos.'

John was studying the position carefully and said 'I'd have recognized this target as Bergen, Mark, even if you had not mentioned it. D'you remember those Royal Marine commandos who were with us a few months ago? The ones with the speedboats?' Mark nodded and John continued, 'Well, the intention was that the Squadron would drop them one dark night into Bergen Fiord. The nose of each boat was crammed with high-explosive and the commandos were to clear the 'chutes after the drop, and then work the boats up to full speed, heading for the entrance to the pens. Once the boats were committed and the tillers lashed, the commandos, who would be sprawled on a sort of wooden platform at the stern, operated a mechanism that would fling the platform clear of the boat. The best those bods could have hoped for was a PoW camp, yet I remember how bitterly disappointed they were when the operation was cancelled!' John looked up and went on 'I was one of the pilots selected for the dropping, and we had to spend hours studying the target photo of Bergen until we could draw it perfectly from memory. The whole success of the operation depended on the boats being dropped in EXACTLY the right spot. It would have been quite an interesting operation, if it had come off!'

He bent forward to study the photograph once more, and Mark said, rising from his seat, 'I don't think there is anything I've overlooked. Have you any questions?' John shook his head and Mark added, 'Your navigator was at the briefing, if there is anything I have forgotten. I air-tested the kite—no snags and no apparent vices!' He smiled, 'If it's all the same to you, John, I'll hare off on leave now—before anyone decides to go sick!' He turned as he reached the door. 'Hope it all goes well, John—lot of responsibility, though, a special target—means that there may be a come-back if she's not sunk, so all success and I'll see you when I return!' 'Cheerio, Mark' replied John, 'Have a nice time on the farm—and don't let your father overwork you!' 'Not much chance of that, John' answered Mark, 'I have my own plans for this leave!' 'Oh, if you do see any of my crew, Mark, let them know that I'm back and I'll see them in the crew-room.' 'Willco, mate' beamed the ruddy-faced Mark, 'Have a good trip!'

The door closed behind him and John pushed his luggage under the bed. 'Time enough to stow that when I return' he thought to himself. He removed his shoes and pulled on his black leather fur-lined flying boots. Then he moved over to his dressing table and methodically emptied his pockets into one of the small drawers, removing all items that could be of the slightest possible use to the enemy. He searched his pockets thoroughly a second time before closing the drawer. He picked up his cap, greatcoat and flying helmet, secreted the target photograph securely inside his battledress top and made his way down to his car. It was now 07.40 hours and the Mess was unusually quiet and the quadrangle deserted. He slipped into the driving seat and was soon passing through the village of Woodhall Spa, heading for the airfield beyond. He drove to the Flight office to sign the authorization book and to check his position in the gaggle. He was greeted by many of the other aircrew and asked about his leave. He checked the location of his aircraft's dispersal and then went across to the parachute section to collect his 'chute. He put this in the boot of his car and drove out to his aircraft, to find his crew assembled beneath the starboard wing.

Lancaster 'G for George' was still minus its mid-upper turret which had been removed for the Tromso attacks on *Tirpitz*. The full crew was still carried, with the mid-upper gunner acting as a relief for the rear-gunner during the flight or manning the front turret, although it was more usual for him to maintain an anti-fighter watch from the astro-dome. Albert Hepworth, the wireless operator, made his way across to the car as John parked it well away from the aircraft. He was from Barnsley, in Yorkshire and was the sole remaining member of the crew that had transferred to 617 Squadron from 207 Squadron in mid-February 1944. The original bomb-aimer, Cecil Pesme, a Canadian Flying Officer, had been killed instantly by shrapnel from a near-miss flak burst over Brest in daylight on 14 August 1944. Originally the whole crew had decided to call it a day when they had completed a 'straight through' 45 trips. Through circumstances of sickness and being detailed to complete other operational crews when required, the members had arrived at the magical number 'out of step' and, true to their original resolve, had ceased to operate.

Although John Pryor himself had reached that figure, he had decided to carry on until Albert had completed his tally, then John would make up his mind about an operational future. Albert Hepworth greeted him warmly and asked about his leave. 'Been a bit of a rush, this one, skipper' said Albert, 'Didn't get back to Woodhall myself until after six this morning, to be greeted with that battle order!' He went on 'But it's my forty-fifth—the one I've been waiting for!—and then an end to it!' John smiled at his wireless operator's obvious delight. 'It's been a long time coming, Albert, but it's here at last!' He knew that Albert planned to marry as soon as his tour was completed and guessed that this also lay behind his obvious excitement.

He gathered his 'chute, helmet and greatcoat from the car, then made his way to the Lancaster with Albert beside him. 'Everyone here?' he asked. 'Yes' replied Albert 'Shirley is manning the rear-turret and Paddy Armstrong will be in the front turret or the astro-dome—they don't intend to swap during this trip—not a lot of point in it, anyway,' he added. John glanced at his watch. 'Time to get weaving, if we're to take-off on time' he observed.

The other members of the crew had completed the ritual of the 'good luck pee' over the tail-wheel of the Lancaster and were gathering their operational items, in anticipation of entering the aircraft. John said, 'Hope you all had a good leave and now we've got to earn it! Let's get aboard.' George Kendrick led the way, since, as bomb-aimer his destination was the nose of the aircraft. He was followed by John Pryor and Warrant Officer Winston, the flight engineer. John tossed his greatcoat on to the rest-bed as he passed it before climbing over the main spar. The navigator, Harold Ellis, followed them, heaving his packed navigation bag over the main spar, surmounting that obstacle and seating himself at the navigation table. Albert Hepworth came next. His small stature enabled him to cope better than most with the commando course which was the fuselage of the Lancaster! Paddy Armstrong, the Squadron gunnery leader, took up station near the rear door and assisted Warrant Officer Ernie Temple DFM (inevitably referred to as 'Shirley' by all and sundry on the Squadron!) up the aircraft ladder. Shirley turned his cumbersome figure to the left and performed the feat of advanced callisthenics which was required of every rear-gunner to gain access to his turret.

Paddy, being something of a 'spare bod' in the absence of a mid-upper turret, would remain at the rear of the aircraft and render assistance in the starting-up procedure, by manipulating the 'GROUND-FLIGHT' switch at the direction of the captain. He checked that the switch was in the 'GROUND' position, then plugged himself into the intercom. He hoisted the aircraft ladder inside and acknowledged the 'Good Luck' waves of the ground crew, stationed around the aircraft for the imminent starting procedure. Closing the door behind him, he secured the ladder firmly in the appropriate stowage. Once all four engines had started and the trolley-accumulator had been disconnected, he would switch to the 'FLIGHT' position when ordered and then take the seat beside the wireless operator for take-off.

The four Merlins started without the slightest fuss or complaint. Cockpit drills and checks were carried out and efficiently completed. John Pryor gave the 'Chocks Away' signal to the ever-watchful ground-crew Sergeant, and very quickly received the acknowledging signal that the chocks were well clear. Then he obeyed the signals of the airman marshalling him from the dispersal and on to the perimeter track, where he was given the final OK and a good luck salute by the airman. He taxied 'G for George' carefully but quickly to the take-off point where he joined the queue of eager Lancasters. Soon the baleful green signal was flashed to him from the runway control cabin and he lined his aircraft up on the take-off runway. The final preparations were made, John gave the crew warning of intent and then the Lancaster was speeding down the runway. John held it down until the take-off speed had been securely grasped and then lifted smoothly off the runway without the slightest protest from the aircraft. Albert Hepworth and Harold Ellis both noted in their respective logs, 'Take-off time 08.40 hours'. For the crew of '*G for George*', the operation against Bergen was under way!

* * *

Preparations for the Bergen operation had begun most inauspiciously for several members of Squadron Leader Tony Iveson's crew. Three of the crew, Flight Sergeants Les Smith, Frank Chance and Des Phillips had been inadvertently missed off the 'early call' list prepared in the Squadron orderly room, and the first intimation they had that their presence was required in the briefing room was when their captain burst into their Nissen hut and awoke them. It was a mad scramble in the dark of that cold January morning to dress in their operational gear and climb into the Flight van in which Tony sat, fuming at the oversight, but eventually they were seated in the briefing room, relieved that the main briefing had not begun.

It was always disconcerting for any aircrew when preparations for an operation got away to a poor start and it never failed to throw a shadow of apprehension over the whole proceedings. For the majority of the crew it was their seventeenth operation. They had been one of the four or five crews that had joined 617 straight from the Lancaster Finishing School at Swinderby, without any previous experience of a front-line Bomber Command squadron. It was a personal experiment in reinforcement, initiated by Sir Ralph Cochrane, AOC, No 5 Group, and these crews had to learn their trades alongside the very much more experienced crews of the Squadron.

Three other members of the crew were commissioned, besides the captain. Flying Officer Jack Harrison (navigator), Flying Officer Tittle (wireless operator) and Flying Officer Ted Wass (rear gunner) had had no call troubles in the Petwood Mess. Frank Chance was the bomb-aimer, Les Smith the mid-upper gunner and Des Phillips the flight engineer. The normal briefing procedure ran its course and the crew had been allocated the general target of the submarine pens. As they stood beneath the starboard wing of their Lancaster '*F for Freddy*', having a final pre-operational smoke, 'Taff' Phillips was more than a little preoccupied with an inner conviction that this trip would be one they would all remember. Les Smith also had presentiments about the operation, sufficient for him to call on the Squadron Adjutant before going out to the aircraft, to request that, if things went wrong for them, he would not aggravate the misfortune by sending the 'next of kin' telegrams the following day (13 January) but to delay them by one day. The mid-upper turret had not yet been restored to their aircraft either and so Les would keep fighter watch from the astro-dome.

They climbed into the Lancaster and settled themselves at their various positions. The run-up procedure and pre-flight checks were carried out, but, just when the aircraft was about to be taxied out of the dispersal, Taff noticed that the brake pressure was not building up. He immediately called the captain's attention to this, and the starboard inner engine was given a surge of revs for a couple of minutes, but the brake pressure stubbornly refused to rise. Tony Iveson gave the 'Cut' signal and the four Merlins faded into silence. 'This aircraft is u/s' he announced to the crew, over the intercom. 'All out and let's get over to the spare aircraft before anyone beats us to it.' There was a mild panic inside the aircraft as crew members disconnected themselves from the intercom and gathered up all the paraphernalia of their callings. The cockpit was a hive of frenzied activity as all services were switched off and left 'SAFE' and they were all in a muck sweat as they climbed into the 15 cwt Standard van, which was their captain's perk as a Flight commander.

As the little van rolled and tossed its way across the airfield, Ted Wass was feeling really 'cheesed off' with everything. When he had gone to the parachute section to collect his parachute, he was chagrined to find that his own 'chute was being repacked and he was supplied with a pilot-type 'chute for this operation. He had protested, knowing that it meant an uncomfortable trip, for the seat in the rear turret was not recessed to accommodate this 'seat-type' 'chute, but the WAAF was unimpressed, saying that there was no other 'chute available and adding, jocularly, 'If it doesn't work, sir, bring it back and we'll change it!' It had taken Ted quite a while to settle into his turret and just when he had managed it, the order to change to the spare aircraft had posed him with the immediate problem of getting out of the turret again! Small wonder that the war was finding little favour in his eyes! The van arrived at the spare aircraft's dispersal and they were relieved to find that it had not been previously claimed. The ground-crew came running out of the dispersal hut to man the starting services as soon as they saw that the spare aircraft was needed.

Meanwhile other Squadron aircraft were taking off for the operation. Iveson's crew made a concerted dash for the ladder of '*M for Mike*' and Les Smith lent a helping hand to Jack Harrison, who was struggling with his navigational load. Les seized Jack's parachute and, with gay abandon, hurled it up the fuselage, towards the nose of the aircraft. 'Don't treat my safety equipment like that, you clown!' yelled Jack. 'Bloody nice if I need it and find it damaged!' 'Sorry, Jack' soothed Les. 'Just trying to be helpful and save time!' Jack was to recall the exchange in the quiet of that evening.

The start-up and checking procedures could not be rushed. There was no sign of any other Lancaster either on the ground or in the air as *M for Mike* eventually taxied to the take-off point. When the green take-off signal was received from the control cabin, Iveson settled the Lancaster on the runway. The Merlins were opened against the brakes, which were then released with a hiss of relief and the aircraft immediately began to roll down the runway gaining speed with every yard. It lifted off unhesitatingly at 09.09 hours, nearly half-an-hour behind the rest of the Squadron. When things had settled down, Jack Harrison came on the intercom. 'Skip, I think it would be better if we fly an interception course, rather than to try and make up time on the planned route. That way we won't waste fuel by haring up to Peterhead, and we should be able to get in our correct gaggle position well before the target.' 'Good idea, Jack' replied Iveson.

The navigator had been working on the problem during the taxying-period and was able to come up with a quick course for the interception. The pilot set this on his compass and turned the aircraft to starboard to pick up the correct heading. Jack calculated that it would be a couple of hours before the interception took place and, once the aircraft had cleared the ambiguous Gee area around the Humber, he soon settled into the almost rhythmic pattern of bomber navigation. His careful work, allied to the knowledge of the route timings of the formation ahead, allowed him to give course corrections at intervals to the captain. At length he warned the crew members in the front of the aircraft that they should sight the other aircraft in about ten minutes. He was very satisfied when the bomb-aimer called out, almost dead on cue, 'There they are, skipper—dead ahead, moving across to our starboard.' Iveson had picked up the Lancasters almost at the same time and was acknowledging the bomb-aimer's message, even as he brought his aircraft round to slide unobtrusively into the formation. He was not long in locating and assuming his allocated position. There was a relaxation of tension inside '*M for Mike*'. It was a beautiful day outside the aircraft. The formation sailed serenely towards the targets. Ted Wass had become more or less used to the unusually cramped conditions in his turret. There was even enough time to snatch a drink from the aircraft rations.

Flight Lieutenant Freddy Watts had taken over the controls of his Lancaster from 'George', the automatic pilot, as Aberdeen appeared on the port beam, preparatory for the approaching turn to the East and the run to Bergen. He listened to the short exchanges between Squadron Leader Jock Calder and the leader of the Mustang escort as the rendezvous was effected and acknowledged. The formation swung to starboard and settled down on the long run to Bergen. At this stage the gaggle formation was a loose one, which afforded relief to the pilots, most of whom re-engaged 'George' when they had settled down serenely on the new course. Freddy was one of these and, released from the chore of flying the Lancaster, he relaxed in the brilliant sunlight that flooded the forward canopy.

He mused on the coming operation. Personally he would have preferred to have been at a much lower height than that which he was then flying. This approach height meant that the ever-vigilant German radar would pick them up at a far greater range and thus the German defences would have that much more time to prepare and ready themselves accordingly. It was never a very comforting thought to bomber pilots that fighter opposition could be expected, especially when that opposition would almost certainly be from Fw 190s. Still, the Mustang escort was there to deal with that hazard and the flak menace had come to be accepted stoically by 617, as an inevitable and unavoidable consequence of the long and accurate run-up to any target. Perhaps, in the overall circumstances, the immediate climb to bombing height after setting course from Woodhall Spa was the best plan, but Freddy was not entirely convinced in his own inner mind.

'Not to worry, Fred mate' he thought to himself as he switched on his microphone. 'Push a few drinks around, Cherry' he said, looking at the flight engineer seated beside him. 'My throat feels a bit dry, what with all this height and it being such a sunny day—and I'm sure drinks all round won't come amiss. A Guinness would go down a treat right now, but I guess we'll have to settle for tea!' The engineer acknowledged the captain's request and stowed his seat, to begin the task of providing drinks. Soon Freddy had a carton of hot tea in one hand and a bar of chocolate in the other. He relaxed, sipping and munching, and revelled in the warm sunshine. 'Almost too nice a day for going to war' he mused, but he knew that appearances were deceptive. He realized that it was bitterly cold outside. His mind tunnelled back over the past months and he smiled contentedly to himself in contemplation of the fact that he was now one of the 'veteran' skippers of the squadron. He had joined 617 on 5 April 1944, after completing his first operational tour with 630 Squadron, also in 5 Group. His heart swelled with pride when he recalled that glorious period—the pre-invasion strikes at the French marshalling yards—D-Day and Operation Taxable—the assaults on the V3 sites in the Pas de Calais—the Saumur Tunnel—the Brest U-boat pens—the V1 storage sites—'and every one a good 'un!' he ruminated with pleasure. Then there had been the three raids on the *Tirpitz*—his was one of the very few crews that had actually bombed the battleship on each occasion. Other crews had operated against her each time, but had brought their Tallboys back on one or other of the raids, unhappy with the bombing conditions.

Thinking of the *Tirpitz* sent his mind off on another track. 'Strange' he thought, 'Literally thousands of bomber aircrew will never have seen Norway, or given it a thought as a target area, yet I've been here so often that it's almost like a second home!' He recalled the long haul to the Russian base at Yagodnik, to be followed by the flight up to Kaa Fiord, the anchorage of the *Tirpitz*, then the direct return from Yagodnik to Woodhall Spa. Two trips up to Tromso, followed by the harassing of German naval units in Oslo Fiord on the night of 31 December 1944, with the German cruiser *Emden* as the main target. Now here he was again, heading in the rugged heights and majestic fiords of Norway once again.

He glanced down into the bomb-aimer's compartment and saw that Mervyn Mackay, his Canadian bomb-aimer, had taken advantage of the long sea crossing to relax himself for whatever lay ahead. He was seated on the lower step in the nose, obviously enjoying his drink and rations. 'A good lad!' thought Freddy. 'We work well together and he never gets in a "flap"—nice, concise directions on the bombing run—and quite a lad in the bar, too!' he remembered. Freddy saw that Charles Housden, the navigator, was standing up behind the flight engineer and having a good look round outside the Lancaster. 'God, he's making the most of it!' thought Freddy, 'Don't often see young Charles away from his "navigation altar"! I expect it's a nice change for him, though.' He caught Charles' eye and winked broadly. 'I intend to have a "shufti" at Norway, Freddy' said the navigator over the intercom. 'Might be worth coming for a visit on holiday after the war!' 'Holiday?' replied, Freddy, 'We've been to Norway so often, we could very well be made *Gauleiters* after the war!' Charles laughed and turned away, to resume his seat and continue with his repast.

Freddy nodded to the unflappable Cherrington, the flight engineer, even now conscientiously compiling his log, and then Freddy looked astern on his port side. Ian Ross and the other two aircraft with special targets were out there, but he couldn't pick them up in the streaming sunshine. Ian and Freddy had been on the same course at No 14 OTU at Cottesmore but had gone their separate ways to main force squadrons at the end of the course. They had never been great chums, but had been delighted to see each other again on 617 Squadron, which they joined at exactly the same time. There was an added bond in the realization that they were the only two crews of that course to have survived a first tour. Ray Ellwood, Ian's wireless operator, was one of the cronies of Freddy's crew—a gap-toothed humorist, who had teamed up with Ian when Gerry Fawke had called it a day with 617 in late November 1944—Cherry had joined Freddy's crew from the same crew. Freddy recalled that Ian was very friendly with Jimmy Castagnola, another of the long-serving captains of the current squadron. One couldn't think of 'Cass' without recalling that terribly decrepit 'best blue' hat that Cass was wont to wear—easily the hat with the most 'service' on it in the whole of Bomber Command! 'My bet is that only a DSO investiture would cause Cass to invest in a new one!' smiled Freddy to himself. He glanced at his watch. '12.05' he observed silently, 'Another thirty minutes and the gaggle will close up, and we'll be on our way to war! What a pity—on such a day!'

* * *

Johnny Fauquier had appeared right on schedule and had made his presence known visually to the Lancaster formation leader, Squadron Leader Jock Calder DSO, DFC. The leading Lancasters began to close up the loose gaggle until they had assumed their correct station for the bombing run, and this was followed by the rest of the formation so that soon the Squadron was in its normal composite whole for the approach to the target. Navigators were tackling the calculations that were necessary to afford the bomb-aimers the correct data of height, true air speed and drift that the SABS demanded to achieve its true effectiveness. The data was passed to the bomb-aimer, as soon as it had been re-checked and, a couple of minutes after it had been fed into the sight, the bomb-aimer was required to read his settings back to the navigator, as a final check.

The rugged coast of Norway was well within sight. It was a day stolen from spring, with clear blue skies, and the formation was bathed in sunlight. There was scattered low cloud, at about 3,000 feet but, for the moment anyway, that was clear of the target area. Bomb-aimers were searching the scene ahead of them, anxious to pick up the pin-points that would head them inexorably towards their targets. Pilots and engineers combined to fix their gaggle position implacably, whilst maintaining the needles of the air speed indicator and the altimeter immovable on their bombing-run readings. It was the period of concentrated endeavour that marked every 617 Squadron raid. Most navigators had left their tables and stood behind the pilot and flight engineer, glad of the short break from the intensive demands of aircraft navigation, yet deeply concerned that the bombing results should make their efforts well worthwhile. Rear gunners braced themselves for the bombing report, but at the same time maintained a very alert search for fighters, with the briefing warnings very much in mind at this stage of the operation. The climax of the operation was fast approaching.

* * *

The target area was still about ten minutes away when Freddy Watts saw the Mustang escort for the first and only time that day. They came swooping out of the higher altitude ahead of the bombers and continued in a dive towards Bergen. It crossed his mind that perhaps they had seen enemy fighters below, or were being detached to the Herdla airfield to prevent the German aircraft from taking off to oppose the bombers. But that was just a passing thought, for his bomb-aimer was reporting heavy ground haze which was reflecting the bright sunlight and making the identification of their special target particularly difficult. 'Can't say if it's industrial haze, Freddy' reported Mervyn Mackay, 'or whether the Jerries have a smoke-screen in operation, but, on this heading, I'll never pick up our ship.' 'I'll turn off and make an approach from a more northerly heading, Mac' answered Freddy and edged his way clear of the gaggle, to position the aircraft for the promised run. The main formation of the Squadron flew steadily onwards, heading for the defined headland which would bring their sights to bear on the Bergen submarine pens. He saw other Lancasters leaving the gaggle and guessed that the crews with special targets were all having location and spotting difficulties. He made a second run, which was just as fruitless as the first, and had broken off for yet another attempt when he heard the interjection 'Fighters!' in his headphones. It was not a member of his own crew and he could not recognize the voice that spat the warning, but he immediately said, 'Keep a very sharp look-out, gunners!' as he brought his Lancaster round to face the target area once again. He heard a voice ask the master bomber if the attack should proceed in view of the fighter report and heard the laconic voice of the Squadron commander break into the ether with 'Carry on as briefed' which flitted a smile across Freddy's face. Johnny Fauquier was having no truck with aborting the operation!

He tried several more runs without success, then heard Jimmy Castagnola informing the master bomber that it was impossible to pick up the special target because of the haze covering that area of the harbour. A short silence and then Fauquier's Canadian tones answered with, 'Bomb targets of opportunity!' which was acknowledged by Cass. At the end of yet another futile run, Freddy said, 'This is getting us nowhere, Mac! See anything else that might not welcome a Tallboy?' 'Well, skip, there's a merchant ship that's heading out of one of the Bergen harbours' replied the bomb-aimer, 'Could be a worthwhile target.' 'Yes, let's try that' retorted Freddy, 'It could have a cargo that the Germans are anxious to safeguard, if it's trying to clear the area during an air-raid.' He wheeled the aircraft out to sea and then brought it gently round until once again it was heading for Bergen. A few minutes later and then, 'Got it in sight, skip' from the bomb-aimer settled the Lancaster on its bombing run.

Freddy opened the capacious bomb-doors, reminded the gunners to keep a sharp lookout for fighters, and concentrated on the run. No flak was aimed at them during the bombing-run, possibly because they were outside the main flak zone and no doubt the flak-gunners had other targets to occupy their attentions. He felt the Tallboy leave a split second before its departure was reported by the bomb-aimer, and he waited for the report from the rear-turret. It was some 25 seconds in coming. 'A near miss—about 50-75 yards on the port beam of the target, skip' came the rear-gunner's voice. 'Well, I have no doubt that that will give them a few problems' said Freddy, 'so it won't have been wasted, I'm sure! Well done, again, Mac!' he called to the bomb-aimer. 'Now, let's close the bomb-doors and see about getting home to Woodhall!' The huge bomb-doors closed and Mervyn Mackay put all the bombing gear to 'Safe' positions as he switched off the bomb-sight. The Lancaster turned in the sky, on to the heading for Lincolnshire.

It was at that moment that another Lancaster flew across the track of Freddy's aircraft. It was about 1,000 feet below and Freddy saw that it was Ian Ross' aircraft. It was trailing smoke and was being hotly pursued by two Fw 190s, one on either side of the damaged Lancaster. Instinctively, Freddy veered his aircraft to follow the combat, at the same time pressing his VHF button to contact the master bomber. There was no time for preamble. 'Watts here, sir! Permission to assist Ross, in trouble with fighters!' but already his Lancaster was diving in pursuit. 'Permission granted!' crackled the voice of the master bomber in his earphones. Mervyn Mackay had divined Freddy's intentions and took control of the front turret. He slipped off the safety catches of the two Brownings and gave mental thanks that he had carried out the full cocking procedure en route for Bergen. He switched on the gunsight and illuminated the graticule for full brightness, then slipped his hands into the control grips and lowered the twin Brownings to get an early sight of the quarry.

Freddy aligned himself on the track of the struggle taking place ahead of him. He was at 8,000 feet, having descended after bombing to below oxygen height for the return run to Woodhall. He closed the throttles and put the nose of the Lancaster down in pursuit. He observed that Ian Ross had feathered both port engines and smoke was no longer visible from the aircraft. He was quite low over the sea, with the two enemy fighters continuing to pour fire at him from the rear. At 5,000 feet, Freddy opened up full power and his aircraft surged forward under the impetus. 'Give each of those bastards a dousing as soon as you can, gunners' he ordered and watched the airspeed building up as the Lancaster charged into the fray. At a height of 2,000 feet, the indicated airspeed was around 350 mph and they were closing rapidly. Freddy was counting on the fact that the German pilots would be intent on their prey to the exclusion of all else, and hoped that his intervention, if not actually shooting them down, would give them a fright sufficient to cause them to break off the action and hare instinctively for safety.

The range had closed to about 250 yards when the Brownings stuttered their anger, first at one fighter and then at the other. The fiery tracer sped across the narrowing gap and over the canopies of the enemy. The reaction was immediate. Both fighters ceased to fire at the crippled Lancaster ahead and broke violently to port where they were quickly lost to view. Freddy lifted the nose of his aircraft and cut the throttles right back until the airspeed had reached a more normal reading. Then he opened the throttles again to give normal cruising revs and wheeled the aircraft to observe the crippled Lancaster, which was now very low over the sea, and flying quite slowly. 'He's going to ditch, skipper' said the engineer. 'No other option, I'm afraid, Cherry' replied Freddy, his eyes glued to the scene. 'Keep a sharp lookout for fighters, gunners' he called over the intercom. 'We don't want to have to join the crew below!'

He watched with bated breath, and his professionalism as a pilot made him burst into mental applause as he watched his fellow-pilot make a copy-book ditching. 'An absolute classic' as he was to describe it later. The huge aircraft settled slowly and gently down on to the calm surface of the sea. It quickly lost forward way and the escape hatches on the top surfaces burst open to allow the crew to congregate on the wings. Freddy circled and counted seven figures, all wearing Mae Wests which even now they were inflating. They waved vigorously to the circling aircraft but Freddy was quite perturbed to see that the aircraft dinghy was nowhere to be seen. 'Jesus! No dinghy!' said Charles Housden, who had watched the drama from the starboard perspex blister. 'Probably destroyed by the fire of those fighters' said Freddy. 'Well, we'll have to do our best to get the Air Sea Rescue alerted as soon as possible' he added. The navigator had seized his map of the area and was pin-pointing the position of the distressed crew. He could make out a cluster of three islands at the mouth of what appeared to be an inlet or fiord. He could see the smoke of the Bergen bombing and flak still hanging in the air to the north-east of their present position, some fifty miles away. Confident that he had established an accurate datum for the wireless message to be sent, he returned to his navigation position, to interpret his observations into a latitude and longitude.

The wireless operator broke in on the intercom. 'Skip, we'll need about 5,000 feet at this range to get a satisfactory message off to ASR and Group' he said. 'Righto, thanks. I'll run away and climb to that height. Meanwhile, you and the nav get the message prepared and then stand by to give all the homing facilities we can to the ASR aircraft.' He set climbing revs and boost on the instruments and made a fairly rapid ascent to 3,000 feet. He then turned the Lancaster, still climbing, until he reached 5,000 feet shortly before they were over the ditched Lancaster again. 'OK, wireless operator, get the distress message off. We're at 5,000 feet and circling the lads now. Don't clamp the key down yet, as all that may do is to invite enemy interest. We'll just send messages for half an hour, before we worry about a continuous homing signal.' The ether crackled with the first distress message. Freddy and the rest of the crew maintained a very sharp lookout for enemy fighters.

He felt a tap on the shoulder and turned to see 'Cherry' pointing upwards. He followed the direction of the gesture and saw, some thousands of feet above them, a loose formation of Lancasters heading homewards. He nodded in acknowledgement to the engineer but thought to himself 'I wonder what the lads down below are feeling about that.' He looked down and saw that the Lancaster was still well afloat and it seemed to be in little danger of foundering for the moment. The aircrew on the wing just gave the occasional wave and he could see them slapping their hands across their chests, to keep some warmth in their bodies. He realized that it must be cold for them, and that danger would grow as the sun lost its strength. Freddy initiated messages to the various controls, giving all possible details and up-to-date situation reports. From his circling position, he could see enemy fighters landing at an airfield, and urged his crew to redouble their watch for fighters. When the wireless operator reported that a Warwick was on its way to the scene from the airfield at Sumburgh, Freddy directed that the control be told that the key would be clamped for five-minute periods, with a ten-minute break, to assist the Warwick with a homing signal.

They circled the area remorselessly, little realizing that they were emulating the action of David Shannon, when he circled at night in the North Sea off the Dutch coast, bringing the RAF rescue launch to the scene of David Maltby's tragic crash. This was on the night of the 14/15 September 1943, the aborted raid on the Dortmund-Ems Canal and Dave Shannon had circled the spot for two hours, desperate to render all the succour he could to another crew. Foremost in Freddy Watts' mind was the realization that below him was the only other surviving captain of his

OTU course, with a very capable and experienced crew. It would be a great tragedy if the North Sea was allowed to claim them.

The voice of the flight engineer cut across his thoughts. 'Skip, I've had a fuel check and if we leave now, we'll have about an hour's fuel in hand when we arrive at base. We've been circling for well over an hour now!' 'Thanks, Cherry' replied Freddy, 'but I want to stay here until we really have to leave, to make sure that the Warwick and all its rescue gear will be able to get to Ross' crew without any need to go into a search procedure. The daylight will be fast going when they arrive in the area. We won't be able to stay until that time, but the least we can do is to give the lads every possible chance.' Cherry nodded, but Freddy kept the matter turning over in his mind. He called the navigator on the intercom. 'Charles, we'll head for Milltown, of blessed memory, when we leave here. That's the nearest suitable airfield and it will give us the maximum time here. Work out the time that leg will take so that we can set course for Milltown at the last possible moment.' 'Roger, skip' came the reply and Charles Housden bent to his new task, smiling as he did so at Freddy's 'of blessed memory' sally. Milltown had been their advanced base for the first tilt at the *Tirpitz* at Tromso, and he recalled that the weather there had very nearly caused them to miss that particular 'party'!

They continued to circle the distressed crew, who were all sitting quietly on the wing. Their Lancaster was still riding well on the water and Freddy marvelled at its continued buoyancy. The wireless operator was busy with messages and the homing signal. He reported that the Warwick was receiving their signal very well and was heading straight for the area. 'Warn control that we will have to leave the area before the Warwick gets here' said Freddy, 'so that they'll know that our signal will cease and it will be all up to the Warwick crew then.' The wireless operator acknowledged the instruction and sent out the information. Charles Housden came back on the intercom with the information Freddy required for the journey to Milltown. The flight engineer looked a bit worried as he listened to the intercom traffic and when Charles had finished, he said to Freddy, 'Should be leaving now, skip, if we are to arrive safely?' 'No, we can give it another quarter of an hour' retorted Freddy. The flight engineer looked across to him dubiously, but was somewhat reassured by Freddy's smiling shake of the head and his 'Thumbs Up' sign.

Twenty minutes later, Freddy said, 'Tell control that we are leaving the area now, W/Op, and will land at Milltown.' 'Willco, skipper' replied the wireless operator. Freddy brought his aircraft over the ditched Lancaster, waggling his wings violently. The crew below stood up and waved their thanks as he reluctantly turned on course for Milltown. 'I hope to God that Warwick gets here in time' he said to the crew at large. 'We've done all we possibly could, Freddy. No need to reproach yourself in the least!' countered the navigator, amid general murmurs of approval from the rest of the crew.

Once the Lancaster had settled down on the course for Scotland,

Freddy beckoned Cherry to lean across to him. The flight engineer appreciated that Freddy had something private to say to him, so he leaned over obediently, tugging his left earpiece away from his head so that Freddy could pass the message. 'Cherry, you remember when we were carrying out the endurance tests with the Lancasters before going up to Tromso . . .' Cherry nodded vigorously in agreement. 'I recall that we discovered that to obtain optimum petrol consumption, we dropped the indicated airspeed by ten knots every hour.' 'I can do better than that, skip' replied Cherry, 'I can calculate the changing revs and boost settings even as we proceed on our merry way now—it'll be the first time I've ever been able to carry out my full function in all the operations I've done!' He smiled happily as Freddy gave him a 'Thumbs Up' sign and leaned across again as Freddy beckoned. 'Don't say anything on the intercom, Cherry' he said, 'I don't want the lads to get concerned with something that's down to us two. In fact, you could pass round a nice hot drink and a few "wads", just to reassure them and keep their minds off things.' Cherry nodded and busied himself with the task of getting the drinks circulated, whilst the navigator continued with his duty of getting the aircraft to Milltown. The Gee signals were soon tall and useful, and it was not long before he was able to give the skipper an accurate ETA. The weather was still on its best behaviour and Charles soon had the wind velocity and other data well taped. Successive Gee fixes confirmed the track made good and the settled ground speed, which in turn confirmed the ETA so that Charles was soon feeling on top of the world, navigation-wise.

Meanwhile, the flight engineer had buried himself in his calculations, relating the changing all-up weight of the aircraft to the maximum endurance possible with the lessening fuel load. Periodically, he lowered the revs and boost, to coincide with the revelations of his checked calculations, which resulted in a drop in the indicated airspeed. The navigator's observations then seemed to indicate that the wind was strengthening against the aircraft until he happened to glance at his airspeed indicator repeater and saw it had dropped by ten knots. 'How do you expect me to get you to Milltown on ETA, skip, if you are going to mess about with the airspeed all the time' he expostulated over the intercom. Freddy winked at Cherry, who was smiling broadly, and replied to the irritated navigator, 'Don't worry your pretty little head about the ETA, Charlie lad! Just concentrate on getting us heading towards home, and we'll let YOU know when we're there!' 'Oh, bloody funny!' retorted Charles, 'You'll let me know what I'm supposed to tell you!' Freddy grinned across at Cherry—nothing like a narked navigator to add spice to the proceedings!

Irritated, Charles swung his seat around, away from his navigation table, when his eyes happened on the petrol gauges on the panel beside him. 'Christ, Cherry!' he said, 'Do you realize that these gauges are all indicating a very low state of fuel?' 'Now, Charles' soothed Freddy, 'Don't go worrying your pretty little head about petrol gauges and fuel, there's a good lad. They always under-read in the lower registers—just like on a car. We've got plenty of fuel for the run to Milltown!' 'I hope you're right, Freddy' replied the navigator, uncertainly. Freddy felt that the rest of the crew might well be feeling somewhat disconcerted by the exchange, so he added, 'We won't stay long at Milltown, lads—just long enough to take on sufficient fuel to trundle us down to Woodhall. We'll get more news of Ian Ross at base than ever we will at Milltown.' He instructed the wireless operator to get a message off to Milltown, requesting refuelling facilities to be made available, and then looked ahead where the Scottish coast was looming up plainly in the late afternoon sunshine.

Cherry made his final alterations to the engine settings, and drew his skipper's attention to the fact that the boost dials were now indicating − 2 lb. He put his hands together, miming in mock horror whilst Freddy grinned widely. As the aircraft crossed the coastline, the pilot said to the navigator, 'Crossing the coast now, Charles. I can see Milltown dead ahead—get set for the landing everyone.' 'I hope it's not going to be an unusually heavy one, skip' replied Charles, 'I don't want to worry you but all the petrol gauge needles seem to have slumped on to the zero mark, mate!' 'Don't worry so, Charles' replied the imperturbable Freddy. 'The fans are all turning merrily and healthily!' They joined the Milltown circuit and were given permission to land. The remainder of the crew waited with some degree of trepidation as he made his final approach and came in for the landing. The wheels kissed the tarmac smoothly and Freddy allowed the aircraft to run the full length of the runway, reducing the speed with judicious use of the powerful brakes. At the end of the runway, he turned the Lancaster to port and began to taxi the aircraft towards the refuelling area, indicated by the control officer. They had travelled some forty yards along the perimeter track when all four Merlins lapsed into complete silence and Freddy brought the aircraft to a standstill on the brakes. There was a moment of complete and absolute quiet in the Lancaster, until Freddy shattered it with a statement made in a most matter-of-fact voice. 'I kept telling you, Charles, that we had enough fuel to get us to Milltown OK, didn't I?' He let out a great roar of laughter, in which Cherry joined, and rolled aside to avoid the good-natured pummelling of his smiling navigator.

Two hours later, adequately fuelled for the journey to Lincolnshire, they were airborne again. Suddenly Freddy emitted a yell which startled all his crew. 'Whatever's the matter, skip?' asked the mystified navigator. 'I'm a bloody fool, mate' moaned Freddy, 'I should have nipped up to the Officers' Mess to see what had happened to that couple of quid Witherick and I left there for drinks after the first *Tirpitz* trip to Tromso!'

* * *

Flight Lieutenant James Castagnola—or 'Cass' as he was invariably known on 617 Squadron—had found the Bergen trip a most enjoyable experience on the way to the target. No troubles with the aircraft, a beautiful sunlit day with almost unlimited visibility, and a long, relaxed run before the Squadron had tightened up formation just before entering the battle zone. The positions of the allocated special targets had been confirmed by the Mosquito, after visual reconnaissance over the harbour.

He had edged off the perimeter of the gaggle to pick up his own target and it was then that his troubles began. A combination of ground mist and smoke, together with the brilliant sunshine, made the identification of his target almost impossible. He had made several abortive runs, but each time his experienced bomb-aimer, Norman Evans, had failed to pick up the target in time for a satisfactory run to be made on it. Cass reported his difficulty to the master bomber and received instructions to bomb a target of opportunity. Obediently, he turned the Lancaster back towards Bergen harbour, looking for business. As he straightened the aircraft from its turn, he heard the bomb-aimer's voice on the intercom. 'Skip, there's a ship moving out of the berth area we were supposed to attack, and it appears to be anxious to clear the area' he reported. 'She'll do nicely, Norman—can't be certain that anything else will oblige. Over to you, lad,' replied the imperturbable Cass.

The navigator and bomb-aimer soon had the bomb-sight primed with all the data for the attack and the bomber began to stalk the unsuspecting target. Cass held the Lancaster rock-steady on course, height and airspeed. Some black bursts of heavy flak appeared in the vicinity, but not near enough to worry them—certainly not enough to deter Cass for a moment. He was appreciative of the fact that, having been assigned this special target, he had no gaggle responsibility, which allowed him to concentrate on the perfect flying required by the bomb-sight, without any distraction about his position in the gaggle formation.

Cass, with his navigator, Flying Officer Jack Gorringe and bomb-aimer, Flying Officer Norman Evans, formed one of the most effective teams in the Squadron. In the higher level formation in the attack on the Kembs Barrage, across the Rhine near Basle, in daylight on 7 October 1944, Cass had calmly piloted the Lancaster for Norman Evans to obtain the best bombing result of the seven Lancasters that composed the element. Norman had been awarded an immediate Distinguished Flying Cross for this outstanding effort. Now Cass listened intently to the commentary emanating from the bomb-aimer. He could tell that Norman was very satisfied with the progress of the run, and was well aware that his bomb-aimer would abort the run if it was anything less than perfect.

Obviously Norman was well-pleased with progress too and his 'Bomb gone' call came over without any undue excitement. The crew waited for the rear-gunner's report with bated breath. It was not long in coming. 'God, a direct hit on the stern, Norman! She's rolling on her side! She can't last much longer!' Cass wheeled the Lancaster hard to port and continued the tight turn in order to get a view of the stricken target but from his angle and the interference of the ground haze and smoke, he was unable to get a glimpse of it until he had traversed the half turn on to a reciprocal course. Chick Henderson, the flight engineer, caught sight of the bombed vessel just before it became but a hole in a boiling sea. He shared the general elation of a target destroyed, but in his heart he felt that a Tallboy on a minesweeper was a bit of a 'mis-match' to say the least. It lacked the satisfaction of a strike on the *Tirpitz* or the *Lutzow* (which they were to effect later in the year)—it was war, but so one-sided in this instance. Cass was barely able to glimpse the superstructure and bows of the ship before they slid beneath the waters of the inlet. 'Christ, that was quick!' said Jack Gorringe, from his position at the starboard blister. 'I don't expect that the arrival of a hungry Tallboy at a fair rate of knots is very conducive to long life' observed Cass sagely. 'Well done, Norman' he continued, 'It might not bring you a Bar to your DFC, but it will certainly bring you a few free drinks in the bar tonight.' 'Thanks, skip' acknowledged the bomb-aimer 'but everything, and everyone, has to be right to get such a result, and the credit is just as much yours and Jack's as mine!'

Some sixth sense caused Cass to look up instinctively and search the sky. He caught sight of a Fw 190 coming down towards the Lancaster from the port quarter high. He gave warning to the crew, even as he spun the bomber into a roll towards the direction of the attack and hurled the aircraft into a dive that would take it into the flak area. It would be unusual for a fighter to pursue a bomber into a flak zone, and Cass preferred to take his chance with the flak rather than a fighter at that moment. He continued the dive across the harbour and the built-up area of the town, before turning off for the open sea and the low cloud sanctuary that it offered in places. He was relieved when his gunners reported that they were unaccompanied and not a little surprised that the aircraft had attracted no attention from the very busy flak defences.

Suddenly, ahead of him he saw a Lancaster belching smoke, flying quite slowly and low over the sea, and under attack by a Fw 190. He urged Norman Evans into the front turret and told him to prepare to open fire on the fighter when the range closed. He opened up his throttles and went in pursuit of the combatants. The two front Brownings hurled a cascade of tracer and bullets at the enemy when the range had closed, and it did a quick flick and turned sharply away. The alerted gunners prepared for possible battle, but the enemy pilot apparently had no wish to continue the acquaintance. Cass closed with the damaged Lancaster and heard Norman say 'Jesus, Cass! It's Ian Ross and his crew!' Cass felt a wave of frustration course through him, at his inability to render any practical aid to his great friend in such dire straits. Ian Ross, the likeable Australian, had been on 617 for a considerable time. He had joined the Squadron soon after Cass, and they had become very friendly, accompanying each other on trips to Boston and Lincoln on the 'stand down' nights. The members of both crews were also on the friendliest terms, and there was complete silence in Cass's aircraft as they watched the unfolding drama. Cass throttled back his engines and watched Ian execute a perfect 'ditching'. The seven members of the crew tumbled smartly from the escape hatches in the top of the fuselage as soon as the aircraft had settled on the calm sea. The Lancaster did not break up and appeared to have settled buoyantly on the surface. 'A marvellous effort!' enthused Norman from the front, 'A superb piece of airmanship—absolutely "copy-book"!' 'Yes, but there's no sign of the dinghy breaking out' observed Jack Gorringe. He watched the drama with a feeling of great regret, for he knew all the crew personally.

On 31 December 1944, Cass had been dubbed 'non-effective' by reason of a heavy cold and his crew had been excluded from the battle order that night. Terry O'Brien, Ian's navigator, had been also made non-effective through bleeding from the ears, and Ian had asked Jack to fly with them that night, in action against German naval units in Oslo Fiord. Jack had willingly agreed, with Cass' blessing, and recalled how they had all wished each other a Happy New Year at midnight, even as they scoured the dark waters below for signs of their prey.

Cass' crew waited in silence, willing the dinghy to appear from its stowage in the starboard wing root, but nothing happened. 'Looks as if the fighter attack has destroyed the quick-release mechanism' observed the flight engineer. 'Jack,' said Cass to his navigator 'Wrap our emergency radio in a couple of Mae Wests as securely as possible, but leave as much of the tapes trailing as possible. When you're ready, open the rear door and stand-by on the intercom—don't forget to inflate the Mae Wests when you've got the radio safely wrapped. I'll fly over them as slowly as I can and as low as I dare, and Norman will give you the signal to launch. With a bit of luck and good judgement, the transmitter will land close enough for them to retrieve it and make use of it. There's not much else we can do, in the way of direct assistance. Once we've got the drop completed, we'll get off the necessary wireless messages to alert the Air-Sea Rescue and get them out here as soon as possible.'

Cass sheered off from the area until Jack announced that he was ready for the drop. Cass lined up on the ditched Lancaster, dropped his flaps to their fullest extent, and brought the aircraft down to about fifty feet above the sea. At an airspeed just above stalling speed, he flew towards the distressed crew. Norman Evans concentrated on this approach with even greater care than he had shown on the operational run. At the critical time, he gave the word 'Launch!' and the bundle fell from the Lancaster. He saw the crew below wave in appreciation and the bundle fell quite close to them.

Cass soared the Lancaster up to just over 500 feet, and Jack Gorringe co-operated with Bill Eaves, the wireless operator, to stream out the information required by the listening Air-Sea Rescue Organization. Jack had obtained a very accurate estimate of the position of the ditched crew, by reference to the geographical features available for identification. Cass circled the Lancaster above his friends. He hoped that the transmitter they had dropped was working and that it would provide a homing facility for the ASR aircraft to use to locate the crew. It wasn't much, but at least they had tried to help.

They had been circling for about ten minutes when the rear-gunner came urgently on the intercom. 'Skip, a Fw 190 is coming towards us from the starboard quarter!' Instinctively, Cass thrust the throttles open and the Merlins surged with the increased power. Cass darted the aircraft into some low cloud that was conveniently near. He stayed within it for some six minutes, flying on instruments whilst, as if oblivious to their own present danger, the navigator and wireless operator calmly continued to send the messages into the ether. Cass emerged gingerly from the cloud, ready to envelop the Lancaster in its sheltering cover if the fighter was still about. He and the gunners searched the area with great thoroughness, but they were alone again. It looked as if the enemy pilot had concluded that they had hared off for England.

'Had the German alerted the German rescue service?' Cass wondered, as he resumed his vigil above the ditched crew. Norman Evans came on to the intercom. 'That Lanc doesn't seem to have sunk one inch since the ditching, Cass' he said. 'It looks as if it will float forever! What an aircraft!' Cass counted seven figures on the wing, and saw that they had huddled together. 'I guess they're beginning to feel the cold, Norman' he said, 'They have no special heated clothing for this caper, and only the gunners seem to be wearing Irvin suits.' 'Might be better for them if the German Air-Sea Rescue got to them first' answered Norman.

Cass had been turning over the alternatives in his mind and he spoke to Jack Gorringe. 'We won't be able to stay here until the rescue aircraft arrives, Jack, and we seem to be attracting some unwelcome attention to this area. How are things back there?' 'We've got off all the information possible, skip' replied Jack, 'and control has replied very strongly in the affirmative. Bill is transmitting an intermittent homing signal at the moment, but there's not much else we can do now.' 'Thanks, Jack' replied Cass. 'We'll stay for a short while longer, to consolidate the homing as far as possible, and then you'd best give me a course for Woodhall, whilst we have sufficient fuel. No point in risking another aircraft.' 'There's nothing else for it, skip' agreed Jack. 'At least the rescue aircraft will have a sound datum to work to and should get here before the daylight goes.' Ten minutes later, Cass made a final, wing-waggling pass over the ditched crew, and there was a lump in his throat as they waved frantically back at him. They realized what he had been doing and were waving their gratitude. Cass only hoped that it was enough as he set course reluctantly for base.

It is a strange fact that neither of the Lancaster crews who ministered to the ditched aircraft was aware of the other's presence in the area. No doubt the gunners were totally involved with a sky search for enemy fighters, whilst the forward crew members strove to assist the stricken crew as much as possible. They pursued their efforts at different altitudes, but the fact remains that it was not until they met up again at Woodhall Spa that either became aware of the efforts of the other crew!

* * *

Tony Iveson had tightened up formation with the rest of the Squadron, as the coast of Norway appeared, well-defined, ahead. Les Smith had taken up his fighter-watch position in the astro-dome, and Ted Wass was scouring the skies from the rear turret. Tony saw the aircraft with the special allocated targets begin to diverge to port, whilst the main formation thundered smoothly on towards the U-boat pens, indicated by the prominent headland of Laksevaag. He heard the broadcast warning of 'Fighters!' in his headphones and awaited the master bomber's reaction. None was forthcoming and so he pressed his VHF button. 'Are we to proceed, in view of the last report, master bomber?' he asked. The reply came almost immediately, in the staccato tones of the Squadron commander. 'All aircraft carry on as briefed' was the uncompromising answer, and the bombing run continued unfalteringly. 'Look out for German fighters, gunners' ordered Iveson, 'But remember there are Mustangs about, too!'

'Not much point in proceeding with this run, skipper' said Frank Chance from the nose of the Lancaster, 'An early bomb has undershot the target and thrown a huge plume of dust and debris in the air—so much so that I cannot pick up the target.' 'Roger, bomb-aimer' replied the pilot, 'I'll break off to port and come round for another run.' So saying, he banked the aircraft to port and commenced the turn that would take it back to a fresh datum. It was obvious that the undershoot had ruined the bombing runs of quite a few of the aircraft, for '*M for Mike*' was in company with other aircraft in the turn. They orbited for a while west of the target and tried another run, but the obstruction persisted and they were forced to abandon the attempt. Again, a turn to port to attain another datum and as they flattened out on the reciprocal track, Frank Chance came on the intercom again. 'Skipper, there's a Lanc out to starboard, weaving like the clappers—no flak anywhere near him!' Before Iveson could pick up this phenomenon, the urgent voice of the rear-gunner broke in urgently. 'Fighter astern, skipper—oh no, it's OK! . . . no, Christ! It *IS* a fighter! Corkscrew port!' Almost simultaneously, the astro-dome look-out burst into the intercom, 'Fighter attacking from starboard, captain! Corkscrew starboard!'

The pilot was caught in two minds by these contrary reports, and he hesitated, uncertain which command to obey. He appreciated that the Lancaster was under concerted attack from both sides, but, before his fighter experience could come to his aid, his aircraft bucked and shuddered under a hail of cannon-shells. Frank Chance saw daylight tracer ammunition passing through and under the port wing. The sight provoked a spasm of fear in his stomach and a certain uneasiness in his nether regions. The wireless operator interjected, 'Port inner engine on fire, skipper' which brought Jack Harrison leaping to his feet. He thrust aside the navigation curtain and saw the port inner engine belching black smoke and tongues of flame. Even as he watched, the conflagration died and the propeller ceased to turn as the alert Taff Phillips obeyed the captain's order to feather the engine and operate the fire extinguisher.

Jack became aware that the Lancaster had now assumed a definite 'nose up' attitude as a result of the damage sustained, but was losing height quite quickly, with the pilot unable to assert any control over the aircraft's behaviour. Taff was leaning across the pilot and both of them were straining to push the control forward. On closer inspection, he observed that the column was jammed deep into the pit of the pilot's stomach and that the combined efforts of the pilot and flight engineer were having very little effect. Just as he moved forward to lend his own considerable weight to the struggle, Iveson flicked on his microphone and broadcast, 'Prepare to abandon aircraft! Prepare to abandon aircraft!' Jack pulled back the pilot's earpiece. 'Not yet, Tony—not yet! Let's have a bloody good "go" before we give up!' So saying, he leaned massively against the recalcitrant column but it still refused to budge.

'No chance of bombing the pens now, skip!' came the bomb-aimer's voice. 'Best to jettison the Tallboy now—we're over open country—might help with the control of the aircraft. Open the bomb-doors and I'll let it go!' The three crew members in the cockpit were devoting their attentions to the control column and it took two more calls from the bomb-aimer before the bomb-doors opened. Frank Chance pulled the jettison handle and the weapon left the aircraft. He noticed that all four off-set vanes were badly-holed and the weapon did not fall with its customary grace, but gyrated and swerved erratically on its downward path. Frank appreciated that the Tallboy had saved the aircraft from even greater damage, and had certainly kept him free from serious injury, if not worse. He called 'Bomb jettisoned "Safe", skip!' and saw the bomb doors close. He gathered up his maps and other gear before pulling aside the india-rubber coverings of the escape hatch, in obedience to the captain's preparatory abandoning order.

Far from relieving the trouble of the three crew members struggling manfully in the cockpit, the release of the Tallboy seemed to have aggravated them. The nose of the Lancaster seemed to have risen slightly and the rate of descent increased—that was the impression on Jack Harrison's mind as he continued to battle with the obstinate column. He was conscious of Ted Wass' voice on the intercom. 'Ready to abandon aircraft back here, skipper!' the rear-gunner reported. Iveson switched on his microphone to give a brief 'OK!' before redoubling his efforts on the control column.

Ted Wass had not had too happy a time in the rear turret. The pilot-type 'chute proved not only to be distractingly uncomfortable, but caused a certain amount of readjustment to his usual sighting stance. He had maintained an unceasing and steady fighter watch throughout the approach to the target and had mentally identified the fighter approaching the Lancaster as a Fw 190, but subconsciously he was heeding his skipper's warning not to mistake their own escort for enemy aircraft. He had delayed his final confirmation almost too late, for even as he opened up with his own Brownings, he saw the winking muzzle-flashes of the Fw 190's cannons and machine-guns. The enemy fighter seemed to brush aside contemptuously his own reply, which appeared to be enveloping the enemy, but Ted was shaken to the core when Les Smith interjected about the further attack from the starboard quarter. In this confusion, he felt the Lancaster shake and shudder as the enemy fire bit home from both sides. His own target disappeared from view and Ted was relieved to find that he had suffered no personal injury.

He swung his turret to starboard and then traversed round to the port beam but there was no further sign of the attackers. He saw that the port tail-plane was badly damaged and that a large part of the metal fabric was missing from the fin and rudder. Black oily smoke was streaming back from one of the port engines and he heard the wireless operator's report that the port inner engine was on fire. The attitude and behaviour of the aircraft told him that there was something seriously wrong, and he was not surprised when the preparatory order to abandon aircraft was given by the captain. He centred his turret and locked it into position, before sliding the exit doors open and heaving himself bodily out of the turret and on to the small catwalk. His unaccustomed 'chute made this more of a contortion than usual, but he managed it without too much stress. Les Smith and Alan Tittle were already at their stations by the exit door. Both had their 'chutes clipped to their chests and the door had been secured in the open position. Les was actually seated on the step with his legs dangling over the side of the aircraft. Ted plugged his helmet into the only intercom socket available in that area of the Lancaster and reported their arrival at the emergency position.

Les Smith had felt a tremendous shock of fear when the fighters attacked and he felt the hammer-blows strike the aircraft. He fought down his fear and strove to grasp the requirements of his duty through the severe mental stress. He listened to the intercom traffic, even as he forced himself to maintain his fighter search and he realized the aircraft had suffered serious damage, although not immediately fatal. He saw Jack Harrison leap from his seat and move to the forward area of the cockpit, but the navigator's black-out curtain prevented him from observing the developments in the cockpit. He appreciated that the captain was fighting to regain, or retain, control of the stricken Lancaster. He prayed hard for some seconds and then felt absolutely calm and braced himself for what was to come.

The captain's order to prepare to abandon aircraft caused him to climb the main spar ahead of the wireless operator, collect his 'chute from its stowage and make his way to the rear door station. He was aware that the wireless operator was close on his heels and he turned to give Alan an encouraging grin. He was appalled by the damage that was so very manifest as they made their way along the fuselage, but he resolved that, as he was the most experienced aircrew in the crew as far as flying hours were concerned, apart from the pilot, it was up to him to set an example. Just as he was about to negotiate the step-down in the area of the mid-upper turret position, another large hole appeared in the fuselage, not far from where he stood, and he realized that the fighters had returned to the attack. Les coolly opened the rear door and fastened it securely, before settling himself for the launch into space. Alan Tittle stood just behind him and Les saw Ted Wass appear from the rear turret and connect himself on the intercom. He sensed that Ted was reporting their state of readiness and he braced himself for the inevitable.

When Ted Wass made his report, he was not surprised to receive his rejoinder of 'OK!' Without further ado, he disconnected himself from the intercom, bent over to Les Smith and yelled 'OK—Jump!' 'Give me a push for luck, Ted' said Les, and Ted duly obliged. Alan Tittle quickly followed without any hesitation. Ted Wass slipped off his helmet and settled himself on the step, facing the rear of the aircraft. When he had composed himself on his strange 'chute, he bent his head between his legs and rolled sideways out of the Lancaster.

Les Smith had counted the regulation 'Ten' before pulling the ripcord and was very relieved when the white silken canopy billowed over his head and his headlong fall was checked with a jerk. He was unable to avoid a collision with the hard rock face of a sheer mountainside and his leg was buffeted as his 'chute dragged him across the unyielding rock. He eventually hit the earth with a very solid thud, and just had time to strike the quick-release catch of his harness before the pain of his injured leg thrust him into unconsciousness. When he regained his senses, he found himself on a stretcher, borne along by four German soldiers.

Ted Wass pulled his ripcord and was soon floating gently down towards the ground. He could see the other two 'chutes in the distance below him and was glad to know that the jump had gone perfectly. He was surprised at the impressive silence after the tumult of the Lancaster and how peaceful everything looked. He noticed that he was above the icy waters of a fiord and raised his arms to the parachute shrouds. A few exploratory tugs gave him the ability to change the direction of his fall and he was soon well clear of the water. He could see the built-up area of Bergen and the harbour with countless flak bursts dispersing in the clear winter air and he estimated that he would land in an area some three miles south-east of the harbour.

As he approached the ground, he became very conscious of the speed of his descent, and he prepared for the impact. He landed quite close to a large fir tree, against which the snow had drifted to a considerable depth and this cushioned his fall considerably. He quickly released himself from his harness and set about burying the harness and 'chute in the mound of drifted snow. He was comforted by the thought that the local population was probably friendly, but his proximity to Bergen did not augur very well for a successful evasion attempt.

He began to make his way towards a timber house, which he could see at a lower level, from which a wisp of smoke was rising. He had just discovered a wide track, which promised to lead him to the house, when he heard the soft sound of bells. He turned to see a horse-drawn sleigh speeding towards him, carrying two men. He waited for it to come beside him and the driver waved in friendly fashion, indicating that he should get on board. When he was settled on the rear of the sleigh, the other man covered him with a somewhat smelly tarpaulin. He sensed the sleigh wheel and race off back in the direction from which it had appeared.

The journey continued for some time before the sleigh stopped and the cover was removed. It was getting dark and Ted observed that he was inside a timber stockade, surrounding a large timbered barn-like structure. His companions took him inside and one, who spoke a little English, indicated that they would try to help him. They prepared some very meaty soup on a large wood-burning stove by the light of a very large oil-lamp. When it was ready, they offered a large helping to Ted. It was very tasty and made Ted realize how very hungry he was. After the meal, he gained the impression that his two companions intended to drive off and seek additional help. They showed him into a room adjoining the dining-room, which had a large bench-like bed and a few blankets. He laid down on the bed, glad of the opportunity to relax for the first time since he had seen the attacking German fighter and very soon he was fast asleep.

He was rudely awakened by the sound of an engine. He stood up and opened one of the window-shutters and was stunned to see a German military car with several men in German uniforms. He had scarcely returned to the bed, when the door burst open and what seemed to be a horde of uniformed men swarmed into the room, with guns drawn. An officer advanced, covering Ted with a menacing Luger pistol and snapped '*Kommt mit, Offizier!*' Ted had no alternative and was directed into the back of the car which then drove off, with drawn guns much in evidence. Ted was glad he had had a few hours sleep for it enabled him to prepare himself for any interrogation that lay ahead.

He was not harmed but delivered to an anti-aircraft unit where he was given some strong black coffee, brown bread and sausage meat. Later he was briefly interviewed by a German officer who spoke good English and to whom Ted gave only his number, rank and name. 'You will be taken by rail to Oslo later today and handed over to the Luftwaffe authorities there' he was curtly informed at the end of the short interview. In the afternoon he was taken under escort to the local railway station, to await the train to Oslo. Whilst he stood on the platform, a Norwegian civilian walked past and said, in a stage aside, 'Good luck, RAF!' Ted bore not the slightest ill-will towards his erstwhile sleigh rescuers. He appreciated that evading in Norway was an entirely different proposition from the Continental mainland. He knew that the Germans had a very good idea of his landing area, especially if they had also picked up Les Smith and Alan Tittle. It was obvious that the war was only going to last a few more months and Ted preferred the discomfort of a short PoW career rather than the responsibility for the untimely deaths of any Norwegian helpers. He was confident that he would meet up with his other crew members in Oslo.

* * *

All the aircrew in the forepart of the Lancaster felt the hammer-blows as the fighter's fire struck the aircraft. Taff Phillips immediately inspected the fuel gauges, studying them intently. He was relieved to see that the fuel state remained unaffected, despite the damage that the aircraft had obviously sustained. He glanced out of the starboard perspex blister and saw a Fw 190 range up alongside the Lancaster, not more than twenty yards away. Taff felt a knot of fear tighten his stomach. It was the first close-up he had ever had of the German enemy. Jack Harrison spotted their tormentor at the same time and both aircrew saw that the German pilot was giving them a frenzied and repeated 'Thumbs Down' sign. Jack's reaction was to think 'If only I'd had a gutful of beer! I could piss all over that bastard and stop his engine!' The Lancaster captain ordered Frank Chance to man the front turret guns. Due to the force of 'g' being generated by the aircraft's attitude, Frank found it more difficult than usual to disconnect the leads of his electrically-heated suit, oxygen supply and intercom in the bombing well and then to lift himself into the front turret. He reconnected his oxygen supply and intercom and had just settled himself when the Fw 190 on their starboard side accelerated ahead of the Lancaster. Frank slipped the safety-catches of the Brownings to 'FIRE'.

The German fighter began a turn to port some 200 yards ahead of the bomber. Frank took careful aim and when the fighter's turn brought it dead ahead of the Lancaster, he pressed the triggers. The Brownings remained mute and only then did Frank realize that he had omitted to carry out the cocking procedure for each gun. The fighter continued its turn until it was lost to sight. The aircrew braced themselves for a renewed onslaught, but none came. Whether the enemy pilot had seen the blossoming 'chutes of the three crew members from the rear of the bomber and assumed that the rest would follow, which left the German pilot free to find another quarry, will never be known. What is fact is that 'M for Mike' was no longer the target of any fighter.

From his previous position in the bombing well, Frank had seen the tremendous efforts being made to force the control column forward. Once he was satisfied that the enemy fighter had left the area, he extricated himself from the front turret and added his assistance. Gradually, but very reluctantly, the column moved forward until the captain was able to get both feet at the top of the control and exert far greater pressure. Suddenly it was free, affording the first small degree of positive control of the aircraft since the fighter's strike. The pilot was able to bring the Lancaster into a 'straight and level' attitude, but it continued to lose height, albeit at a reduced rate. Then a new problem manifested itself. As soon as the pilot removed his feet from the rudder controls, the aircraft would commence a starboard turn. It required the pilot to apply and maintain maximum and unrelenting pressure on port rudder to direct the aircraft on a comparatively straight course and keep it there.

But the relief from enemy harassment was short-lived for the sorely-tried crew remnants. Without warning, heavy flak-bursts appeared all around the bomber and yet again the Lancaster staggered from the weight of enemy blows, as shrapnel tore through the lower fuselage. There was very little avoiding action that could be taken, given the control situation which obtained in the cockpit, but, mercifully, the flak barrage was not repeated and the Lancaster was left to lick its wounds in comparative peace.

Jack Harrison saw Iveson's very real predicament in the matter of the rudder bar, which was making excessive demands on the captain's strength. He remembered that there was a good length of stout rope stowed in the near proximity of the mid-upper escape hatch. He raced to this position and unwound the full length of this rope and cut it with a Scout knife. Even as he sawed away at the rope, he recalled that the knife had been given to him as a 'Good Luck' charm by a neighbour when he had commenced flying duties and he had conscientiously carried it on every flight. It was the first time he had had occasion to use it in an emergency and he gave mental thanks for it, as it made short work of its task. It would have been a very much more onerous job if he had been forced to use the small penknife supplied for use on flying boots.

He returned to the cockpit area and bent forward into the nose, where Frank Chance was checking the preparations for opening the front escape hatch. He beckoned vigorously and Frank came over to him. Jack tugged at Frank's earpiece and said loudly, 'Tony's having great trouble with the rudders. Lash this length of rope around the port rudder control and then firmly to something in the nose, so that Tony can take the stress off his leg and ankle!' Frank seized the rope and studied the problem for a moment. He made a firm connection with the rudder control, then ran the rope over the substantial camera-mounting in the nose. He worked hard and fast and soon had a very tight bond which he secured with very effective knots. When he was satisfied, he said, on the intercom 'The port rudder is firmly lashed forward now, Tony. You should be able to take the weight off it safely now.'

Iveson gingerly released the pressure off his left leg and was grateful to find that the aircraft continued dead ahead. 'Thanks, Frank!' he called 'I needed that!' and began to massage the feeling back into his limb, which had been under great strain. He took stock of their position the while and then spoke to the remaining crew. 'I feel it is better if we bale out over land. There's a very long sea-crossing ahead and we certainly have no controls for landing. The elevator trim is useless, as the control wheel spins like a Catherine Wheel—and God knows what else is damaged at the rear! Ditching would be almost as great a hazard as landing, and we cannot be sure that the dinghy will be available, with all the damage the aircraft has suffered.'

But Jack Harrison had no intention of spending a period as prisoner-of-war, if it could possibly be avoided. 'Hang on for a while yet, Tony!' he urged, 'The enemy is no longer in contact and things have improved since the last strike.' Taff Phillips lent his voice in support of the navigator's urgent plea. 'Let me go down the back, Tony, and inspect the damage—I can study the situation and maybe restore sufficient control to make landing a possibility!' 'OK, engineer' replied the captain 'Get back there and make an assessment—but please be quick about it and let me know what the score is as soon as you can.'

Taff disconnected himself from the intercom and made his way to the rear. As he climbed the main spar, he noticed that the wireless operator was not in his seat, and it also dawned on him that Les Smith was no longer visible. He slithered and fell as his feet shot from underneath him in the pool of hydraulic oil that fractured pipes had sprayed on to the floor of the aircraft. He picked himself up, cursing loudly, and then began his examination of the trim cables, as his instinct and experience told him that these were the most likely chance of restoring control. He found them hanging loosely in the bomb bay. He managed to retrieve them and traced them to discover which were the elevator and rudder trim lines. He quickly worked out which was the tail-up position and then wrapped the cable around his hand and gave a solid pull. To his delight and relief, the aircraft responded immediately and he felt the nose drop almost immediately. He heard the skipper's voice in his ears. 'What have you done, Taff? What's happening down there?' 'I've located the trouble, skip, and have the trim controls in my hand. Now, if you'll give me adjustment directions as I experiment with them down here, you should get enough control to head for home.' Between them, they effected adjustments until at last Taff was able to secure the trim wires to the aircraft's stringers.

He had been so engrossed in this work, and so pleased with his success that thoughts about the missing members of the crew had been driven from his mind. But, now that his initial emergency task was complete, he remembered noting the non-appearance of Les Smith and Alan Tittle. He looked down the fuselage and saw the rear door swinging wildly to and fro. He made his way towards it, to secure it against further damage and confirmed his earlier conviction that the rear turret was empty. Without further ado, he plugged into the intercom and said 'Skipper!'

'What now?' came Iveson's terse voice. 'Both gunners and the wireless operator have gone!' replied Taff. 'Gone? Gone where?' came the almost disbelieving query. 'Baled out—hit the silk' answered Taff calmly. 'The rear door has had the lock shot off and is swinging in the breeze, so I'll jam that shut with the aircraft axe, and then I'll get into the rear turret and try and see the extent of the damage down this end.' Just before he disconnected the intercom, Taff heard Jack Harrison say to the captain 'Course for Sumburgh is 275, skipper.' He smiled as he felt the aircraft turn smoothly on to the required heading. He was pleased that his efforts had restored a great deal of the control to the pilot, and it was obvious that Jack wasn't allowing 'baling-out' thoughts to linger in the skipper's mind.

He entered the rear turret and traversed slowly from port to starboard, through the full 180 degrees of the turret's travel, stopping to inspect the items of damage, so that he could take full note of their extent and weigh up the effect they would have on their survival chances. There was a gaping hole in the port rudder and fin, and a very large hole in the port side of the tail wing itself. There was a great deal of continuous vibration that worried Taff, lest the tail section should be shaken loose and break off. He centred and locked the turret, then made his way back to the front of the aircraft. On the way, he discovered that the main spar had been severely dented by several shells so that it was jamming against the elevator control tube.

When he regained his normal crew position, he rendered a full report to the skipper, emphasizing the vibration in the tail section and added, 'Might be a good idea to get down as low as reasonably possible in the circumstances, skipper. Then if we do get some warning of the tail section going, at least we'll have a better chance of making a successful ditching.' Iveson nodded and took the Lancaster down to about 400 feet in a shallow dive. The control column appeared to be working normally and again Taff was pleased that his skill and application had given the crew a better chance of survival. They were clear of the land and no one seemed in the least interested in them. The weather was still excellent and their survival prospects had suddenly blossomed.

Jack Harrison had been stunned by Taff's report that three members of the crew were no longer on board. He turned events over in his mind and realized that Tony's 'OK' in acknowledgement of the 'Readiness report' by Ted Wass had been taken to mean that the aircraft was to be abandoned. He was sorry to think that they had lost three very close friends and hoped fervently that they would all have landed safely. He personally did not hold out much hope that they would be able to evade capture and reach Sweden—the terrain and the winter weather was against them, even allowing for help from the Norwegian population. The war couldn't last for many more months, so their detention in a PoW camp would not be all that long. What was serious to their present plight was that there was no way of letting the outside world know of their difficulties. Tony had tried the VHF but it was absolutely dead and had no doubt been smashed during the fighter attacks.

Taff's report about the tailplane and the possibility of ditching occupied their minds. The prospect of ditching in the North Sea without any of the rescue services being aware of the emergency was a daunting one. At that moment Frank Chance came on the intercom, 'Bomb-aimer to navigator. How about trying to set up the wireless set? We could bash out a "Mayday" message a few times, then leave the key clamped down, so that ground stations could get a continuous fix on us from then on!' 'Can you set the wireless up OK, Frank?' asked Jack. 'Well, I expect that Alan just switched it off before toddling down the back' replied Frank, 'The chances are that it is on the Group frequency and would be ready to transmit, once it was warmed up. We've got nothing to lose by trying it, anyway, have we!' 'OK, Frank, come up here and we'll see what we can solve between us. My knowledge of the Morse Code will just about allow me to knock a message out at about six words a minute' answered Jack. The pilot's voice broke in. 'Leave the W/T set alone! The transmission might also be vectored by enemy stations, who might then send out a fighter to finish us off! It's not worth the risk!' Jack shrugged his shoulders and returned to his navigational task.

Taff Phillips had kept busy and alert from the time he had returned to the cockpit. He noticed that the petrol consumption had increased noticeably and that there was vibration in the starboard wing. However, the fuel reserves were causing no worries. The Shetlands loomed on the horizon and the IFF was quickly switched on to warn the look-outs in this very touchy defence area that the aircraft approaching them was really a friendly aircraft! As they came over the rugged coast, the bomb-aimer and navigator combined to get off a rapid succession of Very cartridges, regardless of colour, in order to indicate visually to the ground control that the Lancaster was in an acute state of distress and unable to communicate by VHF or W/T channels. The captain made preparations for a 'straight in, no messing' approach and landing. He dropped the undercarriage and was reassured to receive a green by Aldis lamp from the caravan at the head of the duty runway. The Lancaster had just cleared the high cliff on the approach run and was almost committed to landing, when suddenly a Spitfire on the port side and below the Lancaster, turned sharply to port and dived in to land ahead of the bomber. The control caravan tried to divert the Spitfire with a series of red Very cartridges but the fighter pilot chose to ignore these signals and landed on the runway. The Lancaster crew had no option but to raise the undercarriage and turn off for a fresh approach. The Spitfire should have burst into instant flame from the red-hot torrent of abuse that issued from the mouths of the bomber crew! To have survived all that the enemy and the elements could throw at them only to be wiped out by the selfish stupidity of a brash Spitfire pilot really would have been the most ironic end!

Laboriously, the Lancaster was coaxed around the circuit by the captain, whilst a cascade of green signals and a flashing Aldis 'green' from the caravan told them that their path had been definitely cleared for landing. 'Bomb-aimer and navigator—get back to crash positions, just in case' came the pilot's orders over the intercom. 'Flight engineer, strap yourself in your seat and stand-by to help with this landing.' Jack and Frank obediently assumed their crash positions behind the main spar, whilst Taff secured his straps and waited for the Lancaster to be lined up with the runway. The undercarriage was lowered, but no reassuring green locking lights appeared on the instrument panel. Taff blew the emergency bottle but still the lights did not light. 'I'm going in, undercart or not' said Iveson, and the crew braced themselves for the possible collapse of the undercarriage on contact with the runway. Iveson lined the bomber up with the runway and brought it in perfectly, so that the wheels touched down just beyond the perimeter track and runway junction, for the runway was quite a short one for a Lancaster. As Taff throttled back just before the touch-down, the cockpit horn klaxoned forth. He reacted immediately to the signal, and changed the supercharger 'S' gear to the 'M' gear and he appreciated the reason for the rise in petrol consumption during the return flight.

When the wheels touched, Taff knocked off the petrol cocks. With great skill, no rudder control and very little trim control and with one engine feathered, Iveson coped with three big bounds down the runway, before expertly bringing the Lancaster to a halt without the assistance of brakes on a short runway, without over-running. Despite the lashed full left rudder, the Lancaster finished up with a starboard wheel just off the concrete and on the grass verge!

There was a profound silence inside the aircraft as the four aircrew felt themselves unwinding from the tension they had unconsciously been under for the past few interminable hours. Waves of relief and joy began to suffuse their beings as the realization that they were safe and whole asserted itself. They grinned and laughed aloud, shaking hands vigorously and clapping the pilot delightedly on the shoulder, for it was his consummate skill which had brought them to safety in the very present dangers of the approach and landing. Tony Iveson broke in the general rejoicing, 'Right, Taff, let's get everything switched off and safe, and then get out. I'm not going to put this aircraft anywhere else! They can tow it to wherever they want to!' Jack Harrison gathered up his navigation equipment and gear and made his way to the aircraft door. He removed the axe which had held it secure and allowed the door to swing free, as it was not possible to fasten it back. He placed the aircraft ladder in position and had just descended to the ground, when an ambulance and medical staff car swerved to a halt close to the Lancaster. 'Any wounded on board?' asked a medical officer. 'Not here' replied Jack urbanely 'but there could be a few in Bergen right now!' The ambulance withdrew rapidly, almost disappointed, Jack thought jocularly.

Several other lorries and small vans arrived. By this time, Taff Phillips had brought the undercarriage locking struts from the aircraft and was just placing them in position when he was approached by a Flight Sergeant. 'Are you staying for some time, or have you just put in for refuelling?' he asked. Taff smiled and said, 'Chiefy, if you can have the tailplane repaired in an hour, all we'll need is sufficient fuel to get us down to Lincolnshire!' He accompanied the mystified NCO to the rear of the Lancaster. On the way, Taff noticed that both starboard propellers had several two-inch holes punched through each of them, which gave him the reason for the starboard wing vibration in flight.

The accompanying Flight Sergeant gasped in astonishment as his eyes took in this damage but his mouth dropped open in disbelief when they examined the tail area. Even Taff was shaken as they examined the damage together. The extensive havoc Taff had noticed in flight had been supplemented by the peeling back of the metal fabric during the return flight by the action of the slip-stream. How the tail-section had stayed on Taff and the NCO could only ascribe to a miracle as they silently surveyed the full extent of the damage to its main members. 'This aircraft should not have flown, by all the rules and theories of engineering and flight' muttered the Flight Sergeant, shaking his head in disbelief at what his eyes beheld. 'How was it done?' he went on, turning to Taff. 'By the combined determination of the crew, Chiefy' answered Taff. 'Oh, by the way, the captain would like the Lancaster towed off to wherever the chief technical officer decides would be the best place for it. Might be better to tow it from the front, if possible. Tractor strain on that tail-wheel might well cause the tail section to give up the ghost.' The Flight Sergeant nodded, still gazing at the mayhem before his eyes, 'Yes, we'll see to that straightaway.' He went on 'Where did all that happen, sergeant?' 'Over Bergen, a few hours ago' replied Taff. 'Bergen?' repeated the NCO, 'And you trundled all the way back across the North Sea in that?' and he jerked his head at the Lancaster. 'An excellent aircraft, Chiefy' smiled Taff, 'I can recommend them wholeheartedly!'

A crew wagon, driven by a very pretty WAAF, arrived and the four aircrew loaded all their gear aboard and climbed in after it. They were taken to the station intelligence section and given the cursory pro-forma debriefing that was alone possible for them on a Fighter Command airfield. It was nothing like as searching as the debriefings to which they were normally subjected on a return to their own base. The usual mugs of tea were abundantly available, and Taff was surprised to find that his hand was shaking so much that he had difficulty in keeping his mug of tea still. He wasn't sure if this was reaction to the recent experiences or the close proximity of the very shapely WAAF who had smilingly given him the tea!

A Wing Commander appeared, with top button undone, so Frank assumed he was the CO of the fighter squadron in residence. He apologized most contritely for the moronic behaviour of the Spitfire pilot, who had put their lives in danger so selfishly. 'I made him walk out to your aircraft and examine it thoroughly, both inside and out' he said 'so that he might begin to appreciate what you blokes had been through and surmounted—and how his bloody-mindedness could have draped you all over the Shetland landscape, if your pilot hadn't coped so very magnificently with the overshoot! A good dose of extra duties will bring it home to that young laddie that bad manners can cost lives. I can only apologize on behalf of the whole squadron, which I do without reserve.' 'Thank you' replied Iveson 'It all turned out OK in the end, and we're all safe and sound—but it could have been a bit hairy—still, say no more!'

They were taken to the respective Messes—Tony Iveson and Jack Harrison to the Officers' Mess and Frank Chance and Taff Phillips to the Sergeants' Mess. There they were allocated comfortable quarters, and long hot baths restored them to a more peaceful frame of mind after their protracted ordeal. Excellent meals were ready for them when they reappeared and the fighter boys were so very anxious to make amends for the miscreant that quite a session developed. They were very interested in the running fight with the Fw 190s over Bergen and promised to do their best to repay the score if ever they found themselves over Norway.

Next morning, after a lay-in and a leisurely late breakfast specially sanctioned by the messing officer, they were informed that a Lancaster would be landing from Woodhall Spa after lunch to transport them back to their own airfield. The four of them were duly transported to the Flying Control when the Lancaster was almost due, and they watched Flying Officer Arthur Kell, one of 617's Australian pilots, make his approach and landing in 'F for Freddy'—their own aircraft. To their absolute consternation, they saw one of the Lancaster's wheels strike a wheelbarrow which had been overlooked at the side of the duty runway. The wheelbarrow splintered and its large, tyred wheel careered merrily down the runway in the wake of the Lancaster. 'Oh no!' groaned Jack aloud, 'We'll be here another 24 hours now.'

Arthur Kell taxied his aircraft quickly to the control tower. He kept the Merlins idling as the four aircrew made haste across the intervening grass. The rear door opened and the ladder immediately appeared. Arthur's flight engineer scrambled down it and ran to inspect the Lancaster's undercarriage area. He was joined by Tony Iveson and Taff Phillips. They examined thoroughly but could see no serious damage. A 'thumbs up' sign was given to the watching pilot, and then they all scrambled on board, hoisted in the ladder and made swift tracks for the take-off point, before any Sumburgh personnel decided that they needed to clear the aircraft, too!

Jack Harrison returned to his room in the Petwood which he shared with Jimmy Watson, a Yorkshireman and a 'long-distance' bomb-aimer with 617 Squadron. Jimmy had flown with the great Bunny Clayton DSO, DFC, CGM, and had decided to continue with the Squadron when Bunny had been forcibly 'retired' at the end of July 1943. Jimmy had a tremendous sense of humour. He greeted Jack enthusiastically and then said, 'I had to go round this morning collecting all the items of your shaving gear again. I'd given them away, as Sumburgh were somewhat late in letting us know that you had all landed safely!'

Iveson's crew never flew together again after the Bergen raid. Tony Iveson was posted on 16 February 1945 to No 6 Lancaster Finishing School before going on to undergo training for the reviving BOAC airline. All three of the remaining aircrew were absorbed into other crews and remained with 617 Squadron until the end of the war. Jack Harrison had completed his first tour and started on his second by the time the war finished, and has to be one of the very few aircrew who completed a first tour on 617 Squadron!

In July 1945, Taff Phillips was part of a detachment of aircrew that was flown up to Sumburgh to collect 'M for Mike'. A team of Polish repair specialists had toiled to renovate the Lancaster. It had been fitted with an entirely new tail section, two new engines and three new propellers. The W/T set functioned satisfactorily but no VHF set was fitted. They flew the Lancaster to a maintenance unit for further repairs and that was the last Taff saw or heard of an aircraft which he will always recall with genuine affection.

A WAAF girlfriend of Frank Chance's happened, by sheerest coincidence, to be on teleprinter duty at RAF Chicksands when the teleprinter chattered out the news that the aircraft was overdue and listed the crew, with their ranks and numbers. She managed to get a copy of the message and handed it over to Frank when next they met. It was a souvenir that he kept for many years as a reminder of the day when only the 'know-how' of a competent flight engineer and the skill and application of a pilot saved him from a very uncomfortable time—and perhaps worse! Jack Harrison, Frank Chance and Des 'Taff' Phillips finished the war undecorated. The three members who left the aircraft were all taken prisoner and were returned to the United Kingdom at the cessation of hostilities, having suffered the privations which were the lot of so many 'Kriegies' in the last months of the Second World War.

* * *

Over Bergen, John Pryor brought '*G for George*' round for yet another run on the special target. George Kendrick was suffering the same frustrations as the other bomb-aimers in the matter of target location, due to the smoke, haze and brilliant sunshine. The whole crew heard the staccato warning of 'Fighters!' crackle in their headphones and John had urged his gunners to intensify their search whilst he concentrated on getting the bomb on their allocated target. He was not too worried about the fighter warning, expecting that, in the main, the Mustangs would deal with that menace, but nevertheless it was up to the Lancaster crew to guard against surprise attack.

But the new run petered out, as had the many before it. They had now been over the target area for thirty minutes. The force bombing the U-boat pens had finished their task and were even now streaming back for Woodhall Spa. John buttoned his VHF and spoke to the master bomber. 'Six abortive runs on the target so far, sir! Any further instructions?' He waited and heard Johnny Fauquier's voice, 'Try one more run then stand-by! I say again—try one more run and then stand-by!' He acknowledged the order and put the Lancaster into a wide sweep to bring its nose round for a final run on the target. At that moment, Shirley's voice broke in urgently on the intercom. 'Fighter approaching from the starboard quarter, skipper! Stand-by.'

John tensed himself for the action and almost immediately he heard, 'Enemy, skip! Diving turn to starboard!' John Pryor was somewhat disconcerted by this instruction, having been expecting to go into a corkscrew, but he obeyed the rear gunner's instruction and put the Lancaster into a diving turn to starboard. He heard the chattering of the four Brownings and obeyed the evasion instructions as they stemmed from the gunner. At that moment, a giant fist seemed to strike the bomber on the port side. Instinctively, John looked out to port and saw chunks flying off the port outer engine. He was in time to see another Fw 190 breaking away, and speedily appreciated that this fighter had been presented with a 'sitting duck' target by its unobserved and stealthy approach whilst their action against the starboard attack had been in progress. 'Feather that engine!' he barked to the engineer, and continued to study the damage on the port side.

He glanced at his engine dials and saw that he was not getting much power from his port inner, although its propeller was still turning. Both starboard engines were, however, contributing full power. Suddenly, he sensed that he had lost a great deal more power and turned back from his damage study to find that the engineer, in the gripping panic that had inevitably seized him when the attack started, had feathered the starboard outer by mistake. 'Re-start that engine and feather the PORT outer, engineer!' he stormed. The flight engineer, appalled at his mistake, immediately commenced to re-start the starboard outer. Unfortunately, in his determination to right his error, he held the button in until the engine revs had passed the danger 1,800 rpm mark and the engine went into overspeeding, from which there was no return and the engine power was lost to the pilot permanently. The stricken engineer gasped at his elementary error but it was now irretrievable. He took a grip on himself and at last feathered the port engine, but John was left with an efficient port inner engine, a partly-functioning starboard inner, an overspeeding port outer and a useless starboard outer—not a pleasant prospect with two enemy fighters intent on their destruction.

There was a roar of rage from the rear turret as the port outer engine lost its output in the attack and the hydraulic supply to the rear turret failed. Shirley was enraged that a second fighter had stolen in unnoticed and he seized the manual cranking handle for the turret and turned it quickly, endeavouring to bring his turret around so that he could fire at this second foe. The fighter, however, had broken off its attack before the rear-gunner could get a sight on it. A row of neat holes had appeared in the fuselage above the navigator's head as he sat riveted by the churning sensations his emotions had released under the stress of the enemy attack. Wireless operator Albert Hepworth had been subject to internal retching and mind-searing fear when the strikes were made on the aircraft. Instinctively, he had screwed himself up into a tight ball on the wireless operator's seat, to make as small a target as possible, but, even as he did so, his reason said to him, 'This is a bloody silly thing to do!' He gained some scrap of comfort from the contortion, nevertheless, and the futility of his action did a great deal to force down the quaking fear that had seized him.

John Pryor now had his hands full. The survival of his crew now depended solely on his skill as a pilot and his efficiency as a captain. Both outer engines were out of commission and the port inner was offering only fifty per cent efficiency, and the enemy fighters were re-positioning for further attacks. No gunnery defence was now available, except from the front turret and there was very little chance of the fighters making head-on attacks from their present vantage point. John put the nose down and dived for the fiord below whilst Shirley maintained a running commentary on the intentions of the fighters, sweating within his suit as he cranked the manual handle to turn the turret and keep the fighters in view. With uncannily brilliant airmanship which excited the silent admiration of the unhappy flight engineer strapped in the seat beside him, he coolly avoided any further damage to the aircraft from the successive attacks by the enemy fighters.

At what seemed to be merely feet above the surface of the fiord, he pointed the port wing downwards and stood the crippled Lancaster 'upright like a flag-pole' as the engineer was to describe it graphically to Albert Hepworth when they were in German custody later that day. He whipped the aircraft round and caused the frustrated German pilots to over-shoot their runs. He coaxed power from his two remaining engines, and was able to open the bomb doors, so that the bomb aimer could jettison the Tallboy. The bomb fell to the west of Bergen and its explosion on an uninhabited hillside was reported by another Squadron pilot, Squadron Leader Powell, at his debriefing. Relieved of the weight of the Tallboy, 'G for George' spurted for height. John Pryor utilized this newly-won height to skirt skilfully around the mountainous terrain and the sheer cleft sides of the fiords, defeating every thrust of the persistent enemy. Yet all the time his mind was clinically assessing their situation and prospects.

'What's the fuel state, engineer?' he asked, after completing yet another manoeuvre to deny their persistent enemies any advantage. 'We've lost fuel from the tanks in each wing' replied the engineer instantly, 'Could possibly make Scotland, but certainly not Woodhall.' 'Thank you' replied the pilot and continued over the intercom 'All crew prepare for a crash-landing! I say again, all crew prepare for a crash-landing!' He counted the individual responses to this order and satisfied himself that all crew members understood his intention. He felt that his chances of reaching Scotland with his present power state were not good, even if their luck held and they avoided further damage from the fighters. He began to search for a suitable spot to set the Lancaster down.

Albert had been sitting in front of his wireless set, very conscious of his inability to help his captain in the struggle for survival. His fear had subsided somewhat in the face of their continued survival. When he had acknowledged the crash-landing order, he clamped down his transmitting key with the set on transmit, although he had very little faith in the British rescue services being able to do anything other than pick up the signal. He removed his parachute harness and left it on the seat before clambering over the main spar to knock off the upper escape hatch, which was his responsibility. He then settled himself in the crash-position allocated to him in the drills, with his back against the main spar and facing the rear of the aircraft. He was soon joined by the gunners. Their move from their operational positions had naturally taken them off the intercom and they awaited the arrival of the navigator, who would plug himself into the solitary intercom socket in the area and keep them informed of developments.

When Harold Ellis received his captain's preparatory order, he detonated the Gee equipment, before scooping up all his navigational equipment and gear into his large canvas bag. He put his sextant into the bag and then fixed the whole securely under the navigation table, so that it would not become a missile on the crash-landing impact. Meanwhile, John Pryor had been studying the topography of the area and it became very apparent to him that a crash-landing was out of the question. He needed to gain what height he could and put the crew out on their 'chutes. The question was just how much height he could gain for he could feel the power dwindling slowly from the port inner engine. He snapped on his intercom and broadcast, 'Cancel the crash-landing order! Cancel the crash-landing order! Prepare to abandon aircraft! I say again, Prepare to abandon aircraft!'

The navigator had seen the crew members move to crash positions and realized that they would not have received the captain's latest instructions. He disconnected his own intercom and moved quickly to the crash-position area. He lifted Albert's earpiece and said, 'Orders changed! We're now baling out! Tell the others—now that they are all forward, it'll be better if we all go out from the front escape hatch!' Harold Ellis returned to his navigation position and Albert informed the two gunners of the change and the front escape hatch plan. They immediately buckled on the harnesses and moved down the fuselage to recover their 'chutes from the stowages. Albert returned to his seat and resumed his harness, in preparation for the abandonment. He saw that John Pryor was clawing for height and was having some difficulty in persuading the Lancaster to climb. He also saw that one of the German fighters had ranged up very close alongside and slightly above the bomber. The German pilot seemed to be making signs to them to bale out. After a while he flew away and came back to make a dummy attack before gesticulating again. Albert went on to the intercom. 'Skipper, shall I fire off a couple of reds to indicate that we are in distress and will be baling out?' 'Might as well' answered the pilot, 'Just a bit more height and then we can start to go—although I think that bod is trying to tell us that if we don't land, he'll shoot us down and I have no intention of presenting the Germans with a Lancaster, even a shot-up one!' Albert selected the cartridges from the stowage above his head and fired them from the Very pistol in its action station near the astro-dome. The fighter wheeled away and Pryor turned the Lancaster on to an inland heading.

George Kendrick had fully opened the front escape hatch and Albert could see the rugged snow-covered Norwegian landscape slipping by beneath the open hatch. At that moment, the navigator, who had been concerned at the thought of the Loran set falling into enemy hands, unbolted the whole set from its mounting and carried it to the hatch. He tossed it over the head of the bomb-aimer seated on the lower step. The set was seized by the slipstream and whirled instantly from sight.

John Pryor had coaxed the Lancaster up to some 1,500 feet above the ground level and his experience told him that he would not get much more height from his labouring engines and time was running out. 'Get ready to leave when I give the word' he said curtly. 'No hesitation and don't impede the man behind! Don't rush things once you're out! Count the usual "Ten" before you pull the ripcord. Stand-by!' He turned the aircraft on to a seaward heading, waited until they were approaching a large expanse of land and then said 'GO!' George Kendrick was the first to leave and, although Albert's view of his departure was somewhat obscured by the other aircrew, it seemed to Albert that George had left the aircraft rather awkwardly. Warrant Officer Winston launched himself cleanly through the gaping hatch, to be quickly followed by 'Shirley' Temple, Paddy Armstrong, and then Harold Ellis. All the while, alone in the cockpit, John Pryor strained to hold the height so hardly won, but the aircraft was gradually losing altitude. Albert was the last crew member to go. He refrained from making any parting gesture but hurried to the escape hatch, praying the while that the man to whom they all owed this chance of life would be able to save his own. Albert followed the other aircrew into space. The abandonment had gone smoothly and precisely.

Albert felt the impact of the bitterly cold air as soon as he had left the aircraft. He pulled the ripcord and the terrific deceleration as the canopy opened above him made him feel as if he had been hung. The jerk dislodged small pieces from behind his bottom teeth and the area under the lobes of his ears, where ears and face met, were cut and bled quite profusely. Once he had recovered from the initial shock, he enjoyed the sensation of falling through the still air. He managed to pick up the billowing 'chute of one of his comrades against the virgin whiteness of the terrain. Of the other five there was no sign. He swung round to find the Lancaster. It had turned so that it was on the shortest possible run to the sea. It seemed to Albert that it had lost quite a bit of height—perhaps it was more damaged that John Pryor had indicated. He saw something hurtle from the aircraft and watched with a prayer on his lips. The 'chute was scarcely open when the figure struck the ground. He was unable to watch further as he became aware that the ground was approaching him at a greatly-increased speed. He did a rapid revision course, searching his mind for the instructed way to land.

He had just about recalled the drill when he struck the ground with quite a jolt that knocked the wind out of him. He staggered backwards for a couple of yards and the 'chute collapsed around him. The silence was very marked. He was completely alone in what appeared to be a small hollow, some fifty yards by twenty yards, perched on the top of some high ground. He operated the quick-release catch on his harness and slipped it off. His evasion training asserted itself and he quickly gathered up his 'chute and harness, and buried it in the soft snow. He scrambled out of the hollow and looked keenly about him. He observed a figure about 200 yards away from where he was standing. The figure seemed familiar and Albert removed the whistle from its fastening at the collar of his battle-dress and gave a short blast. The shrill sound cut the silence like a whetted knife. The scurrying figure halted and turned. Albert waved and received an answering wave. It was Harold Ellis and his delight was obvious.

Once Hepworth had cleared the aircraft, John Pryor began the preparations to leave himself. He turned the Lancaster on to the shortest heading for the open sea and tried to engage the automatic pilot, but in this he was singularly unsuccessful. He realized that the engine outputs were insufficient to supply the requisite minimum pressures. His attempts to engage 'George' had cost him precious height, but he was determined to keep his aircraft out of the hands of enemy experts, and was particularly anxious not to divulge the Squadron and aircraft letters. He moved from his seat endeavouring to keep the control column steady and discovered that the aircraft tended to put its nose down when the control was released. He stayed until he was certain that the aircraft would find a watery grave and then propelled himself through the lower escape hatch. He knew that he was perilously close to the minimum safety height for safe 'chute opening and pulled the ripcord as soon as he felt the icy embrace of the atmosphere.

His headlong fall was scarcely checked when he hit the earth. Fortunately, he landed in a large snowdrift which effectively cushioned his fall and certainly saved him from serious injury to ankles and legs. He had landed on an outcrop of ground, raised above the surrounding area and was relieved to see that the aircraft was droning on in a gentle dive well over the sea. He felt the bitter cold biting into his body. Like most of the aircrew in the forward area of the Lancaster, he had not been wearing his Irvin jacket for the operation. The combination of the very effective forward heating of the aircraft, added to the warmth of the winter sunshine had induced him to undo his battledress top and remove his tie. He buttoned up as quickly as he could, but was shivering well before he had finished.

He buried his harness but needed the silk of his parachute to protect him from the freezing cold that was engulfing his being. Quickly he swathed the silk around himself and felt the warmth creeping back into his frame. He remembered with longing the warm protective greatcoat he had flung so carelessly on the rest bed. How useful that would have been! Then the thought dawned on him that he would need to buy a new greatcoat when he returned to England and the RAF! When he had regained his composure he took stock of his position, and decided to set off in an easterly direction away from the coast, desperate to obtain whatever help might be forthcoming from the civil population and, hopefully, to give the Germans a run for their money if ultimate capture awaited him.

* * *

Norvald Soetre, on the island of Fosnøy, had been an interested eyewitness of the running battle between the Lancaster and the two

German fighters. He saw the bomber to the east over the Masfjord mountain range, apparently looking for a suitable landing area in the snow, but it seemed to abandon this quest and turned westwards towards the coastline. Smoke streamed from the aircraft as it circled above Fosnøy at low altitude and travelling quite slowly. Two German fighters were around the bomber, appearing to be trying to force it to land at Herdla. Norvald saw the crew abandon the Lancaster, it turned south over Austrheim and then over Hjartas.

He was observing the action from a window in the Municipal Hall and lost sight of the aircraft when it disappeared behind the hills. It was quite low. It reappeared over Aras and the pilot parachuted. He came down on a hill west of the Municipal Hall and some two hundred metres from the road. Norwald and another Norwegian ran outside and down the road to meet the pilot. He recalls a well-built figure walking downhill in the snow and it struck him that he did not appear to be in the least afraid. They were joined by more and more people and Pryor asked to speak to the mayor, who stepped forward. They had some conversation and he directed that the crew should be gathered in the sheriff's office. However, the aircrew walked around quite freely for some time. There was some discussion of possible help from the Resistance, as several of the men present had connections with the movement, but it seemed that John Pryor was against an attempt to hide out, for fear of vicious German reprisals against the local civilians.

Another eyewitness has a bizarre story to tell. After the pilot had left the aircraft, the 'plane continued in a south-westerly direction, with the two German fighters in attendance. It is not clear if one of the fighters made a further attack on the bomber, thinking it was trying to get away, or if the pilot deliberately rammed it, but in any case, there was a terrific explosion which involved both aircraft and the wreckage plummeted into the icy sea, some five miles off the coast. The other Fw 190 circled the wreckage, no doubt searching for his comrade and alerting the German rescue services. Unfortunately for this pilot, he stayed too long and his fuel began to run out. He was making his way back to his base on Herdla when his tanks emptied and he crashed into the Hjeltefjord. He was picked up eventually by a German naval vessel and rushed to hospital, but died due to the exposure his body suffered through the prolonged immersion in the icy winter water. Thus, both tormentors of 'G for George' failed to survive to enjoy their triumph.

Six of John Pryor's crew were quite quickly rounded up by the Germans. Norwegians had speedily reached both Albert Hepworth and Harold Ellis and they were soon reunited with Warrant Officer Winston. There was talk of helping them to evade capture, but there was no organized 'underground' as in France and the other occupied Continental countries. Sweden was a forlorn hope with 400 miles of inhospitable terrain between them and the frontier. The news reached them that a squad of over forty Wehrmacht troops had been deployed in the immediate area, as the Germans had obtained a very accurate estimate of the area of their landing. Reluctantly, the Norwegians agreed that it was safer for all if the airmen were handed over to the searching Germans. The three aircrew agreed readily, for it would have been madness to put the lives of their hosts and helpers in unnecessary jeopardy. They were taken to the office of the local sheriff, which turned out to be the general store, post office and civic centre. They never met the sheriff but two women made them very comfortable and gave them very welcome hot food.

One woman, who spoke some English, asked them to write down their names and addresses, with a brief message. She assured them that the details would be transmitted to England at the first opportunity. In return, the aircrew handed over their silken maps and the Norwegian currency notes from their escape kits. They were warned by telephone that the Germans were on the way to collect them, but were assured that the German officer in charge was a reasonable type and they should come to no physical harm. Albert also learned that George Kendrick's 'chute had not opened and that the bomb-aimer was lying in a critical condition in a village some miles away.

They were duly collected by the German squad and eventually found themselves on a rough quay, awaiting a boat which would take them to Bergen, on the first stage of their journey to Dulag Luft, the interrogation camp outside Frankfurt, in Germany. John Pryor was also brought to the quay, still wrapped in his 'chute. He informed them that a German officer had told him that George Kendrick had apparently struck his chin on the rim of the escape hatch when he had leapt from the Lancaster. This had rendered him immediately unconscious, unable to operate his 'chute and he suffered very severe injuries on landing.

Norvald Soestre saw the beginning of this tragedy, as he was horrified to see that the 'chute of the first man to leave the aircraft did not open, and he crashed to the ground in some dry marshland, about three hundred metres west of the school-house of the village of Little Lindas. He landed on his back and heels, and his knees struck his jaw with the force of the impact. He came down on snow-covered marshland, and sustained appalling injuries, including a broken spine and serious head damage. He was carried very carefully into the school-house, where he was devotedly nursed by the schoolmaster, Mr Anton Unvoy, together with the local doctor and many women from the village. When the Germans came, they were persuaded to leave Kendrick where he was. He was in no condition to be moved and the Germans could see that the injuries were fatal. George died two days later and the villagers wanted to bury him in their own graveyard. They made preparations for the funeral service, and Mr Georg Stellberg composed a very touching tribute as a last salute to the young airman, which was set to music. However, before the internment could take place, the Germans returned and removed the body to Bergen. George Kendrick now rests in the Mollendal Cemetery, in the area set aside as a British Military Cemetery.

The nine survivors from the Lancasters met up for varying periods during the trek to Frankfurt. They endured a few months of prisoner-of-war privation before being released by the advancing Americans and repatriated. Three weeks after reaching home, Albert Hepworth married his girlfriend, Joan.

The news of George Kendrick's tragic death caused great sadness on the Squadron when the news filtered through before the end of the war. The Squadron aircrew recalled his epic fight to regain aircrew standard of fitness after suffering almost fatal injuries to his head in the training accident in the southern Wash area on the night of 20 January 1944. He had rejoined 617 Squadron for operational duty in September 1944, determined to finish his second tour, although he could have retired honourably from the operational scene after the accident. The Squadron watched with quiet pride as he flew operationally, without seeking any special consideration. The manner of his untimely death was a cause of great regret to a group of men who had come to terms with death in its most violent forms and learned to live with that ever-present prospect.

* * *

Aware of the Bomber Command operation against Bergen in daylight on 12 January 1944, Coastal Command had detached Warwick aircraft '*G for George*' of 279 Squadron to the airfield at Sumburgh, on stand-by air-sea rescue call. The Warwick carried a Mark 2 Airborne Lifeboat and two sets of Lindholme gear in the bomb-bay and was captained by Pilot Officer Duthie.

At 14.00 hours a preparatory warning for 'Scramble' was received at Sumburgh, as reports were being received of a ditched Lancaster some thirty miles off the Norwegian coast in the Bergen area. These reports were being transmitted by two Lancasters who were circling the area. The ditching position afforded by each Lancaster provided an excellent cross-check and the navigator was informed that the position was accurate. When the Warwick crew had obtained all the information possible, they adjourned to their aircraft and awaited the 'Take-off' signal.

The Warwick became airborne at 14.43 hours, heading directly for the scene of the ditching. During the flight, a message from their control told them to expect homing assistance of five minutes duration, with a ten minute break, during the run to the target area. Pilot Officer Duthie kept the needles of his W/T homing indicator intersecting on the instrument datum and was pleased to see that the course demanded to keep them thus was almost co-incident with the course his navigator had calculated. It was a perfect flying day, with no weather worries at all and very little wind, from the sea surface indications. They were adequately warned about the cessation of the homing signal but by that time they were well committed to an accurate course for their destination.

Almost on cue, a Lancaster was sighted in the water. It was almost submerged and the crew was standing on the fuselage. No aircraft dinghy was visible. After the normal initial 'dummy run', the airborne lifeboat was successfully dropped at 16.05 hours, about 200 yards upwind of the distressed crew, who were now in the water as the Lancaster had finally sunk. They were making their way towards the lifeboat but some were making heavy weather of it and so Duthie decided to stream a Lindholme gear across their path. He lined the Warwick up for the drop and headed steadily on the cross track. The gear was released but, to his horror, instead of streaming out as designed, the Lindholme remained in one bulky package and sank like a stone! He cursed the incorrect installation of the gear and rapidly retraced his path, to release his second gear. Unbelievably, this gear behaved in precisely the same way and disappeared beneath the waves without operating. Suddenly, one of the lookouts warned 'Fighter! Fighter!' and Duthie caught sight of a Fw 190 investigating the area. It was almost last light but he was able to ascertain that one of the ditched aircrew had managed to climb into the lifeboat, whilst the others were still making their way towards it or were apparently treading water. He took his aircraft low on the sea, so that it would not present a silhouette against the sun in the west, opened the throttles and quickly took his unarmed aircraft from the scene.

Coastal Command laid on a night search, using a Catalina aircraft and another fitted with a Leigh Light in the nose. The datum of the search had been proved by the Warwick and both aircraft searched the area diligently throughout the night, right up to the Norwegian coast, without finding a trace of the sturdy lifeboat or receiving any signals from the sea surface that could have been expected, considering the very adequate supplies of pyrotechnics with which the lifeboats were stocked.

The calm and sunny weather continued next day and Coastal Command mounted an intensive search with three Warwick aircraft, under strong fighter cover, within the ditching area throughout the hours of daylight. Three Anson aircraft of 1693 Flight from Sumburgh carried out an additional search for survivors. These aircraft were airborne at 10.23 hours and landed at 14.06 without finding a trace of the missing crew. The search was called off when night fell. The non-discovery of the lifeboat itself caused the staff at Coastal Command headquarters to come to the conclusion that the crew had been picked up by the German rescue service, who would have taken the lifeboat in tow.

But that did not prove to be the case. Nothing more was heard of any member of Ian Ross' crew until on 13 March 1944, the body of the wireless operator, Flying Officer Ray Ellwood DFM, was found in the sea by a fisherman at the island of Slyngen, in the small Asvaer group of islands. Originally, the body was buried in the Nesna Civil Cemetery, but as maintenance of the grave proved impossible there, the Commonwealth War Graves Commission had it moved to the Trondheim (Stavne) Cemetery where it was reburied in the British sector. The University of Bergen investigated the whole circumstances and came to the conclusion that the body was carried northward in the drift of the Norwegian Coastal Current. None of the other six bodies was ever discovered. One of the mysteries of this situation is why the efficient German rescue service did not react. The Fw 190 pilot, who caused Jimmy Castagnola to seek cloud cover must have seen the plight of the ditched crew and could have been expected to have reported it. Did the damage done by the Bergen operation affect the rescue service, so that no ship could be sent out to the distressed crew? Or were they simply left to their fate?

No one can underestimate the bodily damage that immersion in the sea in those latitudes in winter can inflict. Life expectancy in such conditions was put at not more than fifteen minutes. The crew had been exposed to bitter weather for three hours or more before the Lancaster sank and left them in the icy water, so their resistance had been lowered before their immersion. It can be safely assumed that it was Ian Ross who was seen in the lifeboat by the Warwick crew as they turned for safety. His appreciation of his responsibilities as captain would have made that certain, and his outstanding ability as a swimmer would confirm it. Conditions were against the crew's survival but the remaining unanswered mystery is whatever happened to the sturdy lifeboat? If Ian had been able to release the three huge parachutes on which the lifeboat was dropped, his next action would have been to start the efficient petrol engine and take the lifeboat to his crew members, afloat in their inflated Mae Wests. If he had been overtaken by the effects of his long swim in the icy water, and unable to release the parachutes, then they would have acted as a drag anchor and kept the lifeboat more or less stationary in the calm, almost windless conditions that prevailed on that day and the following day. The datum point was far enough off the Norwegian coast to preclude the possibility of waves bearing the lifeboat to its destruction on the rock-strewn, craggy Norwegian coast during the night of 12/13 January and with the ideal conditions prevailing, the intensive sea search could reasonably have been expected to locate the lifeboat. There are no Luftwaffe records available for Norway after 1941, according to the Military Archives Office in Freiburg, so no help has been possible from that source. It is now probable that the full truth of this affair will never be discovered and it will remain one of the minor mysteries of the war.

Extracts from the official war diary of Admiral von Schrader, commanding the west coast of Norway indicate that the U-boat pens received three direct hits, each of which pierced the roof, which was 2½ to 3½ metres of reinforced concrete. Several workshops, all the offices, many walls and parts of the frontage were destroyed. Two U-boats were slightly damaged but others were untouched. Two men of the Todt Organization were killed and about twelve others wounded. The minesweeper *M1* in Eidsvaag Bay was hit on the stern by a large bomb. The vessel turned turtle and sank within a minute. Three crew members were killed, four badly wounded and ten others wounded. Seventeen others were posted missing. A large bomb exploded close to the German tramp steamer *Olga Siemens* (3,347 grt) causing a bad leakage. The vessel was beached in Sandviken Bay.

Luftwaffe sources admitted the loss of two Fw 190s from 9/JG 5, one of the fighter squadrons operating from Herdla. Both pilots, Unteroffizier Kirchner and Feldwebel Lieber, were lost. The body of Feldwebel Lieber was recovered and is buried at Bergen. An underground radio report to Britain on 13 January reads 'Allied raid on Bergen today seems successful. From observers (second-hand) is reported one destroyer sank in Byfjorden. Bombs hit bunkers at Laksevaag. Excellent. Civil Air Defence says no civils killed or hurt.'

The 617 crews were bitter at the loss of their comrades and very scathing about the protection offered by the escorting Polish Mustangs. It was in sharp contrast to that provided by Mustangs in the latter months of 1944 for daylight operations by the Squadron. The crews averred that once the Polish pilots had the scent of Germans in their nostrils, they completely forgot their role and dived away to beat up the ground defences and kill as many Germans as possible. Werner Gayko, the former CO of 9/JG5, was very surprised to learn in 1978 that there were Mustangs in the area and stated that not one of the Fw 190 pilots engaged that day reported sighting any Mustangs.

The escorting Mustang squadron was No 315, under Squadron Leader Anders. Thirteen Mustangs took off from Peterhead at 10.45 hours and rendezvoused with the Lancasters. Two Mustangs aborted during the flight and returned to Peterhead with mechanical trouble. The remaining Mustangs landed back at Peterhead betwen 14.35 and 15.00 hours. Squadron Leader Ander's post-operational report is interesting. 'Extreme difficulty experienced in escorting the bombers as they bombed the target approaching from different directions. Heavy and light intense inaccurate flak was encountered over the target area. *WEATHER* Scottish coast to 100 miles out. . . Two tenths cloud at 500 feet. *TARGET* Clear with slight industrial haze. Visibility very good.' This report contains no mention of the fighter opposition encountered by the bombers and it can be concluded that the briefing of the fighter pilots prior to the operation failed to prepare them for the very present possibility that the bombing would last for some considerable time. In similar circumstances in 1944, Mustangs wheeled and turned on station above their charges maintaining a vigilant protection for as long as the attacking bombers so required.

The entry in the official German War Diary regarding the sinking of the minesweeper *M1* proved to contain an error in the matter of the location of the sinking. A Norwegian eye-witness observed the 'one ship, one aircraft and one bomb' incident from start to finish. The action happened outside Eidsvaag Bay, a little south of the entrance to the bay and about 600 yards from the shore.

Some 617 Squadron personalities

Squadron Leader Donald Alexander Bell
DFC (RCAF)

No one could say that Don Bell had not been anxious to get into World War 2. He enrolled in the Officers' Training Course at HMCS York on 4 September 1939. In January 1940, he enlisted in the 48th Highlanders, Canadian Militia Regiment. At the age of 25, he left his employment with General Steel Wares Limited in January 1941 to enlist as aircrew in the RCAF. He revealed the injuries he had suffered in a motorcycle accident in 1931 and was rejected. Three weeks later he made another attempt with amended answers to medical questions and was accepted.

After a spell at Trenton, he moved to Initial Training School at Victoriaville, Quebec Province and was directed to observer training, on the strength of his maths ability. He moved to the Air Observers' School, Portage la Prairie, Manitoba, for navigation training and was delighted that this complete change of environment warded off the heavy attacks of hay fever to which he was normally subject in August and September each year. He went to the Bombing and Gunnery School at Macdonald, Manitoba to complete full courses successfully in each skill in November 1941 and obtain his air observer brevet. His final course in Canada was at Rivers, Manitoba, where he completed an astro-navigation course in January 1942, with the ground temperature seldom rising above minus forty degrees Fahrenheit.

Don arrived at the Bournemouth Reception Centre in February 1942 and was posted to the Advanced Flying Unit at RAF Millom, Cumberland in March. This course was followed by posting to No 16 Operational Training Unit, RAF Upper Heyford, Oxfordshire in April, flying Wellington 1Cs. In June 1942, at RAF North Luffenham, Rutland, Don was crewed with Art Jackson from Vancouver and posted to No 158 Squadron at RAF Eastmoor, Yorkshire, flying Halifax 1s. Art Jackson had difficulty in coping with four-engined bombers and the crew was posted to No 425 Squadron, forming at RAF Dishforth, Yorkshire, flying Wellington IIIs.

In September 1942, Don began his first operational tour. After a few mining operations, the emphasis turned to daylight raids on Emden and Wilhelmshaven, which were costly and quickly discontinued. After surviving an emergency crash at RAF Rufforth, Yorkshire, Don's crew were given three days leave. They went to London and into the Canadian YMCA Club at Earls Court to locate successfully a traditional Christmas dinner. This circumstance also led to Don meeting Angela, the girl he was later to wed so happily. Angela helped in the running of the YMCA in her spare time. She was also employed as a private secretary in the Shell-Mex building on the Embankment.

The Battle of the Ruhr had been joined and was decidedly no picnic for the Wellington crews, whilst targets like Frankfurt, Mannheim and Stuttgart meant long flying slogs. In May 1943, six Wellington squadrons, equipped with khaki-camouflaged aircraft, were transferred to North Africa. Don's squadron was based in the desert, thirty miles inland from Sousse and Sfax, and south of Kairovan. The area was really unfit for human habitation in the summer months and the last Arabs were pulling out as the Wellingtons arrived! The Luftwaffe never 'recce-ed' that area, but concentrated on the established airfields along the coast. The 'secret' Wellington squadrons inflicted great damage on the ports of Reggio and Messina a month before the invasion of Sicily. Their attention then switched to the docks at Palermo and Naples.

Don finished his first tour in early August 1943 with a total of forty trips. Twenty-five of these had been with Bomber Command and the remaining fifteen with the British North-West African Air Force. He returned to the United Kingdom in the Dutch liner *Christian Huygens*. No 22 Operational Training Unit, RAF Wellesbourne Mountford became Don's base as a staff instructor in mid-September 1943. It was here that he met Bill Duffy and rapidly became aware that trouble seemed to associate itself continuously with Duffy. Bill Duffy was a staff pilot and absolutely fed up with the routine. He was raising a crew to join No 617 Squadron, an apparently 'suicide' outfit, called upon to perform tasks that greatly appealed to Duffy. However, the Canadian who had agreed to take the navigator post in the crew suddenly decided that the United Kingdom was not a healthy spot for him and rapidly organized for himself a pilot's course in Canada, disappearing only days before the civil Police arrived at Wellesbourne Mountford to make enquiries about him with regard to a fracas in Birmingham. Don agreed to replace him in the crew but when the posting notice came through in January 1944, Don's name had been omitted from the list. Bomber Command regulations stipulated a minimum of six months break between two separate tours and Don was in his fourth month of his rest from operations. He made application to take the proffered month's leave in Canada.

However, in late January he received a telephone call, telling him to be out by the runway at 11.00 hours with all his kit, to be picked up by a 617 Squadron aircraft. A Lancaster appeared on the dot, landing downwind and coming to a very smart halt. Don hauled himself and his kit aboard and was amazed to find that the sole person on board was the pilot, Bill Suggitt. Bill immediately opened up all four engines and took off directly for Woodhall Spa, rarely more than twenty feet above the ground. This was Don's introduction to 617 Squadron and Danny Walker was to tell him later that Bomber Command, unable to get a suitably qualified navigator to complete Duffy's crew, had waived their own regulations and authorized Don's posting.

'Duffy's mob' began operations with 617 on 10 March 1944, against a military target in the St Etienne area of France. By late June, Don had completed a total of sixty operations. With 617, he had operated against the Paris marshalling yards in April, Brunswick, Munich, Operation Taxable and the Saumur Tunnel, as well as the V3 sites in the Pas de Calais. He had also logged three 'Boomerangs'. He was awarded a Distinguished Flying Cross in July 1944.

Leonard Cheshire and most of the long-serving aircrew had been 'forcibly' removed from 617 in late July 1944 and these postings left only one target-marking Mosquito crew on the squadron. Willie Tait assumed the role, using Danny Walker and some other navigators to complete his crew, as required, and Bill Duffy and Don Bell stepped up to fill the other vacancy. Bill Duffy was in his element with this aircraft. Their first Mosquito operation was on 31 July in daylight against a rocket storage site at Rilly-la-Montagne, as back-up markers to Willie Tait. Willie decided that the target did not require to be marked in the very favourable weather conditions. On 4 August, with Willie flying the Mustang in a marker role, Duffy and Don were the Mosquito back-up again. The target was a bridge near Etaples but a malfunction produced no results when Duffy attempted to mark the target with smoke-bombs.

Bill Duffy practised dive-bombing continuously at the Wainfleet range, to reach marking perfection. Don found his stomach unable to face lunch after these morning gyrations. On 7 August 1944 he said 'Hell, Duffy, you can see Wainfleet from Woodhall! I'm going to enjoy a lunch for once and get ready for tonight.' Flying Officer Phil Ingleby jumped at the opportunity of a Mosquito flight and took Don's place. Soon after 11.00 hours on that fateful day, a stunned 617 learned that Mosquito 'N' (*NT 202*) had crashed during dive-bombing practice at Wainfleet and both Bill Duffy and Phil Ingleby had been killed instantly.

Don crewed with the American pilot Nick Knilans DSO, DFC for the first *Tirpitz* raid, flying out to Russia on 11 September 1944 for a hair-raising experience he will never forget. On 17 October he was posted to the RCAF 'R' Depot for repatriation, arriving in Canada in late November. He became a 'personnel counsellor' in the RCAF and this duty allowed him to get back to London in May 1945 to assist the repatriation and demobilization procedures. He married Angela in London a week after VJ-Day.

Don was one of the comparatively few RCAF officers to be offered a permanent commission in the peacetime Service, being granted the rank of Flight Lieutenant. He participated in the geodetic survey of North

America, navigating Lancasters and specially supercharged Dakotas right up to the geographic North Pole, at 20,000 feet. In the Korean War, he navigated North Star aircraft out of Washington State, via the Aleutians, into Japan and Korea as part of the American airlift. VIPs were carried on the outward journeys and stretcher-wounded on the return, which was made via Wake Island, Hawaii and Northern California—70 hours flying per round trip. Don was detached on exchange posting to RAF Air Ministry Intelligence from 1951 to 1953. During this tour, he was detailed to report to the commanding officer of RAF Waddington, Lincolnshire and found himself in the presence of Group Captain Willie Tait. In 1962 Don prepared the intelligence draft for the Cabinet Defence Committee in relation to the Cuban Crisis. This was the first time that the committee had met in peacetime. Don kept up his flying hours throughout his career and qualified for flying pay, right up to the time of his retirement from the RCAF in June 1963, with the rank of Squadron Leader.

Don joined the firm of Matthews and Company to learn the brokerage business. His aptitude and application allowed him to survive several reorganizations and three major mergers and, approaching his seventieth birthday, he is still active daily with the largest brokerage house in Canada. He has managed to attend all the major reunions of the 617 Squadron Association from 1968 onwards and was heavily involved in the arrangements for the reunion in Canada in June 1972. He was one of the two Canadian representatives on the visit to Tromso in the summer of 1984.

The vivid memory of the searing desert heat causes him to seek his vacations in much milder climes. He recalls the several instances of 'changed postings' which apparently saved his life, with his replacements not surviving the war. He found that he was the sole survivor of Course No 31 at the Air Observers' School, Portage la Prairie and, as he contemplates his magnificent view from his Toronto office window, of Lake Ontario and the Harbour, he feels that, thankfully, his guardian angel was always alert and 'on the ball'.

Flight Lieutenant Daniel William Carey DFC

Bill Carey enlisted in the Royal Australian Air Force for aircrew duties, a month before his twenty-third birthday, in August 1941. He was selected for pilot training and was posted to No 4 Initial Training School at Victor Harbour. This course was followed by posting to No 1 Elementary Flying Training School at Parafield and then to No 6 Service Flying Training School at Mallala. He was awarded his pilot brevet on 25 June 1942 and the rank of Sergeant.

He left Sydney for overseas service on 24 August 1942 and arrived at No 3 Reception Centre in the United Kingdom on 18 November 1942.

He was given a course at the No 15 Advance Flying Unit and from there was posted to No 29 Operational Training Unit, RAF Bruntingthorpe, where he was crewed for bomber operations. He and his crew continued through the training schedule of Heavy Conversion Unit and Lancaster Finishing School, to be posted to No 106 Squadron, RAF Metheringham on 3 February 1944.

After a period of additional training on the squadron, Bill was detailed as second pilot with Flying Officer J. Forsyth DFC on the night of 15/16 February. It was quite an experience. The target was Berlin with 10/10th cloud below the aircraft at 20,000 feet. Their bombs were aimed at the centre of three green target indicators and immediately after bombing the Lancaster was hit by incendiaries from another bomber and considerably damaged. They managed to get back to Metheringham and Bill observed that it could only get better after that!

On 20 February, the full crew was detailed for their first operation together. The target was Stuttgart and their operational score began to mount quickly. They took part in the Nuremburg operation on 30/31 March. Three 106 Squadron aircraft went missing that night, out of a Squadron effort of seventeen Lancasters. This was their tenth operation as a crew, and their tour thus far had included one trip to Berlin, as well as the Nuremberg raid.

On the night of 5/6 April 1944, they were briefed for the aircraft assmbly plant at St Martin-du-Touch, Toulouse. As they were about to enter the aircraft, the Squadron commander drove into the dispersal. He had a few words with the crew, wished them good luck and then, as he was about to pull away, he called out 'This will be your last trip tonight, Carey!' and drove off. Bill's temper flared and he tore after the car, shouting 'Come back here, you bastard!' but the car continued on its way. Bill seethed throughout the trip and was scarcely mollified by the full explanation offered to him by the Squadron commander at debriefing. His rather ill-chosen words had meant to convey the news that their application to join 617 Squadron had been approved and the Toulouse trip was to be their last with 106! It certainly could have been phrased better!

Bill was commissioned on 25 September 1943, a birthday present he greatly appreciated. His first promotion had occurred on 25 March 1944, and he arrived on 617 Squadron on 10 April as Flying Officer Carey. He then had twelve operations to his credit. He flew as second pilot to Flight Lieutenant Bunny Clayton against a target at St Cyr in France and was very impressed with the discipline and technique displayed by the whole squadron that night.

Their first operation as a crew with 617 was against the Juvisy Marshalling Yards in Paris on 18/19 April. Their early operations included taking part in the 'spoof' raid on Milan whilst 5 Group pounded Munich on 24/25 April. Bill Carey's crew was teamed with that of Bunny Clayton for the D-Day Operation Taxable, followed by the Saumur Tunnel raid. By this time Bill had become known on 617 as

'The Australian James Cagney'. He was somewhat shorter than the usual run of bomber pilots and he appeared to weigh up the most innocent remark or question to make sure that no 'Pom' was trying to take the mickey out of him. He was very well liked by the aircrew and it was very obvious that Bill was inordinately proud of the Squadron on which he served. Bill had completed 37 trips when the forced-landing in Sweden happened. He arrived back in the United Kingdom from Sweden on 24 November 1944 and rejoined 617 to resume his operational career on 18 December. He brought his total score to 48 by the end of the war. His last duty was to deliver a Grand Slam 22,000 lb bomb to the Farge U-Boat pens in the Hamburg port complex.

In March 1945 Bill was awarded the Distinguished Flying Cross. It was always an honour to be decorated, but Bill was so proud to have gained it on 617 Squadron that he almost burst. It was a pleasure shared by the whole Squadron, at such genuine surprise and delight at being thought worthy. Bill performed instructional duties at RAF Syerston and RAF Gamston after hostilities had ceased in Europe. On 7 September 1945, he was posted to No 11 Personnel Despatch Centre and disembarked in Melbourne on 17 October 1945, having been flown home on the Transport Command routes. After a spell of leave, he reported to No 4 Personnel Depot in Adelaide on 26 November and was demobilized on 5 December 1945, returning to his home in Mount Gambier, South Australia for the period of his demobilization leave.

After his leave, Bill travelled to Adelaide to seek suitable employment but was very disappointed with the situations he was offered and returned to Mount Gambier. His uncle, Ed Molony, persuaded Bill to enter the family hotel business and Bill applied himself diligently to the career. He developed into an astute and capable businessman under his uncle's careful and thorough tutelage and was highly respected on this account in the district. Bill married his wife Margaret on 11 August 1951 and they had two sons, Simon and Timothy. But Bill's interests and commitments widened. He was the inaugural President of the South Eastern Area of the Ryder Cheshire Homes, an office which gave him the greatest pleasure and one he never relinquished. He was a committee member of the South Australian Jockey Club and had syndicate shares in about a dozen racehorses.

Bill returned to England in May 1968 with the Australian members of the 617 Squadron Association to attend the functions to mark the 25th anniversary of the Dams raid. He was being carried away by the euphoria of the commemorative church service in St Clement Dane when he saw the collection plate being moved towards him. To his horror, he discovered that all he had on him was a five-pound note! With something of a gulp he deposited it on top of the plate. It so happened that he was on the front row of pews and his liberality caused great consternation. Silver coins were hastily thrust back into pockets, to be replaced by (at least!) one pound notes. No wonder the Chaplain-in-Chief announced joyously afterwards that it was the highest collection ever taken in the church up to that time! Bill reckoned that he more than recovered the outlay in free drinks received from Association members when he related the episode in the Waldorf Hotel after the service!

Bill was the patron of the East Gambier Football Club for many years and found a very useful honorary membership of the Police Social Club, which guaranteed him an understanding ride home after festive occasions. He was a member of the Mount Gambier Golf Club and served on the committee. He took the local championship three times and reduced his handicap to 3.

Association members all over the world were stunned and shocked by the news in February 1979 that Bill had been killed in a car accident returning, as a passenger, from the races. It was hard to believe that the 'Australian James Cagney' would not be beaming at them throughout the scheduled April 1980 reunion in Adelaide. Even today it is a loss many find difficult to accept. Margie Carey and her second son Tim attended the Adelaide reunion in 1980 and met many of Bill's wartime friends for the first time. They both came to the UK in May 1983 for the reunion weeks that marked the 40th anniversary of the Dams raid. Here they met members of Bill's wartime crew, with their wives, and lasting friendships developed. Margie and Tim spent two weeks with Doug MacLennan's family in Fredericton, New Brunswick before returning to South Australia.

Bill Carey's two sons had benefited greatly from the experience they had gained from their father in the family business when they were suddenly confronted with the running and developing of a large company. Simon in particular, as the eldest, had a tremendous amount to cope with, but has done so in a way that would have made his father tremendously proud and delighted. 'Molony's Hotels Limited' now own eleven hotels and one brewery.

The East Gambier Football Club erected a scoreboard on their oval to the cherished and respected memory of the man who had been a supportive and active patron for many years. Bill was missed in all the circles he had graced over the years. It is impossible to think of Bill Carey without a smile creasing one's face. He inevitably had that effect on all who knew him. With all the sorrow and misery caused by World War 2, it is a sobering thought to remind oneself that, but for that calamity, many lives would now have been the poorer for not having known Bill Carey.

Squadron Leader James Castagnola
DSO, DFC and Bar

James Castagnola joined the Royal Air Force in March 1941 for pilot training and, inevitably, throughout his career in the Service he was affectionately known as 'Cass'. He passed through all stages of his training with high commendation and arrived with his crew at RAF East Kirkby, Lincolnshire, to join No 57 Squadron in December 1943 for his first operational tour with Bomber Command, flying Lancasters.

He completed thirty operations with 57 Squadron, and was awarded the Distinguished Flying Cross for his steadfastness and achievements. He had borne his full part in the bomber battles of the period, including eight operations against Berlin. His crew had been welded into a first-class operational unit and they were welcomed on to No 617 Squadron in May 1944.

Cass and his crew served with distinction under Leonard Cheshire, Willie Tait and Johnny Fauquier, being recognized as one of the finest crews to serve on 617 Squadron, imperturbable and supremely devoted to their every task. Cass was awarded his first Bar to the DFC in February 1945, and this was speedily followed by the well-deserved award of the Distinguished Service Order in May 1945, an honour also bestowed on his navigator, Jack Gorringe, who had shared all Cass' operational career. The end of the war in Europe found Cass with 62 bomber operations to his credit.

Cass stayed on in the Service after the war and was given a permanent commission in 1947. He flew Mosquitos, Vampires and Meteors at the Central Flying Establishment, RAF West Raynham and joined the Empire Test Pilots School at the Royal Aircraft Establishment, Farnborough in March 1950. After completing this course, he was posted as a test pilot to the Aeroplane and Armament Experimental Establishment at Boscombe Down. Between April 1954 and February 1958, he served on fighter squadrons in the Middle East and Germany. He became the Commanding Officer of No 41 Squadron at RAF Biggin Hill, flying Hunter V aircraft. This appointment was followed by a radar control course and a posting as Control Executive at the radar station at Neatishead in Norfolk.

Cass became a Staff Officer at Headquarters No 13 Group at RAF Ouston, and it was from this appointment that he retired from the Royal Air Force in 1961 with the rank of Squadron Leader to enter civil aviation with British Airways, where he flew Comets and Tridents with the same expertise and flair that he had brought to all the other aircraft types he had flown. He finally retired from active flying in 1980 and is now enjoying a well-earned retirement with his wife and daughter.

Flying Officer Frank Robert Chance

Frank Chance joined the Royal Air Force in 1942 at the age of 21. His initial training took place in the United Kingdom and was completed in South Africa. In March 1944 he crewed up with Flying Officer Tony Iveson as bomb-aimer at No 14 OTU, RAF Market Harborough and continued through the heavy bomber training schedule until the crew was posted to join 617 Squadron at Woodhall Spa on 22 July 1944, and discovered that theirs was the first crew to be posted to this Squadron without any previous bomber operations experience.

After the Bergen episode, Iveson left the Squadron and Frank flew with other captains, to bring his operational score to 25 by the end of the war. He had bombed targets in Brest, Lorient and other U-boat lairs, as well as taking part in all three operations against *Tirpitz* and the daylight raid on the Kembs Barrage, across the Rhine, near Basle, Switzerland. Heligoland and the bridges at Arbergen and Neinburg also felt the weight of 'Chance-aimed' Tallboys and he was on the final symbolic raid on Berchtesgarten at the end of the war.

He was commissioned in March 1945 and from July until September 1945, he attended and passed a 'codes and cyphers' course at RAF Compton Bassett, Wiltshire. He was then posted to Germany in November 1945 and remained there until March 1949, mainly as Adjutant at No 418 Air Stores Park, near Celle and then on other units in Germany. He was a signals officer at Headquarters, BAFO during the Berlin Airlift. In March 1949 he was posted for general administration duties at Headquarters, Flying Training Command and was finally demobilized in June 1949.

From October 1949 until April 1983, Frank served with the Civil Service in London and Cheltenham. He then retired and now follows his interests in rugby, photography, reading and tennis, which he still plays regularly.

Warrant Officer Albert William Cherrington

Bert Cherrington completed a joinery apprenticeship in November 1939 and joined the Royal Air Force as a fitter rigger. He was posted to No 15 Advanced Flying Training School at RAF Kidlington, Oxfordshire, where he worked on Harvards and Oxfords, moving to RAF Leconfield where he served until early 1943. A call came for volunteers for aircrew flight engineers for the four-engined bombers with which Bomber Command was increasingly re-equipping. Bert answered the call readily and was accepted, much to the chagrin of his engineering officer.

He underwent a course of training at RAF St Athan in Wales and was then posted with an Australian captain, Pilot Officer 'Sandy' Duff to No 57 Squadron at RAF Scampton, Lincolnshire, to commence a tour of bomber operations on Lancasters. The squadron moved to East Kirkby in Lincolnshire and on their fifth operation against Hanover, their aircraft was attacked by a German 'intruder' aircraft over base on the return. 'Cherry' and the bomb-aimer managed to abandon the Lancaster with barely sufficient height for a safe parachute landing, but the other five members of the crew died, either in the aircraft when it crashed or through their parachutes failing to open fully after they had jumped from the doomed bomber.

After a period of survival leave, Cherry was detailed to fly with a Squadron Leader captain who had had no operational experience and had come practically from years of 'flying a desk'. His unfortunate experience with this pilot on a training cross-country flight, terminating with a heart-stopping landing caused Cherry to opt smartly out of this crew. He was posted to No 9 Squadron at RAF Bardney, near Horncastle, Lincolnshire and was crewed with a Flight Lieutenant Hadland. He completed a further eleven sorties, including seven on Berlin, when Hadland decided to volunteer the crew for 617 Squadron. They joined 617 in March 1944 but after a further seven sorties, the captain had completed his first tour and opted for posting. Cherry found himself in the unenviable position of being an 'odd bod', but he managed to fly operationally with Bill Carey, Dave Wilson and other skippers, as occasion offered.

When there was no longer any call for Mosquito marking aircraft on 617 Squadron, Squadron Leader Gerry Fawke, the 'B' Flight commander formed a Lancaster crew and Cherry found himself flying regularly with this very experienced team. He flew operations against *Tirpitz* and other targets, but when Gerry Fawke ceased operations in late November 1944, Cherry once again found himself without a crew.

Not for long, however. He joined Freddy Watts' crew permanently and flew with Freddy until February 1945. Cherry married his childhood sweetheart on 11 August 1945 with Freddy Watts and crew attending the festivities. Cherry had completed 48 sorties, 32 of them with 617 Squadron. He was posted for instructional duties to No 1668 Conversion Unit at RAF Cottesmore and was demobbed in February 1946.

He returned to his former employers until, in 1949, he moved from the district and started a small building business with a friend, in the Huntingdon area. It was thriving until, in 1960, Cherry fell from the roof of a school they were building. This accident incapacitated him for a year and the firm folded in that period. When he had fully recovered, Cherry obtained several jobs in building administration and design. This led to a position in local government in building control and health departments. He took early retirement in 1982 and now spends a great deal of time with his three grandsons, with gardening as a hobby. He is an enthusiastic member of the 617 Association and likes nothing better than to meet up with his wartime comrades on social and charity fund-raising occasions.

Flying Officer C.B.R. Fish BSc, CEng, FICE

In October 1940, at the age of eighteen, Basil Fish went up to Manchester University from Queen Elizabeth's Grammar School,

Blackburn, Lancashire, to read civil engineering. In early 1941, he joined the first Air Squadron to be formed at the university and, on 3 November 1941, when just nineteen, he enlisted in the Royal Air Force Volunteer Reserve at Padgate. He was accepted for pilot/observer training, but was returned to university to continue combined studies for his BSc degree and Initial Training Wing for the Royal Air Force. In the summer of 1942, he obtained the first part of his degree. He also passed the Initial Training Wing examination and entered the RAF full-time.

He was directed to navigator training and sent to South Africa to follow this course. On 21 August 1943 he qualified as an Air Navigator at No 42 Air School, Port Elizabeth. He returned to the United Kingdom and was posted on a course at No 8 Advanced Flying Unit, RAF Mona, Anglesey and in April 1944 he was posted to No 17 Operational Training United at RAF Silverstone, Northamptonshire, where he crewed with a New Zealand pilot, Flying Officer Arthur Joplin from Auckland. The crew continued through the bomber training schedule via No 1660 Heavy Conversion Unit, RAF Swinderby and then to No 5 Lancaster Finishing School at RAF Syerston, to be posted in mid-August 1944 direct to join 617 Squadron at Woodhall Spa.

There was much to learn and absorb, especially the proper use and demands of the Stabilized Automatic Bomb Sight and the dominant role that accurate bombing played in the lives of all 617 aircrew. At the end of August their bombing results on the Wainfleet Bombing Range reached the standard required of crews operating with 617. On 27 August 1944, the crew carried out their very first bomber operation, a daylight raid in the 'gaggle' formation favoured by 617, against the U-Boat pens at Brest. Their operations were to include two of the *Tirpitz* raids, the Kembs Barrage across the Rhine near Basle, the E-Boat pens at Ijmuiden, Holland and two operations against the Urft Dam in Germany before the crash on their ninth operational sortie left Basil the only member of the crew able to continue his operational career.

After a very brief spell in hospital, Basil was back on 617 and flew further operations with Flying Officer Bill Carey, Flight Lieutenant 'Stew' Anning and Squadron Leader Ward, his last and twenty-fourth operation being the Berchtesgarten raid on 25 April 1945. He had been recommended for commissioning by Group Captain Johnny Fauquier, the 617 commanding officer, and duly became a Pilot Officer on 21 April 1945. He moved to RAF Waddington with 617, to commence training for 'Tiger Force'—the scheduled Bomber Command contribution to the war against Japan. For a while he was also employed on assistant Squadron Adjutant duties.

With the Japanese surrender in August 1945, the Tiger Force concept was abandoned. Basil had been under considerable strain since the crash of December 1944 and after the cessation of hostilities, was given a short spell of hospitalization and a period of leave during which his promotion to the rank of Flying Officer was gazetted. Towards the end of 1945, Basil decided to apply for accelerated demobilization, in order to prepare for the resumption of his studies at Manchester University. This was subsequently granted and his official demobilization was notified to him on 19 April 1946. In October that year, Basil commenced his third and final year at University, obtaining a BSc in Municipal Engineering in June 1947.

Basil then worked for various British international building and civil engineering contractors in different parts of the world before joining the Anglo-American Corporation in 1970 as Managing Director of one of their companies in Zambia. Shortly thereafter, he became the Senior General Manager of the Corporation's Group of Companies on the Copper Belt. He travelled extensively throughout the world on both business and pleasure. He took up flying again in 1982 and obtained a private pilot's licence in April 1982, within four months of his sixtieth birthday. He holds both a Zambian and South African private pilot's licence, each with night ratings and, in April 1985, Basil succeeded in qualifying for the award of a full British private pilot's licence at the age of sixty-two. He has logged several hundred flying hours as a pilot in various parts of the world, on business and pleasure.

Due to his wife's poor health, Basil has now officially ceased working abroad and lives in Surrey. Consultancy work should continue to take him overseas occasionally. Basil has a son and a daughter, both married and who have rewarded him with a total of three grandsons and one granddaughter.

Basil visited 'Joppy' and their erstwhile bomb-aimer, 'Lofty' Hebbard, in New Zealand during the last months of 1984. Basil, Lofty and Frank Cardwell, another New Zealand member of the 617 Squadron Association, staged a 'mini-reunion' during his visit, and drank a toast at the exact moment (allowing for the time difference) when Basil and Lofty had been over *Tirpitz* forty years previously—08.42 hours 13 November 1944 at 15,200 feet, in Lancaster '*T for Tare*'.

A further incident furnished Basil with a unique memory of his New Zealand visit. He was talking casually one day to a lady in a queue in Auckland and it came to light that she had been serving in the WAAF in the Sergeants' Mess at RAF Scampton at the time that 617 Squadron took off for the German Dams raid under Wing Commander Gibson.

Flight Lieutenant J. D. Harrison

At the age of eighteen, Jack Harrison was accepted for pilot training with the RAF and called up just after Easter 1942. He completed initial training in the United Kingdom before being sent to Moncton, Canada and from there to Assiniboia to commence flying training in early January 1943. He was failed at the end of that month, but accepted for navigator training and, on 19 April 1943, arrived at No 7 Air Observer School, Portage la Prairie, Manitoba, to be trained as a navigator. On successfully passing this course he was commissioned and he returned to the United Kingdom in November 1943.

He passed the course at No 3 Advanced Flying Unit, RAF Halfpenny Green and moved to No 14 Operational Training Unit, RAF Market Harborough, where he was crewed with Flying Officer Iveson. The crew continued through the training schedule of Heavy Conversion Unit (at RAF Winthorpe, where Sergeant Des Phillips joined the crew as flight engineer) and the Lancaster Finishing School at RAF Syerston, to be posted to 617 Squadron at Woodhall Spa on 22 July 1944.

After the Bergen experience in January 1945, Iveson left the Squadron, having completed the requisite twenty operations for fulfilment of a second tour and the three remaining crew members found themselves as spare aircrew. Jack soon crewed with Flying Officer Johnny Spiers and was on the operation which devastated the Bielefeld Viaduct. He completed his first tour of thirty operations on 16 April 1945 and was on the final bombing raid of the war against Berchtesgarten on April 25. Jack ended the war with a total of 32 operations. Jack takes pride in the fact that his was the first 'green' crew, without any previous Bomber Command experience, to have been posted to 617 Squadron and is also one of the few aircrew members to have performed a complete first tour on the Squadron.

He had various employments in the RAF after the war and applied for flying duties with Transport Command, only to be told that he did not have enough experience. He decided to put both feet firmly on the ground and served as an operations officer at the headquarters of No 46 Group at Northolt and then for a short spell on loan to BOAC at Northolt. Just prior to his demob, he flew the Atlantic for the first time in a Lancastrian of No 24 Squadron. Jack was demobbed in October 1946.

In November 1946 he joined BOAC as a duty operations officer and was later transferred to an equivalent post in BEA. He progressed to become Senior Operations Officer for BEA in Rome from 1951 to 1956, and filled a similar position at Athens from 1960 to 1963. In 1969 he was promoted to Assistant Operations Control Manager and when the two state airlines merged, Jack became the Manager of Operation Control Services at the Queens Building at London Airport.

He retired in January 1982 and is enjoying a well-earned retirement. Jack proved to be a capable liaison officer between the United Kingdom element of the 617 Squadron Association and members in Canada on the occasions that Jack visited members of his own family living in Canada.

Flying Officer Albert Hepworth

Albert Hepworth, the son of a miner, left school at the age of fourteen in 1935. His elder brother, Cedric, had joined the Royal Air Force in the early 1930s and was to serve for over thirty years, in the United Kingdom, Mesopotamia, Malta, France and, after the war, in Washington DC, USA.

Albert's initial employment was with a bookmaker for a few months (ready money betting) and then for about two years he was a proof-reader's copyholder and junior reporter with *The Barnsley Chronicle*. In February 1939, he became a junior clerk with the Yorkshire Miners Association. In June 1940, with the threat of imminent invasion, Albert joined the Local Defence Volunteers (the LDV, which music-hall comics of the day insisted stood for 'Look, Duck and Vanish') and this volunteer organization was speedily re-named 'The Home Guard'.

In early 1941 at nineteen years of age, Albert volunteered for aircrew duties. He appeared before a selection board at RAF Cardington, Bedfordshire, and was medically examined and attested, before being directed to return home and await call-up for wireless operator/air-gunner training. It was November 1941 before his call-up came and Albert reported to Blackpool for his ab initio 'square bashing' in the 'Blackpool Air Force' and to commence his wireless training in the famous Tram Sheds. He progressed through the training schedule to arrive at No 26 Operational Training Unit, RAF North Luffenham as a fully-fledged wireless operator air-gunner. Here he crewed with Pilot Officer John Pryor, a circumstance to which Albert is firmly convinced that he owes his life.

The crew continued through No 1660 Heavy Conversion Unit, RAF Swinderby, and No 5 Lancaster Finishing School, RAF Syerston, to be posted on 8 September 1943 to No 207 Squadron, RAF Langar, to commence a tour of bomber operations. It was to be a hectic period for the crew. They operated against Berlin nine times, Mannheim, Stuttgart, Modane (Italy) and many targets in the Ruhr Valley, with the superb skill of the pilot and the above average ability of the navigator, Flying Officer Lloyd Pinder, getting them safely through this part of their operational career. Albert missed three of the Berlin operations, being off operations for the period, following a minor operation for removal of a cyst.

After eighteen operations with 207, the Squadron commander suggested to John Pryor that his crew answer the call from 5 Group headquarters for experienced crews to join 617 Squadron. Squadron losses were always known to aircrew and 617 was regarded by many aircrew at that time as an apparently officially expendable squadron, a reputation resulting from the abnormally high losses on the Dams raid and the Dortmund-Ems Canal operation in September 1943. After much discussion amongst themselves, and in the light of John Prior's obvious enthusiasm to join 617, they agreed to move as a complete crew. Approval for the posting came through for 15 February 1944, but the crew operated for 207 Squadron that night against Berlin, before making the journey to Woodhall Spa on 17 February.

They were engaged in the early experimental and development stages of 617's target location, marking and bombing technique, especially in the important duty of laying the target-illuminating flares accurately and on time, and of renewing this illumination as demanded by the Squadron commander. Their operations on 617 included the early French targets, the D-day 'spoof' Operation Taxable, the V3 sites in the Pas de Calais, the Channel ports and two of the *Tirpitz* operations, as well as German targets as the Allied armies rolled forwards. A very close burst of flak killed their Canadian bomb-aimer, Flying Officer Cecil Pesme, at his station in the nose of the Lancaster during a raid on the U-Boat pens at Brest on 14 August 1944. Cecil Pesme had been with the crew from the outset and was greatly missed and mourned.

The flight engineer, Bob Telfer, left the crew and the Squadron on completion of his thirtieth trip and first operational tour and, as their operational score mounted, other members of the original crew opted for posting as they reached the then statutory 45 operations for a continuous 'double-tour' until John Pryor and Albert were the only two remaining. John had actually passed this total but chose to continue to operate until Albert had reached his magical 45, when John would decide his own personal course of action. The Bergen trip was Albert's 45th operation and Fate ensured that it would be his last, although not in the way Albert would have wished. But at least at the end of it he was alive, thanks to John Pryor's skill and captaincy.

Albert was repatriated from the Moosburg prisoner-of-war camp, near Munich, in May 1945. After a period of rehabilitation and home leave, he was eventually granted a Class B demobilization priority and returned to the administrative work with the Yorkshire Miners Association. Albert continued in this employment until his retirement in June 1981. He had put in over forty years with the Association, which became the National Union of Miners, Yorkshire Area in 1945. He was progressively promoted until his appointment as Chief Administrative Officer of the Yorkshire Area in 1952, a post he held for 29 years.

Albert is a very keen supporter of the 617 Squadron Association. He and his wife Joan have attended most of the major reunions and functions that the association has organized since the initial reunion in 1968. In 1984 they were part of a small group of members and wives who attended the ceremonies in Tromso, marking the fortieth anniversary of the sinking of the *Tirpitz*. Former members of the battleship's crew, some with wives, also attended and wreaths were laid from Norwegian naval vessels at the anchorage where *Tirpitz* capsized. There was an air of quiet camaraderie and peace which enveloped all elements at the ceremonies, which was very favourably remarked upon by the Norwegian newspapers covering the events and which met with great approval within Norway. A commemorative memorial, fashioned from steel salvaged during the post-war removal of the battleship's hulk, was unveiled on a site above the anchorage.

Flying Officer Arthur William Joplin (RNZAF)

At the age of eighteen, Arthur Joplin joined the Royal New Zealand Air Force in May 1942 and commenced flying training in January 1943. He received his wings and a commission in July 1943. Overseas service was permitted only with parental consent and, although he was the only son, Joppy persuaded his parents to give their permission and he was duly posted overseas, arriving in the United Kingdom in September 1943. He was eventually posted to No 17 OTU, RAF Silverstone, North-amptonshire, where he became part of a bomber crew. They completed the training schedule for the operation of heavy bombers, to be posted direct to No 617 Squadron, RAF Woodhall Spa, in mid-August 1944. Joppy was twenty years of age.

His first operation was against the U-Boat pens at Brest on 27 August 1944. Other operations followed, including two against *Tirpitz* at her Tromso anchorage and the daylight raid against the Kembs Barrage, across the Rhine near Basle. Tragedy struck the crew on their operation against the oil installation at Politz, north-east of Stettin, in December. Joppy suffered severe leg injuries which handicap him somewhat to this day. By the time his extensive hospital treatment was completed, the wars in Europe and Asia were over and he was repatriated to New Zealand in December 1945. After a period of leave, he was demobilized in February 1946.

His father had co-founded a knitwear manufacturing company in September 1928 and Joppy joined this company, to work in all areas of the organization. He gained a complete working knowledge of the operation. He married his wife, Bette, on 21 December 1954, by sheer coincidence the tenth anniversary of the Politz trip. Unfortunately, due to a recession in the clothing trade and applied financial restraints by the trading banks, the business was sold in 1971, but Arthur stayed on with the new management until 1978 and is still engaged in the knitwear industry.

Joppy is into his second year as President of the Brevet Club (Auckland) Inc, an ex-aircrew club formed in 1946, along the lines of the Brevet Club in the United Kingdom. He has been playing golf intermittently over the years but is now seriously trying to reduce his current handicap of 28. In October 1984, Arthur and his wife were delighted to welcome Basil Fish on the extended visit he had always promised to make. They had a great time and did not forget to mark the fortieth anniversary of their appointment with *Tirpitz* on 13 November 1944. Joppy and Bette are now looking forward to the projected 617 Squadron Association reunion in New Zealand in 1986.

Flight Lieutenant Alexander Millar McKie DFM

In 1938, at the age of fifteen, Alex McKie joined the Royal Air Force as an aircraft apprentice at RAF Halton, Buckinghamshire. He passed out with the classification of 'Aircraftsman First Class' as a Fitter IIE in March 1940 and was posted to No 16 Maintenance Unit, RAF Sealand, Cheshire. Whilst at Sealand, Alex had an accident on his motorbike. Nothing serious in itself, but he developed a hernia when lifting the machine upright. Consequently, at every subsequent aircrew medical in his later career, Alex needed to tighten his stomach muscles as much as possible when asked to 'Cough!' by the medical officer, in order to conceal this weakness. He continued with this deception in order to stay operational, and not leave his crew.

Alex progressed to the rank of Corporal during his stay at Sealand and was then posted to RAF Millom, Cumberland, in May 1941. In 1942 he was accepted for pilot training and commenced the aircrew training schedule. He solo-ed on Tiger Moths at RAF Syston in March 1942 and was thereupon posted to the USA, via Canada, for further pilot training, arriving at the USA Air Base Lakeland, Florida in June 1942. His pilot aspirations came to an abrupt end in July, when he was 'washed out' as a pilot for 'dangerous flying' at Lakeland. He was returned to Canada and proceeded to the RCAF station at Edmonton, Alberta, where he was launched on a navigator course.

He graduated as a navigator, returned to the United Kingdom with the rank of Sergeant and was posted to No 16 OTU, RAF Upper Heyford, Oxfordshire, where he was crewed with Australian pilot 'Bunny' Lee, Gus Hoyland, 'Red' Hunnisette and Frank Richards, as likely a band of 'pirates' as one could hope to come across outside *Treasure Island*. Their training was undertaken in Wellington aircraft and the crew was posted to RAF Swinderby in June 1943 to convert to Lancaster aircraft. Successful completion of this course resulted in the crew being posted to No 106 Squadron, RAF Syerston, Nottinghamshire, to commence their first tour of operations.

Alex' first tour of thirty operations was completed in April 1944. During this tour he operated against Berlin eight times, Ruhr targets, the terribly costly raid on Nuremberg, Schweinfurt and many other heavily-defended German targets. He vividly recalls being coned in searchlights over Berlin at 23,000 feet and the pilot eventually shaking off the tenacious beams at 1,500 feet—Alex never did find his dividers after that plunge! Again a Berlin trip, with Gee unserviceable from the outset. The target was reached without much trouble but the Lancaster became hopelessly lost on the return trip. Alex' astro-navigation indicated that the aircraft was over France when in fact it was over the North Sea and a very thankful crew managed a safe landing at RAF Wing, Buckinghamshire, with very little fuel in the tanks. They came through the Nuremberg raid, with aircraft falling like fireflies all around them to and from the target, unchallenged and unscathed, but on an operation against Stettin, they had several brushes with night-fighters. The rear-gunner was credited with a 'kill' as a result of one of these combats. On the Schweinfurt raid, Alex' oxygen tube became disconnected without him being aware of it. The wireless operator discovered him on the floor unconscious. He was speedily revived and Alex discovered that the aircraft had continued on a southerly course long after it should have been directed on to an easterly course and the lighted towns told Alex that they were actually over Switzerland. He was able to pin-point the Lancaster's position and, nothing daunted, the crew set course for the target. They arrived over Schweinfurt to find that all other aircraft had long since departed and the crew had the place to themselves, with a very warm reception laid on by the ground defences. Apart from these incidents, the tour contained little of note!

Alex was awarded the Distinguished Flying Medal for his services on 106 Squadron. The prospect of joining 617 Squadron proved very attractive to the whole crew and they reported for duty with 617 Squadron on 6 May 1944. Alex was immediately involved with the training and discussion for Operation Taxable, which proved to be the crew's first operation with 617. Alex was commissioned in September 1944 and when Bunny Lee left the Squadron at the conclusion of his second tour, the crew's targets included the U-Boat pens at Brest, the sites in the Pas de Calais and other targets. Alex continued on 617, flying with Bill Carey and other pilots. He was on the first two attacks against *Tirpitz* but was on his 'Swedish Holiday' when the battleship was finally sunk. Alex carried his total score of operations to 46 by the end of the war in Europe. There were some 'incidents' during his 617 operations. Over Brest on 14 August 1944, a burst of flak injured his pilot, Bunny Lee, and plunged pieces of shrapnel into Alex' right calf, with some remaining to this day. En route for the advanced Russian base of Yagodnik, near Archangel, for the first operation against *Tirpitz* in September 1944, his aircraft was damaged by Russian light anti-aircraft fire as it sped across the pine forests and flat-lands. They were unable to use the Lancaster in the operation, but were guests on board other Lancasters of the Squadron for the visit to Kaa Fiord. The forced landing in Sweden made Alex believe that Norway was an unlucky hunting-ground for him.

The end of hostilities afforded Alex the first real opportunity for treatment of his hernia. After hospitalization and convalescence, he initially joined the instructional staff at RAF Swinderby, but was then posted to No 9 Squadron, RAF Bardney, as Squadron navigation officer in January 1945, with the acting rank of Flight Lieutenant. Like so many erstwhile first-line squadrons, their Lancasters were engaged in flying troops home from Germany and Italy for demobilization. In August 1945, with the defeat of Japan, Alex applied for transfer to Transport Command. This was granted and he continued to 'fly the routes' until he was demobbed in May 1946.

He opted for a government training scheme course with J. Lucas, Birmingham, training to become a production manager, but in 1947 he became a professional salesman, and for some years he has been a divisional sales manager with a pharmaceutical company. Alex has two sons. Duncan is the National Accounts Manager for a large company while Roger is a successful businessman with a chain of delicatessen shops in South-west England. The current progeny score is one grandson and four granddaughters.

Alex is very keen on all 617 Squadron Association reunions and functions, and attends all he possibly can. In 1977, with three other Association members, he attended the annual Whitsun reunion of the *Tirpitz* and *Bismarck* Association, held at Lahnstein, near Coblenz and had a memorable time as the welcomed guest of the former enemy.

Warrant Officer Thomas Joseph McLean DFC, DFM

Tom McLean was seventeen years of age when he enlisted in the Royal Air Force, but was not called up to the 'Blackpool Air Force' until June 1940 at the age of eighteen. In the intervening period he had worked with a commercial artist in Glasgow and took to artwork like a duck to water. He had been trained as a barber but did not enjoy the work and welcomed the change. At Blackpool, he was offered training to become a physical training instructor but refused it and eventually trained for ground defence duties at RAF Ronaldsway, Isle of Man in March 1941. He received a very thorough grounding in gunnery and guns which was to stand him in good stead. Even in those early days, gunnery seemed to come naturally to him.

With the call for aircrew volunteers, Tom submitted his application and was delighted to be recommended for training as a 'straight' air-gunner. He passed the medical examination with no difficulty, but it was May 1942 before he was posted to No 2 Air Gunnery School, RAF Dalcross, Inverness-shire, to commence the air-gunners course. During the waiting period for the course, however, he had been able to widen his knowledge of guns and gunnery, even to becoming proficient in the dismantling and reassembly of both Fraser Nash and Boulton Paul gun turrets. His previous experience with guns allowed him to concentrate his mind on the requirements and niceties of accurate sighting, range estimation and deflection shots using the diameter of the 'ring-and-bead' sight and a committed knowledge of the wing-span of enemy fighters.

He was awarded his air-gunner brevet on 7 July 1942 and, as Sergeant McLean, was posted to No 102 Squadron RAF Pocklington, Yorkshire, in No 4 Group, Bomber Command to commence his first tour of operations. He was allocated to a crew which was then converted to Halifax flying within the Squadron resources and, on 28 August 1942, the crew undertook their very first bomber operation. They were to have a memorable demonstration of the calibre of their rear-gunner on this operation. The target was Saarbrucken and the Halifax was attacked on the return trip, just as it cleared the enemy coast. Tom McLean destroyed the Me 109 before it could inflict any damage on the Halifax and the rest of the crew saw the enemy aircraft explode in a sheet of flame as it struck the sea.

Tom's reputation grew as his tour progressed. Following the destruction of two Ju 88s in an operation against Mannheim on 6 December 1942, his seventeenth operation, he was awarded an immediate Distinguished Flying Medal. Unfortunately, his prowess excited not a little jealousy from officers, who seemed to resent the ability of an NCO to protect and safeguard his crew in circumstances where other crews succumbed to enemy attacks. In particular, Flight and Squadron commanders seemed to have resolved to keep this NCO well and truly 'in his place', an attitude that appears incomprehensible from this distance of time. These senior officers lost no opportunity to put Tom down and built up within him a bitter and intense dislike for commissioned ranks that was to be with him for a very long time.

On 16 February 1943, Tom destroyed an Me 110 and claimed another as a probable, during the return flight from an attack on Lorient. In March it was confirmed by intelligence that this probable had also yielded a kill. Tom's first tour of operations ended in April 1943 with his operational score at thirty trips. He became an instructor at various training units within 4 Group when suddenly he was posted to the Coastal Command OTU at RAF Alness, Invergordon, as a gunnery instructor, in itself a most unusual posting for a Bomber Command tour-expired air-gunner, let alone one of such proven capability. Tom soon realized that his abilities and well-intentioned efforts were being wasted in a morass of crass official indifference. He managed to take part in many sea searches, to keep in touch with being airborne and operating a turret, but although these flights were apparently allowed to count as operations by Coastal Command, Tom recorded them merely as 'flying time' in his log book. His morale was at a very low ebb and he was seriously contemplating desertion when the life-line of a tour with 617 Squadron was thrown to him.

He arrived at Woodhall Spa in mid-February 1944 and was immediately impressed by the buoyant and friendly atmosphere in the Sergeants' Mess—but then most operational Sergeants' Messes were places to be recalled with pleasure! He was very relieved that his DFM was in no way remarkable among the decorations on display by a great number of the Mess membership. Inevitably, he had brought with him the seething resentment of commissioned ranks, but as he got to know and appreciate the quality and professionalism of the commissioned aircrew who operated on 617 Squadron this attitude began to undergo a decided change. Bill Duffy, Don Bell and Roy Woods, the commissioned Canadian element of his first 617 crew were able to demonstrate to him that the best type of officer was to be found in the operational squadrons in 5 Group. New ideas, old routines and individuality were all encouraged on 617, providing they added to the efficiency of the

Squadron. Tom found 617 to be an outfit that waged war professionally, with flair and an absolute conviction in its ability to best the enemy wherever he was to be met, no matter what problems such confrontations might initially present.

It was also an outfit that played and relaxed with the same fervour and *joie de vivre*. With such characters in the mess as Paddy Gingles and his all-NCO crew, Mike Vaughan and many others, there were very few solemn and quiet moments. Tom was particularly impressed with the way the aircrew officers and NCOs readily mixed at special celebrations in the Sergeants' Mess. The dance to commemorate the first anniversary of the Dams raid was a case in point. For many of the officers wearing their DFM ribbons with pride, it was a happy reminder of other days and the inevitable presence of many of the station's WAAFs made it a genuine 'Station occasion'. Small wonder that Tom's attitude began to change until he now looks back on his time with 617 as the happiest and most memorable of his operational career.

When he had recovered from the minor injuries of the night of 15/16 March 1944, Tom flew a couple more operations with Bill Duffy and then 'free-lanced' with other crews. He flew against the French marshalling yards at Juvisy and La Chappelle, in the Paris area, as well as against Brunswick, Munich and on Operation Taxable. He flew with Flight Lieutenant Mac Hamilton on the daylight raid against the flying bomb storage depot at Rilly-la-Montagne on 31 July, the raid on which Flight Lieutenant Bill Reid VC, was quite literally knocked out of the sky when his Lancaster was hit by bombs dropped from over-flying main force aircraft. Tom considers that Mac Hamilton was the finest 'low level' pilot with whom he ever flew.

Tom brought his operational tally to 51 having operated with 617 Squadron on 21 occasions. He was awarded a Distinguished Flying Cross and left the Squadron in late August 1944, holding the rank of Warrant Officer. He was presented with both his awards at an Investiture held at Buckingham Palace in December 1945 by His Majesty King George VI. Tom was both surprised and honoured that the Monarch spoke to him at some length at the time of his investiture. The King commended him for his devotion to duty and tenacity, and referred to Tom's success on his very first operation and mentioned his awareness of the services to the country of Tom's father in World War 1 and of his two brothers also in the RAF in World War 2. Tom remembers the total unexpectedness of this audience with great pride to this day.

Tom's DFC citation credits him with having definitely destroyed seven enemy fighters with two more as probables. After the war, in 1948, Tom contacted the Red Cross and eventually established that the two probables were actually kills but he still limits his successes to the seven confirmed in his citation, and there are quite a few ex-aircrew alive today who owe their lives to his skill and prowess with four Browning machine-guns.

Tom stayed in the RAF after the war. He remained on flying duties on various employments at RAF Manby, RAF Driffield and at the headquarters of Flying Training Command, where he collated the results of gunnery tests. In 1954 he forsook flying duties and re-mustered to photographic work at RAF Ballykelly, Londonderry, Northern Ireland, where two Shackleton squadrons were stationed. He finally left the RAF in 1956, after sixteen years of service.

Since 1956, Tom has been a self-employed barber, and a free-lance landscape/seascape painter, as well as a professional child photographer. His second wife, Kay, presented him with a beautiful baby daughter, Rebecca, in May 1979. Over the last few years, Tom has been increasingly troubled with spinal osteo-arthritis, an affliction that strangely seems to have been visited upon many wartime rear-gunners. It has affected his ability to get around but his daily dose of 300 mg 'Fortral L' makes life more pleasurable. It also makes him independently mobile and he attends his local hospital regularly for physiotherapy. When he looks at the lot of some of his fellow-sufferers in the treatment room, he feels that he has nothing about which to complain.

When Tom looks back on his wartime years, the memories of his time with 617 Squadron put his more unfortunate Pocklington experiences in a more acceptable light, but some recollections still rankle. When he recalls these bizarre happenings there is still a trace of bitterness in his voice, mixed with amazement, that such things could have been.

Captain Douglas H. MacLennan, Royal Canadian Service (formerly RCAF)

Doug MacLennan enlisted in the Royal Canadian Air Force at Charlottestown, Prince Edward Island soon after his nineteenth birthday. On 22 September 1941 he was sworn into the RCAF and posted to No 1 Manning Depot, Toronto, from which he proceeded to Initial Training School, Bellville, Ontario. He was scheduled for pilot training and was posted to the Elementary Flying Training School at Stanley, Nova Scotia in February 1942. Successfully completing this course, he went on in June 1942 to the Service Flying Training School, Uplands, Ottawa, Ontario, where he flew in Harvard aircraft. Unfortunately, he was suspended from further pilot training during this course and was subsequently remustered to training as bomb-aimer. In October 1942 he arrived at No 7 Bombing and Gunnery School, Paulson, Manitoba and followed this with a navigation course at No 5 Air Observers School, Winnipeg, Manitoba, being awarded his air observer brevet on 30 December 1942.

Doug was posted overseas and arrived at the Bournemouth Reception Centre in January 1943. He completed an unarmed combat course at Whitley Bay, before being posted to No 5 Air Observers School, RAF

Jurby, Isle of Man in March for a familiarization course. This course was followed by a posting to No 29 RAF Bruntingthorpe, where he crewed with the Australian pilot, Pilot Officer Bill Carey on 15 June. They passed through the training schedule of Heavy Conversion Unit (RAF Swinderby) and Lancaster Finishing School (RAF Syerston), at the conclusion of which they were posted to join No 106 Squadron at RAF Metheringham in February 1944.

Their first operation was against Stuttgart on 20 February and by 5 April they had completed eleven sorties, including one raid on Berlin and the traumatic Nuremberg raid on 30 March. On 7 April, the crew departed for 617 Squadron, following the directive from 5 Group Headquarters to all 5 Group squadrons that experienced and successful crews should be given the opportunity to volunteer for transfer to 617.

On 10 April, Bill Carey flew as 'second dicky' with Flight Lieutenant Bunny Clayton DFC, CGM, and Doug went with Flight Lieutenant J. Cooper, both to gain first-hand experience of 617's methods and technique. The target was at St Cyr and both were very impressed with the efficient way the target was obliterated by very accurate bombing. By 11 August, Doug had completed his first tour of thirty operations. These included Brunswick; the 'spoof' raid against Milan on 24/25 April, to cover the premier target of Munich; Operation Taxable; the Saumur Tunnel; U-Boat pens and the huge sites in the Pas de Calais. They had been somewhat hampered in the course of this tour by the sinusitis troubles of their original navigator, Jock Kerr, and flew with an array of navigators during this period on 617. Doug's rank when he joined 617 was Warrant Officer and he was commissioned to the immediate rank of Flying Officer on 10 June 1944.

The crew continued to operate with 617 and their aircraft was damaged by Russian light ack-ack en route for Yagodnik in Russia on 11 September 1944, when positioning for the first raid on *Tirpitz*. Their Lancaster *'Easy Elsie'* was unable to take part in the actual operation against *Tirpitz*, and the 'Johnny Walker' mines it carried were transferred to the aircraft of Flight Lieutenant Iveson, who had jettisoned his own load of mines prior to making an emergency landing at another Russian airfield. However, Bill Carey's crew did fly against *Tirpitz* by the simple expedient of being 'guests' aboard other Lancasters of the squadron. Bill Carey flew with Freddy Watts and Doug went with Flying Officer Paddy Gingles DFM. The German battleship was to prove an unlucky target for Bill Carey's crew, for on the next operation against her at her anchorage in Tromso, *'Easy Elsie* was hit by flak over the target and in the target area, which led to their 'Swedish Holiday'.

After their repatriation and a period of leave, the crew rejoined 617 and continued to operate. Doug had brought his score to 45 operations by 27 March 1945 when an instruction arrived from RCAF headquarters, ordering ALL aircrew of Canadian origin, wherever stationed, who had completed a tour of operations, to cease operating immediately and to prepare for return to Canada. This very firm edict applied to all

Canadian aircrew and even Group Captain Johnny Fauquier was unable to get special permission to continue to lead 617 personally into battle. Doug was relieved that the order had not come through a few days earlier for on 27 March he had successfully aimed a 22,000 lb Grand Slam bomb at the U-Boat pens at Farge, in the Hamburg port complex. In addition to the two *Tirpitz* raids, targets in his second tour had included the Bielefeld Railway Viaduct, the Dortmund-Ems Canal and vital railway bridges in the campaign to isolate the Ruhr area.

Doug arrived back in Canada in May 1945 and after a period of home leave he was posted to Moncton, New Brunswick in June as a flying control officer. This was followed by a similar post at Goose Bay, Labrador before he was demobilized at Dartmouth, Nova Scotia on 25 December 1945. He served eight years in the Department of Transport as a flying control officer at Winnipeg, Manitoba, Sydney, New Brunswick and Moncton, New Brunswick and then re-enlisted in the RCAF in 1953. He was the officer commanding the Rescue Co-ordinating Centre, Maritime Command Headquarters, Halifax, Nova Scotia when he reached compulsory retirement age in 1970 and retired with the rank of Captain.

Doug and his wife Doris now live in Fredericton, New Brunswick. He has been troubled by a heart complaint which has given rise to serious concern at times, but recent surgery appears to have given him a new lease of life, enabling him to play a good deal of golf, albeit to the neglect of his correspondence in recent months, but he is mending his ways in this respect. His son Ian graduated from the University of New Brunswick with a Bachelor of Education degree and is now a supervisor with the Canada Permanent Trust at their head office in Toronto. His daughter Heather graduated from the University of New Brunswick with a Bachelor of Science degree in Bio-Chemistry and also from the University of Guelph (Ontario) as Bachelor of Applied Science (Applied Human Nutrition). Heather is employed in the Doctor Everett Chalmers Hospital in Fredericton.

Doug has kept in touch with Bill Carey and Gerry Witherick over the years and was very grieved to hear of Bill's tragic death in a motor accident in Australia in February 1979. He attended the 617 Squadron Association reunion in Adelaide in April 1980 and met Margaret Carey, Bill's wife, for the first time. After the Association's reunion in the United Kingdom and France in May 1983, Margie Carey and her second son Tim returned to Canada with Doug and spent a very happy fortnight in Fredericton with the MacLennan family, during which time Ian, Heather and Tim became very firm friends. When Tim married in December 1984, part of the honeymoon with his bride, Beverley, was spent with the MacLennan family, in the course of a world tour and this cemented the relationship.

Flight Sergeant John Desmond Phillips

Des Phillips applied for aircrew training in March 1943. He passed the selection board and strict medical at Adastral House, London, but was told that the pilot training list was full and offered training as a flight engineer. He accepted this, but it was July before his reserved occupation exemption was lifted (reluctantly) by the Ministry of Labour, and Des reported for training at the age of nineteen.

He passed each successive training phase comfortably, finally being sent to RAF Winthorpe, Lincolnshire for a comprehensive and intense engine handling course. He became a fully-fledged flight engineer in May 1943 and was drafted into Flying Officer Iveson's crew when they arrived at Winthorpe from No 14 OTU, to convert to four-engined bombers. The complete crew continued their training schedule, to emerge from the Lancaster Finishing School in July 1944. At this stage of his career, Des had 'amassed' a total of 24 flying hours! They were posted to 617 Squadron direct from RAF Syerston.

Their subsequent operations with 617 Squadron included raids against U-boat pens and the so-called 'V3' sites in the Pas de Calais, the Kembs Barrage and the three raids against the German battleship *Tirpitz*. He recalls very vividly the take-off in the early hours of November 13 1944 from RAF Milltown in the Moray Firth area for the third and final operation against *Tirpitz*. The aircraft was taking off with 14,000 lb overload when the port outer engine cut to less than half power. With tyres screaming, the Lancaster began to swing to port. Quickly Des closed down the starboard outer engine and then gradually re-opened the throttle to bring all four engines into synchronization. Fortunately the trouble in the port outer cleared and all engines rendered full power. The swing was arrested, the aircraft straightened and managed to stagger off the ground, but not before giving John Pryor some very anxious moments as at one stage a collision with John's own fully-laden aircraft en route for the take-off point seemed very much on the cards.

Tony Iveson's departure from 617 without further operation after the Bergen experience made Des a 'spare' flight engineer on 617, but this was to give him operational experience with Group Captain Johnny Fauquier, Flight Lieutenant Alan Quinton and Squadron Leader Brookes before he crewed permanently with Squadron Leader Ward. The Berchtesgarten raid was Des' final operation and brought his total to 35 operations. He moved to RAF Waddington with 617 after volunteering for operations in the Far East. The Squadron was to convert to the new Lincoln four-engined bomber and become part of 'Tiger Force', Bomber Command's immediate contribution to the war against Japan. The unforeseen but welcomed end to the war against Japan cancelled the project. Instead, Des went with 617 to India in January 1946 with the Lincoln bombers and was stationed at RAF Digri in Bengal. The squadron dropped food supplies to the inhabitants of villages in the Burmese jungles, and took part in the fly-past over Delhi during the victory parade.

Des returned to the United Kingdom in April 1946 and was posted to Technical Training Command for instructional duties at Weston-super-Mare, training Fitter II Engineers. He filled this post until his demobilization in March 1947. Des married in April 1948 and for the next fifteen years he was engaged on research and experimental work at the Royal Aircraft Establishment, Aberporth, with the main emphasis on guided missile systems. Then he joined the Central Electricity Generating Board, completing ten years with the Board, ending up in the works study section at CEGB headquarters.

In 1973, Des moved to the economic forestry section of the Ministry of Agriculture as a manager, but had to endure some eight months of unemployment when this section folded in 1974. His next appointment was with the Powys County Council, carrying out surveys concerned with rights-of-way and country walks. In February 1977, Des joined Lockheed Aircraft International in Riyadh, Saudi Arabia and rose to a very responsible superintendent post. In October 1984 he transferred to the Dallah-Avco organization in Riyadh in a similar capacity and is still actively engaged in this employment. If Des' employment contract in Saudi Arabia is not renewed, he plans to return to the United Kingdom and assist in the running of a son's business.

Des was never one to let the grass grow under his feet. He has four sons, three daughters and, at the last count, eleven grandchildren. He had managed to arrange his United Kingdom leave periods from Saudi Arabia to coincide with 617 Squadron Association functions and thus he was able to be present at the dinner given by the Association to celebrate the ninetieth birthday of Sir Barnes Wallis and the first week of the 1983 reunion to mark the fortieth anniversary of the Dams raid. He was accompanied by his wife and daughter Amanda and a lasting memory of this reunion week will always be the totally unexpected presentation on the Association's behalf of a lovely bouquet of flowers to Amanda on the occasion of her twenty-first birthday and during the Association's dinner at Castle Howard, Yorkshire.

Flight Lieutenant Henry John Pryor DFC

John Pryor was born on 5 January 1918 on his father's small farm at Harlow, Essex. The family moved to a much larger farm at Navestock, Essex in 1923. John attended the local village school until he was thirteen years old when he transferred to the Ongar Grammar School. He left school at the age of fourteen to work on the farm.

His reserved occupation caused John problems when it came to achieving his ambition of becoming aircrew. He was accepted for pilot training and attested at RAF Uxbridge on 8 December 1939, but was sent back to the farm to await call-up. His next communication from the RAF was after the 1940 crops had been harvested, but then only to inform him that his documents had been endorsed for a return to farming should he fail a pilot's course, and adding that there was no immediate demand for pilots at that time.

He was called up on 15 September 1941, reporting to the Aircrew Reception Centre at Regent's Park, London. After six weeks of *ab initio* training he was posted to No 13 Initial Training Wing, Torquay for a twelve weeks' course in aviation subjects. John coped well with this course, but had difficulty with the audio Morse due to congenital middle-ear trouble. However, he was passed through to a flying familiarization course at No 6 Elementary Flying Training School RAF Sywell, Northamptonshire, where he logged eight hours Tiger Moth flying.

He moved to Heaton Park, Manchester en route for training in Canada and in April 1942 he sailed in the *Rangitiki* on a nine day voyage to Halifax, Nova Scotia. On board were some of the crew of the German battleship *Bismarck* heading for internment camps in Canada. John's first unit in Canada was No 5 Manning Depot, Lachine, near Montreal, followed by flying training at No 17 Elementary Flying Training School at Stanley, Nova Scotia. John was finding that his restricted schooling required him to apply himself much more diligently to the 'classroom' side of courses than did his fellow-students who had had more advanced education, but his determination saw him through this obstacle. Successful completion of the EFTS course took John back to the Montreal area to No 13 Advanced Flying Unit, St Hubert's where he flew Harvard aircraft. He was awarded his pilot's brevet on 20 November 1942 and was delighted to be commissioned at the same time. Crossing the Atlantic in the *Queen Elizabeth* he arrived in the United Kingdom in time for Christmas leave at home.

He was directed to report to the No 7 Personnel Receiving Centre RAF Harrogate where he opted for bomber pilot training. He converted to twin-engined aircraft, flying Oxfords at RAF Shawbury, Shropshire. May 1943 found John at No 29 OTU, RAF North Luffenham, Leicester, to convert to Wellington aircraft. Here he assembled a crew, confident that in Flying Officer Lloyd Pinder, a Canadian from Burlington, Ontario, he had a first class navigator. Lloyd came from a farming background and was a keen bridge player, which gave them both common interests outside of flying, and which led to a great friendship which has lasted ever since.

The bomber training schedule took them to No 5 Lancaster Finishing School where John picked up Bob Telfer, a flight engineer, to complete his crew. They were posted on 15 September 1943 to join No 207 Squadron at RAF Langar, Nottingham, exactly two years after John had reported to ACRC. John did a 'second dickie' trip to Hanover to give him some experience of German defences and then the crew was ready to operate with Bomber Command.

Their first operation together was on 23 September 1943 with the target being Mannheim. Thereafter their operational score mounted during one of the bitterest periods of the bomber war. On one Hanover operation their starboard inboard engine blew up, but they continued on to the target, inevitably arriving late and being given a rough ride by the German defences. During one of their Berlin raids they were attacked by a fighter, John's skill and the gunners' support enabled the Lancaster to shake off the enemy, but the aircraft was left with no brake ability, no hydraulic services and substantial fuselage and airframe damage. They limped home to make a landing at the emergency aerodrome at RAF Woodbridge, Suffolk, and it was a month before the aircraft was repaired sufficiently for it to be returned to 207 Squadron. After another operation John was presented with an unexploded cannon-shell by the ground crew. It had been taken from one of his Lancaster's fuel tanks! Bomber losses were consistently high at this time, but John became convinced that he and his crew would survive the carnage.

John's operational score had risen to twenty operations in February 1944 when his Squadron commander, Wing Commander P. Jennings sent for him and asked if he would like to take his crew to 617 Squadron, as 5 Group Headquarters had circulated all 5 Group Squadrons for experienced crews to volunteer for transfer to 617. John was enthusiastic but was somewhat taken aback by his crew's initial reaction to the proposition. They talked it out earnestly but after a few hours consideration, they did all decide to make the change. They were due to go to join 617 on 15 February, when Wing Commander Jennings asked if they would do one last operation with 207 that night. John reminded him of the imminent posting but the Wing Commander asked him to telephone Wing Commander Cheshire at Woodhall Spa, to discover if he had any objections to the crew's arrival being delayed by a day or so. John was told by Wing Commander Cheshire that 617 crews were engaged on training and one or two days delay would make no difference. John recorded his ninth operation against Berlin that night.

The crew reported to RAF Woodhall Spa on 16 February 1944. At 207 they were naturally regarded as a senior and experienced crew. With the type of aircrew assembled at 617, they felt very, very junior. John admits that he felt more of a 'sprog' that day then he did when he joined 207. Soon after his arrival John was notified of the award of a Distinguished Flying Cross for his services to 207 Squadron.

To their surprise and amazement, the crew was kept on a training schedule for a month, absorbing the new techniques and attitudes at 617 Squadron. When they eventually featured on the battle order, it was as part of a flare-laying element. John soon discovered that Leonard Cheshire, for all his mild manner on the ground, could be very forthright, testy and critical on operations, expecting illumination where and when he required it. The crew became quite expert at laying the initial flares on time and positioning their aircraft for instant renewal if required. Their success in this role owed not a little to Lloyd Pinder's navigational ability. Subsequently their aircraft always carried a few flares on night operations even when their main load was much more lethal.

The crew operated against the French targets 617 used to develop and perfect their technique, bombing with care and precision to endanger the fewest possible civilian lives. An unfortunate cricket accident resulted in John being the only 617 aircrew on strength to miss Operation Taxable, the D-Day spoof, but he returned to operational duty to fly against the 'V3' sites in the Pas de Calais. When these had been over-run by the Allied ground forces, 617 turned its Tallboys on to submarine pens. On 14 August 1944 during his bombing run on the pens at Brest, a single piece of shrapnel from an ack-ack burst penetrated the bomb-aimer's compartment. It struck Cecil Pesme in the neck, killing him instantly. This was a great blow to the crew, both personally and operationally, as Cecil's ability had always been a big factor in their run of success.

Their operational score mounted and John Pryor's crew became recognized on 617 as a very professional and successful combination operationally. John developed a reputation for being uncompromisingly dogmatic in discussions where he felt he was right. He would never concede a point, even diplomatically, and the more affable and easy-going aircrew of the Squadron found him very irritating on occasion, to say the least!

They had two *Tirpitz* operations to their credit, and during December members of his crew reached the optimum 45 operations for a continuous 'double-tour' and exercised their right for posting. Lloyd Pinder's last operation was against the Urft Dam, in Germany—on 8 December 1944 he returned to Canada. John completed further operations in the late December and then went on rostered leave. His personal score at this time was 49 operations, 28 of which he had completed with 617 Squadron. He knew that Albert Hepworth needed one more operation to register 45 operations, and John had decided that he would see Albert 'over the hump' before deciding his own future. John returned to Woodhall Spa on the morning of 12 January 1945 to operate immediately against Bergen, which was to prove his last operation.

After the Bergen misfortune and subsequent capture and interrogation by the Germans, John finally arrived at Dulag Luft Transient Camp at Wetzlar, forty miles north of Frankfurt-on-Main, to be released eventually on 1 April 1945, when General Patton's American 3rd Army Corps over-ran the area. After repatriation and a period of leave John was posted to West Malling, Kent until July 1945. He was then posted to Elsham Wolds, North Lincolnshire where he trained as a flying control officer. In March 1946 he was posted to Mildenhall, Suffolk, to 15 Squadron as a pilot screening officer. He tried to get accelerated demobilization to return to farming, but ironically, in view of his frustration to join the RAF, because of his farming employment, it took eighteen months for authority to release him to return to the land!

John applied himself diligently to agriculture under the watchful eye and guidance of his father until the unexpected and horrendous loss of both parents in a road accident on 17 January 1973 whilst en route for a holiday. He has made a great success of the farm, as could be expected, never being afraid to make decisions, change direction and make the great changes necessary to keep the farm viable and in good shape. His son Mark is following the family tradition in farming and his daughter Anne presented John with a granddaughter in 1984 to his great delight and appreciation. A life-long and fervent cricket enthusiast, the county's success in recent years has pleased John tremendously. His natural dogmatism has softened over the years but still surfaces on occasions, but then one cannot expect total miracles in this day and age.

Squadron Leader David John Shannon
DSO and bar, DFC and bar

On his eighteenth birthday in May 1940, David Shannon reported to the Royal Australian Navy's recruiting centre in Adelaide, in company with his good friend Batty Marks. They were told that the waiting period for entrants was at least nine months. Batty accepted this, but Dave decided to see what the Royal Australian Air Force had to offer. He discovered the waiting period for the RAAF was six months and so he signed on to wear the famous dark blue serge, little knowing what bearing that decision was to have on his life.

He completed his flying training and was commissioned as a pilot in September 1941. Dave arrived in England by way of the USA and Canada, a journey that made a great impression on the young Australian, in November of that year. After attending No 1 Advanced Flying Training Unit for a month at the RAF College, Cranwell and a short blind approach training course at RAF Swanton Morley, he was posted in January 1942 to No 19 OTU at RAF Kinloss, on the Moray Firth, flying Whitleys in preparation for a bomber pilot's career.

Dave joined No 106 Squadron at RAF Coningsby, Lincolnshire in June 1942 and logged his first bomber operation that same month against Bremen, flying a Lancaster. His first tour was especially noteworthy for that period of the war in that he flew four major bomber daylight operations—Danzig on 11 July, Essen on 18 July, Le Creusot on 17 October and Milan on 24 October. He was awarded the Distinguished Flying Cross and took himself off to join Pathfinder Force at the conclusion of this tour, only to return at the double to 5 Group, Bomber Command at Wing Commander Gibson's telephoned invitation to join a new squadron that was being formed in 5 Group in March 1943.

Dave was twenty years old when he captained a Lancaster on the Dams raid on 16/17 May 1943 and celebrated his twenty-first birthday on the occasion of the visit of His Majesty King George VI to RAF Scampton to congratulate the crews of 617 Squadron on their magnificent achievement. Dave was awarded an immediate Distinguished Service Order for his part in this operation, and the award was presented to him by Queen Elizabeth, the beloved Queen Mother of today.

Dave continued to operate with 617 Squadron until he was 'retired forcibly' and without appeal by Sir Ralph Cochrane, the Air Officer Commanding No 5 Group, to the great relief of his wife Ann, whom he had married soon after the Dams raid. He had accomplished 69 operations without a break, adding six more daylight operations to his previous tally and finished his operational career on 25 June 1944. He had been awarded an immediate first Bar to the DFC for a low-level attack against the Dortmund-Ems Canal at Ladbergen on the night of 15/16 September 1943. An attack against this target had been recalled on the previous night before the aircraft had crossed the enemy coast. Over the two nights, nine crews had been detailed for the operation and of these only three survived. A first Bar to the DSO came at the end of his time on 617 Squadron, with a special mention in the citation of his part as deputy-leader in the very successful attack against Munich on the night of 24/25 April 1944. This operation was also cited in Leonard Cheshire's Victoria Cross award.

Dave was promoted to Wing Commander and posted as Chief Flying Instructor to No 27 OTU, RAF Church Broughton, a unit using Wellington aircraft. This was not Dave's idea of the war and so, after some discussion and 'string-pulling', he relinquished his Wing Commander rank to join RAF Transport Command, flying C 47s and York aircraft with 511 and 246 Squadrons on the trunk routes until he was demobbed in December 1945 in England.

After a few brief months working with Leonard Cheshire on a few hare-brained schemes that just did not jell, he joined the Shell International Petroleum Company. For sixteen years he was on exploration and production assignments in Borneo, Venezuela and Egypt, followed by a period in the London head office, concerned with ventures in North Africa. Later he was a director of Shell companies in Columbia and Kenya. A change of direction was made in 1962 when Dave turned to farming. Farmer Shannon and his wife began to fatten beef stores, set up an intensive poultry unit and to make a name for himself for the breeding of Welsh mountain ponies, although his efforts did occasionally receive caustic denigration from the New Zealand farmer and former 617 Squadron 'original' Les Munro.

In 1968 Dave returned to the world of oil, joining Offshore Marine at Great Yarmouth. His experience of earlier years was of great value. In 1969 he became Commercial Manager and spent a couple of years on projects and developments, being appointed Marketing Director in October 1972. The company won a Queen's Award for export achievement. In 1973 he became Sales and Chartering Director of Offshore Marine, as well as Deputy Managing Director of the company. Dave sold the farm and the Welsh pony stud in 1973 and, later that year, became Managing Director of Offshore Marine, which had by then become one of the Trafalgar House Group of Companies.

In September 1978 he was transferred as Managing Director to Geoprosco Overseas Limited, another Trafalgar House Company. This company contracted oil drilling and work-over rigs in the Middle East and Egypt. He was required to travel, occasionally at very short notice, often and extensively in this capacity until his well-earned retirement in September 1984, an event that met with Ann's great approval! However, Dave has not entirely severed his connection with the oil world, having been retained as a consultant for the Group.

Dave aims to see much more of his daughter and the two grandsons with whom he and Ann have been blest. Earlier in 1984, he obliged a German TV company by appearing on a programme that was being produced for Germany, involving the Allied bombing of the Third Reich, his contribution being about the Dams raid. Dave insisted that as well as interviews in the TV studio, by the German Press and at the Mohne Dam, some 'takes' were done at the Eder Dam, which had been the scene of his personal contribution to the Dams raid.

Despite all the influences of 'anglicization' over the past forty years, Dave still retains that outspokenness and forthrightness which is the acknowledged, and envied, hallmark of all true Aussies—God bless 'em for it!

Warrant Officer Albert Leslie Smith

Les Smith was called-up to Blackpool on 13 September 1940, to commence training as a 'straight air-gunner'. After initial training in foot-drill, etc, he was posted to No 10 Air-Gunnery School at Dumfries in February 1941. He passed the gunnery course and was posted to No 10 Operational Training Unit at RAF Lossiemouth in April, to convert to Wellingtons en route for Bomber Command. In July the aircraft in which he was flying crashed in flames near Keith, about twenty minutes flying time from Lossiemouth. In this accident, the front gunner was killed and the rest of the crew severely injured. When Les was discharged from hospital, graded fit for flying duties, he became a ground gunnery instructor at Lossiemouth.

However, the injuries he had suffered required him to be hospitalized at Peebles for twelve days, followed by ten weeks in the RAF hospital at Matlock. In December 1941, he was finally discharged, fully recovered and he went on a series of staff gunnery instructor courses. On 8 May 1943 he was posted for flying instructional duties at No 1 Air-Gunnery School, RAF Pembrey, South Wales. This proved to be a very hazardous occupation and Les decided to seek the possibly safer life of bomber operations rather than continue in this duty. His request was granted and on 3 March 1944, he reported to No 14 OTU, RAF Market Harborough, where he was crewed with Flying Officer Tony Iveson.

The crew passed through the training schedule, culminating at the Lancaster Finishing School, from which they were posted direct to 617 Squadron on 22 July 1944.

After his traumatic Bergen experiences, Les was eventually sent to Stalagluft 3A at Nuremberg. That camp was hastily cleared with the advance of the US Armies and the prisoners were herded into cattle-trucks and sent to Moosburg, near Dachau, the largest PoW camp in Germany, being heavily attacked by marauding US fighters en route but managing to survive. The camp was liberated on 1 May 1945 by US forces after a short local battle. Les was returned to the United Kingdom on 10 May.

He was finally demobbed on 3 May 1946 and resumed his trade of hairdressing. On 19 October 1944 his daughter Christine had been born and, sadly, in 1950 it was confirmed that she suffered from Muscular Spinal Atrophy. Les and his wife Jess have earned the admiration of the whole 617 Squadron Association for the care and love they have bestowed uncomplainingly on Christine ever since, almost without a break. Not that Christine was prepared to accept her fate without question. She has attended many of the social functions of the Association over the years in her wheelchair and coped adequately with the eight-day visit the Association made to Amsterdam in 1976. She wrote an account of her life, and the manuscript was finally accepted and published under the title *Clouds got in my way* in the Year of the Disabled, 1981. She also produces excellent paintings, holding the brushes dexterously between her teeth.

Les and Jess have nevertheless found time to become actively involved in fund-raising for the Cheshire Homes, the Sue Ryder Homes and the Muscular Dystrophy Group of Great Britain, of which they are founder members. The cumulative effect of the injuries he suffered during his wartime flying career has required Les himself to have spinal operations and his left leg is half-dead, due to the nerves being severely damaged. He now needs sticks to get around and has great difficulty in sitting comfortably. He has been medically declared fifty per cent war disabled. Despite all this, Les and Jess maintain a cheerful outlook on life which is an example to all.

Warrant Officer James Theodore Thompson

At the age of eighteen, Jim Thompson (or 'Tommy' as he inevitably became in the Royal Air Force) presented himself to the RAF Selection board at Oxford. He passed the selection tests and the stringent medical examination and was accepted for wireless operator/air-gunner training. Tommy was called up into the 'Blackpool Air Force' in February 1941 and did his *ab initio* training, stamping around the streets of Blackpool and his wireless training in the famous tram sheds on the South Shore (no joke in the northern winter!). He passed the final Morse test at twelve words per minute and moved to the No 2 Signals School, RAF Yatesbury, Wiltshire in December 1941. Here he completed his wireless operator course, having raised his Morse speed to eighteen words per minute and become competent in all aspects of the wireless transmitting set. Tommy then moved on to the air-gunnery school at Walney Island, Lancashire in November 1942. On the successful completion of this course, he was awarded his brevet and posted to No 19 OTU, RAF Kinloss, Morayshire in January 1943.

At Kinloss he was crewed for bomber operations, flying Whitley aircraft. The crew was posted to the Bomber Command Detachment at RAF St Eval in April 1943 at the completion of their OTU course. Flying Whitleys operationally, the crew carried out six ten-hour anti-U-boat patrols in the Bay of Biscay. On their sixth patrol, a U-boat was attacked with depth-charges and the photographic evidence taken at the time of the attack suggested that the U-boat had been severely damaged. In June 1943, the crew was posted to No 1654 Heavy Conversion Unit at RAF Wigsley, Lincolnshire to continue the training schedule leading to operating in four-engined bombers. After completing this training in full, they were posted to No 619 Squadron at Woodhall Spa to operate on Lancaster aircraft. Tommy's captain at this time was Flying Officer Malcolm Hamilton.

On 9 January 1944, 619 Squadron moved to RAF Coningsby and 617 moved from Coningsby to Woodhall Spa. With his operational score at twenty sorties, including ten to Berlin, Tommy moved with his crew back to Woodhall Spa, when their application to join 617 had been approved in February 1944, meeting up with two former crew from 619 who had joined 617 previously—Nicky Knilans and Bob Knights. By June 1944, he had completed his first tour of thirty operations, and his targets with 617 included Angoulême, Lyons (twice), Toulouse, Brunswick, Munich and the D-Day Operation Taxable, as well as the Saumur Tunnel raid and the Le Havre U-boat pens. Like all good bomber crew, he put his anti-U-boat patrols down to experience rather than count them in his operational total.

The crew decided to carry on operating to mount a second tour. This they did very successfully, against U-boat pens, the massive sites in the Pas de Calais and two of the *Tirpitz* operations. With his operational score at 45 sorties, Tommy decided to continue on 617 Squadron, even though most of his crew opted for posting. He joined Flying Officer Joplin's crew in the role of rear-gunner. It is interesting to note that one of Tommy's previous 617 operations had been with Bill Carey's crew as front-gunner against one of the Pas de Calais sites. 617 aircrew were nothing if not versatile and willing! The episode of 22 December 1944, which incidentally was Tommy's twenty-second birthday, was his last operation, with his final score at fifty sorties.

After he had recovered from his spinal injuries, Tommy had some innocuous postings and was demobbed in November 1945. He married his wife Elsie in January 1946 and in the fullness of time was blest with two daughters. Tommy admits to having changed jobs 'more times than Tommy Cooper changed hats' in the post-war period but, in 1971, he joined a manufacturer of fine precision castings in Ryde, Isle of Wight, engaged in radiography and film processing. In 1981, the company was forced by the onset of the recession to cut its X-ray staff but Tommy was re-located in the inspection department. He has his fingers crossed that the next three years will pass to his retirement date without further employment complications for himself, or better still, that the forecast industrial upsurge will actually arrive to reinstate him in his former radiography duties.

Tommy is very proud of his daughters and is more willing to talk about them than his own life. His elder daughter, Christine, is a teacher at the Wandsworth Boys' School in South London and Valerie is a medical secretary at the All Saints Hospital in the Medway Area of Kent. Both are married and Tommy has two splendid sons-in-law who behave as good sons-in-law should. They regularly hammer him at chess and golf, but do not neglect to push the boat out in way of compensation. All in all, Tommy is grateful for a closely-knit and happy family.

Flight Sergeant Frank Tilley

Frank Tilley reported to the Aircrew Reception Centre, Regents Park, London in June 1943, having enlisted for flight engineer duties. He went to the Initial Training Wing at Torquay for his *ab initio* training and introduction to the specialist aircrew subjects. He was posted to the Engineer Training School, RAF St Athan, South Wales, in September 1943 and successfully passed the course in March 1944. He was sent to the Heavy Conversion Unit, RAF Swinderby, where he was crewed with Flying Officer Arthur Joplin and completed the training schedule for heavy bombers, at which point his crew was posted direct to 617 Squadron at Woodhall Spa.

The disaster on 22 December 1944 was his tenth bomber trip, as he had performed one with another crew during his stay with 617. His injuries resulted in a stay at RAF Hospital Rauceby, near Sleaford, Lincolnshire. When he had recovered, he was transferred to the RAF convalescent wing at Hoylake and stayed there until August 1945. He was posted back to RAF Woodhall Spa where he stayed for a few weeks before travelling across Lincolnshire to join 617 at RAF Waddington. The Squadron had its full complement of aircrew and Frank was posted to RAF Catterick 'surplus to requirements' for re-mustering to another trade. He was given a clerical grade and posted to a Polish Transport Command airfield at Chedburgh, where he found himself in charge of air publications (engineering). He was posted in August 1946 to RAF Whytleaf for clerical duties at Croydon Airport, assisting in the documentation of personnel from all three Services repatriated from overseas service. He was eventually demobbed in February 1947.

Frank decided to make his career in office and business machines. He quickly found employment with the National Cash Register Company but after six months moved to the Hollerith Punch Card Systems and joined the British Tabulating Machine Company Limited. He started as a field engineer and was quickly promoted in the rapidly expanding company, which became International Computers Limited and then Standard Telephones and Cables. The company was among the first to design and develop computers and Frank found it an ideal environment in which to develop his career. He held several senior positions in various engineering activities, covering field engineering, technical support, world-wide technical services and, finally, repair workshops. Frank counts himself fortunate in that his work was also his hobby and he spent a completely happy time with the company, retiring on 31 December 1982.

Frank met his wife, June, in 1947 and they married at Thames Ditton Parish Church in July 1949. They have two sons. Richard achieved a first class honours degree in engineering at Bath University. A spell at British Leyland decided him to seek fame and fortune overseas. He now holds a very senior position with one of the major American computer companies in their South African organization. Frank's second son, David, also went into engineering. He spent a few years at the British Aircraft Corporation and then took courses in works and methods study. These qualifications brought him a responsible position with Sperry, New Holland, Lincolnshire but when this American company decided to close down its European operations, David emulated his brother and sought his fortune successfully in South Africa. He now works for Soilmasters in Johannesburg. Their sons have provided Frank and June with a grandson and two granddaughters but unfortunately visits are somewhat few and far between, although letters and photographs try to bridge the gap.

June and Frank are still enjoying a full life. They play golf regularly, albeit they are members of different clubs. Frank follows the usual hobbies of gardening and house-decoration. He maintains their two cars and finds time to pursue his love of classical organ playing. Frank belongs to an organ club in the Hitchin, Hertfordshire, area and happily serves on the maintenance team which keeps their pride and joy—a 1936 Christie, three manual, cinema organ—in majestic voice and power. On a purely voluntary basis, but motivated by his love of machinery and its development, Frank assists in the maintenance and development of the ICL Museum. This holds a fund of knowledge, literature, films, photographs and quite a selection of the hardware, tracing the growth of information technology from Babbage's time in 1833 to the present day.

Squadron Leader Edward A. Wass AE

Ted Wass enlisted in The Royal Air Force Volunteer Reserve as an equipment assistant in May 1939. The enlistment took place at No 7 FTS, Westwood Airfield, Peterborough and was ostensibly for a period of five years part-time service. He was mobilized for full-time service on 1 September 1939. His first posting was to RAF Waddington, Lincolnshire and then to the Equipment Training School, RAF Cranwell for specialist training.

He spent a year at RAF St Athan, South Wales and was then posted to the Middle East in June 1941. He served with a mobile stores unit in Egypt, Syria and the Lebanon, supporting fighter squadrons and mobile repair units in the field. He responded to a call for volunteers for training as air-gunners, was accepted, and returned to the United Kingdom in July 1943 for training.

He passed through all stages of training successfully and on 22 July 1944 he joined 617 Squadron at Woodhall Spa for his first tour of bomber operations. He was a member of Flight Lieutenant Iveson's crew, all of whom were having their first contact with bomber operations. They undertook operations with the squadron, including the three attacks on the *Tirpitz* and the operation against the Kembs Barrage across the Rhine, near Basle. In November 1944, Ted was appointed to commissioned rank and continued operating until baling out over Bergen in January 1945. He attempted to evade the enemy but was captured by the Germans and eventually finished up in Stalag 13D, on the site of Hitler's Nuremberg Stadium. He was subjected to a forced march similar to those experienced by most PoWs in April 1945, but later that month his camp at Moosburg, east of Munich, was liberated after a short battle, by General Patton's American Army and Ted found himself back in England on 10 May 1945.

After a short period of rehabilitation and leave he was returned to duty as a supply officer in September 1945, pending demobilization. However, in January 1947 he accepted a permanent commission in the supply branch. Over the next 28 years, Ted had progressive appointments in charge of supply squadrons, at command headquarters and at branches of the Ministry of Defence. He also had overseas tours of duty in Egypt, Germany and Norway.

His two years appointment at NATO Headquarters, Oslo, Norway, was of great nostalgic interest. He found the cells at Fornebu Airport where he and several other 617 aircrew had awaited transportation to Germany in January 1945. He revisited the Hotel Holmenkollen on the outskirts of Oslo which was the Luftwaffe headquarters in Norway during the war and which held memories for him, but he never managed to get to the Bergen area, scene of his bale-out.

Ted retired from the Royal Air Force in October 1975 with the rank of Squadron Leader, at the age of 55. He recalled with a wry smile that, under the terms of his original part-time engagement, he had been required to serve seven days full-time training with the Service during the week ending 1 September 1939. In the event that week extended into 36 years of unbroken service, and a rewarding life of travel and comradeship throughout the world.

Ted joined an East Anglian garage group as Sales Administrator for a period of five years. He is now enjoying full retirement in his own leisurely way and actively serves on the civilian committee of No 115 Squadron (Peterborough) Air Training Corps.

Flight Lieutenant Arthur James Ward DFC, Mention in Despatches

Arthur Ward left the Auxiliary Fire Service to join the Royal Air Force on 3 September 1940, for wireless operator/air-gunner training. His training became prolonged, as he was posted to serve as an 'under-training' wireless operator at RAF Scampton and then on flying boats at RAF Invergordon. He eventually qualified for his brevet and was crewed up to operate in Blenheim aircraft in the Middle East. At the last moment, this posting was cancelled and he was switched to further training courses for duties on heavy bombers.

Arthur joined No 467 (Australian) Squadron at Bottesford, Lincolnshire and undertook his first bomber operation against Hamburg on 3 March 1943. Later that same month he was posted to No 97 Squadron at Woodhall Spa, where he joined an experienced crew under Flying Officer Harrison. He completed five more operations with this crew, only to find himself transferred in July 1943 to Flight Lieutenant Tom O'Shaughnessy's crew and posted, together with crews from other 5 Group squadrons, to form the new 619 Squadron at Woodhall Spa. He had flown 25 operations when his crew answered the call for experienced reinforcements for 617 at RAF Coningsby. When 617 transferred to Woodhall Spa in early January 1944, Arthur found himself once more comfortably ensconced in the Petwood Hotel, which was the Officers' Mess for 617 Squadron.

After his full recovery from crash injuries, Arthur rejoined 617 in May 1944 and continued to operate, bringing his operational score to 53 sorties. His 'Mention in Despatches' was awarded for the long and carefully-coded wireless message he had sent during the return flight from Tromso on 13 November 1944, announcing to 5 Group in particular and the world in general that the German battleship *Tirpitz* had been sunk at her Norwegian anchorage.

Arthur left 617 Squadron in June 1945 and was demobbed on 1 November that year. He joined an advertising agency and, after a long and successful career, retired in 1979 to enjoy his hobbies of gardening and watercolour painting.

Flight Lieutenant Frederick H. A. Watts DFC

Freddy Watts was born in Kensington, London and was training as a metallurgist at the AEC Company, Southall, Middlesex when war broke out. At the age of nineteen, he immediately attempted to join the London Scottish Regiment, but was sent back to his civilian occupation which was reserved at that time. He later volunteered for the Royal Air Force as an air-gunner, since men in reserved occupations could be accepted for aircrew duties. He was offered pilot training after his selection board interview and gladly accepted. There followed a period of deferred service before Freddy entered the 'training treadmill', obtaining the coveted pilot's brevet in October 1942.

After completing operational training and 'heavy conversion' in 1943, Freddy joined No 630 Squadron at RAF East Kirkby in October 1943. After fifteen operations with 630 Squadron, Freddy was approached for transfer to Pathfinder Force duties but expressed a preference for 617 Squadron, as he wished to stay in 5 Group. He moved with his crew to 617 at RAF Woodhall Spa in April 1944. He bombed *Tirpitz* on all three operations against the German battleship and was a credit to many of the other operations of the Squadron. He completed his second tour in January 1945, but continued to fly with the Squadron until February 1945, by which time he had raised his operational total to 52 sorties, 37 of these with 617. He was awarded the Distinguished Flying Cross in November 1944, the citation including references to his operations with 630 Squadron. He was delighted when the same award was made to his navigator, Charles Housden, and his Canadian bomb-aimer, Mervyn McKay in January 1945.

Freddy had a short spell on fighter affiliation duties, which was followed by a posting to No 83 Squadron as squadron instructor, responsible for converting crews to Lincoln aircraft in preparation for the Far East war. The code name for the squadrons being so prepared was *Tiger Force*. In November 1946, he captained one of the three Lincoln aircraft which flew to Santiago, Chile, representing the British Services at the inauguration of the Chilean President. It is believed that they were the first Bomber Command aircraft to overfly the Andes.

In 1947, Freddy commenced a four-year stint test flying Meteor aircraft at No 32 Maintenance Unit, RAF St Athan. During this period Freddy had the great pleasure to make the acquaintance of Sir Arthur Whitten-Brown, the Atlantic pioneer of 'Alcock and Brown' fame. This grand old gentleman was an honorary member of the St Athan Officers' Mess and Freddy enjoyed many mutually interesting and stimulating conversations and discussions with him. On 12 October 1948, Freddy felt honoured to be the pilot chosen to fly the aircraft charged with the duty of scattering Sir Arthur's ashes over the broad Atlantic. The last rites were pronounced by an RAF padre, the only other person on board the aircraft, and carrying out Sir Arthur's last request gave Freddy a rare sense of occasion.

In 1953 Freddy was offered a permanent commission in the RAF which he accepted. He continued on various tours of flying duties, interspersed with two ground tours on schools liaison and recruitment. His final tour of flying duty was with the Cambridge University Air Squadron and he retired from the Service in June 1964. He joined Barclays Bank that same month and worked for the bank until August 1984, when he retired to lead a much more leisurely life.

Freddy and his crew rendered sterling service to Bomber Command and 617 Squadron during their operational career. On 617 they were looked upon as one of the 'backbone' crews, always contributing to the successes of the Squadron. Freddy had a great sense of humour and when the two Londoners, Witherick and Watts, got together on festive occasions, the wit and raconteuring kept the laughter flowing. One cannot think back to the wartime 617 days without recalling Freddy Watts with pleasure and the inevitable smile.

Flight Lieutenant Gerald Witherick DFC, DFM

Gerry Witherick joined the Royal Air Force on 14 September 1936 on a nine year engagement. In September 1939 he was a driver (petrol) with the rank of Leading Aircraftsman serving on No 47 Squadron and stationed at Khartoum. When war was declared on 3 September 1939, he felt reasonably safe since he figured that the nearest German was about 2,000 miles away and he put the extra hour that the canteen was allowed to remain open that night to very good use!

In April 1940, 47 Squadron moved to the Red Sea Hills, as the Italians had been staging Savoia bombers through Khartoum for the previous two months to their East African colonies and it was obvious that some major move was afoot. The actual RAF station at which the squadron settled down was RAF Erkowit.

On 10 June 1940 he was inevitably in the NAAFI tent when the news came through that Italy had issued an ultimatum which meant that, if its demands were not met, a state of war would exist between Italy and Britain as from midnight. All hands turned to, to fuel and bomb up the five Wellesley bombers with which the Squadron was equipped. Before leaving Khartoum, the airmen had been to see Errol Flynn's film *The Dawn Patrol*, so what they didn't know about war in the air was nobody's business! The five aircraft took off at one minute after midnight to bomb the large Italian base near Asmara, the capital of Eritrea. They arrived over their target to find that the Italians were holding a grand parade on the barrack square. As the Wellesleys swept over the parade ground, the crews noticed that slit-trenches had been dug all over the camp, but there was no anti-aircraft opposition. Each bomber dropped 48 25 lb anti-personnel bombs during the raid and machine-gunned the area thoroughly in repeated sweeps.

In the course of later raids, the Squadron began to suffer casualties. Pilots were 'ten a penny' but air-gunners were at a premium and so a call was issued for volunteers to be trained as air-gunners. Gerry stepped smartly forward, mesmerized by the offer of seven shillings a day pay! The course was shown a Lewis machine-gun and its dismantling and re-assembly was practised until each airman was proficient in this skill. Each one was then allowed to fire a few rounds at the butts and then they were declared 'air-gunners' and awarded the 'Golden Bullet'.

Gerry's first operation was in a Wellesley against the Italian base at Zula (Eritrea) on 20 July 1940. The formation was attacked by Italian CR 42 and CR 32 biplane fighters and a fair little battle ensued. The fighters were armed with .5 calibre machine-guns against the Wellesley's .303 calibre gun, and so they could sit back at 600 yards range and fire at the bombers, whose return fire was impotent at that range. However, no bomber was lost or damaged and no fighter appeared to be distressed, so honours were declared even.

Not so on the next operation against Gura (Eritrea). The bomber formation was attacked very strongly and one of the gunners, Sergeant Pope, was killed. All the bombers suffered machine-gun fire damage, but the strangest incident occurred after the action had apparently ceased. The target had been bombed and the bombers were heading for base when a lone CR 42 ranged up into the formation vic of Gerry's flight and settled down comfortably behind the Flight leader. It was too good a chance to miss! All three gunners took careful aim and opened up almost simultaneously. The fighter tipped over on to its back and spun down to crash into the desert below in a burst of flame and smoke. Gerry was credited with one-third of a CR 42 for this combined effort. After several more operations from RAF Erkowit, the Squadron returned to Khartoum, a move which brought targets in Italian Abbysinnia within range. They attacked a large petrol and ammunition store at Mattemma, using 250 lb bombs and incendiaries. The attack went in at 500 feet and the target was soon blazing and exploding merrily.

Gerry had completed the stipulated two years in desert conditions and was posted to No 70 Squadron at RAF Kabrit on the Great Bitter Lake, Egypt. He spent a month converting to Wellington bombers and mastering the intricacies of power-operated turrets and sighting, before the Squadron moved up the line to RAF El Adem in Libya, an ex-Italian airfield that the desert war had delivered into British hands. In April 1941, the Afrika Corps with its attendant Luftwaffe groups had arrived to stiffen the Axis effort in the Western Desert and things were never quite the same after that. The Squadron operated under desert conditions, which were uncomfortable, to say the least. Gerry had amassed 37 operations in the Sudan and Egypt when higher authority decided to use him as a secret weapon and launch him against the Fatherland. He was returned to England via South Africa and to this day has happy memories of that wonderful place with its wonderful people.

He arrived back in the UK in February 1942 and was pushed around various training establishments until finally arriving on No 405 (Canadian) Squadron at RAF Pocklington in Yorkshire, where he became a rear-gunner on Halifax bombers. His captain's name was Blizzard and Gerry carried out five operations with this captain, including the 'thousand bomber raids'. He also had the experience of 'baling out' over RAF Binbrook in Lincolnshire. The next operation was to Duisburg, at the apex of the Ruhr complex. It proved to be the usual run-of-the-mill operation until they returned to Pocklington. The pilot landed the Halifax off the runway. It careered through two Wellington bombers which the station engineer officer had lovingly rebuilt from the wrecks of other Wellingtons, and came to rest beside a hangar. Gerry was the first out of the aircraft and sped to open the door of the aircraft so that the rest of the crew could escape. He shouted in to see if any assistance was needed and, with many lurid Anglo-Saxon expressions, his fellow crew members assured him that this was so. It was subsequently learned that the pilot suffered from continuous double-vision so that he always saw two runways but up to that time he had managed to select the correct one on which to land!

With a new skipper, Gerry's tour developed along the usual main force lines, with targets mainly in 'Happy Valley' and the Rhineland. In September 1942, his crew was detached to RAF Beaulieu in Hampshire, to assist in Coastal Command operations. They carried out eleven anti-submarine patrols and one dinghy search without seeing a submarine or one single German, which made a change from the hectic bomber life. He was awarded the Distinguished Flying Medal and posted for instructor duties to RAF Topcliffe in Yorkshire.

He spent a year on these duties, hating every moment of it. With his record of 57 bomber operations and eleven submarine patrols, he felt that he would be condemned to the instructional role for the rest of the war. He was greatly intrigued by the Dams raid operation and when, later in 1943, he heard that this Squadron was accepting only aircrew who had at least one tour of bomber operations to their credit, he sent off his application to join 617 with great alacrity. Subsequently, his posting was approved and he joined 617 at their base at RAF Coningsby in Lincolnshire in October 1943. He was welcomed into the Officers' Mess by a most wonderful man, with a chestful of operational medals. This Wing Commander greeted him with 'Hello, Gerry! I am Leonard Cheshire. Welcome to the Squadron!' and shook him delightedly by the hand. Gerry unashamedly admits that he has been a Leonard Cheshire man ever since!

Gerry became one of the many characters on 617 Squadron. His abilities, both operationally and party-wise, were always commented upon most favourably and he flew with many of the colourful and rumbustious captains and crews that inhabited the squadron during his period on 617, particularly in the latter stages with the Australian Bill Carey and his 'chickens'. He was awarded a well-merited Distinguished Flying Cross for his services on 617 Squadron and finally left the

Squadron and the operational scene on 4 May 1945.

He had accomplished 104 bomber operations in various theatres of war, but mainly in the bomber war against Germany from England. This total did not include the five 'early returns' (known as 'boomerangs' among the aircrew fraternity) due to aircraft failures, or the eleven anti-submarine patrols and the dinghy search, as Gerry steadfastly regards these to be in the nature of a rest from the strains of the bomber offensive rather than operations in themselves.

He finally left the Royal Air Force in October 1945, being demobbed from the centre set up in Olympia, London for that purpose. He found it difficult to get a job but the parents of his fiancée Pauline, who ran 'The George' public house in Clapton, London, took him under their wing and taught him the ropes. Gerry married Pauline and took over his own pub, 'The Shipwrights's Arms' in Tooley Street, London. They made a success of this venture and moved to 'The Reindeer' in Slough where they ploughed a successful furrow for about four years. They bought 'The George' at Burnham, Buckinghamshire, where they stayed for about three years. Lesley, their daughter, was born in 1950 and they returned to run a guest house in Slough.

The years as 'mine host' had taken Gerry's weight up to 17 stone and he decided that he had to do something about this excess weight. He took a very dirty and demanding job in a scrap-metal works and the physical demands of the job slimmed him down to 13 stone after about three years. He successfully moved into the world of commercial travelling and finally settled down with Superflexit Limited, a firm on the Slough trading estate. This company made pipes and fittings for the car and aircraft industries. He had a very happy working life with this company and retired in 1980. He and Pauline have made a happy home in West Sussex, with quite a few other wartime members of 617 Squadron in the neighbourhood and surrounding district.

No reunion or gathering of the 617 Squadron Association is really complete unless Gerry is present. He is a natural raconteur and his terrific memory and fund of stories always serve to enliven the proceedings. Members affectionately recall that no wartime occasion, operational or social, was ever complete unless Gerry was there to comment in his usual forthright and colourful manner on events as he saw them. To call Gerry Witherick to mind is to bring an involuntary smile to the face and a knowledge that many lives were enriched and encouraged by the larger-than-life presence of this man on the wartime 617 Squadron.

Flight Lieutenant Roy E. Woods DFC, Mention in Despatches (RCAF)

Roy Woods enlisted in the Royal Canadian Air Force on 21 August 1940, aged 22 years. He was sent to the Toronto Initial Training School for aircrew trade selection, and then proceeded to the Montreal Wireless School, followed by a course at Jarvis Bombing and Gunnery School. He was posted overseas, arriving in Scotland on 25 April 1941. His group was the first to arrive at the Bournemouth Reception Centre, Hampshire. Roy completed a course at the wireless school at RAF Cranwell and he was posted to No 22 OTU, RAF Wellesbourne Mountford, near Stratford-on-Avon. Here he switched to bomb-aimer duties and was given some navigation training. On completion of the OTU course, his crew, without a pilot, was posted to No 419 (Moose) Squadron at RAF Mildenhall, flying Wellington Mark 2s.

Roy's first operational trip was against Cologne, the first 'thousand bomber raid', on 15 May 1942 and his captain for this and his second trip was 'Moose' Fulton, from Kamloops, British Columbia. Flight Sergeant Jack Wiggins, from Winnipeg, Manitoba, a pilot who had considerable operational experience on 419 Squadron, became their regular captain and Roy's operational career progressed with him, until an operation on Hamburg. Their aircraft came in for a great deal of attention from the German defences and the 'Wimpy' finished up at roof-top height, machine-gunning the tenacious searchlights and light-flak emplacements. The dive from height adversely affected the eardrums of the navigator, who was taken off operations as a result. Jack Wiggins decided to call that the end of his first tour and once again Roy found himself and the remaining members of the crew without a captain. There was an English pilot, Sergeant Maddock, who had been posted to this Canadian outfit by mistake. He was awaiting re-posting to an RAF Squadron, but had settled down happily on 419 and did not wish to leave. Strong representations were made in the right quarters and Sergeant Maddock was allowed to remain with 419 Squadron and flew with Roy. The Squadron moved to RAF Leeming Bar in Yorkshire on 12 August 1942, when No 6 (Canada) Bomber Group was formed.

Roy completed his first tour, with an operational score of 37 trips, on 6 November 1942. He was posted back to Wellesbourne Mountford as a staff instructor (bombing). During this instructional tour, he was detached to various bombing courses at the air armament school at RAF Manby, including a very thorough course on special bomb-sights, which was to stand him in good stead later in his career. He had been commissioned on 20 September 1942 and was one of the two chief instructors at Wellesbourne Mountford. A month's leave in Canada was available to all Canadian Air Force personnel between the ending of an instructional tour and the commencement of a second tour of operations, and Roy was preparing to take advantage of the concession. However, a certain Flying Officer Warren Alvin ('Bill') Duffy was beavering away at Wellesbourne Mountford to form a crew of experienced aircrew to join 617 Squadron. Somehow, Roy knew instinctively that he just HAD to be part of that crew. He forfeited his month's 'home leave' in Canada to take the bomb-aimer spot in Duffy's proposed crew. Roy had the greatest difficulty in extricating himself from the clutches of the station armament officer, Squadron Leader Redford. The latter was determined to retain his star instructor. But Roy's unequivocal insistence on leaving, coupled with Duffy's own unrelenting campaign to secure Roy's services, eventually won the day and 'Duffy's mob' arrived at Woodhall Spa. Soon after their arrival, they learned that Roy had been 'Mentioned in Despatches' for distinguished service relating to his instructional tour at Wellesbourne Mountford. Bill Duffy was greatly amused by this, referring to it as a 'Bomb Aimer's AFC'. He had his own special translation of these initials which had certainly not endeared him to many senior officers he had encountered in the training sphere.

Duffy's crew were soon held in high regard on 617 Squadron, and in awe in some other quarters. They developed a fierce commitment and loyalty to the Squadron they had applied to join. For all the outward appearances of indiscipline, Duffy ruled them firmly and tolerated nothing less than the highest standards at all times in the air from every member of his crew. They showed nothing but the greatest respect for Leonard Cheshire, and later Willie Tait, not that the rest of the Squadron aircrew would have permitted anything less. But their other paths through Squadron life were liberally littered with outraged senior officers, affronted by the casual and forthright observations 'Duffy's mob' were noted for making on all aspects of Service life and institutions. The latest 'Duffy outrage' would initially take away the breath of the incredulous 617 aircrew before they dissolved into almost uncontrollable mirth. Both Chesh and Willie knew the tremendous and applied professionalism of Duffy's crew in the air, and had a soft spot for them on the ground, albeit they both needed to keep a straight 'official' face when dealing with their escapades.

The Mosquito accident on 7 August 1944 at the Wainfleet Bombing Range, in which Bill Duffy and Phil Ingleby were both killed, left the whole of 617 Squadron stunned. Duffy was buried in the Regional Cemetery, Harrogate on 11 August 1944. Roy Woods was the officer in charge of the funeral party. Somehow the sun never seemed quite as warm again at Woodhall Spa that summer. A small, intangible, but very real, element went out of the Squadron's life with Duffy gone, but the more outrageous episodes are still recalled with relish at Association reunions.

Roy Woods continued to operate with 617 Squadron. Bill Duffy's growing interest in Mosquito flying and operating had led to Roy flying with other captains prior to Duffy's death. He became Squadron bombing leader in July 1944, when Keith Astbury left the Squadron. His wide and effective instructional experience was a great asset to him and he proved to be more than capable of the task. Roy crewed permanently with Squadron Leader Gerry Fawke when Gerry formed a Lancaster crew once 617 had no further call for Mosquito target marking. He was in the crew for the trip to Yagodnik, some forty miles south-east of Archangel, on the river Dvina, when the Squadron positioned for the first raid against *Tirpitz* at her anchorage in Kaa Fiord well inside the Arctic Circle. His final operation was against the Kembs Barrage, across the Rhine near Basle, in daylight on 7 October 1944 and his final operational score was 64 trips. To this day his crew are convinced that if Roy had been with them on the first operation against *Tirpitz* at her Tromso anchorage on 29 October 1944, the third and final operation against the German battleship on 13 November would not have been necessary.

Roy was awarded a well-deserved Distinguished Flying Cross for his superb service to 617 Squadron. He returned to Canada during October 1944, arriving home on 11 November, to be posted as bombing leader at the Fengal Bombing and Gunnery School, moving later to the Mountain View Bombing and Gunnery School. He had a gut feeling that he was being scheduled for operations against Japan. Turning this possibility over in his mind, he figured that his luck could just run out. He was also engaged to be married and, despite advice to stay in the RCAF and make a career in the Service, he applied for discharge, which was granted on 16 March 1945.

He joined the staff of Bright's Limited, Canada's largest winery and settled down in Niagara Falls with his new wife, Eve. He was soon promoted to be in charge of the shipping department of Bright's, retiring after 38 years of continuous service in September 1983. Roy's organization of the visit to Niagara Falls during the 617 Squadron Association reunion in Canada in June 1972 was one of the highlights of the occasion.

1984 was a poor year health-wise for both Roy and Eve. They both underwent major surgery during the course of that year, which happily has proved very successful. Roy fought back with all the application and tenacity that he had shown throughout the war years. Two weeks holiday in Hawaii, with Eve's sister and brother-in-law, speeded their recovery and they now face the future with every confidence.

Glossary

Aldis Morse Code signal lamp: colour of beam changed by glass shutters.

AOC Air Officer Commanding.

AOC-in-C Air Officer Commanding-in-Chief.

ASR Air Sea Rescue.

ATA Actual Time of Arrival.

AWOL Absent without leave.

Boomerang Early return from an operation.

Bull Anything incorrect or unbelievable. Also applied to the 'spit and polish' requirements of a parade.

Chiefy Flight Sergeant.

Coronation The medal struck to mark the Coronation of His Majesty King George VI in 1937.

Cranwell Stickmen Allusion implying that pre-war Cranwell officers were of one mould, and as indistinguishable from each other as the matchstick men portrayed in the paintings of L. S. Lowry, the Manchester artist.

DFC Distinguished Flying Cross.

DFM Distinguished Flying Medal.

Ditching Forced-landing of an aircraft in water.

DSO Distinguished Service Order.

Elsan Chemical toilet at rear of aircraft.

ETA Estimated Time of Arrival.

Fido Fog dispersal system which burned paraffin in large quantities to clear a runway in dense fog.

Fish-heads RAF term for Royal Navy personnel.

Flak Anti-aircraft fire.

Flying bullet Sometimes known as the 'Golden Bullet'—pre-war RAF insignia worn by air-gunners —a winged bullet, in brass.

Gash Unattached or surplus to requirements.

Gharri Small transport van.

Goons Culled from characters figured in 'Popeye' cartoons. Any unprepossessing character.

Grass Description of the appearance of the German jamming on the Gee radar time bases.

Green endorsement Or simply 'Green'. A commendation recorded in an individual's Flying Log Book. Written in green ink.

Griff Reliable information.

Hairy Uncomfortable or somewhat dangerous.

Happy Valley RAF aircrews rueful name for the Ruhr Industrial Basin.

HCU Heavy Conversion Unit where crews were introduced to four-engined aircraft for the first time.

Irvin Trade name of the sheepskin-lined leather jacket issued to aircrew in the early years of the war.

Johnny Walkers A football-shaped hydrostatically-fused weapon of about 350 lb. They sank to a pre-set depth and were then forced upwards by jets of compressed air. If they struck an object on the way, they exploded, otherwise they submerged again to the pre-set depth and then off-set jets of compressed air shot them upwards on a different track. Designed to damage or hole the hulls of ships.

Kite Aircraft.

LAC Leading Aircraftsman.

Lead into the Luft Get airborne.

LFS Lancaster Finishing School, providing experience on Lancasters after the Heavy Conversion Unit course.

Mayday A corruption of the French *M'Aidez!* . . . a distress call.

MO Medical Officer.

NCO Non-commissioned officer.

Non-effective Officially medically categorized as temporarily unfit to perform flying duties.

Nuffield Scheme A leave scheme available to all aircrew. Free board and lodging at first-class hotels all over the United Kingdom, funded by Lord Nuffield of Morris Motors.

Oboe Electronically-controlled marking system, very accurate for area bombing but it had a limited range.

Pancake Landing.

Penguins Officers of the non-flying branches of the RAF.

Petrol bowsers Tanker vehicles for refuelling aircraft.

Petwood Petwood Hotel, Woodhall Spa, Lincolnshire, the Officers' Mess of the wartime 617 Squadron.

Red endorsement Or simply 'Red'. Adverse report of involvement in a flying incident, entered in the individual's Flying Log Book in red ink.

R & I Section Repair and Inspection Section of the ground servicing trades.

SABS Stabilized Automatic Bomb Sight.

SBO Senior British Officer.

Scrub Cancellation of operations, parades, etc.

Shaky Do Unnerving experience.

SHQ Station Headquarters.

SIB Special Investigation Branch.

SMO Station Medical Officer.

SP RAF Service Policeman.

Spam Aircrew reference to the 1939–43 Star, as it then was, later to become the 1939–45 Star. The medal ribbon colours matched those of the wartime tins of Spam cooked meat, imported from America.

SSQ Station Sick Quarters.

Straight gunner An air-gunner not additionally trained in wireless operator duties.

TOT Time on Target.

VC Victoria Cross.

VHF Very High Frequency communication channels.

Willco Acknowledgement of receipt and understanding of instructions and intention to comply with same.